THE BIBLE INSTRUCTOR

Upper: Bible Instructors in Evangelistic Campaign in a New England City, Showing Uniform. Lower: Evangelistic Team in Field Training School in Great Lakes Area. Row 1 (Center) Directing Evangelist and Wife; Bible Instructor (the Author) at Right. Row 2, Bible Instructors and Ministers' Wives Showing Short-Cape Uniform. Row 3, Ministerial Interns Serving as Personal Workers

The
Bible Instructor

IN PERSONAL AND PUBLIC EVANGELISM

By
LOUISE C. KLEUSER

TEACH Services, Inc.

PRINTED IN
THE UNITED STATES OF AMERICA

World rights reserved. This book or any portion thereof may not be copied or reproduced in any form or manner whatever, except as provided by law, without the written permission of the publisher, except by a reviewer who may quote brief passages in a review.

The author assumes full responsibility for the accuracy of all facts and quotations as cited in this book.

COPYRIGHT, 1949, BY THE
REVIEW AND HERALD PUBLISHING ASSOCIATION

Copyright © 2007 TEACH Services, Inc.
ISBN-13: 978-1-57258-517-1
ISBN-10: 1-57258-517-X
Library of Congress Control Number: 2007933154

Published by

TEACH Services, Inc.
www.TEACHServices.com

Foreword

THOSE who read the pages of this volume will be gripped by its logic and moved by its appeal. It is neither academic nor amateurish. It came into being to meet a long-felt need and to answer the specific call of the General Conference for the preparation of such a manual.

The call of the hour is for greater evangelism. But, in the last analysis, the cause of evangelism is bound up with personal work for the lost. Men and women are brought into the kingdom as individuals. To this end we must not look to mass movements, but rather to the power of individual appeal through the ministry of the Word.

Evidence of one's call to the work of evangelism is the ability to meet and win people for Christ. In this the writer has excelled. Because of her long experience in Christian leadership and successful soul-winning service, Miss Kleuser was called to Washington, D.C., in 1941, as one of the secretaries of the Ministerial Association of the General Conference. Since the session in 1941 the author has given herself, in field and classroom, to the building up of a greater concept of personal soul winning. We rejoice that the vital cause of the Bible work has received a new inspiration.

This present volume is the result of thirty years of preparation, and the principles here presented have been tested and proved. Nor is it the outgrowth of one mind, for others have associated with the author in the production of this excellent treatise. Furthermore, it is not the cloistered product of theoretical argument but the expression of a vital, living evangelism. Its chapters have literally taken shape on the evangelistic firing field. The message of this book comes hot from the heart, and speaks in terms of actual life.

Bible instruction in the homes of the people is not new. It was an apostolic method. Paul reminds the Ephesian elders that he had taught them "publickly, and from house to house." The great revival movements of the past, led by such men as the Wesleys, called for much visitation among the people. Many missionary societies today use "Bible women" as the spearhead of their missionary endeavor. As teachers of the Word, they go to the homes of the natives, and in that sense could be classified as Bible instructors. But the ideal of building a complete structure of present truth and leading families step by step in the acceptance of the full message of God for these last days has not been a vital part of the work of such revivalists and missionaries.

However, from the earliest years of the Advent Movement such a method as is outlined in this book has been followed. And, to a large degree, the success of the Advent message has been bound up with this type of evangelism. It is a "heaven-born idea." When the hour struck for the heralding of the imminent return of Christ, a sense of urgency demanded a review of the great foundations of the everlasting gospel. This was done, not only through the soul-stirring sermons of powerful prophetic preachers, but also by the work of God-fearing men and women, who entered the homes of the people to establish them in the way of truth. Thus an apostolic method, long since forgotten, was revived in order to prepare men and women to meet their God.

The purpose of this present volume is to chart the course for the professional Bible instructor. It will become a guide in the special techniques of public and personal soul winning that will bring greater efficiency to the cause of the Bible work. Much instruction has come from the pen of the messenger of the Lord to the remnant church, instruction which outlines very definitely the pattern for such work. But these counsels have not hitherto been brought together. Now that they have, the result is a unified picture.

The Bible instructor, like the ordained minister, must be conscious of a divine call to this heaven-appointed work. A beautiful illustration of such service is revealed in Acts

18, when Priscilla and Aquila, having been gripped by the eloquence of Apollos, came to him tenderly and "expounded unto him the way of God more perfectly." That "way of God" was a way of life. It was the outgrowth of a full understanding of the apostolic message. These workers were more than gospel visitors. They were instructors capable of expounding the Word and the way of God even to such a leader as Apollos.

The picture is clear. It was not only Priscilla who was the Bible instructor; Aquila shared this privilege equally with her. The apostolic pattern reveals that this is not a work for women only. The great apostle had a number of associate workers, both men and women, in his evangelistic program, and the success of his work was due, in a great degree, to the devoted services of such helpers. How affectionately Paul writes concerning these loyal workers in Romans 16:3, 4! He mentions them by name as "my helpers in Christ Jesus; who have for my life laid down their own necks: unto whom not only I give thanks, but also all the churches of the Gentiles."

Not only the churches of the apostles' day but many churches of our own generation could express in similar language their gratitude to God for the sacrificial services of such godly Bible instructors. Not only have families been won for Christ, but at times whole churches have come into being under the benign influence of faithful Bible instructors.

The variety of talent in Paul's evangelistic teams may well be a pattern for our time. The chapters in this volume which emphasize the importance of team relationships will be studied with great profit both by our evangelists and by our conference administrators.

The program of Bible work that took shape under the great Second Advent Movement a century ago needs reviving. Rightly understood, the Bible instructor's work is more than the visiting of homes to bring people to public meetings. A trained Bible instructor should be prepared to give definite instruction "precept upon precept; line upon line," expounding in all the Scripture the things concerning our Lord and His message, that men and women may behold the complete revelation of God and be prepared to meet our Saviour when He appears in glory.

Miss Kleuser not only is an able soul winner but also possesses the ability to inspire and lead others in that service. Bible instruction has been a vital part of the author's ministry ever since she entered the work of God. While carrying responsibility in other fields of Christian endeavor—such as conference secretary for the Sabbath School, Young People's Missionary Volunteer, Home Missionary, and Educational departments, she found in all these different avenues of service an opportunity to engage in and promote a definite program of individual soul winning. Understanding the problems of the work of these important departments within our church organization, and knowing too the joy of bringing many souls to the Saviour, she now places within the hands of her fellow Bible instructors a guide which will greatly strengthen their service.

Some sixty readers have studied this manuscript, including evangelists, pastors, Bible instructors, conference administrators, educators, chaplains, and editors. It is, therefore, sent to the field with confidence that it will prove eminently useful. A valuable feature of this book is the fact that it does not come from one pen. Scores of Bible-study patterns and other counsels from associate workers have been included. Consequently, it contains the winnowed wisdom of many minds. As you read it, fellow worker, may the Spirit of God inspire you to a new appreciation of the high privilege of personal soul-winning service.

R. A. A.

Introduction

THE Bible-reading plan is a "heaven-born idea" used in the teaching of the Advent message since its very beginning, but its importance in evangelism is receiving a new emphasis. At the 1941 General Conference, provision was made for a secretary to sponsor the interests of the Bible work and to help strengthen our methods for this profession. At times it had become evident that this noble field of service was in danger of losing its significance in our midst. There was need, therefore, for its objectives to be clarified, if its true pattern was to be preserved.

After the appointment of a secretary to the Bible work, and under the guiding counsel of the Ministerial Association, the task of first investigating all the available counsel pertaining to Bible work given in God's Word and the Spirit of prophecy was prayerfully undertaken. We soon discovered a very clear pattern for the Bible instructor. As our study continued, we were amazed at the detailed information regarding techniques to be followed in our personal work for souls. It was evident that Bible work as a method of evangelism had not been left to uncertainty. In the book *Evangelism,* a companion handbook for *The Bible Instructor,* these very methods have been set forth in much detail.

Many excellent progressive methods to feature, enlarge, and expedite Bible instruction for those investigating our message have already been introduced into our evangelism, but in Heaven's conception of the plan none of these can take the place of personal Bible work. Accepting the doctrines of present truth is a step of great significance in the life of the inquirer. He needs clear, individual understanding and the personal touch of a teacher. Therefore the heavenly pattern of our denominational Bible and personal work should be well preserved for our future as well as present evangelism.

The plan of a book for Bible instructors has long been in the mind of the Ministerial Association. The idea that this work should include those special plans, methods, and techniques developed in our denominational Bible work has been greatly urged by the field. The organization of this book has grown out of our Bible instructor's course at the Theological Seminary, where Bible instructor methods have now been well analyzed. But in the preparation of this handbook the author was asked to meet the needs of our field Bible instructors. For that reason this work is not primarily a college textbook, although it will well serve as a true guide to those preparing themselves for conference Bible work. And although some problems discussed here are not common to lay Bible instructors, the material presented will be an inspiration to them.

PART ONE of this volume provides the background and methods for the Bible work. The Spirit of prophecy has indeed supplied a wealth of valuable counsel for the Bible instructor, which we desire to stress in all our methods. Although soul-winning and Bible-work methods have been featured in some of our other denominational literature, this handbook is unique in that it aims at providing guidance and an analysis of problems pertaining to a more professional type of personal ministry.

PART TWO sets forth some ideals for a more challenging Bible work and its developing plans. In recognition of the fact that there are specialists in certain phases of the work, some of their material is included to stimulate any latent talent which might be utilized in making greater appeal for the message.

PART THREE briefly sets forth some counsel and policies that all ministers and Bible instructors should understand. It is practical information based on experience. Younger workers especially will appreciate an acquaintance with our working policies in this phase of evangelism, which are hardly discussed elsewhere.

Introduction

PART FOUR features the art of giving Bible readings, and will interest all evangelistic workers, including laymen. Though maintaining the individualistic style of each contributor's material, these studies still suggest unity in approach, build-up, and appeal. Here are the types of Bible readings used by our workers in the world's larger and smaller cities, with other studies designed to meet the needs of inquirers in less-privileged areas. The contributors to these Bible studies represent a large section of the world field. There are also sanitarium-type Bible studies, which though featuring health primarily, do not overlook the broader needs of evangelistic instruction. Some studies have been inserted for the purpose of preserving to the Bible work particular techniques of presentation.

The publishing of *The Bible Instructor* is not the finale for setting forth Bible-work skills. If this volume has lacked space to include some method, particular project, or need, our Bible instructors are invited to suggest it for a future treatise. *The Bible Instructor* now goes on its mission with our sincere prayer that it will encourage our workers everywhere to do a more urgent and effectual Bible work in the proclamation of our fast-closing message.

THE MINISTERIAL ASSOCIATION
GENERAL CONFERENCE OF S.D.A.

Acknowledgments

Indebtedness is here expressed to the large reading committee for constructive counsel regarding the material which comprises this handbook for the personal worker. The committee included officers of the General Conference, conference executives, college Bible teachers, evangelists, pastors, and more than twenty-five Bible instructors. The counsel of college teachers helped to expand this work to include instruction for the trainee and beginner.

Appreciation is also expressed to my co-workers in the Ministerial Association. Their interest, encouragement, and helpfulness have greatly contributed toward the publication of *The Bible Instructor.*

The appearance of this volume is a significant event in the lives of our veteran Bible instructors. The author is deeply indebted to their counsel, guidance, and contributions. Their vision and cooperation have made this book possible. In listing their names we are not unmindful of a host of others, both men and women, who rendered helpful service.

Mary E. Anderson	Jessie Heslip	Margaret Reeves
Rose E. Boose	Mayme Hollingsworth	Ella M. Robinson
Dorothy W. Conklin	Addie M. Kalar	Marie Schmidt
Ellen H. Curran	Lucia Lee	Thelma A. Smith
Alma DuBois	Rachel M. Lemon	Grace Stewart
Abbie Dunn	Alma McKibbin	Ruth Tinkler
Ena Ferguson	Inis Morey	Maybelle Vandermark
Vinnie L. Goodner	Bess Ninaj	Mary E. Walsh
Elva R. Heald	Etheline V. Porter	

Contents

Foreword—R. Allan Anderson	5
Introduction	9
Spirit of Prophecy Counsel	15
Bible Instructor Badge	24

PART ONE
Bible and Personal Work

1. The Bible Instructor	27
2. Men as Bible Instructors	31
3. Qualifications and Training	33
4. Guiding the Beginner	39
5. Making Contacts and Building Interest	44
6. Developing the Conversational Art	47
7. The Pleasing and Inspiring Teacher	51
8. Bible-reading Skills	56
9. The Role in Public Evangelism	63
10. Clinching and Conserving Interest	67
11. The Challenge of Present Truth	74
12. Illustrating Truth	77
13. Continuing to Build Truth	82
14. Skillful Group Instruction	86
15. Methods of the Master Teacher	94
16. Progressive Teaching for Decision	98
17. Teaching God's Great Plan	105
18. Light Through the Sanctuary	107
19. Modern Sabbath Issues	115
20. Teaching the State of the Dead	118
21. Our Reformatory Message	123
22. The Health Evangel	129
23. Life and Stewardship	132
24. Presenting Prophecy	135
25. Souls in the Balance	140
26. Textual Argument in Decision	146
27. Overcoming Evil Habits	153
28. Dress and Other Standards	162
29. Preparation for Baptism	171
30. Integrating New Believers	176
31. Teaching Prayer Habits	181
32. Establishing in the Faith	185
33. Gaining Friends for the Truth	187

PART TWO
Featuring a Larger Bible Work

1. Evangelism for Children and Youth — 193
2. A Health Program in Evangelism — 207
3. Sanitarium Bible Work — 219
4. Artistic Bents and Skills — 230
5. Skills in Meeting People — 233
6. Developing Literary Ability — 278
7. Secretarial and Other Skills — 284
8. Training Personal Workers — 289

PART THREE
The Bible Instructor's Personal Problems

1. Worker's Influence in the Church — 311
2. Daily Work Program — 314
3. Finding Time for Study — 317
4. Filing Notes and Materials — 321
5. Dress of the Bible Instructor — 325
6. Home and Personal Problems — 331
7. Preserving the Worker's Health — 337
8. Hints by a Minister's Wife — 340
9. Professional Relationships — 343
10. Greater Power and More Efficiency — 349

PART FOUR
Bible Readings by Our Bible Instructors (See Index)

Illustrations, Charts, and Diagrams

Bible Instructor Uniforms	Frontispiece
Progressive Doctrinal Studies	102
Scofield's "Dispensations"	242
The Seventy Weeks in Prophecy	398
From B.C. to A.D.	399
The 2300 Days	400
Cleansing of the Sanctuary	401
Law and Grace	409
Flesh Food From Eden to Eden	432

Spirit of Prophecy Counsel
The Bible-Work Plan

1. Work Marked Out by Our Heavenly Father.—"Our work has been marked out for us by our Heavenly Father. We are to take our Bibles, and go forth to warn the world. We are to be God's helping hands in saving souls,—channels through which His love is day by day to flow to the perishing. The realization of the great work in which he has the privilege of taking part ennobles and sanctifies the true worker. He is filled with the faith that works by love and purifies the soul. Nothing is drudgery to the one who submits to the will of God. 'Doing it unto the Lord' is a thought that throws a charm over whatever work God gives him to do."—*Testimonies*, vol. 9, p. 150.

2. Bible Work a Heaven-born Idea.—"The idea of holding Bible readings is a heaven-born idea, and opens the way to put hundreds of young men and women into the field to do an important work, which otherwise could not have been done.

"The Bible is unchained. It can be carried to every man's door, and its truths may be presented to every man's conscience. There are many who, like the noble Bereans, will search the Scriptures daily for themselves, when the truth is presented, to see whether or not these things are so. Christ has said, 'Search the Scriptures; for in them ye think ye have eternal life, and they are they which testify of Me.' Jesus, the world's Redeemer, bids men not only to read, but to 'search the Scriptures.' This is a great and important work, and it is committed to us, and in doing this we shall be greatly benefited; for obedience to Christ's command will not go unrewarded. He will crown with especial tokens of His favor this act of loyalty in following the light revealed in His Word."—*Testimonies on Sabbath School Work*, pp. 29, 30.

3. Plan Demonstrated by Two Bible Workers.—"I saw two Bible workers seated in a family. With the open

Bibles before them, they presented the Lord Jesus Christ as the sin-pardoning Saviour. Their words were spoken with freshness and power. Earnest prayer was offered to God, and hearts were softened and subdued by the softening influence of the Spirit of God. As the Word of God was explained, I saw that a soft, radiant light illuminated the Scriptures, and I said softly, 'Go out into the highways and hedges, and compel them to come in, that my house may be filled.' "—*Evangelism,* pp. 457, 458.

4. BIBLE READING OPENINGS THE OBJECTIVE.—"Elder and Mrs. Haskell were conducting Bible studies in the forenoons, and in the afternoons the workers in training were going out and visiting from house to house. These missionary visits, and the sale of many books and periodicals, opened the way for the holding of Bible readings. About forty men and women were attending the morning classes, and a goodly number of these students engaged in the afternoon work."—*Review and Herald,* Nov. 29, 1906.

5. PLAN USED IN 1844 MOVEMENT.—"In the messages of the first and second angels, the work was done in this manner. Men and women were moved to search the Scriptures, and they called the attention of others to the truths revealed. It was personal labor for individuals and families that gave these messages their wonderful success."—*Ibid.,* Jan. 27, 1885.

6. ASSOCIATED WITH LITERATURE WORK.—"We are to give the last warning of God to men, and what should be our earnestness in studying the Bible, and our zeal in spreading the light! . . . Let the workers go from house to house, opening the Bible to the people, circulating the publications, telling others of the light that has blessed their own souls."—*Gospel Workers,* p. 353.

Call to the Bible Work

1. BOTH MEN AND WOMEN CALLED.—"The Lord has a work for women as well as men to do. They may accomplish a good work for God if they will first learn in the school of

Christ the precious, all-important lesson of meekness. They must not only bear the name of Christ, but possess His Spirit. They must walk even as He walked, purifying their souls from everything that defiles. Then they will be able to benefit others by presenting the all-sufficiency of Jesus."—*Gospel Workers,* p. 453.

2. WOMEN CALLED TO WORK WITH FAMILIES.—"The Lord has a work for women, as well as for men. They may take their places in His work at this crisis, and He will work through them. If they are imbued with a sense of their duty, and labor under the influence of the Holy Spirit, they will have just the self-possession required for this time. The Saviour will reflect upon these self-sacrificing women the light of His countenance, and will give them a power that exceeds that of men. They can do in families a work that men cannot do, a work that reaches the inner life. They can come close to the hearts of those whom men cannot reach."—*Review and Herald,* Aug. 26, 1902.

3. MINISTERS TO DO BIBLE WORK.—"A minister may enjoy sermonizing; for it is the pleasant part of the work, and is comparatively easy; but no minister should be measured by his ability as a speaker. The harder part comes after he leaves the desk, in watering the seed sown. The interest awakened should be followed up by personal labor,—visiting, holding Bible-readings, teaching how to search the Scriptures, praying with families and interested ones, seeking to deepen the impression made upon the hearts and consciences."—*Testimonies,* vol. 5, p. 255.

4. YOUTH CALLED TO BIBLE WORK.—"There are many lines in which the youth can find opportunity for helpful effort. Companies should be organized and thoroughly educated to work as nurses, gospel visitors, and Bible readers, as canvassers, ministers, and medical missionary evangelists."—*Counsels to Teachers,* p. 546.

"In order that the work may go forward in all its branches, God calls for youthful vigor, zeal, and courage. He has chosen the youth to aid in the advancement of His cause. To plan with clear mind and execute with courageous hand demands fresh, uncrippled energies. Young men and women are invited to give God the strength of their youth, that through the exercise of their powers, through keen thought and vigorous action, they may bring glory to Him and salvation to their fellow-men."—*Gospel Workers*, p. 67.

"There is need of young men and women who will not be swayed by circumstances, who walk with God, who pray much, and who put forth earnest efforts to gather all the light they can."—*Ibid.*, pp. 69, 70.

5. LAYMEN TO GIVE BIBLE READINGS.—"There should also be in our larger churches special training-schools for young men and women, to fit them to become workers for God. And far more attention should be given by our ministers to the matter of assisting and educating younger laborers."—*Ibid.*, p. 75.

6. WORK CALLS FOR MATURITY AND EXPERIENCE.—"Those who desire to give themselves to the work of God should receive an education and training for this work, that they may be prepared to engage in it intelligently. They should not feel that they can step at once upon the higher rounds of the ladder; those who would succeed must begin at the first round, and climb upward step by step. Opportunities and privileges are granted them for improvement, and they should make every effort in their power to learn how to do the work of God acceptably."—*Ibid.*, p. 73.

"Ministerial labor cannot and should not be intrusted to boys, neither should the work of giving Bible readings be intrusted to inexperienced girls, because they offer their services, and are willing to take responsible positions, but who are wanting in religious experience, without a thorough education and training. They must be proved to see if they will bear the test; and unless there is developed a firm, conscientious principle to be all that God would have them to be, they will not correctly represent our cause and work for this time."—*Fundamentals of Christian Education*, p. 113.

"Young men should not enter upon the work of explaining the Scriptures and lecturing upon the prophecies, when they do not have a knowledge of the important Bible truths they try to explain to others. They may be deficient in the common branches of education, and therefore fail to do the amount of good they could do if they had had the advantages of a good school. Ignorance will not increase the humility or spirituality of any professed follower of Christ. The truths of the divine word can be best appreciated by an intellectual Christian. Christ can be best glorified by those who serve Him intelligently. The great object of education is to enable us to use the powers which God has given us in such a manner as will best represent the religion of the Bible and promote the glory of God."—*Testimonies*, vol. 3, p. 160.

Women Well Fitted

1. THEIR INFLUENCE IN THE HOMES.—"If half the time now spent in preaching, were given to house-to-house labor, favorable results would be seen. Much good would be accomplished, for the workers could come close to the people. The time spent in quietly visiting families, and when there speaking to God in prayer, singing His praise, and explaining His Word, will often do more good than a public effort. Many times minds are impressed with tenfold more force by personal appeals than by any other kind of labor. The family that is visited in this way is spoken to personally. The members are not in a promiscuous assembly where they can apply to their neighbors the truths which they hear. They themselves are spoken to, earnestly, and with a kindhearted solicitude. They are allowed to express their objections freely, and these objections can each be met with a 'Thus saith the Lord.' If this work is done in humility, by those whose hearts are imbued with the love of God, the words are fulfilled, 'The entrance of Thy words giveth light; it giveth understanding to the simple.' "—*Evangelism*, pp. 463, 464.

"There are numbers of families who will never be reached by the truth of God's Word unless the stewards of the manifold grace of Christ enter their homes, and by earnest ministry, sanctified by the endorsement of the Holy Spirit, break down the barriers and enter the hearts of the people."—*Ibid.*, p. 158.

2. MAKE TEACHERS OF MORAL COURAGE.—"There are noble women who have had moral courage to decide in favor of the truth from the weight of evidence. They have conscientiously accepted the truth. They have tact, perception, and good ability, and will make successful workers for their Master. Christian women are called for."—*Review and Herald*, Dec. 19, 1878.

3. TYPE NEEDED—BLEND MARTHA AND MARY.—"All who work for God should have the Martha and the Mary attributes blended,—a willingness to minister, and a sincere love of the truth. Self and selfishness must be put out of sight. God calls for earnest women-workers, workers who are prudent, warm-hearted, tender, and true to principle. He calls for persevering women, who will take their minds from self and their personal convenience, and will center them on Christ, speaking words of truth, praying with the persons to whom they can obtain access, laboring for the conversion of souls."—*Testimonies*, vol. 6, p. 118.

The Bible-Work Method

1. PEOPLE SAVED AS INDIVIDUALS, NOT IN MASSES.—"Salt must be mingled with the substance to which it is added; it must penetrate and infuse in order to preserve. So it is through personal contact and association that men are reached by the saving power of the gospel. They are not saved in masses, but as individuals. Personal influence is a power. We must come close to those whom we desire to benefit."—*Mount of Blessing*, p. 59.

2. ONE OF THE BEST METHODS OF INSTRUCTION.—"House to house labor with our literature and the giving of Bible

readings in the family is one of the best methods of giving instruction. Such work has been done by Eld. Haskell and his fellow-laborers in New York City and in Nashville, but there should be many companies trained for this work."—MS. 26, 1905.

3. BIBLE WORK NOT A HURRIED WORK.—"We must search the Scriptures, not merely rush through a chapter and repeat it, taking no pains to understand it, but we must dig for the jewels of truth, which will enrich the mind, and fortify the soul against the wiles of the arch-deceiver."—*Signs of the Times,* June 10, 1886.

4. REACHING WHOLE FAMILIES.—"Many workers are to act their part, doing house-to-house work, and giving Bible-readings in families. They are to show their growth in grace by submission to the will of Christ. Thus they will gain a rich experience."—*Gospel Workers,* p. 355.

"Women as well as men can engage in the work of hiding the truth where it can work out and be made manifest. They can take their place in the work at this crisis, and the Lord will work through them. If they are imbued with a sense of their duty, and labor under the influence of the Spirit of God, they will have just the self-possession required for this time. The Saviour will reflect upon these self-sacrificing women the light of His countenance, and this will give them a power that will exceed that of men. They can do in families a work that men can not do, a work that reaches the inner life. They can come close to the hearts of those whom men can not reach. Their work is needed. Discreet and humble women can do a work in explaining the truth to the people in their homes. The word of God thus explained will do its leavening work, and through its influence whole families will be converted."—*Testimonies,* vol. 9, pp. 128, 129.

5. NOT TO BECOME MECHANICAL.—"All who engage in this personal labor should be just as careful not to become mechanical in their manner of working as should the minister who preaches the word. They should be constantly learning.

They should have a conscientious zeal to obtain the highest qualifications, to become men able in the Scriptures. They should cultivate habits of mental activity, especially giving themselves to prayer and to the diligent study of the Scriptures."—*Gospel Workers,* p. 193.

6. TEACHING PEOPLE THOROUGHLY.—"In every city that is entered, a solid foundation is to be laid for permanent work. The Lord's methods are to be followed. By doing house-to-house work, by giving Bible-readings in families, the worker may gain access to many who are seeking for truth. By opening the Scriptures, by prayer, by exercising faith, he is to teach the people the way of the Lord."—*Testimonies,* vol. 7, p. 38.

7. INDOCTRINATE FOR FUTURE TESTS.—"I have been shown that many who profess to have a knowledge of present truth, know not what they believe. They do not understand the evidences of their faith. They have no just appreciation of the work for the present time. When the time of trial shall come, there are men now preaching to others, who will find, upon examining the positions they hold, that there are many things for which they can give no satisfactory reason. Until thus tested, they knew not their great ignorance."—*Gospel Workers,* p. 298.

8. BEST BIBLE WORK DURING PUBLIC MEETINGS.—"The best work you can do is to teach, to educate. Whenever you can find an opportunity to do so, sit down with some family, and let them ask questions. Then answer them patiently, humbly. Continue this work in connection with your more public efforts. Preach less, and educate more, by holding Bible-readings, and by praying with families and little companies."—*Ibid.,* p. 193.

9. TO FOLLOW UP PUBLIC MEETINGS.—"Of equal importance with special public efforts, is house-to-house work in the homes of the people. As the result of the presentation of truth in large congregations, a spirit of inquiry is awakened; and it is specially important that this interest be followed up

by personal labor. Those who desire to investigate the truth need to be taught to study diligently the Word of God. Some one must help them to build on a sure foundation. The Word of God is to be their counselor. At this critical time in their religious experience, how important it is that wisely directed Bible workers come to their help, and open to their understanding the treasure-house of God's Word."—*Review and Herald,* Feb. 21, 1907.

10. Evangelism Weakened Where No Strong Bible Work.—"Many a laborer fails in his work because he does not come close to those who most need his help. With the Bible in hand, he should seek in a courteous manner to learn the objections which exist in the minds of those who are beginning to inquire, 'What is truth?' Carefully and tenderly should he lead and educate them, as pupils in a school. Many have to unlearn theories which they have long believed to be truth. As they become convinced that they have been in error concerning Bible subjects, they are thrown into perplexity and doubt. They need the tenderest sympathy and the most judicious help; they should be carefully instructed, and should be prayed for and prayed with, watched and guarded with the kindest solicitude."—*Gospel Workers,* pp. 190, 191.

Bible Instructor's Badge

THE field has awaited the announcement of a special badge to be used by our Bible instructors. The call was for some type of emblem pin which would distinguish the personal Bible teacher as a professional worker connected with the evangelistic company. The General Conference was asked to give study to the preparation of such a badge for the purpose of making it available to all our conference-employed Bible instructors.

The Bible instructor's badge is in the form of a most attractive convex shield 1½ by 2 inches. A pleasing medium blue is the general background. The other colors are yellow gold and white. The emblem used is a hand holding up a lighted torch against an open Bible. The name "Bible Instructor" is in neat print and easily readable. It is made of a new composition plastic material fastened to a sturdy, untarnishable pin, which can be adjusted without difficulty. This badge will also serve as a cape fastener.

The badge may be ordered by the employing conference from the Review and Herald Publishing Association at a nominal price.

PART ONE

BIBLE AND PERSONAL WORK

Truth Melts Its Way

Let strong reasons for our faith be presented from the Word of God, and let the truth in its sanctifying power melt its way to the hearts and minds of those who are under conviction. As the helpers give Bible readings in the homes of the people, the Lord just as surely works on minds as He does in the public services.—Evangelism, p. 489.

PART ONE ★ CHAPTER ONE

The Bible Instructor

Before a detailed discussion of the various needs of the Bible work is entered upon, our Bible instructors are invited to catch a bird's-eye view of this type of gospel service as it is carried on today. While an endeavor is being made to build this profession on Bible methods and the counsel of the Spirit of prophecy, some special needs in the fast-developing work are not being overlooked. This gospel ministry cannot ignore the progress of time; and although the program of the Bible instructor has of necessity become more streamlined than when the pioneer workers gave their first Bible readings, the principles they then applied are still workable, but with adaptations.

Our modern living and transportation facilities in larger cities materially affect the Bible instructor's daily program. The use of the automobile in evangelism, the service of the telephone and various other commodities—all these enter into the planning of a day's schedule. Because time is now at a premium in every modern activity, these conveniences are no longer considered a luxury. But garage and parking problems in busy centers are typical of the dilemma presented when these utilities are employed for greater efficiency. These were not problems to our pioneer Bible worker, but they have a definite bearing on our Bible work today.

What influences the Bible instructor also affects the lives of those for whom she labors. Daytime visitation by the Bible instructor is growing more complicated in our age, because many former housewives have now become businesswomen. Two recent wars have greatly changed the home routine, because of new industrial and housing problems. The Bible instructor must now visit many families in apartment houses, or in furnished rooms, and is happy when she can arrange for a visit even after nine o'clock at night. Many with whom she comes in contact do not have a home of their own, and this lack presents other problems, making necessary a different type of Bible work from that which formerly concerned families, even those which enjoyed only the privacy of a humble home. These last-day problems, with their pressure on all, only accentuate our great task—speedily to bring the Bible into the lives of these busy and often sin-weary souls who desire to be saved.

As we emerged from World War II we became exceedingly conscious of the fact that we are not living to ourselves but are a part of an important whole. Even as nations need leadership for well-laid plans, so in the church's evangelism there is a great need for leadership that inspires united action. Each new evangelistic series now presents more baffling problems than the preceding one, and untried methods are a constant challenge to all who minister in the Word. Our methods are not confined to the traditions of the past, but it is evident that those working principles early given to us through the Spirit of prophecy, with proper adaptation to modern needs, are still applicable today. In adherence to these sound principles lies the real strength of our present-day Bible work.

The streamlining of some of our methods of Bible work does not imply that instruction of new believers is to be less thorough. For the purpose of reaching more people, group study for the interested while they attend our public meetings may now be emphasized, but this school plan should still have all the elements of inspirational and personal attention. Here Bible instructors may lead out in imparting information on a progressive scale while guiding whole groups of people to take definite forward steps toward the acceptance of all revealed light, which we term "present truth."

The city evangelistic center is now a business office, overseeing and mailing out thousands of carefully prepared Bible lessons. A well-planned program of truth-filled literature follows up the original interest, and then many contacts are made by groups of personal workers who visit homes in the immediate city area as well as in its outlying districts. Such an office also becomes a study-and-counsel center where Bible instructors function as receptionists. This service requires the development of a gracious, pleasing personality which has the power to attract inquirers to the message, even before a keen interest in Bible study has been established.

Younger Bible instructors also have unique opportunities to make their distinctive contributions to evangelism. Spiritually radiant youth will attract other promising youth to the third angel's message. Today young people are not afraid to face facts, and there is something challenging in the study of the Bible as suggested by Seventh-day Adventists. Mature Bible instructors should cheerfully make room for this youthful service in the Bible work, since the success of our message is dependent upon both the experienced, well-weathered worker and the inspirational, youthful type.

During evangelistic campaigns the aim should be to continue the training the youth began in college. As young interns associate with workers of more experience in field evangelism, they may be quickly developed into successful soul winners. This is a "wisely-directed Bible work" and should receive strong emphasis in all efforts. In this way beginners enter right into a program of active service and immediately realize the joy of the gospel ministry.

Bible work is not confined to merely one type of gospel service. Neither is it limited to cooperative labor with an ordained minister. Herewith are listed its broader possibilities as set forth in the inspired counsels of the church.

Types of Bible Instructors

1. The Bible worker connected with city evangelistic efforts. The spirit of inquiry is stimulated by public meetings. Doors open to workers; prejudice is not pronounced.

2. The Bible worker capable of winning town folk and those in rural areas. Quiet, neighborly friendliness helps to break down barriers. The worker may use special approach methods such as literature distribution or health instruction, etc.

3. The Bible worker with special talents that serve as interest-builders and levers to move hearts toward the message. The Bible instructor, for example, with musical or art gift, training in nursing or dietetics, etc.

4. The Bible correspondence worker. Interest in evangelism, with a preparation and experience in school teaching, provides background for the worker who qualifies for this branch of service. Guiding interested people into the full Advent message through correspondence lessons goes hand in hand with field Bible work and prepares the way for contacts leading to decisions for the truth.

5. District leaders. There is a place for the Bible instructor carrying district leadership besides her regular Bible work for non-Adventists. This assignment requires personality, interest, and a preparation for church work and shepherding of the flock in the more isolated districts. Not an ordained man or woman, nor one experienced in public preaching, this type often leads out in unique, intensive soul-winning plans.

6. The experienced Bible instructor, employed regularly or temporarily by a conference or union for training the laymen of our churches in Bible reading and personal-work skills.

7. The institutional type of Bible instructor employed in our sanitariums, perhaps sharing with the chaplain the responsibility of instruction in Bible for nurses in training. This worker also develops interest in the study of our message, and follows up the interest after the patient returns home.

The task of the Bible instructor is vigorous soul winning rather than the perpetuation of traditional methods. Wrestling with every type of error and every problem of sin, Bible instructors today need a constantly fresh supply of progressive methods as well as an increasing Bible knowledge. As the attention of our workers is directed to the divine counsel upon which many methods in this handbook are built, our ministers and Bible instructors are invited to find their application in up-to-date evangelism. Then Bible work will continue to grow in usefulness until the last soul has been brought into the remnant fold.

PART ONE ★ CHAPTER TWO

Men as Bible Instructors

Much instruction has come to us regarding the importance and value of giving Bible studies in the homes of the people. Thus far we have largely employed women as conference Bible instructors, and they have done effective work. In volume 9 of the *Testimonies*, page 128, we are instructed to employ men also to do this type of work. In this field of service there is urgent need for both women and men to teach the truth by personal contacts in the homes of the people, many of whom will never attend public services.

It is evident that if men, properly trained and efficient, could be employed to conduct cottage meetings, to give Bible readings, and to labor in various proved spheres of service, a larger proportion of men could be won to the truth than when only women are employed as Bible instructors. Some men are prejudiced against receiving instruction from women, and some women will not give studies to men. The preponderance of men in our churches in many mission fields may be largely due to the exclusive employment of men as workers.—H. C. OLMSTEAD, *The Ministry*, Oct., 1941.

This need is urgent and universal, and it is hoped that hundreds of young men will eagerly respond to such an opportunity for service.

* * * * *

There are several advantages in using men as Bible instructors in city evangelism. From the very beginning of an effort the Bible instructor is before the eyes of those in attendance at the meetings. He is often seen on the platform with the evangelist, offering prayer, making announcements, or assisting in other ways.

Thus, the people think of him as an associate minister. They feel that they know him, for he has been at the door to bid them farewell, and to invite them back again, and they gradually grow to have confidence in him. Consequently, when such a worker calls upon interested ones, he receives a hearty welcome. Both homes and hearts are opened to his visits and Bible studies.

The interested man especially enjoys having one of his own sex call upon him to help him with his problems. He feels that this worker can understand his position, having, in many cases, struggled in the same way. This is especially true in regard to the problems of Sabbath observance and of the tobacco habit. A man is naturally reluctant to confide his troubles to a woman Bible instructor. And the man's wife, looking upon the worker as a minister, feels free to talk to him also.

Even in this enlightened age there are many people who are a little skeptical of a woman's fitness to study the Bible with them. They believe that authority in spiritual things is the special province of a minister.

There are untold opportunities for the Bible instructor to improve his own work while associated with an older minister. He can observe the effect of all the work that is carried on, and can see what reaction comes to each attack made upon the prospect's former position. As a result he will be able to conduct a much more aggressive campaign of his own.

Many decisions for the message have been made because the truth has been forcefully brought into the very life of the prospect by an evangelist's assistant. A young man, thoroughly grounded in the Scriptures, can most effectively build into the minds of his prospects the foundation of Bible doctrines that must be the bulwark to hold them in the message.
—G. H. Boehrig, *The Ministry*, Oct., 1941.

PART ONE ★ CHAPTER THREE

Qualifications and Training

The call to soul winning demands the highest qualifications. Together with the Spirit-filled life there must be a culture of heart and mind which provides the proper capacity for growth. The Bible instructor must be well read. She must know *how* to read. She must know how to cull from professional as well as current reading material a background of factual knowledge. Such reading must not be too laborious, for the time for reading is limited. A good knowledge of history and biography inspires confidence, and makes the message vital with human interest.

With the growing needs of our work today, the Bible instructor has a broader sphere of influence than she had some years ago. Our expanding program of evangelism, the intensity of the task, and the shortness of time in which to perform it suggest that we become experts in soul winning. There is still a true need for simplicity and humility, and yet we must avoid an inferiority complex that is not helpful to us personally, nor inspiring to confidence in others.

The Bible instructor must know from personal experience what God expects of His children; she must also know the power of God to save, and of Satan to destroy. There are eternal decisions lying in the balance, and not merely human friendships to win. Men and women are judgment bound, and so her appeal must have fervor, sincerity, and point. Appeals cannot be constantly repeated from person to person without the gospel worker's entering anew into the crisis of each individual. It requires "fresh ideas" and new lifting power to avoid monotony or having one's efforts become stereotyped. That natural, urgent appeal of a heart overflowing with soul-winning love is essential.

A life dedication which is born out of a conviction that she has "come to the kingdom for such a time as this," gives zeal and poise to the worker. Human beings still need words of appreciation, but a worker who constantly needs praise and humoring is blocking the wheels of progress. She must "know what Israel ought to do," and her satisfaction lies in the task well performed under the guiding hand of God.

Although success in soul winning brings poise and confidence, the dignity of womanly meekness is a rare gem for the teacher. Some Bible instructors have a personality that revels in leadership, and they exercise it even to the point of becoming masculine in their ways. The gentler, wooing graces—those unselfish, unobtrusive efforts to do helpful things because the impulse flows from a tender, loving heart—are the true graces of Bible work. It is on this point that the leadership of love, and not of show and power, is felt. There is, however, a charm to meekness which is capable of strong action when called for.

What quality is more necessary in Bible work than common sense or sound judgment? Shall we suggest that its twin sisters, vision and intuition, are also dire needs? The worker lacking these does not succeed. Although balancing gifts may bring her into demand in various places, the work of the one lacking good judgment is constantly limited because of this handicap. The ability to see a problem in its broader expanse, and then to weigh its dependent decisions wisely, must be cultivated by every Bible instructor. Intuition is often motivated by good judgment, and this womanly gift aids tremendously in Bible work.

And what about individuality? How much might be said in its favor! How many cautions might be suggested to the worker who is apt at copying another, and often unconsciously mimicking her weaker points as well as stronger traits! Let the Bible instructor be herself, but without any attempt to make over every other individual. God approves individuality, and enjoys variety. She therefore should not exert such an influence on her readers that they are stamped by others as a "second edition" of herself. It is her privilege to help to develop in each soul the best of his true self, which may even be in decided contrast to her own personality. She is to lead people to think for themselves, and to respect the rights of others.

In the training of young women for personal work a preparation for preaching and ministerial duties does not count so much as the development of skills for home evangelism. During their college training, students are greatly helped by occasionally sitting at the feet of experienced Bible instructors who know the art of entering homes and leading whole families to Christ and into the church. In view of their long contact with many types of evangelistic meetings, these tried workers are able to bring to their students the wealth of their own experience. Most desirable is their leadership when students in their senior years of college join them in actual field evangelism.

This thorough Bible instructor training in our schools develops a practical and superior type of womanhood for the gospel ministry. There is a challenge to a profession that uses young women for the gospel ministry. There is a challenge to a profession that uses young women as home visitors, wise spiritual counselors, understanding friends of childhood and adolescence, who then become masters at the art of winning personal decisions for Christ. The young student may be trained to teach groups as well as individuals, developing skill and poise in conducting attractive classwork in doctrinal teaching, health instruction, and cookery.

There is a mature group of workers in the field today who have proved themselves to be most successful soul winners, but who have not had the educational background now recognized as essential. Because of their consecration and soul-winning personality, they have been encouraged by conference leaders to enter denominational work. These women have become most proficient in teaching our doctrines, and have made distinctive contribution to our evangelism. They were usually molded according to the Bible work patterns of ministers they assisted, many of whom built wisely for the profession. Having the ability to get along with others, these women have continued in Bible work. Although experienced, they could greatly increase their efficiency by occasional brief periods of study. Away from their work, they could join other mature, studious workers who are also desirous of refreshing their store of knowledge. (Courses given at the Theological Seminary, Takoma Park, D.C., are designed to meet these needs.)

It is entirely unfair to consecrated women now in the profession for conferences to select in preference to them new recruits who may have the background of a course of training but not the necessary heart experience. These need more than an average mental equipment and an even, balanced temperament. They must know personally that they have been saved by grace, and that evidence of it must be demonstrated in every act of their service. The conference committee would not pick ministers, teachers, or nurses without due caution, and they dare not lay hasty hands of selection on Bible instructors. There should be thorough investigation of each candidate by the committee.

The title Bible Instructor should be sacredly guarded in our ranks. When temporarily or more permanently it becomes necessary to draft extra helpers for a larger evangelism, untrained recruits should first qualify before being recognized as full-fledged Bible instructors. This work cannot be learned overnight; nor does the wearing of a Bible instructor's badge or uniform qualify even a consecrated prospect for a profession comparable only to the gospel ministry. On this point our denominational policy is stated in the *Church Manual.*

The following is a list of the various qualifications for the Bible work. This list has been more thoroughly developed in the book *Evangelism,* pages 477-481, to which close study is invited. Pondering on these qualifications, the Bible instructor becomes convinced of the high calling of her profession. As each Bible instructor endeavors to pattern her work according to God's standard, the Bible work will continue to develop into a noble service.

Bible Instructor Qualifications

(Based on *Evangelism,* pages 293-295, 429-495.)

I. *Spirituality.*
   1. A background of Christian experience.
      a. Being truly converted.
      b. Experience in Christian living.
      c. Meekness and humility.
   2. Love for souls.
      a. The social touch.
      b. Winning souls one by one.
      c. Tender solicitude.
      d. Distinct channel of love.
      e. Sacrificing spirit.
      f. Bearing burdens for Jesus.
   3. In touch with God.
      a. Spirit's guidance in soul winning.
      b. Spirit-directed words.
      c. Possessing righteousness of Christ.
      d. Speaking naturally of God's love.
      e. Freshness and power in appeal.
      f. Dispelling indifference.
      g. Interceding for sinners.

4. Uplifting influence.
    a. Personal influence and attracting power.
    b. Reaching the heart, "inner life."
    c. Power of persuasion, prayer, love of God.
    d. Transforming influence.
    e. "Vital current diffusing life and joy."

II. *Personality.*
    1. Sympathetic, understanding.
    2. Kind and helpful.
    3. Warm, fervent, cheerful.
    4. Persuasive powers.
    5. Tactful, adaptable.
    6. Ability to plan and execute.
    7. Courage, force, energy, perseverance.
    8. Practical.
    9. Cooperative.
    10. Representative in dress.
    11. Discreet toward opposite sex.

III. *Health and Vigor.*
    1. Living health principles.
    2. Teaching health.
    3. Force, power, vivaciousness.
    4. Keenness of perception.
    5. Endurance.

IV. *Mentality.*
    1. Preparation and training.
       Modest, representative, intelligent workers.
    2. Thorough Bible knowledge.
        a. Worker with training and background.
        b. Understanding of warning message of hour.
    3. A studious spirit.
        a. Going to bottom of every subject.
        b. Constantly learning; "able in the Scriptures."
    4. Teaching ability.
        a. Simple, clear, plain language.
        b. Teaching in an "easy style."
        c. Ability to address audiences.

V. *General.*
    1. Bible work a profession.
        a. A ministry for life.
        b. Candidates to be wisely chosen.
        c. Worker with natural ability.

PART ONE ★ CHAPTER FOUR

Guiding the Beginner

The work of the Bible instructor requires ability to plan and execute one's daily program rather independently. Unless the worker is associated with an evangelistic team that receives constant direction, it may be necessary for her to develop in her work without much counsel. This is always a difficult experience for the younger worker. She may be preceding the evangelist several months before he is scheduled to hold his public meetings. Perhaps she is located too far away from the conference office, from which she might seek advice, if proximity would provide an occasional interview with the president of the field. When asked to labor under such isolated conditions, she will be looking forward to the conference workers' meetings, where she may receive help from other Bible instructors.

Not all beginners, however, enter the Bible work under similar conditions. Some are carefully directed and guarded by their leaders; others must learn many lessons in the school of hard knocks. The former is the desirable experience, but it is not the usual one. For this reason the beginner will appreciate receiving some valuable suggestions from one who is still conscious of some specific problems at this stage of development. A successful younger Bible instructor, Marzellas Sell Miller, here provides some helpful suggestions.

First Impressions as a Beginner

"When first beginning the Bible work, a new worker is faced with the realization that classwork and Bible-study preparation have given only a small background for the actual experience of meeting people and presenting Bible doctrines to them.

"Often the task of meeting people and answering their questions nearly overwhelms one. I have found that beginning one's work in an evangelistic effort is ideal, for when the work is all organized and plans are laid as a working group, the Bible instructor feels better prepared and knows what is expected of her. A good start goes a long way in making one's future work successful.

"There are a few pitfalls that I have found Bible instructors should avoid in beginning their work. One is that after having presented the people with literature or announcements several times and having become acquainted, we permit our calls sometimes to become mere social contacts. It is our purpose to open the Bible and present at least a thought or a text and have prayer. And people come to expect it if one begins right away. But if a worker does not do that as soon as she is invited into the home, she sometimes finds it a little awkward to begin later on.

"A beginner has to cultivate the ability to turn the conversation into spiritual lines. Usually the least reference to world conditions can lead to the subject of the second coming of Christ, and many other subjects that one approaches can also be turned into spiritual lessons.

"One must learn how to create interest so that future studies may be arranged for. Frequently the Bible instructor meets one who is full of questions which she tries to answer all in one sitting. If she can cause the person to see that the subject in which he is interested would take a half hour to explain and that she does not have time right then, but suggests some other day or next week, she can often begin a series of lessons, which otherwise could not have been begun if she had answered all their questions sufficiently to satisfy their curiosity the first time. These are a few lessons I had to learn, and am still learning, which may be helpful to other new workers.

"Association with an experienced worker is a real advantage to anyone just entering this field of service. When first beginning, I spent one day a week with an experienced worker simply making contacts and missionary visits. By observing her methods of approach and her answers to different questions that were brought up I received some invaluable training. Later in the effort we spent the day in visiting different people in my territory who were puzzled on certain points, and those whom I had found difficult to convince of various doctrines. This help is priceless to a beginner.

"I have found it a wonderful help to attend a full series of another Bible instructor's studies and take detailed notes. It is surprising how many different points she stresses which can be worked right into your own set of studies. New thoughts and new light on different texts always help one to gain new insight and give fuller meaning to the subjects she is presenting.

"I sincerely believe that studying the Bible in the home with a one-person audience or a larger group brings more satisfaction and greater compensation than any other work one might attempt."

* * * * *

The many and varied problems of the new Bible instructor cannot be discussed at length, but some pointers helpful to the beginner are listed here. These brief suggestions will bring to the young worker an awareness of certain needs and will invite closer study of some specific problems which are now likely to develop.

Helpful Pointers for the Beginner

1. Know that God is leading you personally, that you have been called to the Bible work.

2. Ascertain what plans the conference has for you, your relation to the local church, to other churches in the district.

3. Make friendly contacts with associate workers and local church officers.

4. Properly locate yourself. Neatly organize your little home.

5. Be regular about your rising time. Guard your devotions and study periods.

6. Plan a daily program, even though your work at present suggests no pressure. Keep finding new interest. List all prospects for visits.

7. Use a map in organizing your visits. Get your directions well in mind. Thoroughly acquaint yourself with transportation facilities.

8. Follow a definite plan for visiting the homes in your territory. Be alert to new leads for increasing your list of interested people.

9. Arrange for regular Bible-reading appointments.

10. Consider your work a happy venture for God. Be enthusiastic.

11. Be dignified, yet sociable. Convey the impression that you know how to improve the hours of each day. Let all your visits be purposeful.

12. When assigned a part in the program of some department of the church, be prepared and know your message.

13. Check each day's effort and analyze your results. Learn where to strengthen the weaker places in your work.

14. Be resourceful and not afraid of hard work.

15. Calmly do your best and remain optimistic. Success follows sincere effort.

16. Write to your conference president about once a month. Inform him about the progress of your work and also seek his counsel. He is a busy man, so come to the point at once.

17. Be prompt about sending in your laborer's report. Seek help on special problems, financial or otherwise.

18. Budget your expenses and remain within your budget. Practice economy in order to give more liberally to God's cause.

19. Avail yourself of every opportunity to attend conference workers' meetings. Be on time. Be friendly with your fellow workers.

20. Go the extra mile to help people. Place your strokes where they will count. Successful Bible work is more than keeping very busy.

21. Truth has its opponents, but it always conquers. Meet objections in a tactful way, making friends for the truth.

22. In a crisis, keep prayerful and hopeful. Conservatism and caution never go amiss.

23. Guard your appearance. Let your dress speak for your profession. When in doubt on some point of propriety, be ultraconservative but never odd.

24. Have a hobby, but use it as a diversion in your work and as a blessing to others.

25. Refrain from advertising your good works. Let these be discovered by their influence.

Helping the Tiny Folk

Bible instructors are often confronted with the problem of young infants who must be amused while they endeavor to enlist the interest of their parents for the study of the message. These "bits of heaven" may become a problem, if not a real obstacle, in holding the parents' interest. Bible instructors should be prepared with plans for quieting babies and for capturing the attention of tiny folk who simply must be kept occupied during the Bible study. They must tactfully come to the mother's aid when she fails in her attempts to amuse her three-year-old. It then pays to be able to do some simple drawing to interest the child or to have in the handbag a few colorful bits of pictures to show the child. In this way they endear themselves to these "lambs" of Christ's flock, who will also look forward to their next visit. Missionary Volunteers may be enlisted to make some cloth booklets with pasted-on colored pictures. Drawing projects, sewing cards, beads to string, or various other easily carried articles to entertain the little king or queen of the home are practically indispensable in Bible work. Sunday school supply houses will send catalogs of such devices upon request.

PART ONE ★ CHAPTER FIVE

Making Contacts and Building Interest

The Bible instructor's first business in evangelism is to become acquainted with people. She belongs to them in every sense of the word. She trains herself to use every opportunity to meet people so that she may lead them to Christ. Her work is not done in an office or at home. She goes forth to meet the people—in sunshine or rain, in heat or in cold. As in the lot of the fishermen, she too knows little about regular hours for her "fishing." She also must watch the tides to catch her "fish," at any hour and in every season. She does not wait to be handed lists of names to call on; if she is a real Bible instructor, she is constantly alert for new contacts, wherever she is, for this is her very life.

A consecrated Bible instructor truly loves her work and takes it seriously. From the first moment she meets a prospective reader to the time she sees him established in the church that person is her responsibility. If it is a family, perhaps every member of it is guided by her devoted interest. That is Bible work!

She may have to make her little home in a crowded apartment house of a big city. There, contrary to the customs of other tenants who are not especially concerned about their neighbors, she will carry a burden of soul for the tenant next door to her, or the one across the hall, even before she meets him. She wonders what she can say to the grocer, or to the milkman who daily delivers the milk. She finds suitable youth literature for the newspaper boy. She goes out of her way to meet Sunday school teachers, to converse with them about the Word, and to deepen the interest thus begun.

When invited to a social gathering, there, too, she looks around for someone who may need her particular help, or for

Making Contacts and Building Interest 45

some new contact for the message. She may make new friends at a wedding, or her thoughtful, comforting ways may break down the prejudice of unbelieving relatives at a funeral. While on vacation, away from her work's routine, she still spends herself in order to win some new friends for God. No, this is not the picture of a saint; it is a heavenly portrait of a Bible instructor!

A Bible instructor knows how to follow up the interest of a soul-winning colporteur. She is always delighted with contacts which suggest prospects with whom to study truth. During the lulls between intensive evangelistic meetings she may join lay members in their search for promising people for further study of the message. Whenever possible, she visits the Missionary Volunteer meetings for such contacts. She notices the juniors of the church because she loves them. This may be long before the Week of Prayer indicates that some may be desiring baptism and that her instruction might now be timely. In counsel with the pastor and church school teacher she may organize a class of active boys and girls for the study of Bible fundamentals and doctrines. She may use the occasion of a hike with the young people to create a better understanding between them and the church, or to interest some youth to attend a Christian school. The good Dorcas sisters are her helping hands, and many a promising prospect for the church may be suggested by them. Soul winning is the vital interest of her life. Her influence, therefore, in leading souls to Christ, is continuous and yet unobtrusive.

Because of a shortage of these professional women in our work, today our larger city churches lay claim on our Bible instructors. Here the expanding evangelism program often calls for a full team of workers, and Bible instructors make their special contribution. Too often public evangelism becomes so intensive that workers find it necessary to sidestep every other opportunity to teach the interested, except to follow up those names which have been apportioned to them by the director of the effort.

If the Bible instructor is experienced at her work, she will have at her command a few apt lay sisters who will be her assistants, and who will, under her direction, build up the interest of many prospective readers. The strain of concentrating on the many names which must be handled in a larger interest is strenuous, and extra helpers are appreciated. There is nothing to fear in this plan if the church's talents have been previously developed, and if trained laymen are used. But interest in the message cannot be measured by numbers alone, nor by the scores of name cards procured by the evangelist's skillful public appeals. What worker of experience does not know the toilsome effort of chasing down one name after another, only to find very few good prospects. The more personal contacts for the message there are, the more promising are the results. That name that is associated with the face which has indicated some degree of interest is a good name to follow up. This requires a "watching for souls" in a very practical sense.

An opportunity that needs to be more utilized in our evangelism is the making of the public meeting hall the "fishing pond" for interested people. This is best done before and after the evangelistic service. (*Evangelism,* p. 429.) The strenuous daily visitation program of Bible instructors may tend to bring some rather late to the evening meeting. They then fail to improve the excellent opportunity for making contacts before the song service begins. Bible instructors of experience know that it is a mistake to plan too full a day's program. The visits before meeting bring many fine contacts with people who are interested enough to get there early.

In the thoroughly organized public campaign, workers need not vie with one another in the contacts made prior to the regular evening meeting. Workers are to be a cooperative team. They should graciously help to introduce visitors to each one of the evangelistic group. More and more people will then make every effort to come a little earlier, merely because they find these chats with friendly Bible instructors so helpful. Soon they begin to discuss various points of the message with them, and will casually reveal their special problems. It becomes a natural procedure for the worker to suggest that she will be in their neighborhood on a certain afternoon during the week, and will be happy to "drop in" to further explain these queries. This tactful suggestion usually brings a warm invitation to visit the home at the worker's convenience.

As contacts in the homes are established, more members of these families will begin attending the meetings. At the suggestion of the Bible instructor some become enthusiastic enough to open their homes for a neighborhood study group, on an evening when there is no public meeting. Soon there are many of these little groups studying the message in various sections of the city and its suburbs. An expanding personal work of this type suggests a promising evangelistic harvest. More than is often recognized, the Bible instructor's skilled Bible work is responsible for what may be called a "good interest."

PART ONE ★ CHAPTER SIX

Developing the Conversational Art

"The success of the gospel message does not depend upon learned speeches, eloquent testimonies, or deep arguments. It depends upon the simplicity of the message and its adaptation to the souls that are hungering for the bread of life."
—*Christ's Object Lessons,* p. 231.

The problem of bringing our message to the people is not always as simple as it might seem. Some are not so readily approached, and yet they may be the cautious type who develop into strong leaders when once won over to the cause. It is therefore important that the Bible instructor familiarize herself with every avenue to the human heart. She must be a close student of human nature and of soul-winning principles. Her textbook of method is the Bible, supplemented by the instruction of the Spirit of prophecy. She also learns methods from successful workers.

The graces of Christian culture should charm each step of the Bible instructor's path, and win for her that ready entrance into homes of refinement which the uncouth and uncultured fail to find. This is not all attained through educational advantages. She must know good taste in dress for the sake of winning others.

The Bible instructor's speech must be well chosen and informative. This requires that she constantly fill her mind with interesting things to talk about, as well as with Bible argument. She must learn to live with the people, not merely because she *has* to do it to find access to them, but because she *loves* to and is intensely interested in every phase of human life. If she aims to win the better class, the others will also be reached.

The conversational art is one that is absolutely essential in Bible work. It should not be merely friendly talk or chatter with little point except to make the people feel good. The Bible instructor's conversation must have depth of purpose. Primarily it should guide ordinary conversation into helpful religious discussion, which may later lead into obedience to God.

It is not altogether a matter of stating facts of truth, but much is involved in the way they are stated. Pointed statements, especially on unpopular truth, may be related in the spirit of good will and spiced with humor, so that honest, common sense will want to respond to friendly appeal. Nothing is gained by thrusts, especially in religious discussion, but much is gained by sincere friendliness and kind frankness.

This is an art which many workers must continue to practice to make conversation of point as well as of good will.

If there is ever a time when conversation counts for winning the interest of an individual, it is right at the beginning of one's acquaintance. Then the Bible instructor must make herself especially winsome for God. There must be no delay, because opportunity may not again present itself. For this reason it is important to find the proper point of contact.

There is some interest in every home that may be used to guide household conversation into purposeful religious discussion. The babe of the family may become the incentive for the mother to acquaint herself with the Scriptures so as to be able to teach them to her child. Again, it may be the appeal for spiritual guidance for a young man in his country's service. Often it is the invalid's need that creates an opening for Bible study for the entire family. When other suggestions are not evident, the turbulent conditions of the day never fail to arouse an interest in learning what the Bible has to say about current signs of the times. This is one of the standard methods of leading inquirers into a series of Bible readings.

Although in a few instances it may seem expedient, it is hardly necessary to go through the formality of asking for the privilege of reading from the Bible. This privilege is simply accepted from God, and the Bible is made the tool of one's profession. Christianity is not in its experimental stages today, so when the gospel worker calls, it is rather expected that she will use Christian tools, techniques, and appeals. For this reason the Bible instructor always keeps her Bible handy so that she can produce it inconspicuously. She so naturally and gracefully goes to the Word for her authority that there need be no confusion as to propriety. In this initial technique lies much of the secret of her success in continuing Bible studies in any particular home.

The reading of half a dozen interesting Bible texts during the first visit usually impresses the listener to exclaim, "How

I wish that I knew my Bible as you know yours!" What better opportunity might be wanted than this expressed interest! So now the Bible instructor tactfully suggests that she has weekly calls in the neighborhood and would be happy to give the reader a little of her time also for a better understanding of the Bible. She continues naturally by explaining that Bible teaching is her chosen profession. Perhaps she adds, "Isn't it high time for all Christians, of every faith, to show interest in a prayerful study of God's Word?" This suggests a favorable response and brings the invitation for future Bible readings. It also relaxes any tension regarding the worker's church affiliations. This skill requires tact resulting from practice, but it need not lead to any deceptive strategy about her denominational identity, for it always pays to be cautiously aboveboard.

In the course of conversation some definite doctrinal questions may have been asked the instructor by the one she hopes to interest. It then seems appropriate for her to suggest that she will be happy to take a little longer time at her next visit to explain these points in more detail. The next visit will usually find the inquirer waiting to receive her with a welcome. She has thought of some more questions, and may have invited a relative or neighbor to be present for this visit. After a brief consideration of the particular points in question, it is now good procedure to build a series of studies, even though the Bible instructor may not think it best to announce her intention. She perhaps proceeds with a study on the return of Christ, or a similar foundation subject.

Before the topic of conversation is left, mention of the rather rare grace of listening attentively to what others have to say must not be overlooked. Remember that paradoxically the conversational art has its rest periods, when it quietly listens in good taste to permit the other person to do some of the talking. Then the Bible instructor does not act bored or interrupt with what she wants to present, but she uses these moments to reflect with composure on the individual's various interests, without losing any points which may even seem uninteresting talk. It must all be of interest to the Bible teacher, who uses this information in her analysis of the narrator and in the building of future approaches.

PART ONE ★ CHAPTER SEVEN

The Pleasing and Inspiring Teacher

The Speaking Voice

Our lofty message should be expressed in the purest, noblest, most convincing language. A Bible instructor should try to develop a simple style of speech which has become natural to her. Her voice should match her personality. Some Bible instructors unconsciously adopt the expressions, mannerisms, and voice of those with whom they work. But adopting another's style of voice or speech to the extent that it throws one's individuality out of focus is annoying to the listener. It may suggest at least a limited inferiority complex, and also reveals a self-consciousness which hinders poise and destroys interest in the speaker.

Simplicity in speech is most effective, but it must not be confused with a stunted speech development, either physical or scholastic. True, much of what is conveyed to others may be said in the simplest words, but who would deny the enjoyment that is derived from the expressions of one who has learned to use a cultivated vocabulary? Words should be well chosen and well thought through, whether of one syllable or more.

A Bible instructor may have given much attention to the physical and psychological aspects of voice training, and yet her voice may not be at all pleasing to her listeners. Those who have determinedly taken themselves in hand to correct speech defects under their control, often develop the most charming speech. Once they have mastered their weaknesses, their attainment produces an individualistic type of speech power.

A soft, musical voice is far more effective for the Bible instructor than the harsh, raucous voice which sets the listener on edge. The voice should not be weak, however. And for a Bible instructor to develop a voice which, though musical, is strong enough to be heard in a larger assembly, does not suppress feminine charm. A baby-type voice will never challenge decision for obedience to this forceful message; neither will the harsh, commanding, self-sufficient tone be winsome in appeal.

It is most annoying not to hear what is said, and the efforts of the mumbling Bible instructor are just a waste of energy. The sparkling eye must follow the certain thrust of the word, resting with appeal on the one who is addressed. Looking steadfastly and openly into the face of the reader is the secret of many spontaneous decisions.

In the training of workers the need for a pleasing voice must be stressed. The Spirit of prophecy has provided most practical instruction which is available to all. Professional voice training can be recommended to evangelistic workers generally, but those still denied a cultural training may well profit by giving attention to a few simple rules. A study of the following outline will benefit every Bible instructor.

Development of the Voice
RUTH TINKLER
(Based on *Evangelism,* by Ellen G. White)

I. *Importance of Proper Speaking.* (Pages 504, 505, 665, 667-669.)
  1. The gospel worker is God's mouthpiece.
  2. Imperfect utterance dishonors God.
  3. Truth is marred if communicated through defective utterance.
  4. Voice tones affect hearts of hearers.

5. The voice is a precious gift from God.
6. Perfection of speech and voice should be urged.
7. Bad speaking habits hinder work.

II. *How to Speak.* (Pages 508, 665-668, 174, 175, 183.)
   1. Speak in full, round tones.
   2. Enunciate every word clearly.
   3. Read with soft, musical cadence.
   4. Speak correctly and forcibly, with expression.
   5. Avoid talking in loud voice or high key.
   6. Talk slowly, deliberately.
   7. Preserve pathos and melody of voice.
   8. Cultivate its musical quality.
   9. Speak advisedly, never impulsively.
   10. In reproving, speak with Christlike tenderness and love.

III. *Christ's Example.* (Pages 670, 56.)
   1. He spoke slowly and calmly. Hearers caught meaning.
   2. He gave vital force and impressiveness to all His utterances.
   3. He did not raise His voice to an unnatural key.
   4. His hearers caught every intonation of His voice.

IV. *Voice in Song.* (Pages 496-512.)
   1. Avoid loud singing.
   2. Stress clear intonation, correct pronunciation, distinct utterance.
   3. Cultivate voice for singing.
   4. Modulate the voice. Soften and subdue.
   5. Seek to glorify God with the voice; it is more pleasing to God than musical instruments.

V. *Physical Aspect.* (Pages 669, 668, 667.)
   1. Observe proper breathing. Use diaphragm.
   2. If the voice is used correctly, you may speak to thousands as easily as ten.
   3. Voice training is important in physical culture.
   4. When organs of speech are strained, modulations of voice are lost.
   5. Vocal organs become enfeebled if used improperly.

Truth's Radiating Power

The presentation of our truth-compelling message, whether in public or in private, must be with power. A simple, unostentatious style allows the force of conviction to flash through the Bible teacher's speech and personality. The effectiveness of the message is produced by deep earnestness born of personal conviction of its importance.

Paul's noblest theme was the cross of Calvary. The cross must now be our stimulus for teaching truth. A skillful handling of the Word, with all its sound logic, must not eclipse the cross. The listener's attention must not be focused on the subject of communication; it must be pointed to the direct object of salvation. A Bible reading should vibrate with inspiration and offer a challenge to obey what the Book teaches.

The Spirit of prophecy has told us to avoid "tame and lifeless" teaching. If Bible readings are to maintain force and power, they must be polished and repolished, or they will soon lose their primitive luster. John the Baptist was a "burning and a shining light." We must speak with an authority which grows out of a background of unhurried prayer and personal preparation.

Clarity of Thought: Effective Expression

I. *Truth—Its Radiating Power.* (*Evangelism*, pp. 457, 458, 191, 648, 649, 195, 146, 147, 178.)
   1. Truth in demonstration and power.
   2. Converted teacher to radiate Christ.
   3. Vital, heavenly fire.
   4. Words of freshness and power.
   5. Truth in clear, connected manner.
   6. Avoiding tedious, dry, abstract teaching.
   7. Not stale, oft-repeated ideas.
II. *Examples of Animated Expression and Poise.*
   1. Christ. (*Evangelism*, pp. 55, 56.)
      a. Simplicity of language, beauty of truth.
      b. Vital force and impressiveness of utterance.
      c. Lighting up of hearer's countenance.
   2. Paul. (*Acts of the Apostles*, pp. 237, 245-247, 252, 270, 322, 216, 435, 240, 241, 270.)
      a. Uplifted the cross of Calvary.
      b. Poured out a soul burden.
      c. Presented the fundamentals.

The Pleasing and Inspiring Teacher 55

    d. Studied effects of his message.
    e. Impressed jailer and Agrippa with his tranquillity.
    f. Drew idolatrous listeners.
    g. Won Apollos by clear teaching.
III. *Steps in Effective Expression.*
  1. Knowledge of the subject.
  2. Related material and background.
  3. Selection of material.
  4. Orderly arrangement.
  5. Unfolding progressively.
  6. Introduction of details.
  7. Fitting into occasion.
  8. Clarifying unfamiliar expressions.
  9. Measuring capacity of the listener.
  10. Holding to the point.

Heavenly Power

How oft the power of words prevails,
  Instead Thy Word of power;
How oft we turn to human strength,
  When in that very hour
    Thy mighty Word,
    That Word of God,
In all its truth should tower!

How prone we are to look for force
  Within our words and aims,
And then expect these human plans
  To serve the latter rains—
    The Spirit's gift,
    That gift of God,
Which every doubt explains!

How much Thy Spirit longs to do
  These staggering tasks we face.
O'er which we wrestle in our strength,
  And fail oft in disgrace!
    Help us to feel
    Our need of Thee,
And all Thy power embrace!

> Lord, save us from these carnal ways,
> Reveal Thy Spirit's might;
> Thy boundless store of help divine
> To turn men to the light—
> The light of God,
> That light from heav'n
> That penetrates earth's night!

PART ONE ★ CHAPTER EIGHT

Bible-reading Skills

It was during the early '80's that the "heaven-born" idea of teaching by means of Bible readings was first introduced into our work. The Lord then directed in this plan of using Bible texts to meet doctrinal inquiry. We smile a bit as we remember that the first Bible reading used by our Bible instructors consisted of about one hundred and fifty questions answered by Bible texts. Indeed, progress has been made in this holy art, for the textual argumentation has been trimmed down and the plan itself has increased in favor.

Trained Bible instructors may not need some of the Bible-reading techniques in this manual. Experience has taught them many points on the proper use of texts, logic, and sequence, so important in developing comprehensive and convincing Bible studies. They have worked their hands into this Bible-reading art even as the good housewife discovered the very "feel" for making nutritious and well-baked bread. But others are still growing into the profession. All may continue to improve by observing at least where the emphasis on these techniques should be placed.

The work of evangelist and Bible instructor is interdependent in the winning of souls, the true objective of personal work, but the instructor must remain a teacher even as the evangelist in his public sphere is primarily a preacher. It is expected, however, that as a Bible instructor she will add teaching dignity to her profession by her ever-broadening knowledge of the Bible and increasingly successful teaching methods.

A Bible reading is not a sermon. A Bible reading consists in the compilation of texts and their comparison one with another, whereas the usual sermon is an exposition of a single text, or at least a single idea. Bible instructors who listen to many sermons and lectures on doctrine must guard their teaching technique if the Bible reading is not to take on preaching and lecturing aspects. But there are many advantages of the Bible reading over the sermon or lecture. The former is not so complex, and is most suitable to the average individual's inquiry. The Bible reading confines itself to letting God's Word provide the answer to the problem under consideration. It also lends itself to the needs of smaller and larger study groups who are interested in personally investigating Bible truth. There is great power in the Bible reading with all its directness. It creates a wholesome type of expectancy on the part of the learner, stimulating in the study of present truth.

The Bible Study

But let us now stress a few other techniques necessary for a helpful Bible reading. These points must be stated briefly. Our denomination has made definite progress in the development of Bible-teaching methods. Today a Bible study may be selected from sets of printed patterns in our correspondence courses. These courses, developed out of broad experience in progressive evangelism, may vary in approach, development, and appeal, but the purpose of each set is indoctrination of our message. They suggest sound methods that Bible instructors of limited experience may use as models for effective, provocative teaching of truth.

Although these prepared lessons supplement and expedite the process of teaching our truths to non-Adventists, they also serve to establish those who already believe the message. The influence of these courses is world wide, for correspondence schools function at the home base and also overseas. Since this plan of truth instruction is growing in popularity, it is necessary for the Bible instructor to fit into its objectives. This plan breaks the ground for expansive evangelism. Here is a caution for Bible instructors: It is the *planned* lesson, not the *canned* lesson, the Bible instructor is to use! Though these sets of Bible lessons are for truth seekers generally, the teacher should at least adapt each lesson to the needs and capacity of the individual.

Title of the Study

Choosing an appealing title for the study must be more than just giving it a name. The signs of the times may be the topic, but why not stimulate the reader's imagination in suggesting an interest-provoking title? Mrs. Smith's husband is deeply concerned about modern management and labor problems. He will be much more impressed with a study announced as "Management and Labor in Conflict" than by generalizing on the signs of the end. Now he alertly sits up to find out what his informer may know about a problem he may think belongs solely in the jurisdiction of businessmen like himself. It is now only a problem of the worker's making good her claims. The Bible instructor must not overlook this point of suggestive titles, for it will keep her out of the rut of monotony.

The Introduction

Of course, some real study must be given to the *introduction* of the Bible reading. It must be gripping in its forecast and sincerely honest in its claims. Again, it should be brief, and yet it must also lay a good foundation. The introduction should meet the need and mental capacity of the reader. For instance, statistical facts on the signs of our times must not be exhausted on a Grandma Green, who now needs far more the security of Jesus than an array of facts. A brief suggestion of the problems and general beliefs on the topic may be a sufficient introduction. A strong text or two may also open the mind to Bible-directed thinking before the main points are built up in a more thorough way. The introduction is the interest gripper, and when it has been gripped, then the reader is ready to enter into an investigation of the evidence.

The Body

For the *body* of the Bible study the instructor will need to be well prepared with argumentation, much of which will be restrained until required. Again, this section of the Bible reading should be adapted to the needs and interest of the pupil. The points should be organized against error in battle array, but the spirit of the study must not be militant or dogmatic. Truth should be built up by exalting Jesus, the Truth. Then points of truth should be tied together with the bands of sound logic. Truth must bear investigation.

The Close

The *ending*, or closing, of a Bible reading suggests summarizing, clinching, appealing, or forecasting; not all for the same study, however. It is not necessary to announce any of these objectives, and especially not the appeal. In fact, an appeal at the climax of the study should be the outgrowth of a series of either less-pointed appeals or perhaps those progressive, more-imbedded appeals which are convenient elsewhere in the study. But now is the proper time in the study for the Bible instructor to guide the thinking of her reader toward a spontaneous committal regarding the points of truth already reviewed. Any pressure must be guarded against, for it would merely bring embarrassment, which will lead the reader to seek excuses for evading such a committal in the future.

Use of Texts

No definite rule can be laid down as to the number of Scripture passages to be used in Bible reading. Fifteen to twenty texts would be sufficient for the average reader, and the study should be from forty to sixty minutes' duration; however, other factors might suggest a deviation from this plan. Some Bible teachers have the gift of using conveniently a textual vocabulary without appearing professionally stilted. (Recommended by Mrs. White, *Evangelism*, p. 204.) Again, it is one thing to "go to the bottom of every subject" when the Bible instructor is preparing an outline of material for herself, but quite another matter when the reader's mental and physical capacity must also be considered. When arguments become too explicit and prolonged, the interest is lost. One or two texts on a point in question are usually sufficient evidence, but where confusion must be cleared away, then the teacher will do wisely to reduce the discussion on some other points planned for the study. Progression of thought should mark the order and arrangement of texts. Transition from one text to another should be natural, without force or strain. It adds to the effectiveness of a Bible reading to occasionally use a fitting illustration especially on such points of new truth to the reader which require more clarification. Bible examples are most appropriate, but apt illustrations from modern life also have their special value.

Notes, References

Regarding the use of notes, Bible teachers will vary in their opinions. Those who speak loudest in favor of not using notes at all still feel that a limited use of notes assures poise and organized progression to the teacher. In first organizing a study one should not be sparing in jotting down sufficient points to round out the subject. This is most helpful for the instructor who will live with these notes until they become a part of her instruction. The teacher need not be riveted to these various points, however, and may select those that are most important to the reader. She will look at her pupil while she teaches, glancing at her notes only occasionally.

Building Truth

A Bible instructor is a builder of God's temple of truth. An inspiring work, indeed! Her objective must be worked out in the experience of her pupil, who, guided by her, will soon be building truth into his own life. She builds according to the divine blueprint. Naturally she must have a well-thought-through plan on all the details of her building program. There is a definite place for each stone she will be using in the structure. She does not begin in this prejudiced age with a study on the mark of the beast, but later in the series this subject, which needs foundation teaching, will carry great weight, and often becomes the crowning theme of the whole series.

Hit-and-miss subjects usually miss far more than they hit. They are largely to blame for the disappointing results of the slipshod methods of instruction employed by the rush-and-run type of worker. The very nature of our unfamiliar message requires a most thorough indoctrination. If solid instruction is not given before burial with Christ in baptism, it surely must be given immediately after. It is far better, however, to postpone the time of baptism until the reader is reasonably well established in the message. It pays to give even a brief series of studies which will include at least all the chief points of our doctrines. To further emphasize by repetition those doctrinal points and practices that are not as generally accepted by other denominations, is sound reinforcement of present truth.

Interpreting Scripture

Because whole fallacious systems are today being built on faulty interpretation of Scripture, this outline of suggestions for the Bible instructor will be helpful for personal study.

I. *Authority of the Bible.* (See such sources as C. B. Haynes, *God's Book,* pp. 117-128; H. L. Hastings, *Will the Old Book Stand?* etc.)
   1. Unity of Bible writers. *God's Book,* 37-47.
   2. Reliability and power. *Ibid.,* 48-91.
   3. Prophetic writings. *Ibid.,* 92-116.
   4. Inspiration of Scriptures. *Ibid.,* 129-149.
   5. Scientific accuracy. *Ibid.,* 150-170.
II. *Interpreting God's Word.* (See William Evans, *How to Prepare Sermons,* chap. 4, Moody Press.)
   1. Literal interpretation. A. J. Wearner, *Art of Personal Evangelism,* 140-142; *God's Book,* 215-220.
   2. Figurative language. *Art of Personal Evangelism,* 147-149; *God's Book,* 213, 214.
   3. Apocryphal writings. A. J. Wearner, *Fundamentals of Bible Doctrine,* 24, 25; *God's Book,* 126-128.
   4. Versions of the Bible. *Fundamentals of Bible Doctrine,* 22-24; *God's Book,* 171-184; Edgar J. Goodspeed, *How to Read the Bible,* chap. 23, John C. Winston Co.
III. *Problems for the Bible Teacher.*
   1. Bible its own interpreter. *God's Book,* 211-221; Ed 190.
   2. Holding to the affirmative. GW 358; 9 T 147, 148; Eze. 13:4-14 (false prophets); AA 257.
   3. Not for argumentation. GW 259.
   4. Teaching Christ. *God's Book,* 185-195, 45.
   5. Harmony of Old and New Testament. *Ibid.,* 104-113.
   6. Importance of Bible for all mankind. GC 69, 521; FE 444.
   7. Proper attitude of searcher. GC 599, 600; CT 450; Ed 188, 189, 192.

PART ONE ★ CHAPTER NINE

The Role in Public Evangelism

ELLEN CURRAN

The world today is accomplishing tremendous things in a short time. Scientific invention and increased knowledge are crowding decades into hours, as it were. In order to give the last warning message to this fast-moving world, Bible instructors too must expand their vision. True, the great message will always be the same, and their only hope for results remains the same—the power of God in their labors. But God calls them to put forth every effort to gain greater efficiency and larger results in their work.

The Bible instructor's work is strenuous but most enjoyable. Hers is the privilege of getting into close contact with the people. Some Bible instructors give their whole time and effort to obtaining open doors where they may regularly study the Bible with a few people in their homes. Others assist in public efforts by giving Bible studies and doing personal work in connection with the effort. A Bible instructor with public ability follows a different program in public meetings from that which she would follow in association with local church endeavors. She would lessen her value to the evangelist if she were to be tied down exclusively to the few that she would be able to study with regularly each week, and have no time left to reach the masses. This is not what most evangelists want or what the public effort demands. Let us note five points toward efficiency in large effort work.

1. FRIENDLY CONTACTS.—Seek a friendly contact with as many people as possible, because you do not know who will accept the truth—this one or that one. Therefore be friendly with all. This, however, must be done with tact and wisdom, for it can be overdone.

When the meetings first begin, a friendly "Good evening" or a quiet smile may be better than much handshaking and asking for names. The same is true as the people leave. A cheery "Good night" and "Come back again" will be sure to make friends.

When cards are passed for names and addresses, the same thing is true again—make as many short calls as possible, the more the better, at first, to find out where the interested ones are. Use the telephone for making contacts. If you cannot get around to all, mail out postal cards asking people to obtain their promised literature from you at the meetings. Urge everyone to come to the meetings. Talk up the meetings and the preacher. Tell them that you will be looking for them personally—at the meetings. There is the place you want to see them—not in their homes. You cannot see all of them in their homes every week. But soon you will see definite interests developing, and these should have first attention.

2. List of Special Interests.—Besides a general visiting file, keep a separate list of outstanding interests. Keep this list up to date and on your mind and in your prayers. Some Bible instructors segregate names according to where the people live, grouping those together who live in the same localities. This may work at first, but I believe that from the very beginning the visiting file should contain a separate list of those interests that could be developed ahead of the rest. If these names are left scattered among the other cards, they may be forgotten at the crucial time.

The Bible instructor should ascertain the reactions of the interested ones each time a subject is presented, answer their questions, and study with them, or give them printed lessons to study on all essential lectures they may have missed. Help them to make decisions as they progress. We are certainly blessed these days with all the truth-filled literature and printed lessons we can give to the people to study at home. We find that God's powerful Word works in the lives of men and women who will study for themselves. With the permission of the evangelist, set up a little "headquarters" right in the foyer or at the entrance, where a file with printed lessons and literature on all the various subjects may be kept, and as the people's needs are revealed by visiting with them before and after meetings, provide them with lessons to study. Make appointments according to the needs of interested ones and record them in a daybook.

Invite the interested people to the Sabbath services as soon as advisable, and be there to meet them.

3. "This One Thing I Do."—Cause the people to know by your actions that your main job is soul winning. Let no person or persons monopolize your time with social affairs or otherwise. Most people can readily see that you are interested in all the people—that you love them all. They will understand and appreciate this fact, and will not needlessly take up your time. In making calls, maintain this same attitude—let the people know you are there for one purpose only —to help them love the Lord more than any earthly thing. Enlist the new members as your partners to help win souls by having them introduce you to their friends. Then they will not feel neglected after they are baptized.

4. Indoctrination Classes.—If possible at all, conduct classes for indoctrination and baptismal instruction. Fortunate is the Bible instructor who is associated with an evangelist who believes in Bible classes in connection with his meetings, not just a class conducted by the Bible instructor, but a class that is really "under his wings," and a definite part of his program. He should support it and build it up with his strong influence, as only the evangelist can do. Such a class will not only prove a definite factor in developing interest but will also take care of many, many Bible studies which would otherwise have to be given in each of the homes. In this way the Bible instructor has much more time for general calls and for helping the people when they most need her.

The more the evangelist builds up the Bible instructor before the people, the more results her work will produce.

5. CONCENTRATE.—While you keep your finger on the pulse of the general interest, concentrate on those who may be brought to a decision with the proper help. Keep the evangelist informed of their special needs. Know your people as individuals. Watch the developments in their lives and keep very close to them at the critical time.

One prominent evangelist tells what he expects of a Bible instructor. He said, "I want a Bible instructor who knows how to take off the cream when I bring it to the top." Then he added, "Many just stir around in it until the cream is mixed back with the milk." What an apt illustration! Much interest can be lost by not taking care of it at the proper time. The devil knows who is about to make a decision, and he stays very close to that individual. The Bible instructor too should stay very close. Watch whether each particular one is at the meetings or whether he is absent. Some will tell you when they are having battles to fight; others will not tell you, and you must sense their need and get close to their hearts. A personal experience illustrates this point.

Among those whose interest was developing very well was a good man who had been attending the meetings regularly and also the classes at the reading room. In fact, he told me that he had been attending Elder K's meetings off and on for ten years. He had now begun to attend Sabbath services, but I missed him one Sabbath morning at church. He did not come to the baptismal class in the reading room that afternoon. I thought, "Perhaps he is ill, but he will surely be at the meeting Sunday morning." He was absent from all the meetings that Sunday, but I could do nothing about it until the classes were ended at the reading room, which was about nine-thirty that night. Another worker and I drove over to this man's home. He came to the door with an open Bible in his hand, but it was apparent all was not well.

"Brother Arnold, we have missed you. I hope you are not ill," I said. He answered no.

"What's wrong? Has someone been discouraging you?"

"Well, some of the people from the other church have been talking to me, and I decided I would just stay away from everybody and read my Bible at home."

"Brother Arnold, remember, it's always darkest just before the dawn. The devil knows you are taking your stand, and he is making it hard for you, but you are going to come out all right. God is going to help you. You will be stronger than ever because of this battle. It's late now, but tomorrow morning come over to the reading room, and we will go through all the doctrines with you again, and I'm sure God's Word will settle it for you." He promised he would come, and at ten o'clock the next morning he was there. The man's faith in this message returned fully, and he said, "Now it is settled forever. No one will shake me again." Before he went away he said, "After you left my home last night I thought to myself, 'Who am I that they should care that much—to come here this late after a long, hard day? They really care. There is something to this religion.' "

He was baptized with the very next group and is now a faithful member and trustworthy helper at the reading room.

So, while you watch the general interest and find new interests, concentrate on the outstanding interests.

PART ONE ★ CHAPTER TEN

Clinching and Conserving Interest

Mrs. J. E. Whelpley

Should the Bible instructor carry on regular Bible studies during the evangelistic effort, or will her work consist mainly of making contacts with the people and keeping them attending the meetings? There is much to be said on both sides.

If the Bible instructor has been working in a city, giving studies prior to the beginning of the evangelistic series, she will not want to lose contact with these interested ones. If her readers are able to attend the meetings, then she will have no difficulty in keeping in contact with them. But on the other hand, if readers are situated so that they cannot attend the meetings, or if they are well along in a series of studies, the Bible instructor will need to continue the studies until the readers have been led to a decision. In this event her readers will then be ready for the first baptism in the effort.

Whether or not the Bible instructor carries on regular Bible studies during the effort may be a question; however she will endeavor to keep those on her calling list abreast of the public meetings. Her first call on those whose interest has been aroused by the effort will be short, and often she may not even enter the door. The object of this call is to encourage the people to keep coming to the tent or hall. So she will mention the topics to be considered by the evangelist each night of the current week and especially try to arouse an interest in "tonight's" subject.

At the evening meetings the Bible instructor will make it a point to greet and shake hands with those upon whom she had made her initial call, endeavoring as soon as possible to be able to call them by name. It will not be long before she will be invited into the home when she calls, and then she can really go to work. She will avoid asking Mrs. Smith, "How did you like the sermon?" But she will ask her whether the subject was clear and whether there are any questions in her mind regarding it.

The worker will answer questions and clear up any points that were not understood, but she will be careful not to answer questions on any subject not yet presented by the evangelist. If questions on future subjects are asked, she might answer, "That's a good question! No doubt there are many people wondering about the same thing. Why not put it in the question box? I believe I have a question card right

Clinching and Conserving Interest

here in my handbag. Would you like to write it out and drop it in the question box, so that the evangelist can answer it tonight?" Such questions give the evangelist an opportunity to arouse an interest in topics to be used in future meetings.

The worker will endeavor to keep each one she calls on interested in the progress of the meetings. Unless she does this, it will require much more time and effort later on to bring these persons to a decision. She will help Mrs. Smith to take her stand on each point as it is presented. If she does this, it will not be hard for her to make her decision on the Sabbath and other testing truths of the message.

If Mrs. Smith, who has been attending each night, is absent one evening the Bible instructor should let her know that she has been missed, and that she missed an interesting lecture. For example, she might say, "I am so sorry that you had to miss that sermon on heaven. It was one of the most interesting lectures that Evangelist Green has given. He showed us where the redeemed will spend eternity and that we shall be real people in a real world. Why, did you know that each of us is going to have a mansion in that holy city as well as a home in the country, too? We are going to build our own homes in the country, and raise our own gardens. Oh, I wish you could have heard it."

Help for Those Who Missed Meetings

By this time Mrs. Smith is sorry that she did not attend that meeting. The instructor may continue, "It is too bad to have to miss a single meeting. It is like breaking a link in a chain. No doubt you have noticed that one subject is closely related to the others, and when you miss one topic you have lost a link. By the way, Mrs. Smith, if you wish, perhaps I could give you just a few of the high lights of what Evangelist Green said, so that you will understand it."

The reader, feeling that it would be asking too much, will probably reply, "I would appreciate it if you have time." So a short Bible study on the subject is given her.

Mrs. Smith now agrees that what Miss Bible Instructor told her was very interesting—and if this is a taste of the good things presented, then the lecture must have been wonderful. She is sorry that she missed that meeting, and is now determined that she will not miss another of the series. In this way the Bible instructor can do her part in helping Mrs. Smith to pick up the lost thread of topic interest, and at the same time keep her coming to the meetings. Of course, this should not be done if the individual attends the meetings only occasionally, as some do, because there would then be too much to cover in Bible studies. Such interest should be handled by the Bible instructor, who would give a series of progressive Bible studies of her own.

The worker must constantly keep her finger on the pulse of those on her calling list, watching their development and counteracting any influence which might tend to detract from their interest. Especially is this true when the Sabbath is presented. She will know when Mrs. Smith is troubled over the Sabbath, and will help her in making the right decision. Turn to the book *Gospel Workers* and read: "My brethren and sisters, in your ministry come close to the people."—Page 37. "Many a laborer fails in his work because he does not come close to those who most need his help."—*Ibid.*, p. 190.

Since the Bible instructor knows that Mrs. Smith is deeply concerned over the Sabbath, she drops in, between her regular calls, when in that neighborhood. She says, "I was just passing by, Mrs. Smith, and thought I would drop in a moment and see how you are." Only a friend "drops in" when passing by; hence, the bond between Mrs. Smith and Miss Bible Instructor is strengthened. They become friends, and Mrs. Smith will naturally turn to this friend when she needs help and counsel in making her full decision.

Perhaps Mrs. Smith's minister has been to see her, or one of the members of her family has been trying to overthrow the Sabbath truth. By "dropping around" between calls, the worker has an opportunity to counteract this influence before it has time to get a foothold. She can instantly detect a change in Mrs. Smith's attitude, and it is not long before she can find out in a tactful way where the trouble lies. She can then help remedy the difficulty, and again Mrs. Smith is in harmony with the message. At the proper time the Bible instructor should invite the evangelist to visit Mrs. Smith. After all, no one can help her to make a decision better than the evangelist who first aroused her interest.

After the Sabbath is presented and the people are invited to attend Sabbath services in the tent or hall, the Bible instructor will make it a point to drop in and see Mrs. Smith near the close of the week, preferably on Friday. "I have brought you a *Sabbath School Lesson Quarterly*, Mrs. Smith, on the lessons we are studying in our Bible school. I thought you might like to look it over so that you will be familiar with it." This gives the worker an opportunity to urge Mrs. Smith to attend the Sabbath services. Such a personal invitation is often effective. When Mrs. Smith comes to the Sabbath service, she should be greeted and made to feel at home. If possible, the Bible instructor should sit with her during her first Sabbath service, so she will not feel alone. At the close of the service she should be introduced to some of the church members.

Throughout the series of meetings the worker carries these interested ones on her heart. She prays for them by name in her private devotions, as well as in the workers' meetings. She must also pray with and for them when they are in the valley of decision.

The Bible instructor is the tool the Lord uses to cultivate the soil in which the evangelist has planted the seed. But only God can cause the plant to bear fruit. Only He can change the heart; only He can lead this soul to a decision. If the worker will stay close to this source of all power, if she is willing to be a tool in the hand of God, then God can use her effectively to bring souls to Christ,

Personal Work in Evangelism

"Personal influence is a power. The more direct our labor for our fellow men, the greater good will be accomplished.... You must come close to those for whom you labor, that they may not only hear your voice, but shake your hand, learn your principles, and realize your sympathy."—*Evangelism*, pp. 438, 439.

I. *Personal Work in the Closing Message.* (Based on *Evangelism*.)
   1. Awakening interest in eternal life. 430.
   2. Speaking words of encouragement. 430.
   3. Following up spirit of inquiry. 429.
   4. Helping inquirers to build on sure foundation. 429.
   5. Ascertaining reactions on how message received. 429.
   6. Turning men's minds to serious thinking. 431.

II. *Illustrations of Personal Work.*
   1. Hiding the truth in hearts. 469.
   2. Inviting men to the "gospel feast." 433.
   3. Fishing for souls. Jer. 16:16.
   4. Visiting, seeking, as hunting. 433, 437, 463.
   5. Digging confused out of debris of error. 444.
   6. Deepening impressions "made upon hearts and consciences." 438.
   7. Tendering the heart. 460.
   8. Flashing on the light of God's Word. 438, 577.
   9. Sowing and tilling gospel truth. 490, 429, 432.
   10. Raking, gathering, caring for the harvest. 443, 438, 462.
   11. Picking most accessible berries first. 293, 294.
   12. Making truth clear as mileposts. 439.
   13. Bearing the censer of love to homes. 349.
   14. Growing flowers for God's garden. 98, 99.

III. *Finding Way to the Heart.*
   1. Personal work an adventure and discovery. 483.
   2. Softening the heart by sympathetic interest. 430.
   3. The delicate touch; opening the heart. 483.
   4. Doing the little things. 329.
   5. Visiting and laboring for people. 306, 307.
   6. Doing a special work for sinners. 306, 307.
   7. Speaking to people at public meetings. 429.
   8. Helping mothers with home problems. 459.

Clinching and Conserving Interest 73

    9. Showing an interest in the sick. 459.
   10. Using our literature. GW 353; 7T 38.
   11. Creating a desire for Bible study. 481.
   12. Breaking down prejudice. 445.

IV. *Bible Study and Personal Work.*
    1. Praying with people; giving them Bible readings. 457.
    2. Deciding truth by what God has said. 481, 464, 433, 485, 457.
    3. Persuasion, prayer, love of God. 459.
    4. Teaching doctrine; how to surrender to God. 465, 430.

V. *Personal Work and Bible Study.*
    1. An understanding of human nature. 486, 487.
    2. Simple, spirited Bible readings. 481.
    3. Clear, definite instruction. 475.
    4. Teaching to create and hold the interest. 459, 491, 493, 483.
    5. Vitality and freshness of ideas. 487, 458, 478, 481.
    6. Talking naturally about God's love. 459, 466, 484, 485.
    7. Teaching that reaches the heart. 460, 474, 475.
    8. A soft, refining influence for truth. 472.
    9. Quiet visiting, teaching, and praying. 463.
   10. Instructing meekness and tact. 466, 487.
   11. Teacher's sympathetic touch. 461, 467.
   12. Persuasiveness in teaching. 459, 489.
   13. Intelligent, persevering, patient teaching. 466, 467, 472.
   14. Spirit-controlled lessons. 474, 475.
   15. Teacher's pleasing way with children. 460.
   16. Comforting sick. 460.
   17. Uplifting and educating. 465.
   18. Awakening desire and faith. 487.
   19. Teaching with earnestness. 487-489.
   20. Teaching to meet objections. 477, 484, 483.
   21. Truth to stand out against error. 170, 624.
   22. Doing a large, far-reaching work. 465, 474.

PART ONE ★ CHAPTER ELEVEN

The Challenge of Present Truth

The Advent message has been grounded in sound Scriptural argument. Seventh-day Adventists are prone to refer to it as "the truth," and when this expression is adopted into the vocabulary of a new believer, we feel that the message has taken proper root in his life. We amplify this term by applying *present* to *truth*, to characterize its urgency.

The Bible instructor is a teacher of present truth. The principles of righteousness by faith brought to light during the great Reformation are today re-emphasized by us. Whereas at that time great truths were restored to the church, reform in doctrine generally was soon arrested. These arrested truths must now constitute the preparatory message for the second coming of Christ. Modern erroneous teachings will be exposed in their true nature as these present-truth doctrines are now properly revealed.

In these pressing times a series of twenty present-truth studies is perhaps the very maximum of subjects that can be taught to an individual or group. Some readers may require more instruction, but many will never receive that much. Therefore, these truths must be presented with terse directness. There is no time now to generalize on Bible teaching. With a little building at the foundation, the Bible instructor must soon come to the point by teaching the Sabbath, state of the dead, and the reform subjects. But although she must be terse, she should not overlook the fact that she is teaching the "everlasting gospel." The fundamentals of the Christian faith must be soundly built into present truth.

Frequently a Bible instructor will adopt an arrangement of lessons suggested by some evangelist whose sequence and logic have impressed her. But what appeals to one may not appeal to another, and therefore each lesson should be planned around the needs of the reader. The forcefulness of a Bible study may lie in the teacher's thorough, personal preparation and in her unique presentation. Each topic should be presented so that it will bring new delight to the instructor and a new appeal to the pupil. Present truth will then grow in the work of the teacher as well as in the hearts of her readers.

Building a Seventh-day Adventist Philosophy

The Bible teacher, who is a skilled personal worker as well, will build into her teaching many helpful points which will clear the way for the acceptance of our entire message. This personalizes her Bible readings and gives power to her teaching. The reader will then become conscious that our induction into belief through a process of instruction is vastly different from just being asked to join a church. He will see a message as well as its cross, and will be building up a wholesome concept for present truth, instead of shrinking from Seventh-day Adventism.

Merely presenting a series of lessons on our message does not necessarily bring conviction to the hearer to walk in all its revealed light. Truths recognized should be speedily lived if a definite reform is to take place. To assist in the reader's conversion as well as conviction to the truth, the instructor should weave lessons of practical godliness into a series of doctrinal and prophetic subjects.

Advancement into the full light of truth will be far more evident where prayer does not need to be restrained because of the reader's home problems. Even the dulled senses will be awakened under the influence of prayer, and soon may be seen the faintest glimmer of light pointing in the direction of complete obedience. Prayer always works marvelous changes in the perception of the truth as well as in one's attitude toward its acceptance. The reader will soon be building a new philosophy of life—Adventism!

Prayer is also most important in the experience of the Bible instructor herself. Since whole systems of finely spun error must be challenged with present truth, honest souls are often so confused by the various fallacious teachings of our times that more than the power of clear-cut argument must be employed by the teacher. There must be the Holy Spirit's witness to "the power of persuasion, the power of prayer, the power of the love of God."—*Evangelism,* p. 459. The simple Bible reading will reveal point and force when the spiritual Sword is bathed in prayer. Though the Bible teacher must ever be a close student of the mysteries of the Word, her readers should not merely see truth flashing forth when she teaches, but should also come under the influence of the Spirit of truth. This experience always comes in answer to the worker's sincere prayer.

Teaching Present Truth

I. *Truth Analyzed.* (COL 39, 40.)
   1. What is truth? Prov. 22:21; John 17:17; 1 John 2:4; Ps. 119:142, 151, 160.
   2. What is present truth? 2 Peter 1:12.
   3. Present truth topics suggested by Ellen G. White:
      Sure Word of Prophecy. GW 147-149.
      Christ's Second Coming. AA 513.
      Signs of the Times. AA 535, 536; GW 57.
      Matthew 24. GW 148.
      Divinity of Christ. GW 405.
      Sin—Origin and Results. AA 503.
      New Earth. AA 601.
      Kingdom of Grace and Glory. MB 159.
      Law and Gospel. GW 161, 162.
      Commandments and Faith. GW 162.
      Two Laws. AA 553, 190.
      Obedience to God's Law. MB 83, 116.
      New Covenant. MB 80, 81.
      Sanctuary. AA 228-230, 246, 247.
      2300 Days. GC 429, 457.
      Judgment. GC 489, 490.
      Prophecies of Daniel and Revelation. AA, Chap. 57.

Three Messages. EW 258.
Sabbath—Sign and Test. GW 148, 149; 9T 234.
Resurrection. AA 320.

II. *Building Truth.*
1. Line upon line; precept upon precept.
2. Logical textual sequence and argument.
3. Rightly dividing the Word.
4. Building character while building truth.

III. *Steps in Presenting Truth.*
1. Capturing attention.
2. Holding the interest.
3. Clinching points of present truth.
4. Gaining decision for its acceptance.

For Us

It was for us
Those hands became nail pierced!
That brow so noble,
Blood stained from its crown of thorns,
Those arms outstretched
With love embraced humanity,
That by His grace
Again we may be born!
—Helen M. Weston.

PART ONE ★ CHAPTER TWELVE

Illustrating Truth

Plans for Illustrating

We now live in a picture age, and the Bible teacher who knows how to interest people in the study of the message by means of illustrations, charts, diagrams, or teaching aids will add to her success. Visual education not only appeals to many;

it also fastens the more solid facts in the mind. Prophecy especially is more readily comprehended when devices are employed to clarify symbolic truth.

In presenting prophetic subjects, Bible instructors have long found it helpful to use charts and diagrams. The prepared cloth charts used in evangelistic work in the past still have their place of usefulness. Smaller lightweight cardboard charts are also practical for the Bible instructor's use. With the development of newer artistic skills, the image of Daniel 2, the beasts of prophecy, and other prophetic symbols have now been reproduced in plywood cutouts of sizes suitable for home evangelism as well as for smaller and larger public meetings. Photography is also employed in reproducing charts. Some workers are skilled at wood carving, and others use personally made, artistic felt cutouts which adhere to a felt background representing a sea or land scene. The whole field of illustrating is still wide open for new suggestions, and some Bible instructors have already made their practical and artistic contributions.

Whatever type of symbol is used by the worker, it is important that certain psychological principles be kept in mind. There is teaching value in a diagram that is produced before the eye in a progressive way, being drawn or mechanically built up, step by step, as points are explained. Some charts are too complicated, and become confusing. It may be that the date stressed at the end of the diagram catches the eye even before the beginning is clearly recognized. Then at times a student may become definitely prejudiced on some minor point that may not look right to him at the outset, but if built up gradually, the questionable feature becomes clear in the process of illustrating. (See *Evangelism*, pp. 203-206.)

There is true psychological value in the use of the blackboard for explaining time periods of prophecy such as the 2300 days, 1260 days, or the millennium. A portable blackboard is indispensable to the Bible instructor. When a blackboard is not available, a piece of cardboard or heavy paper will answer the purpose, especially when the group is small and the illustration is given to a few who may be seated close to the instructor, perhaps around the dining room table.

The use of the stereopticon and moving-picture machine is growing in approval. Although their constant use is not commendable, these mechanical helps have their place. One may interest a group of children or young people more readily by means of picture devices than without them. Often the very suggestion of a picture lecture in the home will create keen interest where other methods might fail. It is a better plan, however, for the study group to learn to use their Bibles. Each text is then investigated, and this makes a far deeper impression than when texts are merely shown on the screen to be read by the teacher.

The Place of the Story in Illustrating

There is one field of illustrating in which all may develop more proficiency—the use of the human-interest story. The Saviour truly understood this art. His skill lay in His uniqueness of style and simplicity of method. The incident in which He wrote the sins of the Pharisees with His finger in the sand is worthy of our study. But we never find Him using an illustration from either life or nature without there being a real need for it in helping to clarify truth.

Bible instructors too may find suitable illustrations in everyday life. They are to be found at every hand, and the successful teacher of the Word will learn to supplement and to enforce her own teaching by means of these homey and practical lessons. They appeal to the listener because of their familiarity. Stories serve as windows to an otherwise dim structure of truth. The simplest type of story will sometimes present the most illuminating or touching appeal. The teacher need not resort to volumes of stock anecdotes and illustrations, since these are likely to be used too generally in evangelism, and may not fit into our message.

The Bible teacher should have a fund of suitable stories properly organized and filed. Those of the great Reformers of the church, and of noted missionaries and Christian heroes, have built faith and doctrine when properly told and duly applied, and never cease to grip interest. They have their special appeal when valor and courage are needed by youth who must take their stand for unpopular truth.

A versatile Bible instructor will have an array of children's stories stored in the mind for ready use, and new stories will be constantly added to this collection. She will develop the skill of storytelling, but this does not mean that she specializes in dramatics. The practical value, not the entertainment feature, suggests such an equipment.

Awakening an interest in the study of God's Word requires various skills. There may be a laddie in the home whose mother will be pleased when you relate an appealing story for his benefit. The aim, of course, should be to grip his mother's interest for a series of Bible studies at the same time.

The following story by Inez Brasier, entitled "Father, Come!" is suggestive of how a Bible instructor may proceed to introduce a study on Christ's second coming.

A Story for the Child—and His Mother

A little boy of three awakened as the morning sunshine slanted across his hospital bed. He climbed up on his pillow, where, by stretching as tall as possible, he could see down the street. This was the morning that father was coming to take him home!

Eagerly he watched the cars going past. Breakfast time brought his tray, but he scarcely touched the fruit and cereal. Father was coming! Quickly he climbed up again to watch for the one car he knew. Minutes grew longer and longer to the lad, yet father surely was coming. Had he not promised only the evening before as he tucked him, nearly well, into bed? So Jimmy watched, but no familiar car stopped.

"Daddy come! Daddy come!" he sang over and over through his morning care and between sips of orange juice.

"Daddy come! Daddy come!" he repeated as his eyes closed and he swayed on the pillow.

But he must not sleep. Father was coming. He rubbed his eyes and stood a little straighter. Then there were familiar steps beside his bed. "Daddy come!" and he was in father's arms, laughing and rubbing away the happy tears.

This story has a beautiful appeal. It is a simple matter to follow such a story with a dozen pointed texts on the subject. The child should be directly addressed when the story is begun. The mother will be listening attentively. As an appeal is made to the mother, the worker might add: "The Bible tells us, Mrs. Smith, that Jesus' coming is very near. We desire to be ready for His coming, do we not? Let us read a few Bible promises pertaining to the soon return of Jesus." (Now open your Bible and proceed with your study.)

Although stories have their place in evangelism, the teacher must guard against moralizing. A good story well told will produce the right effect without pointing out the moral. For the story enthusiast who is in danger of cluttering up the Bible reading with too many illustrations, another caution is timely. In this case one story often detracts from another, and the appeal is likely to be neutralized. Although the Bible instructor should be alert in using stories, she should be aware that some Bible studies are more effective without them.

For the worker who has sufficient skill to use her chalk or pencil artistically, many occasions for their use will present themselves. The future holds a wide field of usefulness for Bible instructors who will develop their artistic talents.

In the field of illustrating and visual aids, constant improvement is being made. Consult *The Ministry* and write to the Ministerial Association for helps and suggestions. Workers should become acquainted with denominational and general supply houses. Catalogs of their supplies are usually furnished upon request.

PART ONE ★ CHAPTER THIRTEEN

Continuing to Build Truth

The consecrated Bible instructor is truly a builder for God. She helps her readers to raise a solid doctrinal structure for truth. She must build wisely and carefully, for the Master Builder Himself examines her work, and there must be no weak places in any part of her construction. Every truth she teaches should fit into a structure of which Jesus, the truth, is the sure foundation. As the building progresses, our teachings on various doctrinal points develop a beautiful edifice. Indeed, we do not build merely doctrine but rather living material. Each one saved in the kingdom of heaven must become a pillar in the spiritual temple of God, and therefore doctrinal building should mean that character is also being built in the lives of readers.

The zeal of the messenger affects the reception of the message. A Bible instructor who has herself come into our work from another church affiliation may better appreciate what skill and earnestness is necessary in bringing people out of their former beliefs into the Seventh-day Adventist Church. There is a very definite experience behind this step. There is reality to these questions and doubts, tests and struggles, anxious days and sleepless nights, heartaches and persecution, which may be a part of the reader's experience in taking his stand for truth. But where the teacher does not have this particular background, she may have other experiences that will be equally as helpful.

Those who have lived this message, or who were "born in it," as we often express ourselves, should be aware that new converts to our faith have a great deal to learn. As the reader's former house of fallacious doctrinal faith gradually topples to the ground, this experience will affect his whole emotional life. Then as each added point of truth is brought into clear focus, new convictions will undermine the reader's former beliefs built on tradition. To him it is a disappointing experience at first, and the teacher must be very sympathetic. But soon an interest to defend truth is definitely aroused, and the teacher realizes that her student is beginning to cooperate in building upon the sure foundation of God's Word. Here and there unfamiliar points of truth will need to be buttressed, but on the whole, each additional Bible reading now adds to the erection of truth's structure. Simultaneously, a deepening of the reader's spiritual life takes place as practical truths are also built into this framework.

Leading Along

An early decision for baptism is often quite foreign to the thinking of the prospective convert. He now desires to make certain that his next step is a right one, and may suggest by his attitude that he wants sufficient time to think it through. Though procrastinating to their own detriment must be guarded against, the soul in the balance must now feel the firm support of an understanding friend. Here a womanly touch is needed, and happy the worker who is skilled in this feminine art of "leading people along."

The truth seeker may now express his emotions by saying to his instructor, "The Bible has become a new book to me!" This registers favorably in the mind of the teacher that the interest is being secured. Each point of truth must now be clinched "as a nail in a sure place." The planks of truth and the girders of faith have all been properly measured so that each new doctrine will fit into its special place. Sequence and logic count in the reader's recognizing the perfection and unveiling of God's over-all plan.

In efforts to teach the truth to others, problems on attitude are bound to arise. The enemy is not sitting idly by, but stirs up relatives, neighbors, or friends, and especially those with whom the reader formerly associated in church fellowship. If Mrs. Brown herself has not thought of some questions suggesting doubt, these may be brought to her by others. Controversial arguments may now need to be handled with great tact and skill. Though registering each remark, it never pays for the teacher to make much point of some casual statement of doubt. Better build it into a future lesson. The truth eloquently defends itself, and the student will soon be exclaiming, "How clearly the Bible speaks on all these different questions!" The teacher must have more than ready argument to meet objections, for Bible work is far more than textual versatility. She will need a background of Bible knowledge to draw from the past fitting examples and apt illustrations to strengthen her argument, or to make an appeal for obedience.

Digressing From the Planned Series

Even though the Bible instructor has her topical series of Bible studies well in mind, its regular sequence may be disturbed. To clarify a position of truth, it often becomes necessary to introduce additional lessons. Or again, the teacher may feel impressed to digress from the regular sequence by introducing an entirely different line of doctrine. While studying with a very sincere woman I met a snag on the immortality question. A number of studies did not altogether clear up the difficulties. I was then impressed to leave this theme, suggesting that we study the sanctuary. After a very few lessons I was again teaching the nature of man, but from another angle entirely. In this case my explaining Psalms 37:20 in connection with the Old Testament sacrifices bridged over the earlier difficulties regarding our teachings on the state of the dead. The object lessons of the sanctuary taught points that were hard to comprehend otherwise.

Although our workers usually agree on a rather unified sequence, there are also various topical arrangements which may be used. Here, again, one should consider the background of the student or the group. Whereas the state of the dead may not especially upset the more liberal-minded types of religionists, one soon discovers that great caution must be used in dealing with Methodists, Baptists, and others who dogmatically teach an ever-burning hell. Again, where the reader has previously become acquainted with the doctrines of Seventh-day Adventists, it might be a very simple matter to begin with an explanation of our reasons for keeping the seventh day instead of the first, whereas this plan might prove disastrous with those already prejudiced. This is equally true of the health subject. Some may already show interest in this direction, while others bristle at any suggestion of its introduction. In order to assure unbiased study, the teacher must first build an approach to that particular topic. This same principle exists on other points of our reformatory teachings, such as dress reform, tithing, and the Spirit of prophecy. In this respect good judgment on the part of the instructor is most essential.

Our message is anchored in the great Bible prophecies, which should be well understood by all. These great lines of prophecy inspire the reader to see the mysteries God has revealed to His children. Besides introducing into our methods a uniqueness which grips the interest of the pupil, the study of the prophecies brings assurance, and this will lead to decision resulting in obedience.

One of the outstanding features of Bible work is clearing up doubt and answering questions. Tests must be applied to a doctrine before the reader recognizes its truth. This builds confidence for the message and the messenger. The following thoughts are for the Bible instructor's reflection and study.

Meeting Doubt and Questions

I. *Faith and Doubt.* (*Steps to Christ*, chap. "What to Do With Doubt.")
   1. Inquiry followed by doubt. DA 356.
   2. Points on which doubt enters. Isa. 1:18; 1 John 5:3, 4; Ex. 19:5; 16:4, 29; Ps. 78:19; Mal. 3:10; 1 Peter 3:3-5. (Forgiveness, faith, law and the Sabbath, diet, tithing, dress, etc.)

II. *Encouraging Questions.*
   1. Questions tactfully suggested. Luke 24:26; 2 Tim. 2:23.
   2. Bible answer to questions. Acts 16:30-32; Matt. 19:16, 17.
   3. Truth revealed; truth to be revealed. Deut. 29:29.
   4. Sincere inquiry omen of progress. John 3:9; 4:11.
III. *Testing Doctrine.*
   Isa. 8:20; John 10:35; Matt. 15:9, 13; 22:29; Eph. 4:21.
IV. *Meeting Doubt.*
   1. Using Scripture. John 18:37, 38; John 7:16.
   2. By experience. 2 Kings 5:15.
V. *Building Confidence.* (GW 496, 497.)
   1. In Bible as supreme authority. Isa. 34:16; Rev. 22:18, 19.
   2. In message of the hour. Rev. 14:6-12.
   3. In instrument presenting message. John 1:23; 5:34, 35; 6:66-69.
   4. In God's power to help. Heb. 7:25; Mark 9:23.

PART ONE ★ CHAPTER FOURTEEN

Skillful Group Instruction

The plan for gathering groups of interested people for Bible study greatly conserves time for the worker, and quite generally intensifies the interest. One must make certain, however, when to use this method, especially in connection with our public meetings. Many a good prospect for individual study has been diverted by an unskillful or too previous an attempt to transfer an interested individual to a study group, or perhaps a community Bible school.

Observations of the experiences of class instructors lead to the conclusion that whereas some are skillful in dealing with people individually, they fail decidedly with a group. It is still believed that experienced workers can master this skill, and should not be afraid to persevere. In dealing with groups, however, the Bible instructor may expect that some will lose interest, but this will be true in working with individuals. The worker who becomes apt at conducting larger classes thereby greatly multiplies her usefulness and her results in Bible work. Every added contact counts in evangelism, and though the work is not just mass production, it is wise to consider every agency or method which promises larger returns.

The suggestion to the more timid Bible instructors—those who may become a bit panicky when dealing with groups—is that each study her ability, and then endeavor to work in her own harness. A word of caution should be added, however, regarding a too rigid attitude on the part of any worker who hesitates attempting a new way for soul-winning efficiency. There is danger that one may become too set in her ways, a course that often retards progress. Many who are today capable group instructors merely persevered in their timidity until they mastered the art. The individual instruction method may be easier, but the group method speaks for skill and is more productive.

Class instruction in connection with present-day evangelism made definite progress with the appearing of printed Bible lessons. These lessons, written by workers of evangelistic experience, are designed to meet the common needs of the many interested people with whom one labors. They may be used for correspondence courses or home Bible studies conducted with a teacher for the group. Such courses now fill a real need.

These uniform Bible lessons may become the basis of the Bible instructor's own studies, but they should not, however, become the only pattern. A doctor does not cure everybody with the same medicine or the same treatments. A thorough diagnosis of each case will reveal the many factors that decide the nature of the treatment. Some idiosyncrasies will suggest smaller doses of medicine or less frequent treatment. This same caution would also apply to the Bible instructor, who would do well to follow the fine logical sequence of a prepared series, but adapt the lessons to meet the needs of individuals. Then one of these printed lessons left with her readers after she has presented her own study will be helpful in reinforcing her instruction.

In the conducting of a successful Bible class certain points should receive consideration. To bring the importance of this type of classwork to the attention of an evangelistic audience, it is essential that the evangelist himself publicly, and urgently, invite people to attend. Whether the class instructor is a sister or a brother associate, the class plan will require an enthusiastic build-up on his part. The presence of the evangelist at the class meeting, at least in the earlier part of the class, will be considered its best endorsement. No class instructor works at an advantage without his strong backing. There must be thorough advertising to get the group together, but after that the personality and ability of the teacher may have much to do with assuring regular attendance. This type of instruction still necessitates some home calls by the teacher, but these are now for the purpose of becoming personally acquainted with the pupils and their problems.

The use of the projector as an interest builder for a group is to be recommended. We now have access to excellent filmstrips designed to supplement the evangelist's instruction. But the projector plan is not the only plan, neither is it without its limitations. There is nothing more effective than the teacher's best tool—the Bible itself. In dealing with a group one should aim to stimulate and hold the interest by introducing a variety of methods. This requires more than just showing pictures. A stimulating and perhaps even a primed question will often introduce interest for a study topic. There soon comes a time when it is advisable to let the whole group handle the Word themselves, not using the projector at all. But the projector may still be used occasionally in summarizing or reviewing subjects already presented.

Skillful Group Instruction

Whereas it may be best to limit class enrollment to a definite expiration time, and also to the number attending, little is gained by a too rigid use of the school-bell method. Allow for elasticity which considers a few tardy folk who must catch up with the class, or perhaps even need to be humored a little to get started. Such personal work must never be lost sight of. Class psychology means genial good will and mutual cooperation to learn.

In anticipation of the time when the class will be facing decisions for the various truths of the message, the teacher should be building up group action. The concert recitation of a text, an enthusiastic class committal on a recognized duty toward God, and even an extemporaneous testimony— all build toward witnessing for truth. The teacher's aim should be to gradually limber up the group for future, more pointed class response.

But she should watch out for the too aggressive leader in the group who may upset her equilibrium, or for one who may even attempt to counteract her efforts, especially at the time of an important decision. Such an individual needs to be held in check by timely visiting when various points of disagreement can be handled privately. This builds for mutual understanding. Before aiming at class decision, the teacher must always know her leaders. She should have discussed with them individually, and in a friendly solicitous spirit, the blessing gained by leading out in witnessing for new light. A tactful suggestion to each that he is being counted on to lead out soon in a public expression of obedience will help to get the right reaction. Today the stronger types of Christians must be guided to lead the weaker ones, because people will move forward with a group.

The time will come when those in the group will show various stages of development. The more progressive thinkers should not be held back by those who act more slowly. It may be best to find some tactful plan to reclassify the more advanced students without discouraging the slower thinkers. A baptismal class may readily result from this practical plan.

The use of better techniques for indoctrinating those who have more recently embraced our faith should be stressed. The pressure of the evangelistic program will not allow for much personal instruction after baptism, but it is well to gather these new people into groups for at least another briefer course of instruction. Points that will help to ground them in the message and to fortify them against apostasy may then be most profitably presented.

While the public Bible class, or the "Pictured Truth" class, is gaining momentum at the meeting hall, the visitors' class in the Sabbath school should also be attracting the newly interested. Much could here be said about Sabbath school evangelism, for the proper location of such a class, and for the right instructor, but space is lacking. The worker should co-operate with this department so that the Sabbath school and its lessons will fit into the experience of these visitors.

A sound plan for instructing the children of these interested people should not be overlooked. They must be guided into classes where pleasant teachers will give them a welcome. Sabbath school teachers who fail in making these visiting children a part of the school's interest often bring problems to our evangelism. Where children of interested families do not enjoy our Sabbath school, parents find it difficult to develop enthusiasm for our church. The evangelist may have worked hard to stimulate interest for attending the Sabbath school, but such a setback too often results in the actual failure of some to accept our message. For this reason all Sabbath school teachers should be well instructed as to how to foster the developing interest.

Our medical leaders also have good plans and helpful material for conducting evangelistic health classes. Back numbers of *The Ministry* may be consulted for suggestions and techniques. The timing of this health instruction should be carefully studied in the setting of our other evangelistic objectives. Some evangelists are more health conscious than others, and may use health education as the entering wedge. Some, however, prefer using it as a follow-up feature after baptism. The instructor of the group should be well qualified for her work. Helping this class to visualize facts by means of pictures, charts, and diagrams builds interest and is illuminating. The demonstrating of treatments and the the actual preparing of healthful foods to replace a harmful diet rate high as teaching agencies.

Mention should be made of the effectiveness of the child-evangelism class. This provision for the children may become a great asset to the evangelistic program. The teacher of such a group should also be evangelistic and well prepared for her work. She must have a loving interest in them. Featuring the youth of a community at our evangelistic services holds great possibilities for winning their parents, relatives, and friends to the church. It also helps to break down prejudice where this may have arisen. (See *Evangelism,* pp. 579-584.) Child-evangelism classes may be coordinated with the soul-winning program of the Sabbath school. Bible instructors who are not yet informed on these particular plans for winning children would do well to write to their conference Sabbath school department for special helps in children's evangelism.

Class Instruction in Evangelism

ENA FERGUSON

I. *Purpose of Evangelistic Bible Class.*
 1. To gather specialized study groups from larger audience.
 2. To form more personal contacts.
 3. To aid development in friendly study atmosphere.
 4. To handle suggestions that arise in public meetings.
 5. To save Bible instructor's time on visitation program.
 6. To meet large city needs where home contacts are difficult.
 7. To supplement the lecture subjects from a different angle.

II. *Organizing the Class.*
 1. Evangelist's enthusiastic support.
 2. Proper advertising on handbills and from pulpit.
 3. Securing of suitable meeting place.

    4. Time of meeting to be arranged for.
    5. Cooperation of associate workers.
    6. Relationship of class to general visitation program.
    7. Class records.
    8. Teacher to familiarize herself with names and faces of those in large class (sometimes seventy-five or more) by means of test papers. Class members submit test sheets to teacher. As each is handed to her, she quickly glances at name. Teacher now calls individual by name, and this helps her to associate name with face. After test sheets have been graded, another opportunity is presented to note who responded to name called.

III. *Spirit of the Class.*
    1. Each member brings Bible.
    2. Class held to schoolroom plan.
    3. Friendliness and class response encouraged.
    4. A studious interest developed.
    5. Help of members in building up class attendance.

IV. *Conducting the Lesson.*
    1. Opening prayer by an associate worker.
    2. Class enlisted to read texts in unison.
    3. Occasionally a good reader called on to read text.
    4. Each point of lesson clinched.
    5. Class assent and response solicited.
    6. At first meeting class program outlined. Make it plain that time is limited; make best use of every moment. Aim to cover lesson, and therefore cannot encourage round-table discussion.
    7. Announcement of plan for occasional question evening. Opportunity thus afforded for questions by class. Cordially solicit these as well as remarks. Ask class members to write out questions and mail them to teacher, to eliminate spirit of argument, and yet show that teacher is not afraid of questions.
    8. Teacher must find time for personal interviews. Such interviews often important for results. Teacher must remain alert to recognize opportunities for personal work.
    9. Summarizing lesson points.
   10. Closing with prayer.
   11. Dismissing in orderly way.
   12. Reserving seats in larger auditorium for class members.

V. *The Evangelistic Lesson.*
    1. Provision for a series of typed, mimeographed, or printed lessons.
    2. Studies built on a theme.

3. Theme suggestions:
    a. God's Great Plan of Salvation.
        These lessons deal with such topics as (1) purpose of the Scriptures, (2) pre-existence and incarnation of Christ, (3) second coming, (4) faith, (5) grace, (6) repentance, (7) conversion, (8) obedience, (9) baptism.
    b. Great Controversy Between Christ and Satan.
        Beginning with study on reign of Satan, nearly any present-truth doctrine can be taught from this angle. This theme especially adaptable to law, change of Sabbath, manner and purpose of Christ's coming, Christian temperance and healthful diet, worldly amusements, and so forth. New earth would be good conclusion, indicating controversy ended.
    c. Science and the Bible.
        Teacher can originate a series using such studies as astronomy and the Bible, evolution and the Bible. This series will be be especially helpful for those who are perplexed in thinking that science and the Bible are not in harmony. Helpful conclusion to series is a study on the science of salvation.
    d. Present Truth for This Generation.
        This series can be made very pointed. Signs of Jesus' return, Daniel 2, the judgment, the 2300 days, the sanctuary, the mark of the beast—all these lend themselves to this theme.
    e. Meaning of Sanctuary and Its Services.
        A fascinating theme for a series. It makes good Seventh-day Adventists, for it gives a solid foundation. Twelve lessons on the sanctuary are none too many.
4. Six to twelve lessons, a series on each of these themes. Depending upon objectives of series, or time of baptism, lessons can be introduced as it seems practical. Same students who attend first series usually attend succeeding series. Therefore not necessary to cover every phase of present truth in each series. With beginning of each series evangelist makes public appeal for new recruits. Best to attend to this a week or two before new series is to begin. New members may now be added to replace those who have dropped out of previous course.

VI. *Follow-up Methods.*
   1. Prompt, courteous attention to all letters.
   2. Teacher mentions to class query notes received. (These query notes are written on test sheets when they are returned to the teacher.)
   3. Thanks class for remarks of appreciation.

4. Responding to mail.
   a. Writing detailed letter a reply.
   b. Sending brief note and inserting tract or *Present Truth*.
   c. Lending library books for further study.
   d. Making follow-up visit to home.

PART ONE ★ CHAPTER FIFTEEN

Methods of the Master Teacher

In the field of personal work there is no better example than the Master's. Bible teachers do well to make the study of His life and methods paramount. Young Bible instructors unconsciously adopt many of the ways and expressions of those for whom they work. Youth look around for heroes to emulate, and the ability to adopt their style and ways is pronounced at this stage of their development. At times the personality traits of their associated workers leave a very definite imprint on their own. The young worker must therefore spend much time with the Master, with the objective in mind of learning mostly from Him.

Many and varied are the types of approach Jesus used. We observe His skill in building up points of truth as He spoke to the woman of Samaria. We marvel at His method of clinching that interest as He guided it toward a decision for eternal life. We note how His appeals varied with the different types He would meet, and how He developed in these new believers the burden for winning others. They beheld Him in His work, and then caught the burden to become fishers of men.

An outstanding trait of Jesus was His deep love for souls. He completely forgot Himself in His soul-winning task. With a deep appreciation of the sinfulness of sin, He longed to win for God each soul He met. The sincerity of His purpose made His appeals earnest and genuinely effective. Because of the seriousness of the hour, time and again He would urge some soul to speedily make the right decision. He truly knew men, not from outward appearance, but from motive. He could discern between the searcher who had become confused by skeptical suggestions, and the stony heart of skepticism.

Christ's discernment was evidenced by His understanding of Nicodemus's problem. Humbly ignoring the flattery of His admirer, He straightway came to the point, "Ye must be born again." That point was not lost, even though it required a timely illustration of the wind to explain the mysterious work of the Holy Spirit. Well-known Scripture found a new application as Jesus revealed His vicarious sacrifice to one who should have been well versed in the types and ceremonies of Israel. Delicately, yet nevertheless definitely, the Master told this great teacher that his fear of man must be overcome. It may have taken months to bring this truth to fruition, but it was this same Nicodemus who later, in the hour of crisis, boldly took his stand for unpopular truth.

The faint cry of faith by Bartimaeus was not missed by Jesus. He stimulated his weak faith and so won an ardent disciple for the cause. Zacchaeus had a number of wrongs to make right, but Jesus went to his home and helped him to carry out all his newborn purposes. Nathanael's honest inquiry was not judged by his youthful and apparently skeptical assertion; the Master judged his motive—and it was, oh, so guileless! True, his faith needed deepening, but the Great Teacher knew that this would follow his complete acceptance of the Christ.

At Calvary, in Christ's midnight hour of grief and pain, He could still win a hardened soul to God. In the faith of the thief beside Him, Christ saw the souls you and I must find—those who may have wasted their lives, but who will in the hour of death, reach out for a place in God's kingdom. These remaining few moments were freighted with the destiny of a soul. Here was not the occasion for intricate prophetic dissertation; all that mattered for this thief was a place with Him! What wonderful discernment and delicate skill!

May every Bible instructor spend more time in learning the ways of the Master Teacher. You are invited to consider prayerfully the following points in an outline that might require many chapters to tell in detail the story of the Prince of Evangelists. You are a Bible instructor, and will be able to supply for yourself those points that can merely be suggested by the outline. Meditate on other types of cases reached by the Master Teacher.

The Master's Methods For Personal Evangelism

I. *Winning the Woman of Samaria.* (John 4; DA chap. 19.)
   Type: The prejudiced, simplehearted.
   1. Christ's soul-winning purpose.
      a. Aimed to win confidence. MH 143.
      b. Met people on their own ground. DA 253.
      c. Used personal-interview method. 6T 115.
      d. Had earnestness for audience of one. DA 194.
   2. Manifested friendly manner. DA 183, 184.
      a. Natural request made point of contact. John 4:7.
      b. Interest laid in immediate surroundings. Verses 6, 7.
      c. Used "tact born of divine love."
      d. Trust awakened trust in others.
      e. Aroused curiosity to awaken interest. Verse 10.
      f. Met prejudice by creating curiosity, not by dispute. Verse 10.
      g. Point of interest—common need, but *living* water. Verse 10.
   3. His bid for interest. DA 184-187.
      a. Curiosity provoked thinking. Verses 10-12.
      b. Met prejudice with suspense, not explanation. Verses 12-14.
      c. Built confidence through familiar truth. Verses 13, 14.
      d. New truth proved He had message. Verse 14.
      e. Captured interest by creating desire for water to satisfy personal need. Verse 15.
   4. Deepened interest. DA 187, 188.
      a. Awakened conviction of a lack. Verse 15.
      b. Relieved embarrassment by commendation. Verses 17, 18.
      c. Won confidence by His discernment. Verse 19.
      d. Retracked when sidetracked. Verses 19, 22.

Methods of the Master Teacher

5. Intensified interest. DA 189.
    a. Question-provoking methods used. Verse 20.
    b. Guided questions toward truth. Verse 20.
    c. Built up truth to destroy error. Verse 21.
    d. Clinched truth in face of preconceived ideas. Verse 23.
6. Gained decision. DA 190.
    a. Appealed for truth while imparting information. Verses 23, 24.
    b. Opened mind for present truth (Messiah). Verse 25.
    c. Used psychological moment for decision. Verse 25.
    d. Revealed truth in clear, brief, pointed manner. Verse 26.
7. Christ's methods successful. DA 187, 191-195.
    a. Woman's pleasure at finding living water. Verses 28, 29.
    b. Interest in truth eclipsed all else. Verse 28.
    c. Compelling power of truth. Verses 28-30, 39.
    d. Advertising method: "Come, and see!" Verse 29.
    e. Magnetic power of truth. Verses 40-42.
    f. Triumph of truth in all Samaria. Verse 39; Acts 8:5, 14.

II. *Nicodemus, a Great Teacher in Israel.* (John 3:1-21; DA chap. 17.)
   Type: A rather self-sufficient scholar.
   1. Flattery of inquirer ignored by Jesus.
   2. Came right to point: "Ye must be born again."
   3. Began with known truth; added points of interest.
   4. Illustrated from nature—wind.
   5. Explained well-known incident.
   6. Tactfully rebuked fear of man.

III. *Bartimaeus, the Sick Beggar.* (Mark 10:46-52.)
   Type: A sick, poor, neglected sinner.
   1. Cry of faith detected.
   2. Made interview possible.
   3. Sent message to stimulate faith.
   4. Inquired into need and met it directly.
   5. Won new disciple.

IV. *Zacchaeus, Rich Publican.* (Luke 19:1-10; DA 553-555.)
   Type: A fraudulent businessman.
   1. Seeker handicapped by stature.
   2. His sincere desire detected.
   3. Singled out in crowd; personally appealed to.
   4. Call made at home despite public prejudice.
   5. Home interview for best results.

6. Willing listener became believer.
7. New supporter for God's cause.

V. *Nathanael, Skeptic Toward New Truth.* (John 1:43-51; DA 139, 143, 293.)
Type: A skeptical but guileless youth.
1. Invited by Philip to investigate.
2. Seeker sincere in quest.
3. Effort commended by teacher.
4. Spontaneous decision resulted.
5. Won confidence in His Messiahship.
6. Taught proper basis of faith.
7. Assured greater demonstrations.

VI. *Malefactor on Cross.* (Luke 23:39-43; DA 749-751.)
Type: A repentant sinner facing immediate death.
1. Last opportunity to save.
2. Conversation brief because of circumstances.
3. Forgiveness in face of death.
4. Promised place in kingdom.

PART ONE ★ CHAPTER SIXTEEN

Progressive Teaching for Decision

In presenting a series of doctrinal subjects, the Bible instructor may lead the student into definite themes of study, in which natural decision places are progressively reached. Step by step, as new light is received, the heart must respond to walk in that light. When the Bible instructor follows the progression of the evangelist's subjects, he usually sets the pattern for her sequence, whether she teaches individuals or groups. But there also are occasions when the Bible instructor must build a series quite independent of any evangelist's help, and she should understand the principles involved in the building of a series of studies designed to lead inquiring souls into our message. Since there is much discussion in this field of logical sequence, a practical suggestion is herewith submitted, but other arrangements are equally as good.

On the chart on page 102, the first six lessons of this series of Bible readings reveal God's plan for His kingdom. There is today much confusion regarding God's kingdom. His kingdom will come soon, when Jesus returns to this earth, and sin and sinners will be destroyed. The new-earth lesson is an appeal to prepare for His soon-coming kingdom. Here is an excellent opportunity definitely to enlist the reader's interest in becoming well acquainted with God's plan as revealed in the Bible. (It may not be necessary to give topics 1 and 2 to those already familiar with the Bible, but many today will still need these introductory lessons.)

Topics 7 to 10 teach salvation in Christ and His atoning work. Seventh-day Adventists are often accused of stressing the law more than the gospel. The reader should understand the right relationship between these two. This is laying the proper foundation for teaching Sabbath truth. The 2300 days should reveal the Christ of prophecy, as well as the close of time. (Because evangelists frequently present the 2300 days before the sanctuary study, this sequence has been followed.) The sanctuary truth presents Christ's high-priestly ministry in behalf of all.

The third group, topics 11 to 15, presents the restoration of the lost Sabbath truth. Each study in this group should aim at restoration, and make clear that the Sabbath is the sign of creation and also sanctification. Previous lessons should have already stressed the significance of God's eternal law.

The theme for topics 16 to 19 is *life*. Our denominational teachings on the state of the dead and destruction of the wicked are apt to be controversial subjects with many, especially in some sections of the world. They require a build-up before the plan and the purpose of God is understood. Where controversy is apparent, emphasis should be given to the fact that immortality may now be ours by faith, on condition of obedience to the Creator. In this present life we learn to live for God. If we live right, we shall die right. In the course of the discussion life and immortality should be accentuated instead of death and extinction. At present we are merely stewards of God's blessings of health, time, talents, and means. Each study should bring to the reader's attention a clearer conception of the *life* in Christ and the need for his full dedication to God in order to enjoy life on this earth in all its fullness. Immortality will become a reality when Jesus returns, but not before. Such an approach with the prejudiced paves the way for more pointed doctrinal truth on this subject. Where the case does not suggest such prejudice, the state of the dead may be presented earlier in the series.

The last studies, lessons 20 to 25 of this series, are great truths which should urge home the need for our message of a sanctified life. At the climax of this entire series truth is presented in contrast with error and tradition. With each successive study the reader should be deciding more definitely that he will press on toward perfection. Next he will want to seek entrance into the true church by baptism. God's special gift to His remnant church concludes the series.

It is not recommended that this sequence of Bible lessons be followed arbitrarily, or even exclusively. It is given merely to suggest how the teacher may group her topics into various fields of thought. Beginning with the kingdom truths, the teacher leads her pupil into the salvation and sanctuary service topics. These lay a sure foundation for the Sabbath. Next the more abundant life is taught, including man's complete consecration. The reader must now separate himself from every evil habit, and press on to perfection in Christ. As the teacher aims to build toward these definite objectives, timely decisions will need to be made, and the opportunity for committal on each truth will present itself more naturally.

There are some rather similar, as well as more varied, topical arrangements based on this principle of theme classification. Grouping the topics into fields of thought will result in a broader scope of truth teaching, and also provide natural climaxes for making specific appeals. The arrangement of a series of Bible readings has been well featured in our other evangelistic literature and sets of prepared Bible lessons. There is still room for individualism, despite the fact that our progressive message will follow a certain definite sequence of subjects. Further study is invited to some excellent suggestions by two experienced Bible instructors who have analyzed their sequence of topics in a very detailed way. (See "Bible Readings as a Continued Series," by Mayme Hollingsworth, in *The Ministry*, February, 1944, p. 11; "Logical Sequence of Subjects," by Mary Anderson, in *The Ministry*, January, 1948, p. 14.)

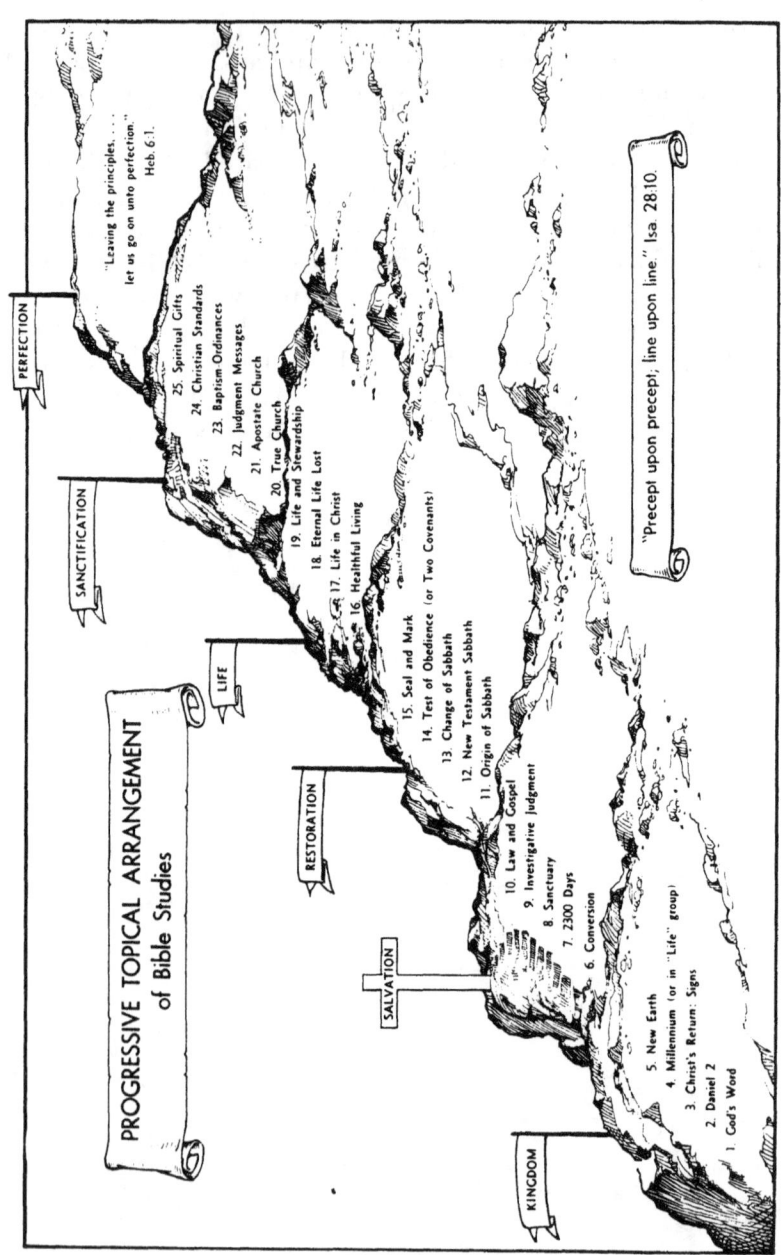

Topics for Bible Readings
Ida Poch
Series I

1. God's Plan—Christ.
2. Origin of Evil—Satan's Plan.
3. Daniel 2—Prophecy of Kingdom.
4. Return of Jesus—Object.
5. Millennium.
6. Matthew 24—Signs.
7. Life Only in Christ.
8. 2300 Days—Prophecy of Christ.
9. Sanctuary—the Whole Plan of God.
10. The Creator.
11. The Law of the Creator.
12. The Sabbath Institution—a Memorial.
13. New Testament Sabbath.
14. Daniel 7.
15. The Change of the Sabbath.
16. Seal and Mark—U.S. in Prophecy.
17. The Messages—Plagues.
18. The Judgment.
19. The Covenants—Experience.
20. Justification—Sanctification.
21. Bible Temperance.
22. Stewardship.
23. Holy Spirit's Work
24. Spiritual Gifts.
25. Spirit of Prophecy.
26. Baptism.
27. Dress.
28. Ordinances.

Series II
Mary E. Walsh

1. The Bible—Its Origin and Canon.
2. The Bible—The Living Word.
3. Why the Apocrypha Is Rejected.
4. Signs of Christ's Coming.
5. The Second Coming of Christ.
6. The Millennium.

7. State of the Dead.
8. Everlasting Fire.
9. Spirits in Prison.
10. To Depart and Be With Christ.
11. The Rich Man and Lazarus.
12. The Sanctuary.
13. The 2300 Days.
14. The Investigative Judgment.
15. The Two Laws.
16. The Commandments Before Sinai.
17. Christ in the Sabbath.
18. Sunday—The First Day of the Week.
19. Daniel 7—Change of the Sabbath.
20. Is God Particular?
21. Paganism, Papacy, United States.
22. Seal of God and Mark of the Beast.
23. The Seven Last Plagues.
24. The Coming of Elijah.
25. The Ordinance of Baptism.
26. The Greatest Question Ever Asked.
27. The Ordinance of Humility.
28. The Lord's Supper.
29. God's Storehouse and Gospel Financing.
30. Light for God's Children.
31. Spirit of Prophecy.
32. The Two Covenants.
33. Standards of Church Fellowship.
34. The Three Gospel Calls.

PART ONE ★ CHAPTER SEVENTEEN

Teaching God's Great Plan

Two vital problems affecting our evangelism today make it important that we teach well God's purpose in Christ. One problem is suggested by the various types of confusion regarding man's nature at creation. It also embraces the problem of his eternal destiny. The other deals with God's eternal and unchangeable law. The first of these problems must be well met in studying with the majority of Christians, and especially cultists. The second problem is presented by the dispensational teachings of our times. Since these groups in their perversion of Scripture are definitely gaining ground, our instruction on the various points of truth must become more specific. Dispensationalism believes in a never-dying soul as well as dispensation of the law being in the past. Cultism stresses many and various shadings of confused ideas pertaining to man's inherent nature, and it also quite generally ignores the importance of God's Ten Commandments.

As in the earlier days of Christianity, the nature of the Godhead has again become a point of speculation. The deity of Christ and His divine-human nature enters into this problem. Speculations as to the nature of man and his destiny once more give rise to such pagan ideas as pantheism and the transmigration of the soul. These fallacious mysticisms are now becoming so deeply entrenched that the Bible teacher cannot ignore them, since they are believed by the studious as well as the less careful Bible searchers. Cultists, Modernists, and some Fundamentalists share these errors, so our instruction must meet the present needs of honest inquirers.

Although Dispensationalism is Protestant, it denies the Bible claims of orthodoxy. It is Satan's masterpiece of error under the guise of Scriptural truth. It strikes at the very heart of prophecy, and claims the imminent climax of all things, even as does the Advent message. Its Satanic meanderings are aimed at undermining God's unchangeable law. It hobnobs with cultism, and yet adds to its confusions by an even more unique and fanciful mysticism. It represents the thinking of the more sincere type of Christians, and has already become a mighty challenge to us as Bible instructors. It cannot be ignored, for it must be met.

More than the casual meeting of the rapturist doctrine must now be our approach with dispensationalists. It requires on our part a thorough knowledge of God's eternal purpose in Christ and the ability to teach that truth with objective and force. "No prophecy of the scripture is of any private interpretation." 2 Peter 1:20. When once the true nature of the Scofield Bible is recognized by the inquirer, then its interpretation in the light of Peter's foregoing argument quickly helps to unveil the whole dispensational fallacy. But this principle must be recognized by the pupil, and not just condemned by the teacher.

I have found it important in meeting dispensationalists to suggest to them a mutual Scriptural investigation on a few underlying doctrines. These are built into the general series of Bible readings. When to introduce each of these topics should be decided by the needs of the student. The following sequence is merely suggestive: 1. God's Eternal Purpose in Christ. 2. Personality of God; Divinity of Christ. 3. Origin of Evil and Fall of Man. 4. Life in Christ Only. 5. Purpose and Perpetuity of God's Law. 6. The Mystery of Iniquity.

"The principles of God's government and the plan of redemption must be clearly defined. The lessons of the Old Testament must be fully set before men."—*Prophets and Kings,* p. 700.

"He [the Bible student] should gain a knowledge of its grand central theme, of God's original purpose for the world, of the rise of the great controversy, and of the work of redemption. He should understand the nature of the two principles that are contending for supremacy, and should learn to trace their working through the records of history and prophecy, to the great consummation. He should see how this controversy enters into every phase of human experience; how in every act of life he himself reveals the one or the other of the two antagonistic motives; and how, whether he will or not, he is even now deciding upon which side of the controversy he will be found."—*Education,* p. 190.

Observe the foregoing instruction. The whole controversy centers in the "grand central theme"—"God's original purpose." Helping the student to understand the nature of the two contending principles unmasks Satan's plan. The reason for this method is that the reader may see his own case as related to the contest. Heaven suggests this technique to meet the problems of this hour. By this method the Christ of the great controversy stands out in bold relief. He points to Himself as the way, the truth, and the life. A typical Bible reading on this topic is suggested on page 365.

PART ONE ★ CHAPTER EIGHTEEN

Light Through the Sanctuary

The outstanding truth of Seventh-day Adventists is the sanctuary. It serves as a mighty weapon against the increasing doctrinal confusions of our day. Our clear-cut teachings on this subject revive the spirits of those who in their former church affiliations were awaiting a revival of Bible teaching. When they once grasp the importance of the sanctuary theme as fitting into the judgment hour, its verities anchor their faith.

The sanctuary truth is the very heart of our message, and should be presented as such. To wait with its presentation until the Sabbath, state of the dead, and reformatory doctrines have all been taught—with the sanctuary subjects used only as fillers—is a wrong conception of its significance. It belongs in the earlier stages of the series in order to reveal the Christ of prophecy in all His beauty and importance. This mighty theme also adds luster to the law and force to the Sabbath. Properly introduced, it safeguards a legalistic approach to our studies by exalting the everlasting gospel.

When to Present the Sanctuary Truth

Usually the time for presenting the sanctuary and kindred doctrines is preceding the study on the Sabbath. It is through the sanctuary that we magnify the atoning work of Christ, and thereby declare ourselves straight on those fundamentals of faith that evangelicals like to claim Seventh-day Adventists disregard. Before the Sabbath question must be met in rebuttal, the relationship of the law and the gospel should be well established. This procedure will at least materially trim down the attacks on our "old covenant experience." In our clear teaching that it is the shadows and types of the Old Testament that are fulfilled in Christ, we reveal our consistent stand on the ceremonial law. The prophetic setting of the investigative judgment gives authority for teaching the epochs of the two resurrections and the return of Jesus with Bible certainty. Again, who can gainsay a definite time message for the Second Advent in the light of the first? Adventists are unique on this point.

Not the *furniture* of the sanctuary, but the *services* of this economy should be stressed by the teacher. The inexperienced Bible instructor is likely to elaborate on the furniture rather than emphasize the significance of the daily and yearly services. Making an "end of sin" in ancient Israel pointed to Christ's atoning work on Calvary. The imminence of His return is revealed in the 2300-day prophecy. Teaching the cleansing of the sanctuary urges a preparation of heart for this event. One's sincerity is revealed by the last-day Sabbath test, which is deeply grounded in the sanctuary. In this respect the sanctuary doctrine safeguards a superficiality of life. Its keynote is a freedom from sin for Christian service. These principles are not new.

Sanctuary Embraces Present-Truth Doctrines

A point of special significance regarding the sanctuary truth should be noted. Every other doctrine we hold as present truth may be taught through a study of the sanctuary. Our various doctrines are like the spokes of its wheel, with Christ as the hub. The sanctuary truth unifies our whole message. (See "Sanctuary the Heart of Our Doctrine," by Dorothy Whitney Conklin, in *The Ministry*, September, 1946, to January, 1947.)

But this great truth is more than a doctrine. Living in the judgment hour, a time which necessitates a heart preparation, the church is enjoined to "worship God." (Rev. 14:6, 7.) The mind's assenting to the acceptance of the sanctuary doctrine must be perfected in the experience of His believers in their true worship of God. For this reason our sanctuary teachings, even as the Spirit of prophecy, are doctrines that deepen the Christian experience of all, but especially of new believers. Because of their importance as well as novelty to the young convert, a review course on the sanctuary truth should be included after baptism in our plans for establishing those who have recently embraced the faith.

We refer Bible instructors to the material in *Evangelism*, pages 221-225. They will here find information as well as method and caution for presenting this subject to their readers. The subject has not been exhausted by any means, and this material could be used for a research project of one's own, and other valuable points added as they are discovered. A subject as important as the sanctuary should invite a close study on the part of every worker.

The Sanctuary Truth in the Spirit of Prophecy
ALFRED RICHLI

We should be intelligent.

"We should not rest until we become intelligent in regard to the subject of the sanctuary, which is brought out in the visions of Daniel and John."—*Review and Herald,* Nov. 27, 1883.

"The death of Christ elevates the Jewish system of types and ordinances, showing that they were of divine appointment, and for the purpose of keeping faith alive in the hearts of His people."—*Signs of the Times,* April 15, 1875.

Old truths are to be understood before the new can be comprehended.

"In every age there is a new development of truth, a message of God to the people of that generation. The old truths are all essential; new truth is not independent of the old, but an unfolding of it. It is only as the old truths are understood that we can comprehend the new. . . . But it is the light which shines in the fresh unfolding of truth that glorifies the old."—*Christ's Object Lessons,* pp. 127, 128.

"Around the sanctuary and its solemn services mystically gathered the grand truths which were to be developed through succeeding generations. There has been no time when God has granted greater evidences of His grandeur and exalted majesty, than while He was the acknowledged governor of Israel."—*Review and Herald,* March 2, 1886.

Important truths are taught in types and symbols.

"Important truths concerning the atonement are taught by the typical service. A substitute was accepted in the sinner's stead; but the sin was not canceled by the blood of the victim. A means was thus provided by which it was transferred to the sanctuary. By the offering of blood, the sinner acknowledged the authority of the law, confessed his guilt in transgression, and expressed his desire for pardon through faith in a Redeemer to come; but he was not yet entirely released from the condemnation of the law. On the day of atonement the high priest, having taken an offering from the congregation, went into the most holy place with the blood of this offering, and sprinkled it upon the mercy-seat, directly over the law, to make satisfaction for its claims. Then, in his character of mediator, he took the sins upon himself and bore them from the sanctuary. Placing his hands upon the head of the scapegoat, he confessed over him all these sins, thus in figure transferring them from himself to the goat. The goat then bore them away, and they were regarded as forever separated from the people.

"Such was the service performed 'unto the example and shadow of heavenly things.' And what was done in type in the ministration of the earthly sanctuary, is done in reality in the ministration of the heavenly sanctuary."—*The Great Controversy*, p. 420.

"He who created the mind and ordained its laws, provided for its development in accordance with them. In the home and the sanctuary, through the things of nature and of art, in labor and in festivity, in sacred building and memorial stone, by methods and rites and symbols unnumbered, God gave to Israel lessons illustrating His principles, and preserving the memory of His wonderful works. Then, as inquiry was made, the instruction given impressed mind and heart."—*Education*, p. 41.

"The tabernacle was to be sacred to the service of God. It was to stand continually in the sight of more than a million people as an illustration of the perfection of Christ's work; and all that was done in its building was to represent this perfection."—*Review and Herald*, June 24, 1902.

God's truths are to be carefully searched out.

"Satan invents unnumbered schemes to occupy our minds, that they may not dwell upon the very work with which we ought to be best acquainted [the investigative judgment]. The arch-deceiver hates the great truths that bring to view an atoning sacrifice and an all-powerful Mediator. He knows that with him everything depends on his diverting minds from Jesus and His truth."—*The Great Controversy,* p. 488.

"The precious gems of the righteousness of Christ, and truths of divine origin, are to be carefully searched out and placed in their proper setting to shine with heavenly brilliancy amid the moral darkness of the world."—*Review and Herald,* Oct. 23, 1894.

"Many people are sadly ignorant in regard to the plan of salvation; they need more instruction upon this all-important subject than upon any other."—*Gospel Workers,* p. 158.

"In the ministration of the tabernacle, and of the temple that afterward took its place, the people were taught each day, by means of types and shadows, the great truths relative to the advent of Christ as Redeemer, Priest, and King; and once each year their minds were carried forward to the closing events of the great controversy between Christ and Satan, the final purification of the universe from sin and sinners. The sacrifices and offerings of the Mosaic ritual were ever pointing toward a better service, even a heavenly."—*Prophets and Kings,* pp. 684, 685.

The heavenly sanctuary reveals Christ's work and our duty today.

"Many and earnest were the efforts made to overthrow their faith [of those who came through the disappointment of 1844]. None could fail to see that if the earthly sanctuary was a figure or pattern of the heavenly, the law deposited in the ark on earth was an exact transcript of the law in the ark in heaven; and that an acceptance of the truth concerning the heavenly sanctuary involved an acknowledgment of the claims of God's law, and the obligation of the Sabbath of the fourth commandment. Here was the secret of the bitter and determined opposition to the harmonious exposition of the Scriptures that revealed the ministration of Christ in the heavenly sanctuary. Men sought to close the door which God had opened, and to open the door which He had closed."—*The Great Controversy,* p. 435.

"The condition of the unbelieving Jews illustrates the condition of the careless and unbelieving among professed Christians, who are willingly ignorant of the work of our merciful High Priest. In the typical service, when the high priest entered the most holy place, all Israel were required to gather about the sanctuary and in the most solemn manner humble their souls before God, that they might receive the pardon of their sins, and not be cut off from the congregation. How much more essential in this antitypical day of atonement that we understand the work of our High Priest, and know what duties are required of us."—*Ibid.,* pp. 430, 431.

Our eyes are to be fixed on the heavenly sanctuary.

"God's people are now to have their eyes fixed on the heavenly sanctuary, where the final ministration of our great High Priest in the work of the judgment is going forward, —where He is interceding for His people."—*Review and Herald,* Nov. 27, 1883.

"Those who would share the benefits of the Saviour's mediation should permit nothing to interfere with their duty to perfect holiness in the fear of God. The precious hours, instead of being given to pleasure, to display, or to gain-seeking, should be devoted to an earnest, prayerful study of the Word of truth. The subject of the sanctuary and the investigative judgment should be clearly understood by the people of God. All need a knowledge for themselves of the position and work of their great High Priest. Otherwise, it will be impossible for them to exercise the faith which is essential at this time, or to occupy the position which God designs them to fill. . . . All who have received the light upon these subjects are to bear testimony of the great truths which God has committed to them. The sanctuary in heaven is the very center of Christ's work in behalf of men. It concerns every soul living upon the earth. It opens to view the plan of redemption, bringing us down to the very close of time, and revealing the triumphant issue of the contest between righteousness and sin. It is of the utmost importance that all should thoroughly investigate these subjects, and be able to give an answer to every one that asketh them a reason of the hope that is in them."—*The Great Controversy,* pp. 488, 489.

The understanding of the sanctuary truth will prepare God's people for Christ's appearing.

"The great plan of redemption, as revealed in the closing work for these last days, should receive close examination. The scenes connected with the sanctuary above should make such an impression upon the minds and hearts of all that they may be able to impress others. All need to become more intelligent in regard to the work of the atonement, which is going on in the sanctuary above. When this grand truth is seen and understood, those who hold it will work in harmony with Christ to prepare a people to stand in the great day of God, and their efforts will be successful."—*Testimonies,* vol. 5, p. 575.

"But the people were not yet ready to meet their Lord. There was still a work of preparation to be accomplished for them. Light was to be given, directing their minds to the temple of God in heaven; and as they should by faith follow their High Priest in His ministration there, new duties would be revealed. Another message of warning and instruction was to be given to the church. . . . This work is more clearly presented in the messages of Revelation 14. When this work shall have been accomplished, the followers of Christ will be ready for His appearing."—*The Great Controversy,* pp. 424, 425.

"The enemy will bring in false theories, such as the doctrine that there is no sanctuary [in heaven]. This is one of the points on which there will be a departing from the faith."—*Review and Herald,* May 25, 1905.

"Christ is not entered into the holy places made with hands, which are the figures of the true; but into heaven itself, *now to appear in the presence of God for us.*" Heb. 9:24. (Also see *Evangelism,* pp. 221-225.)

PART ONE ★ CHAPTER NINETEEN

Modern Sabbath Issues

We are living in the time of the world's greatest apostasy. Babylon the great has many daughters. A confused world is being deceived by a revival of heathen philosophies, papal mysticisms, and the irresolute teachings of fallen Protestantism. Our message today must meet great systems of error. It must strike at the very heart of God's law as it challenges a generally blinded Christendom to return to God's original holy, seventh-day Sabbath. Tactfully, but nevertheless definitely, we must point out the great papal deception as being responsible for the transference of the sanctity of the seventh day, the sign of His sovereignty, to Sunday, the first day of the week.

The Bible teacher must observe how adroitly Rome is shifting her positions on the important Sunday issue. Catholics, with deceived Protestants, now loudly declare that the Sabbath belonged to the ceremonial law, and was therefore fulfilled at the cross. Protestantism is laying new stress on an observance of the "spirit" instead of the "letter" of God's law. A close student of prophecy must see how these two religious forces are blending their arguments in support of Sunday. Then there is Jewry to be heard from on the same question. Here we perceive a complete lack of vision, with absolutely no courage to return to Jehovah's neglected Sabbath. The fathers of this race once boldly contended for strict Sabbath observance, but Jews today have become indifferent on the question. The result is often stark atheism on the part of many who were once orthodox.

It becomes more evident that a remnant will soon be standing alone in defense of God's true Sabbath. The Sabbath was instituted at creation, and today, when evolutionary teachings prevail, our worship of the Creator as called for in the first angel's message is not without significance. This is a vital point which the Bible teacher can afford to stress in the setting of the judgment-hour message.

One would hardly begin a series of Bible readings by presenting the Sabbath truth. Unless this unpopular subject has first been given a build-up, few will be prepared to receive it. Bible instructors have therefore found it helpful to precede their Sabbath studies with the sanctuary topics. When the reader once grasps God's plan of atonement, and when he senses the importance of the law in connection with it, the Sabbath harmonizes with redemption and presents but little difficulty. It is most helpful to teach the law and the gospel prior to introducing the Sabbath.

History so well supports our arguments on the true Sabbath that honest Christians will not fail to acknowledge the source of Sunday observance. Neither is there much question on the Sabbath as a Christian institution after one has really studied into the practices of the early Christians. Another point of force is the presentation of the Sabbath in prophecy as well as history. As the periods of Sabbath neglect are now pointed out, and the reader observes what dire calamities resulted, these Sabbath prophecies speak with new significance for obedience to it. He begins to see that the Sabbath is in God's divine plan. It is the sign of His creative and re-creative power. The Sabbath was made for man, and therefore belongs to the Christian as well as the Jewish church. It is not affected by "dispensations," races, or creeds.

Because of strange interpretations of the prophecies of Isaiah and Micah as pertaining to the law, new zeal for the observance of God's law is now recognized among many Christians. Much is made of the text, "Out of Zion shall go forth the law, and the word of the Lord from Jerusalem." Isa. 2:3. In this connection there is a revival of emphasis on the teachings of the return of the Jews to Jerusalem. Zionism fits into the political picture of our times, and dispensationalism engenders doctrinal stimulus by means of perverted prophecy. This emphasis for observing the Ten Commandments as shared by Christians and Jews alike hardly touches the principle of true law observance. But, nevertheless, this setting of an awareness for keeping God's law gives the Bible instructor a more ready approach on this important subject. One may point out to the reader that although the nations will fail in bringing about worldwide law observance, God has provided for a message of Sabbath reform which will produce a law-abiding remnant before Jesus' return.

The Papacy's present overture to her "straying children" —those still in Protestant churches—presents another point of interest with many readers. The Pope's long-coveted role as the world's peacemaker now brings him into great prominence. Even Protestants are being confused on the authority of his leadership in the present crisis. Again, those issues that gave rise to the various branches of Protestantism at the time of the Reformation, are now being seriously minimized by Protestants as well as Catholics. It is difficult to interest Protestants in doctrinal study. We should be challenging them to maintain Bible truth.

Lest our younger Bible instructors read into these suggestions and cautions a need for recasting their entire array of topics and textual argumentation, let it be stressed again that it is their *methods* of approach that should become more dynamic, with an up-to-the-minute appeal. To do this, the Bible teacher need not enter into fields of speculation on prophecies still in fulfillment. This hour demands an acquaintance with those great issues that are affecting the very principles of God's government. We must recognize on Rome's part a scheme of Satan to set up a rival government, noting the modern developments that reveal the subtle tactics of truth's great adversary.

This method of teaching requires more than our usual argumentation based on an array of proof texts pertaining to the Sabbath. There are significant issues at stake, and when presented by the teacher in an intelligent way, people who think for themselves will in turn become leaders for these same principles.

For further study of the problem we recommend the following reading: *Evangelism,* pp. 225-237; *The Great Controversy,* pp. 563-652.

PART ONE ★ CHAPTER TWENTY

Teaching the State of the Dead

Some workers are laboring under a growing impression that Bible instructors frequently teach too negatively our doctrines concerning the state of the dead and the destruction of the wicked. One does become conscious that some Bible studies present at the outset a whole array of negative

Teaching the State of the Dead 119

points which tend to stir up opposition, and fail to bring about a decision in favor of the truth. It is possible that constant usage of strong argument may lead some teachers to become too dogmatic. This especially applies to points which are taken for granted by the teacher, but which are not generally accepted by the reader.

Again, the problem of teaching individuals in their homes is different at times from that of the evangelist who presents the truth to larger audiences. He is to "blow the trumpet in Zion," and is not likely to be publicly challenged by his listeners on points of disagreement, whereas the Bible instructor, who is not teaching in a rented hall, is considered a guest in the homes she visits. She must be most diplomatic and must make herself very agreeable if she is to continue her work with these families. The evangelist is decidedly in place blasting at the rocks of error with Bible dynamite, but the Bible instructor must use milder measures. This may not be necessary after the reader has become used to the evangelist's dynamic ways. Too often, however, the Bible instructor will still need to be pouring oil on the trouble spot while also aiming at being most definite in what God's Word teaches. Neither would we now argue for watering down our distinctive message on the state of the dead.

Bible instructors need to seek God's help for a new approach to the problem of death, so accentuated by war and its catastrophes. Death has cut deeply into the tender tissues of the human heart, and its bleeding wounds and unsightly scars bring us face to face with life's tragedies. The need today is for teachers with deep understanding and sympathy, who will convince people as to the reasonableness concerning what the Bible teaches regarding the state of the dead. Too many nervous cases suggest that workers refrain from giving a gloomy, merely factual presentation of this topic. The prophet Isaiah warns us, "Comfort ye, comfort ye My people."

Bearing in mind that our state-of-the-dead teachings incite more controversy in some sections than others, the Bible teacher will need to be governed by the conditions and reactions in the area in which she is laboring. Where there is no background of prejudice, the Bible instructor should feel free to introduce these issues early in the series. It is then not necessary to wait until the Sabbath truth has been presented. The main point is to study divine counsel and caution and to tactfully carry the people along for the full acceptance of truth. The following suggestions will prove helpful to the less experienced worker.

Pointers on Teaching State of Dead
(See *Evangelism*, pp. 246-249)

I. *Finding a Kind, Positive Approach.*
   Stress the following points:
   1. Introduce God's great purpose that man shall *live* forever. John 3:16; 2 Tim. 1:9.
   2. *Life,* not death, is man's privilege and his right. John 10:10.
   3. Heaven risked all that man might have *eternal life.* Rom. 8:32.
   4. Life is in Christ only. Phil. 1:21.
   5. Man is not left to die, unless he *chooses to.* Deut. 30:19.
   6. Eden was planned by God to last *forever.* Isa. 51:3.
   7. Sin did not surprise God; He was prepared for it. (John 1:29, 36; Rev. 13:8.) The provision for the Lamb of God to take away the sins of the world was made before the entry of sin.
   8. God has to eradicate sin. Nahum 1:9.
   9. The destruction of the wicked is a *"strange act"* by God, but it also displays His heart of love. It is associated with fear, suffering, and great anguish. Destruction in the lake of fire will not be instantaneous. It will be *everlasting punishment.* The sinner is *destroyed forever.* Isa. 28:21.
   10. *Everlasting fire* is prepared for the devil and his angels, not for man. Only when man's nature becomes Satanic will he share in Satan's destruction. Matt. 25:41.
   11. Man need not perish; he should not perish! John 3:16.
   12. We may now have eternal life "in hope." Titus 3:7; 1:2.
   13. In the grave the righteous are still "prisoners of hope." Zech. 9:12.

14. The gospel "abolished death" and "brought life and immortality." 2 Tim. 1:10.
15. "Who shall change our vile body . . . like unto His glorious body." Phil. 3:21.

II. *Meeting the Reader on His Own Ground.*
   1. Most people believe in the conscious state of the dead. Ask questions to draw out their ideas. Avoid abrupt statements of new truth.
   2. Lay a foundation by presenting God's plan for man to have eternal life and immortality.
   3. Study well the parable of the rich man and Lazarus. Here Christ used ideas common to the Jews of His day. He built on these, but did not abruptly upset the thinking of the people. Also study His methods in revealing God's purpose to Mary and Martha. (John 11.) Observe how He here introduced and unfolded the doctrine of death as a sleep, and then the truth of the resurrection. Also notice how the resurrection is associated with the "last day" instead of an immediate entering into God's presence at death. John 11:24.
   4. At first bring out those gospel facts on which you can agree with the reader, then tactfully but definitely build new truth. (*Evangelism,* p. 446.)
   5. Avoid argument when answering common objections, guiding these toward Bible truth. Always let the Bible speak. If necessary, reinforce truth with additional texts, but avoid too many concepts in one study. Handle other points gradually as questions arise.
   6. Although points of truth may be clear when first presented, some doubts are bound to arise, and these confusions will need to be straightened out.
   7. State-of-the-dead truths lend themselves to fitting illustrations for building confidence in God's Word. Use those that break down prejudice. Avoid gruesome tales and deathbed stories, always stressing the joy and hope of the resurrection.
   8. If your reader finds difficulty in grasping texts, do not hammer them in. Encourage praying about the matter, and urge the careful reading of helpful literature on the subject. (*Evangelism,* p. 441.)
   9. If difficulties continue, try teaching similar truths through the study of the sanctuary. David's feet had almost slipped, until he grasped God's plan for the destruction of the wicked through an understanding of this economy. (Ps. 73; 37:20.) Many a

reader soon recognizes God's plan for man's temporary mortal nature by studying the types and the shadows of the sanctuary.
10. Do not press the issue too hard, but continue studies on other subjects. After the Spirit of prophecy is accepted, many difficulties on the state of the dead will be cleared away.
11. Expect that it will take time for some elderly people to grasp various points of these doctrines. Handle them gently. Pray with them. They may continue to speak in a confused way on some points already taught, but do not take this too seriously. Patiently educate, repeat, clarify, and win friends for the truth.

Modern State-of-the-Dead Issues

Evangelism, pp. 246-249; *The Great Controversy,* pp. 540-550.

1. Error on state-of-dead doctrine almost universal; doctrine most stressed. GC 543, 547.
2. Error one of Rome's poisonous drafts of Babylon. GC 536, 549.
3. Our duty to expose pagan errors. GC 548, 549.
4. Universalism teachings result of error. GC 537-539.
5. Unsound reasoning of texts; texts out of their context. Result: unsound conclusions.
6. Danger in presenting state-of-dead topic too soon. *Evangelism,* 246.
7. Topic restrained even as Sabbath question. E 246, 248.
8. When reader's heart melted, then present topic. E 248.
9. No place for "combative armor" or "debating spirit." E 249.
10. Satan's first sermon on immortality, a last-hour deception. GC 533.
11. Our approach: *Life in Christ only.* E 247; GC 540.
12. Life in Christ on condition of accepting God's offer. GC 540.
13. Place of human will, God's law, and proper choice by obedience. GC 541-543.
14. Death and the grave the lot of every human being. GC 544.
15. Two classes at the resurrection. GC 544, 547.
16. An intermediate state or second chance not in Bible. GC 546.
17. Reward of saints not at death but after investigative judgment. GC 548, 550.
18. Death like a sound slumber; awakened when Jesus comes. GC 550.
19. Each know personally what Bible teaches. GC 540, 542.

PART ONE ★ CHAPTER TWENTY-ONE

Our Reformatory Message

Health Reform

The teaching of health in connection with the Advent message always adds power to its proclamation. The world at large has become exceedingly health conscious. What at one time was considered by many the "fanatical" teachings of Seventh-day Adventists, has now been adopted by science and informed Christians as well. We too now point with just pride to the ancestry of our health reform practice. It is to be regretted that we failed at times to bring some of its great principles into prominence before science presented them to a listening world. God planned that His people at all times should be the head and not the tail, and this would include a knowledge of healthful living and God's methods for treating diseases.

In our presentation of health to the public, certain approaches have been helpfully used by evangelists who have a background for health teaching. Public health lectures in an evangelistic series have always been a great attraction. The methods, however, should vary according to the ability of the evangelistic company. Here again our Bible instructors have made their contributions, for a representative number are graduates of the nurses' course. But the majority are not trained nurses, and will need to continue improving their more limited knowledge in the field of health. Our message should definitely include health reform, and the best methods of instruction should be employed.

Scientific Yet Simple Method

Because of science consciousness today, our approach to health teaching should be scientific. But physicians who have this knowledge sometimes fail to get down to the level of the ordinary man in presenting their instruction in a simple and practical way. Therefore a Bible instructor with simplified technique is often better suited than a doctor to grip the interest of these new believers. This should encourage her to persevere in becoming more and more skillful in teaching practical health to those with whom she studies. There is no room, however, for the overenthusiastic health reformer—that fanatic or faddist type of Bible instructor whose claims are all based on the Bible. Neither the Bible nor Spirit of prophecy should ever become a "club" for the transgressor, or for the ignorant; but in them may be found an authoritative appeal to healthful, clean, and sanctified living.

When our health message first holds a definite conviction for the teacher, then her message will have weight with her readers. Others may be careless in living these timely health principles, but never should this be said of the Bible instructor! There must ever be a deep sincerity in her life. She is not to be found with those who engage in borderline practices. She does not "break over," to become the reproach of the critical, but neither does she lose out because of her extreme positions, which may be undermining her own health. She maintains a middle-of-the-road position by keeping herself in a sanctified state of mind and body while she continues to study God's Word and the Spirit of prophecy. She faithfully reads our current denominational health literature, and at least one other recommended non-Adventist health journal.

Various Approaches

Just where in a series of studies the Bible instructor should bring in the health message depends entirely upon the person with whom she studies. There may be occasion to introduce it early in the series. With others, it may be presented soon after the Sabbath truth is introduced. Again, some readers must be carefully carried along until sufficient background indicates that they are actually ready to cease their health-destroying practices. The experienced worker will understand that the Holy Spirit definitely guides in this. Where interest has been previously awakened in health and diet, the way has been prepared for an earlier presentation.

As you study the diagram of the topical arrangement on page 102, observe where this lesson may best fit into the entire series. Here is found a practical approach as it is presented in connection with those subjects that relate to the more abundant life. Before the state of the dead is presented, the readers should be taught how to live better and longer. The emphasis must always be on vibrant Christian living, and not on the moroseness of dying. When the sinner eventually dies the second death, it is because he has neglected every opportunity of living in harmony with God's laws—moral or physical.

Suggestions by an Evangelist

The following suggestions by an evangelist of wide experience may well be observed by the home Bible teacher.

1. Be practical rather than technical.
2. Be positive, not negative. Avoid gruesome things.
3. First stay within general fields—do not attempt anything too specific.
4. Consider the economic problems of the community.
5. Illustrate your talks by personal experiences.
6. Keep a sense of humor.
7. Make your appeal spiritual.
8. Avoid referring to funerals and undertakers.
9. Never make claims that cannot be substantiated by scientific investigation.
10. Remember that health reform is progressive. Do not attempt to teach everything at once.
11. Capitalize on health consciousness of nations today.
12. Continue to give a progressive health message from the Scriptures.

Well-balanced Health Instruction

Although health reform is very important in our reformatory message, it still remains only its "right arm," not the head or the whole body. This divinely balanced counsel defines its rightful place in the presentation of our doctrines. Where this advice is followed our health program will be soundly balanced with other doctrines that are equally intended to prepare a people for Christ's return. Bear in mind that health reform should always be progressive, and that the young Christian must be carefully led along into its fuller blessings. Another principle to stress is its local, yet universal, application. Health reform belongs to every nation, kindred, tongue, and people. Local conditions vary its application, but these never minimize its world-wide importance.

Health and Evangelism
LeRoy E. Froom

I. *Descriptive Terms Employed.*
  1. Right hand (to open door for body to enter). MM 238; R&H, June 7, 1902.
  2. As hand to body. CH 21, 73; R&H, June 20, 1899.
  3. God's helping hand. MM 240; CH 514.
  4. Right arm. 6T 327; MM 237; R&H, June 20, 1899.
  5. Door—means of entrance. MM 241.
  6. Entering wedge for other truths. 6T 327; R&H, June 20, 1899.
  7. Pioneer work of gospel. MM 239.
  8. Part of gospel. MM 259.
  9. 'A new element. MM 319.

II. *Inseparable Relationship to the Gospel.*
  1. "Gospel of health is to be firmly linked with the ministry of the word." MS. 172, 1899.
  2. Linked—not to be separated. 9T 171; CH 497.
  3. Combined. MM 320. "Combine medical missionary work with the proclamation of the third angel's message."
  4. Keep to the front. GW 348.
  5. Advance together. 6T 379.
  6. Go forward together. 9T 113; 6T 327.
  7. Neither complete without other. CH 514.

Our Reformatory Message

   8. Appointed work. CH 40; CDF 458.
   9. To be part of ministerial preparation. CH 538, R&H, Jan. 14, 1902.
  10. Baleful effects of negative attitude. NP Leaflets, Method, no. 5.

III. *Fundamental Purpose of Health Message.*
   1. To lessen suffering. 9T 112, 113.
   2. To prepare minds for reception of truth. CH 22.
   3. To rescue from evil habits. 6T 378.
   4. To develop body, mind, and soul. MH 146; CH 390.
   5. To prepare for Christ's coming. 3T 161-165; CH 20, 21.

IV. *General Scope and Limitations.*
   1. With every city effort. MM 299, 300, 304; GW 347; R&H, Jan. 7, 1902; MS. 1, 1910.
   2. In foreign field, homeland, and new fields. CH 389, 390; MM 246, 239.
   3. By health demonstrations and cooking schools. MM 265, 267, 270, 306, 322; CDF 254, 255; 9T 112, 161; 7T 113; R&H, June 6, 1912; Letter 55, 1905; Letters 106, 166, 1903; Letter 343, 1904.
   4. Through temperance lectures. CH 449.
      Cooperation with other temperance organizations.
   5. Instruction should include:
      a. Preservation of health (laws of life—hygienic agencies, pure air and water, proper exercise, sleep, rest, clear conscience, healthful diet and dress, health foods). 7T 247; MM 259, 275, 105; MH 292, 293, 382, 383; MS. 10, 1898.
      b. Relationship of mind and body.
      c. Nonuse of tea, coffee, tobacco, flesh meats. MM 222, 266.
   6. Prevention of disease. MM 221.
   7. Simple treatments and care of sick. R&H, June 9, 1904; MM 29, 222, 227.
   8. In homes of people. CH 497; R&H, March 4, 1902; Jan. 1, 1901; Aug. 3 & Nov. 23, 1905.
   9. Not assume functions of physician. 2T 375; CH 161.
  10. Sometimes must act part of physician. MM 253.
  11. Health books and papers. CH 428, 446, 447, 462; CDF 461, 462.
  12. Health foods. CH 492.

V. *Avoidance of Extremes and Negativism.*
   1. Varying world conditions to be recognized. (Different diet in different countries.) MM 289, 261; GW 239; 9T 162, 163; CH 118, 137, 153, 156; CDF 94-96.
   2. Not to be deprived until substitutes provided. MS. 165, 1899.
   3. Extremes and narrow views to be avoided. MM 269.

4. Meat eating not a test. Methods, no. 5, pp. 2, 3.
   5. Not yet time to discard butter, eggs, and milk. MM 289; 9T 162, 163; CH 136.

VI. *Relation to Prayer and Anointing of Sick.*
   1. Sick to be prayed for as did disciples. R&H, June 9, 1904; GW 215; 2T 147.
   2. Praying for sick not to be "discarded." CH 380; 5T 196; PFS 41; R&H, July 19, 1898.
   3. Conditions and restrictions. MH 227-231; 2T 146-149; 2T 350; CDF 400.
      a. Confessing sin.
      b. Submitting to God's will.
      c. Forsaking evil habits and indulgences.
   4. Relation to remedial agencies. MH 231-233.
   5. Cooperation with means for recovery. Letter 17, 1892.

Health in Relation to Religion
Mary McReynolds, M.D.

I. *Health and the Gospel.*
   1. The "Gospel of Health." 7T 137; 6T 327; MH 115.
   2. Health work not to promote physical well-being only. 7T 120.
   3. Not only health, but perfection, the great object. 1T 554.
   4. Part of third angel's message. 1T 486, 559; 3T 61, 62, 161.
   5. An important place in the work of salvation. 9T 112.

II. *A Reformatory Work.*
   1. For purifying His church. 9T 112, 113.
   2. Its great object spiritual. 1T 564, 565.
   3. Sanctification impossible when under control of appetite and passion. 3T 570.
   4. John the Baptist a reformer. 3T 60-63.
   5. Christ first reformed physical habits. 3T 486.

III. *Health and Temperance.*
   1. Eternal destiny dependent upon strictly temperate habits. 3T 489.
   2. Every practice which destroys physical, mental, or spiritual energies sin. MH 113.
   3. A sin to abuse health. 3T 150.
   4. In worst sense transgressors of God's law. 3T 165.
   5. Impossible for those who indulge appetite to attain perfection. 2T 400.

The Health Evangel 129

IV. *Diet Important Today.*
   1. Diet and appreciation of truth. 2T 364.
   2. From a religious standpoint. 3T 170.
   3. Relation to the loud cry. 1T 486.
   4. The truth not appreciated. 6T 371.
   5. Those who conquer appetite able to conquer on other points. 3T 491, 492.
   6. Failure to overcome appetite, failure in other victories. 3T 490.
   7. Sin to eat too much. 2T 412.
   8. Discern right and wrong. MH 128.
V. *Diet and Translation.*
   1. Relation to translation. 2T 63; CDF 380, 381.
   2. Hope of Eden, firm denial of appetite and passion. 3T 491.
VI. *Health a Boon to the Church.*
   1. Religion a continual wellspring. CH 28.
   2. Christ's love a healing power. CH 29.

(For health teaching plans and Bible study material see next chapter.)

PART ONE ★ CHAPTER TWENTY-TWO

The Health Evangel

There is no doubt but that the knowledge of health principles which Seventh-day Adventists hold enhances to a marked degree the Bible doctrines which they propagate. In *Medical Ministry,* page 320, the instruction from God's messenger is that we are to "combine medical missionary work with the proclamation of the third angel's message."

The Bible instructor who practices and teaches healthful living has a great advantage over the one who does not. This is true for several reasons, the chief of them being that she herself will enjoy better health. Another benefit is the added respect which she will merit from her readers, for the majority of those whom she meets are selfishly interested in their physical well-being. Their interest in a future life is secondary in importance. Thus the teaching of health in its various phases becomes the entering wedge for teaching those truths which we hold to be of first importance.

The knowledge of health doctrines is a sound base upon which a satisfying Christian experience can be erected, for is not the body the "temple of God"? It is through the physical channel that man perceives spiritual truth, so it follows that the healthier the channel, the better prepared is one to receive that truth. A good Christian principle is more effectively taught if it is first exemplified in a sound body.

How may the Bible instructor's knowledge of physiology, simple preventives, remedial treatments, fundamentals of nutrition and cookery, be an asset to her in teaching the doctrines of the Advent message, the second coming of Christ, the state of the dead, or the Sabbath?

Just watch the interest awaken and grow as the instructor prefaces her study before an apparently apathetic group in a cottage, with a simple, tactfully presented study on a health topic. Her audience becomes not only friendly but also quite cooperative as she attempts to bring to them the points of our doctrine. Especially when she sends up a petition for anyone in the home who is ill, calling the name if possible, are seeds of faith sown, which God jealously watches and cherishes.

The Bible instructor is wise who is alert to discover an illustration from the fertile fields of physiology to apply the spiritual truths she is trying to instill. Such association formed between the physical and the spiritual would result in bringing the spiritual to mind whenever the physical is remembered. See how often in His lessons with ancient Israel, God uses these illustrations to impress some obscure lesson.

A Bible instructor who is acquainted with the interdependent action of the mind and body can with God's help prepare her readers for the perception and the acceptance of God's will by inviting them to practice the principles of healthful living for a while, to see for themselves how much better they feel, and how much easier it is to understand the Bible when they study it in the fresh air, or after a moderate meal of wholesome food, or after abstaining from tobacco for several days.

It is a challenge to readers and a thrill to the instructor to watch the transformation achieved after these principles have been practiced for only a short time. The testimonials of victory over wrong habits and ignorance truly furnish inspiration to the worker.

Whenever possible the Bible instructor may invite one of her readers or a family to dinner, and serve a tasty, well-balanced, well-prepared meal. The results are always worth the effort and expense. They can only be measured in eternity. This is one form of good news which *does* travel, and fast, too. As a result of such a meal a cooking school may be organized.

Whenever a crisis occurs in a home, when first aid is essential, the Bible instructor who can fit in right then and there may not only save a life but, by her calmness and efficiency, her trust in God and faith in prayer, be placed in a singularly favorable light. She must not attempt to take the place of the doctor or the trained nurse after they come, but who is to say that she is not to serve to the best of her ability until they are accessible? In wartimes, when medical helpers are so scarce, and in rural or remote areas, she can enlist the aid of holy angels in ministry to the afflicted in times of emergency.

A rousing interest in the study of health principles can be developed by the instructor in our churches, and sometimes can be more effective than the same efforts put forth by the minister. "The refining, softening influence of Christian women is needed in the great work of preaching the truth."—*Review and Herald,* Jan. 2, 1879.

Of first importance is example. The Bible instructor must be an example in healthful dress, healthful diet, and the observance of health habits. Practice should precede preaching, it is true, but in the field of health evangelism there must be the preaching too. God has signally blessed, and will continue to bless, the army of His evangels of mercy, who, like His own dear Son, "went about doing good, and healing all that were oppressed."

PART ONE ★ CHAPTER TWENTY-THREE

Life and Stewardship

The question of Christian stewardship holds a large place in the progress of the message. Every new convert to the faith should be well instructed regarding his personal responsibility and relation to it. Stewardship must include our time, talents, strength, means—yes, everything God has given man. Becoming a part of the Advent Movement requires the same consecration that was demanded of the disciples in Christ's day. Leaving their fishing nets signified to the world their "all-out" policy for His gospel work.

Presenting God's plan in tithes and offerings needs no apology on the part of the Bible teacher. This duty is viewed in the light of God's fast-closing work, and the truth seeker is invited into the blessed experience of having a part in it. However, it is well to await the direction of the Holy Spirit as to the proper time to present this topic. I recall an experience which came to me when I was rather new in the work. I felt impressed to present the study rather early in the series because of the questions asked by a sincere inquirer, and had the joy of immediately seeing that individual's faithfulness as she promptly entrusted her tithe to me each week. This took place several weeks before the reader was ready to leave her former church fellowship, where tithing was not practiced. Many similar experiences since then have encouraged me to present God's claims to the tithe whenever the Holy Spirit so indicated,

As the new convert faithfully tithes the means God gives him, the blessing of partnership with the Master in winning souls is realized. Then as the various calls for home and foreign missions multiply, he learns a new economy. Where the family is united in this new-found truth, these sacrifices become an act of devotion in which all in the home are interested. But when just one person in the family takes his stand for an unpopular message, a conflict often begins.

At first the new believer may find himself in trying straits because of this new financial responsibility. God now comes first, and then his family. He needs constant encouragement to be faithful in that which is least. A timely lesson should be impressed upon the new believer—love is to become the ruling motive in every service for the Master. Tactful guidance during a new member's early training in church responsibility will help him solve his problems according to principle rather than emotion.

Modern business methods sometimes creep into the promotion of our church campaigns. It may be well to check our experience as leaders, for our example counts with new believers especially. Since they watch us, and also copy our ways, how important it is that we implant real principles of righteousness in their lives. Souls won for the kingdom must be the true goal of every church project. Never must we stoop to the ways of the world by methods of unsanctified competition. This stretching ourselves to outdo another's attainment is not the way of Christ. Neither zeal nor strenuous labor can atone for our lack of vision in this respect; and yet there still is a place for sanctified enthusiasm, devotion. The true Christian is free from all self-glory, envy, and pride.

There is another important feature that must be watched in the convert's early zeal for the truth. During a church campaign new believers frequently show more enthusiasm than the established members. To suggest a working load equal to one's spiritual strength and experience is far more wholesome than to overestimate this newborn zeal for service. The latter often kills enthusiasm after the first few years. We sometimes stress money and time spent in service rather than loving, increasing devotion to the Saviour. Perhaps the Bible instructor can be as helpful now as anyone, for these new people in the faith enjoy working with those who brought them into the church.

A special caution should be remembered when dealing with juniors. True, they are active and willing, and are thrilled to be doing exploits for God and man. Yet we must consider unfavorable reactions which may mar their young lives. Therefore, the principle of stopping while the work still appeals, applies to more than food. A meal may be eaten with relish, but health reform would suggest to us that there is a limit to one's appetite. Likewise, as directors of God's work, let us plan as sensible men and women who have the responsibility of these developing workers on our hearts.

At the proper time new believers should be informed concerning the disposal of their possessions in case of decease. All workers, including our Bible instructors, should be conversant with the plans proposed to us by God's messenger. They wield a great influence over those lives God has entrusted to them, and the many occasions to speak a word in season may best be tactfully improved in this stage of the reader's experience. Had we as workers been more faithful to duty in teaching new converts the right disposition of property, God's cause would today realize more of the means that too often flow into the coffers of the world.

It takes time and effort to make really strong Adventists, who will be pillars for the message. Too many today have but a flimsy grip on the rugged truths which will figure in the testing experiences of the future. May we as Bible instructors be clear before God that we have fully taught our readers and have grounded them so well that they will add strength to the Advent Movement in its closing days.

Teaching Stewardship Principles

I. *Stewardship for the New Convert.* (CS 19; chap. 24; 298.)
   1. Complete dedication of the life.
   2. Time, opportunity, talents, strength, means.
   3. Tithes and offerings.
   4. Practice of Christian economy.
   5. Faithfulness against opposition.

II. *The True Motive in Giving.* (AA 278, 280, 342, 541-543; CS 16; MH 500-503; AA 338-344; CS 25, 65, 68, 107, 176, 180, 299, 300, 344.)
   1. Giver actuated by love.
   2. Principles of stewardship taught.
   3. Competitive methods not helpful.
   4. Righteousness by faith, not works.
   5. Our many sacrifices recorded in heaven.

III. *Advanced Instruction.* (CS 53, 74, 78.)
   1. The sacredness of vows.
   2. Wills and legacies. CS sec. 14.

PART ONE ★ CHAPTER TWENTY-FOUR

Presenting Prophecy

In the teaching of present truth it is necessary that the instructor stress the great present-day issues of prophecy. This means that Bible truth should be clearly taught in contrast with tradition, and that those chapters in Daniel and Revelation which reveal these special issues should receive their proper emphasis. Today whole systems of fallacious teachings must be exposed by the searchlight of prophecy. The Bible student must be led to see the foundation of his faith; whether it is grounded on the solid rock of the Word or built on the sinking sand of tradition. Before he considers taking the serious step which involves changing his rest day from the first to the seventh day, he should recognize its importance through a study of these special prophecies which pertain to this important truth.

Prophecy helps the Bible student to see the true problem of sin and righteousness. This issue centers on the great question, What is truth? Prophecy here throws the spotlight on the man of sin as well as on the sinless Saviour. In the prophetic portraits of nations we perceive the immutability of God's throne. Again prophecy presents a clear picture of the true church as compared with the apostate Babylon. Here are revealed the reward of obedience and the consequence of disobedience.

Through a study of the prophetic portions of the Word the Bible student will see God's wise over-all purpose in a way that doctrinal study alone cannot supply. Bible teachers should balance their doctrinal instruction with prophecy. Doctrine and prophecy must again be balanced with practical truth.

I. *Well-balanced Truth Teaching.* (Based on *Evangelism.*)
   1. Doctrinal subjects. 361-364.
   2. Prophetic studies. 193-199.
   3. Practical lessons. 124.
      a. Teachings of Jesus. 172, 199.
      b. Practical godliness. 178, 142, 400, 200.
   4. Witnessing experiences. 186, 187, 485, 486.
II. *Stressing Principles.*
   1. Principles of Bible truth. 374, 195.
   2. Doctrines vitalized by principle. 557.
   3. Truth reflected in principle. 483.
   4. Principle not obscured. 357.

Denominational Bible work is not merely a plan for giving proof texts in defense of our doctrines, important as this duty may seem. Therefore our workers are invited to study a point which needs more consideration—the teaching of *principles* of truth, and not just doctrines of truth. The present intricate dispensational confusions cannot be met with only proof texts, for this and other last-day fallacies require a thorough acquaintance with the principles of God's governing purpose as against the principles of Satan. That purpose, of course, is founded on Scripture, and Bible texts must be supplied. The messenger of the Lord states that doctrines such as the sanctuary, the Sabbath, the state of the dead, health and dress reform, and the Spirit of prophecy should be taught by stressing the *principles* of these truths. When teachers get hold of this point, their teaching will hold a new appeal.

In our emphasis on teaching the principles of a doctrine let us take as an illustration that familiar topic "The True Church," based on Revelation 12. This lesson would usually be given near the close of the series. If we bear in mind that we are still aiming at explaining the problem, *What is truth?* our Bible study should be providing an answer. Some teachers, perhaps, might think that the historical aspects of the church should here be stressed, but Revelation 12:17 suggests that the eternal principle of God's law be stressed. Even in these lawless last days a remnant will be keeping His commandments. The gospel church began in pristine purity, but because of persecution passed through stages of temporary retirement. Prophecy reveals her emergence from obscurity. In earth's closing hours, when all the world wonders after the beast, the true church gloriously demonstrates that the law is a principle of the everlasting gospel. From this study the reader must catch the idea that the law as well as the gospel is an eternal principle. The Sabbath, therefore, must abide on principle, and should still be kept by us today.

There are other grand prophecies in the book of Revelation that teach the principle of the immutability of the gospel —the seven churches, seven seals, the sealing, the three angels' messages, et cetera. The Bible instructor should become skilled in presenting these prophetic studies with interest, point, and decision. The principle of the controversy between Christ and Satan presents the theme for these topics.

As the prophetic clock keeps striking the last hour, the reader must become more concerned about his own case pending at the judgment bar. Stimulated by the Holy Spirit, the reader's imagination will often get ahead of the teacher's points of instruction. It is not because the Bible instructor is reluctant to expose the whole truth that she may restrain some points; it is rather because of her desire to be tactful and considerate in presenting new truth. Yet the Word of God makes no apologies for any man's feeling; it cuts to the quick! Prophecy points an accusing finger at the man of sin; it dramatically reveals the great Babylon; it unflinchingly points to the consequences of lawbreaking—the lake of fire.

To expedite decision on the part of the reader, the Bible instructor should emphasize the characteristics of the apostate church by a study on "Babylon and Her Daughters." The way having been prepared by the Holy Spirit, she may now give a clear call to the reader to come out of this great confusion. There is inspiring and convincing proof for Babylon's sins in Revelation 17 and 18. It may be necessary for the instructor to point out flagrant apostasy, but the effect of this should be a deepened conviction that truth requires absolute and immediate obedience. Rome's traditions and backslidings must be merely incidental.

Personalities should never be attacked by us as teachers. A negative spirit will only tend to defeat truth's noble objectives. There is today a growing conviction that there is good in all religions. Bible instructors know there are sincere souls in every religious body, and what the readers need is a clear call to leave their former Romish practices. Truth, like a great magnet, attracts to herself all the children of truth. She is mighty to defend herself, and does not need unwise zeal to give her added support. Therefore let us guard these principles of truth from becoming submerged by details of such a nature as will amuse only shallow minds. Methods of ridicule and attack produce an adverse effect on the broad-minded and informed. Emphasizing the great principle of God's sovereignty bears much weight especially when presenting the Sabbath truth.

Pedagogy suggests that a contrasting of two or more objects, principles, or systems is strong teaching. (See *Evangelism*, p. 24.) We see the strength of a Bible doctrine by comparing it with tradition. Truth or error, sin or righteousness, light or darkness, life or death, are evaluated by their contrasts. Then as the reader learns to reason from cause to effect, guided by both knowledge and experience, he will be helped to make right decisions. This explains why a prophetic subject assists the teacher in gaining the reader's prompt decision to accept God's revealed light.

Even though the element of emotion may enter into the final decision to walk in all revealed truth, it certainly should not predominate. Purely emotional decisions usually last as long as a stimulus is being supplied; decisions made on principle will last after the worker has been transferred to another field of labor. So while the student of prophecy learns to weigh and compare truth, he is also being taught to do his own thinking—an experience that will speak well for the Bible instructor's methods.

Two problems today suggest that prophetic teaching be re-emphasized: first, that the more doctrinal type of lessons do not crowd out this method; second, that our caution in interpreting unfulfilled prophecy will not cause us to shy away from prophetic analysis entirely. Prophecy must remain strong in the Advent message. The challenge comes to every Bible instructor to become a closer student of prophecy, fulfilled and fulfilling, and then to receive a new endowment of God's Spirit for presenting prophetic truth in the same undaunted spirit as did the prophets of old.

(For prophetic studies see pages 457-468.)

PART ONE ★ CHAPTER TWENTY-FIVE

Souls in the Balance

Winning men and women from sin to righteousness is God's work. True, He has purposed to use man, with his human limitations, to help lift souls out of the kingdom of darkness into the light of the gospel, but we must never lose sight of the fact that "as the Spirit comes with more direct appeal, the soul gladly surrenders itself to Jesus," and that winning souls is "the result of long wooing by the Spirit of God,—a patient, protracted process."—*The Desire of Ages,* p. 172.

Bringing individuals to a decision for Christ and the message is not accomplished in a moment; nor does it come as a result of half-hearted, intermittent effort. There must be a background for such a weighty decision, and the human and the divine element must combine to bring this about.

The gospel worker must understand the forces involved in the issues of such a decision. He must remember that the controversy between truth and error, especially today, is a grim battle against indifference, bigotry, unbelief, and fear. The enemy has become skillful in the subtle art of confusion, and procrastination and truth defiance are its by-products. He has so blinded the hearts of men that to them darkness appears as light, or light as darkness. The foe holds back no fiendish weapon, obstacle, or supposed benefit to the deciding soul.

When the hour of decision arrives—and there is an hour when such a stand is not only opportune but definitely urgent to salvation—then action on the part of the wavering soul must follow. The human instrument making the appeal must use the full force of a sanctified personality to help effect the decision. The appeal must become the very call of God to that struggling soul. It is imperative in this hour that the

Bible instructor's relationship with God be such that He can use her words as a winsome appeal in wooing souls from error into truth. In a certain sense a work of mediation takes place. "Be ye reconciled to God" is the import of the call to the deciding one.

The "engrafted word . . . is able to save your souls." James 1:21. The worker must have a thorough knowledge of the Bible. It is the "sword of the Spirit," which the soldier of Christ uses to storm the citadel of the soul effectively. The reader must clearly recognize what God expects him to do in this critical hour. Scripture, timely and pointed, must be tactfully, persuasively, and directly aimed at the soul in the balance. Men may try to evade all human appeals, but they cannot forever dodge God's claims or change His word. No argument is more important, and no better method to bring about the right decision is known.

The soul winner must keep in mind that God did not make men according to one pattern. A special supply of grace is needed to be able to "discern the spirits" of men. Jesus beautifully mastered this art. "He knew what was in man." John 2:25. We must know *men* before we may hope to know the methods by which to win them. A sympathetic touch is vital at this stage of the effort. Out of the memory of the anguish of our own soul's Gethsemane will come those sympathetic expressions that will strike a responsive chord in the experience of the struggling soul. It is indeed a "delicate work" requiring gentleness, pathos, patience, and persuasion. As God uses the consecrated soul winner with power, the stony heart is softened, the barriers of prejudice break down, and procrastination is changed into decision.

After an experience of successive victories in gaining decision for God, there is always grave danger that the worker may begin to feel that she is mastering the only methods and the soundest technique to be found. But professional confidence may rob her of the power and glory which are due God alone. In one who has this self-confidence the keen, soul-winning senses will become blunt. Her experience may be similar to that of the professional nurse who becomes so hardened to the scenes of the sickroom, that though her actual skill in nursing may be improving, her own heart becomes calloused to the true anguish of the world's sorrows. This may also become true in the field of spiritual nursing.

I recall frequent experiences when I was awakened in the hours of the night with strong impressions crowding into the mind regarding one for whom I was laboring. There followed clear conviction about the next step to take in helping this soul to gain the victory—even the very words to be employed in making further appeals would fill the relaxed mind. Needless to state, as these impressions were followed, the decision came quickly and easily. I recall that this was especially true when dealing with the more temperamental kind of individual. Moods materially affect reactions, and they are often baffling to the Bible teacher, who must be in constant touch with God to know how to deal with all kinds of people.

Persuading souls for God is not the experience of the ordinary agent who goes from door to door selling encyclopedias, household articles, and the like, although some of the same techniques are employed. It is not a battle of wits, high pressure salesmanship, or stampeding a person into a decision. The earnest wooing of a soul to yield to God is what counts the most in the decision. The conviction must be present that the worker is "a teacher sent from God." Then the tendency to delay or to escape taking a stand for truth is more often changed into action and unreserved surrender.

The fruitage that remains firm through spiritual test and storm is a heavenly miracle, with no place for human glory. It is a process that never can be completely analyzed in human terms or by commercial comparisons, and the warmth of this spiritual experience is always chilled by the cold professionalism that employs the measuring rod of statistics.

In this critical hour of decision the worker must exhibit the qualities of Elijah and John the Baptist. She is a messenger of God with the solemn message, "If the Lord be God, follow Him," and "Repent: for the kingdom of heaven is at hand." The word of the Lord speaks through her, and it must be fearlessly given to His children. It is not an easy task, but it is her bounden duty nevertheless. Even in our day God has been pleased to use human instruments to such a degree that souls who were facing decisions actually saw Christ in the messenger, and dared not reject His message. Oh, for more of this power in our ministry for hesitating souls!

Gaining the Final Decision

(Based on *Evangelism*)

MAYBELLE VANDERMARK

I. *Decision Methods.* (293, 295, 432, 433, 437, 442, 443, 457, 462, 464, 481, 485.)
   1. Winning souls compared to harvesting.
   2. Gathering souls into gospel net.
   3. Picking accessible berries first.
   4. Keeping "on track of souls."
   5. Making quick decisions.
   6. Weighing each decision carefully.
   7. Deciding truth by what God says.
   8. Avoiding premature decisions on part of new convert.

II. *The Promised Harvest.* (443, 459, 481, 490.)
   1. Husbandman to *till* and *sow*.
   2. Humble worker crowned with success.
   3. Fruitfulness of persuasive, prayerful, loving effort.
   4. Definite results, the aim.
   5. Harvest raked, gathered, and cared for.

Decision Principles in Evangelism

(Based on *Evangelism*)

I. *Decision.* (Pages 279-283.)
   1. There are undecided souls in every meeting. Some may be listening to their last sermon, and the grand opportunity may be lost.
   2. "If words are not spoken at the right moment, calling for decision from the weight of evidence already presented, the convicted ones pass on without identifying themselves with Christ,

the golden opportunity passes, . . . and they go farther and farther away from the truth, farther away from Jesus and never take their stand on the Lord's side."
3. "In every discourse fervent appeals should be made to the people to forsake their sins and turn to Christ."

II. *Methods.* (Pages 281-311.)
1. "Declare the whole counsel of God." Do not appear provoked or speak "in a harsh un-Christlike manner."
2. "Lift up Christ before his hearers. Christ's claims upon them are to be made plain."
3. "Make scripture explain scripture." "A plain Thus saith the Lord" will impress the people.
4. "No unnecessary words."
5. Calls should be made for those who believe the truth to stand. Prayer should be offered for them.
6. "Direct the mind to Him who guides and controls all things."
7. "Lead the people to think that there is life or death in these solemn questions, according as they shall receive or reject them."
8. "As you present testing truth, ask often, who is now willing, as they have heard the words of God, pointing out their duty, to consecrate their hearts and minds, with all their affections, to Christ Jesus."
9. "Jesus Christ should be presented distinctly," as John declared, "Behold the Lamb of God, which taketh away the sin of the world." "Christ, Christ, Christ is to be in it everywhere."
10. Personal inquiry should be made. "Each one should be asked how he is going to take these things, if he is going to make a personal application of them."
11. Put away evil speaking and selfishness, and continue in prayer and humble yourself before God.
12. "Make men to know how much Jesus loves them, and what evidences He has given them of His love."
13. "Cultivate earnestness and positiveness in addressing the people."
14. Speak "with such certainty that those who hear may know that the truth is a reality to you."
15. "Pray with these souls, by faith laying them at the foot of the cross; . . . and fix the eye of faith . . . upon Jesus."
16. They should be *led* along.
17. "Be very careful how you handle the Word."
18. "Hold to the affirmative."
19. "Avoid any severity of speech that might give offense."

Souls in the Balance

   20. "It is the duty of the pastor to have special meetings. . . . Give them Bible readings, converse and pray with them, and plainly show the claims of the Lord upon them."

III. *Conversion.* (Pages 287-292.)
   1. All people are not alike. "Often souls have been drawn to Christ when there was no violent conviction, no soul rending, no remorseful terrors."
   2. "The conversion of the human soul is of no little consequence. It is the greatest miracle performed by divine power."
   3. "The conversion of souls to God is the greatest work, the highest work, in which human beings can have a part. In the conversion of souls God's forbearance, His unbounded love, His holiness, His power, are revealed."

IV. *Problems.* (Pages 286-306.)
   1. "Satan's batteries will be opened upon those who advocate the truth, and the standard bearers must expect to meet many sneers, and much reviling that is hard to bear."
   2. "The work for our time is attended with the same difficulties that Jesus had to meet, and that the reformers of every age have had to overcome."
   3. "There is in the heart of man that which is opposed to truth and righteousness." (Prejudice.)
   "We must expect to meet unbelief and opposition."
   4. "Every teacher of the truth, every laborer together with God, will pass through searching, trying hours, when faith and patience will be severely tested."
   5. Some are weary of sin, but do not have the courage to claim themselves to be children of God.
   6. Others claim to be children of God, but do not show true conversion.
   7. Some may delay in presenting the Sabbath question through fear of consequences.

V. *Baptism.* (Pages 306-320.)
   1. "Repentance, faith, and baptism are the requisite steps in conversion."
   2. "The new converts to the truth should be faithfully instructed in the plain 'Thus saith the Lord.' "
   3. "When they give evidence that they fully understand their position, they are to be accepted."
   4. "The principles of the Christian life should be made plain to those who have newly come to the truth."

5. Parents are to be instructors and guardians of their children, to bring them to Jesus and baptism.
6. "Show that true conversion is a change of heart, of thoughts and purposes."
7. "Evil habits are to be given up. The sins of evil-speaking, of jealousy, of disobedience, are to be put away."
8. "Before baptism, there should be a thorough inquiry as to the experience of the candidates."
9. "The words of Scripture in regard to dress should be carefully considered. . . . Even the style of the apparel will express the truth of the gospel."
10. "Ministers . . . should not feel content, nor that their work is ended, until those who have accepted the theory of truth realize indeed the effect of its sanctifying power, and are truly converted to God."

PART ONE ★ CHAPTER TWENTY-SIX

Textual Argument in Decision

Deciding for Christ

Whereas in our present-day evangelism the Sabbath truth might be considered the crucial point of decision, the presentation of any other doctrine may also bring about the final surrender to accept Christ. Many types of obstacles and excuses may stand in the reader's way for taking this last step, and therefore the personal worker must know the art of dealing with each of these problems specifically.

When the teacher draws from the experience of some Bible character in order to set forth a Scriptural principle against which the reader may be struggling, its too direct personal elements will then be hidden under the garb of common humanity. This type of appeal is usually most effective, and may become the quickest means to win the right decision.

As the teacher draws his lesson from some Bible pattern, the imagination will often supply more than just scenery for truth; it will also stimulate the hesitant reader into action for God.

Frequently the emotional element of an important decision for the pupil may bring to him embarrassment as well as confusion of thought. There is so much at stake for the deciding one, who now seems to need a guide. It helps to have the teacher apply a Bible verse which very directly points the way or supplies the answer to the problem under consideration. It is an effective way to clinch a decision. Knowledge and skill must here be combined, and the teacher's familiarity with the Bible as a whole, and with human nature in general, will direct her in the choice of such scripture.

Another method that has been found to be very successful at the decision stage is the use of a Bible text that suggests a specific prayer. The Scriptures provide abundant prayer verses, and these have led many a perplexed soul over the final hurdle of indecision. Stressing such a verse in our petitions for the struggling one, or suggesting that it be used by him personally as his covenant with God to obey truth, often makes a strong impression. If the decision cannot be immediately reached, this particular verse will continue to sound its message of warning and surrender. Readers frequently testify to the fact that they were unable to find peace of mind until they finally obeyed the Scriptural command that would keep ringing in their ears. It is God's way of revealing the converting power of His Word.

The Sabbath Decision

To one who has already been led to realize the importance of Scripture, no argument is more convincing than a "Thus saith the Lord." After the true Sabbath day has been pointed out to the reader, the suspending decision is based on what the Bible teaches on this question. Perhaps no other truth lends itself better to a clear-cut decision influenced by the Word than the Sabbath.

As prophecy and the Sabbath of history are studied by the Bible student, he becomes convinced that the original rest day still remains. The commandment cannot be changed, and Christ's example, as well as His atonement for man's transgression of the law, presents the strongest proofs in favor of Christians still observing the seventh day. When proof for the correct seventh day is next taken care of, the adversary will try to resort to other doubts to harass the reader. He builds up excuses why the Sabbath cannot be kept in our day. These are usually his stock arguments, but occasionally the Bible instructor faces something that appears to be entirely new in the category of excuses. Handicaps of all kinds will be presented by the reader's loved ones and friends. He will be reminded by them of his health, his family responsibility, and his financial obligations. And what an array of them can be presented to some overwhelmed soul who must now take his stand!

The decision of changing over to another rest day is indeed a great experience. It is then that the mind is likely to become so agitated or confused that the inquirer may become discouraged in his effort to keep the right day. Although he may have already admitted that the Bible clearly teaches his duty, he now lacks the courage to step out. It is then that the help of an understanding Bible instructor is so much needed. This is not the work of a novice, and yet God is pleased to use the beginner also. For the encouragement of the more inexperienced let it be said that God at such times always provides a double measure of His grace.

But these excuses cannot easily be brushed aside; they exist as real problems. Those Bible instructors who have had to meet them previously in their own lives can understand why the sense of their reality can never be lost. For that reason the beginning Bible instructors should realize the importance of the following techniques.

Textual Argument in Decision 149

Let us begin by considering the case of a man who is buying a house. Payments on it must be met regularly. He must find some definite assurance that he can buy that home and still keep the Sabbath. But he must first see another point: the buying of that home may, or may not, be God's will for him! First, it requires faith to surrender all to God; next faith to fully believe God. Since this man's whole interest is centered in his house, the text of appeal should include the word *house* or at least a reference to a temporal abode. So Psalms 127:1 might be suggested: "Except the Lord build the *house,* they labour in vain that build it."

Now, the person who is buying an automobile when the Sabbath comes to his attention has the same economic battle as the man who considers buying a house. Since automobiles are not directly mentioned in the Bible, perhaps Isaiah's "chariots," with their lesson of idolatry as set forth in Isaiah 2, may here find an application. Of course, a theological discussion on these chariots will not be entered into, because the point now is the getting of the decision. These chariots, however, are included with the last-day idols (Isa. 2:2, 7), and any idolatry which sets God aside might well be applicable. Here the automobile must be laid on the altar of sacrifice if the reader's Sabbath victory is to be assured. There must be something specific in dealing with that problem, and God's Word abounds in fitting parallels for the teacher's use. If you know of a better way by which to teach surrender on this point, by all means apply it. The plea is for more originality in the securing of decisions.

Peruse carefully the material under "Meeting Sabbath-keeping Arguments." As you think yourself into the various situations for the variety of these excuses, you will get the idea that the applied texts must be well related to the particular obstacle that is withholding the decision. For instance, if the problem is fear, then the fear complex, which might also involve a job, a diminishing bank account, poor health, and so forth, must be specifically handled. If the textual argumentation deals with a particular problem, it is remarkable what a "Thus saith the Lord" will settle. Without question it is God's most powerful weapon for truth. The Bible instructor who knows how to use it has learned a valuable technique for getting decisions.

The following outlines of textual argumentation for winning decisions are merely suggestive. The teacher's study of the Bible will bring to mind many varied Scriptural appeals. These must never be used mechanically, however; they should always be Spirit directed. Since the beginner in Bible work may need to drill herself constantly on texts for ready usage when confronting excuses, these outlines may be helpful in guiding the younger teacher. When decisions are born in the atmosphere of a revival, not only the mind but the heart as well will respond to obedience. There is indeed a Christian experience connected with such conversions, and the results will be enduring.

Texts for Hesitating Souls

I. *"Not Today! I'll Take My Stand Later On."*
  1. "Choose you this day." Josh. 24:15.
  2. "How long halt ye?" 1 Kings 18:21.
  3. "Boast not thyself of to morrow." Prov. 27:1.
  4. "While He may be found." Isa. 55:6.
  5. "Why tarriest thou?" Acts 22:16.
  6. "Now is the accepted time." 2 Cor. 6:2.

II. *"Too Late! I Have Waited Too Long!"*
  1. "If the wicked turn . . . , he shall live." Eze. 33:19.
  2. "Him that cometh to Me." John 6:37.
  3. "Whosoever shall call upon the Lord." Rom. 10:13.

III. *"I Tried Once; I Am Afraid to Try Again."*
  1. He is able—
    "to deliver." Dan. 3:17.
    to fulfill promises. Rom. 4:21.
    to guard your treasure. 2 Tim. 1:12.
    to save to the uttermost. Heb. 7:25.
    "to keep you from falling." Jude 24.

Textual Argument in Decision

IV. *"How May I Know My Sins Are Forgiven?"*
   1. "If we confess . . . , He is faithful . . . to forgive." 1 John 1:9.
   2. "Whoso confesseth and forsaketh." Prov. 28:13.
   3. "Sins be as scarlet, . . . white as snow." Isa. 1:18.
   4. "Sins into the depths of the sea." Micah 7:19.

V. *"Some Things Are Not Yet Clear."*
   1. "The secret things belong unto . . . God." Deut. 29:29.
   2. "Thou shalt know hereafter." John 13:7.
   3. "It is not for you to know." Acts 1:7.
   4. "Now we see through a glass, darkly." 1 Cor. 13:12.

VI. *"I'm Not So Bad!"*
   1. "He that believeth not is condemned already." John 3:18.
   2. "He that believeth not . . . the wrath of God abideth on him." John 3:36.
   3. "All have sinned." Rom. 3:23.
   4. "The wages of sin is death." Rom 6:23.
   5. "How shall we escape, if we neglect?" Heb. 2:3.

VII. *"God Is Love; He'll Save Me Anyway."*
   1. "Cast him into outer darkness." Matt. 22:13.
   2. "Except ye repent, ye shall . . . perish." Luke 13:3.
   3. "If God spared not the angels." 2 Peter 2:4.

VIII. *"There Are Too Many Hypocrites in the Church."*
   1. "The hypocrite's hope shall perish." Job 8:13.
   2. "Judge not, that ye be not judged." Matt. 7:1.
   3. "Every one . . . shall give account of himself." Rom. 14:12.

IX. *"The Step Will Cost Me Too Much."*
   1. "What shall I render unto the Lord?" Ps. 116:12.
   2. "What shall it profit?" Mark 8:36.
   3. No man has left all who shall not receive manifold. Luke 18:29, 30.
   4. Who "bare our sins in His own body on the tree." 1 Peter 2:24.

X. *"I Cannot Leave My Relatives and Friends."*
   1. "Thou shalt not follow . . . to do evil." Ex. 23:2.
   2. "He that walketh with wise men shall be wise." Prov. 13:20.
   3. "Not unequally yoked together with unbelievers." 2 Cor. 6:14.
   4. "Be not deceived: evil communications corrupt." 1 Cor. 15:33.

XI. *"I Fear to Be Persecuted."*
   1. A blessing is connected with it. Matt. 5:11.
   2. It lifts the soul to the plane of the prophets. Matt. 5:12.
   3. All godly people expect it. 2 Tim. 3:12.
   4. It leads to a crown. Rev. 2:10.

Meeting Sabbathkeeping Arguments

I. *"How May I Get a Living and Keep the Sabbath?"*
   1. "Take no thought . . . , what ye shall eat." Matt. 6:25, 26.
   2. Not begging bread. Ps. 37:25.
   3. "Not want any good thing." Ps. 34:10.
   4. Found a living. Isa. 57:10, 13, margin.
   5. "He is thy life." Deut. 30:19, 20.
   6. "For a piece of bread that man will transgress." Prov. 28:21.
   7. "More than my necessary food." Job 23:10-12.

II. *"But My Job May Be at Stake!"*
   1. "Fear ye not . . . men." Isa. 51:7.
   2. "Establish thou the work of our hands." Ps. 90:16, 17.
   3. "Put my life in mine hand." Job 13:14, 15.
   4. God's law "better . . . than thousands of gold and silver." Ps. 119:72, 127.

III. *"How Can I Pay for My House?"*
   1. "Except the Lord build the house, they labour in vain that build." Ps. 127:1.
   2. Foolish man built his house on sand. Matt. 7:24-27.

IV. *"I Am Buying a Car and Must Pay for It."*
   1. Chariots may become our idols today. Isa. 2:7, 8.
   2. "The idols He shall utterly abolish." Isa. 2:18.

V. *"I Must First Lay by a Little Surplus."*
   1. "Seek ye *first* the kingdom of God." Matt. 6:33, 34.
   2. "Blessing of the Lord, it maketh rich." Prov. 10:22.
   3. Riches without God's blessings bring sorrow. Prov. 28:20, 22.
   4. "The expectation of the wicked . . . tendeth to poverty." Prov. 11:23, 24.

VI. *"I Don't Think God Expects Me to Deprive Myself."*
   1. "My thoughts are not your thoughts." Isa. 55:8, 9.
   2. "Blessed is the man . . . that keepeth the Sabbath." Isa. 56:1, 2.

VII. *"Because of Poor Health I Am Afraid to Change My Religion."*
  1. "He sent *His word*, and *healed* them, and delivered." Ps. 107:20.
  2. Health springs forth when Sabbath truly kept. Isa. 58:8, 12, 13.
VIII. *"I Am Afraid to Go Ahead."* (Various fear complexes.)
  1. "Fear thou not; for I am with thee." Isa. 41:10.
  2. "Neither have our steps declined from Thy way." Ps. 44:17, 18.
  3. "I made haste . . . to keep Thy commandments." Ps. 119:57-60.
  4. "Turn away thy foot from the Sabbath." Isa. 58:13.
  5. "Remove thy foot from evil." Prov. 4:26, 27.
  6. Workers of iniquity turn aside from the Lord. Ps. 125:4, 5.
IX. *"This Is So New to Me—What Should I Do About the Sabbath?"*
  1. "How long halt ye between two opinions?" 1 Kings 18:21.
  2. "Ask for the old paths, . . . and walk therein." Jer. 6:16.
  3. "Do His commandments." Rev. 22:14.

PART ONE ★ CHAPTER TWENTY-SEVEN

Overcoming Evil Habits

The following principles from the Bible and Spirit of prophecy should be well understood by every Bible instructor. The outline "Building Faith for Overcoming," p. 157, suggests principles which may be followed, at least partially, in instruction on overcoming evil habits. Since this need is so general, these principles should be very clear to the teacher so that she can help to make them plain to others. One who is struggling for victory over appetite or vice must be guided by more than sentiment. There should be an experience with God that will bring assurance of complete victory in the struggle.

The sinner must first meet God's conditions for forgiveness. He must also become acquainted with God's promises to forgive. Each step in this process of overcoming must be an experience in victory promising lasting results. These are principles more than they are doctrines. The definite steps of conversion may well be taught from the book *Steps to Christ*. For this reason I have found it practical to give a little pocket edition to each of my readers. When the Bible instructor underlines these various steps in conversion in her own copy of the book, the reader will be inspired to do likewise. Before wrong habits disappear in the life of the young Christian, a new life of faith must first be built up step by step. These steps will need to be reviewed frequently.

Observe from the outline on page 157 how the first need of the sinner is to recognize his sin. To try to excuse it would be a mistake. This should mean that tobacco is not merely a wasteful habit; it is positively sinful. Liquor is not only a despicable thing; it is a definite curse. Pork is not just harmful physically; it is an "abomination" to God. The reform therefore must also be as definite. In each case there must be a strong loathing of sin, with a firm conviction of its destructive power.

The incentive to reform must be a distinct call from the Lord to the individual. He must turn away from that particular evil habit, and must now concentrate on that as a necessary step in overcoming. This instruction is not just for or by the church; it is from God and to each individual. It is well that this point be understood, for it is not the church that prohibits the use of tobacco, liquor, pork, and so forth; it is simply that the Christian cannot turn a deaf ear to God's call to him personally to forsake his sin.

To depend on some medical remedy for overcoming liquor or tobacco may help to some extent, but though a crutch is a valuable help to one whose leg has been amputated, it is not his real limb. Just so the right and only sure cure is for the overcomer to lean on Christ. Here is true overcoming power, and here only! It must be emphasized that it does not matter how bad or deep-seated the habit, there is victory in Christ. Right at the start of one's efforts to overcome there must be no question about the certainty of overcoming. Christ has already obtained the victory for the sinner; it is now up to him to claim it on those conditions which He has provided. Acceptance of Christ is the beginning of victory.

The next experience in overcoming is prayer. The teacher must guide the Bible student in prayer but the reader must also learn to pray for himself. With every craving to return to his former evil practice prayer must become that mighty weapon which completely destroys the very desire to indulge in it. The victory should be immediate, but again it may not be without a resisting "unto blood." (Heb. 12:4.) The victory must be "stedfast" and "in the faith." (1 Peter 5:9.) Then there is another stern duty—to make the devil flee from us. (James 4:7.) We are not to argue a point with him in any way. The tempted one should fix each step of this overcoming process definitely in mind, making a sure work of grace.

As the heart then yields to Christ, the conscience is quickened. The sinner will catch a vision of His sacrifice on Calvary. He cannot crucify the Son of God afresh; he must most definitely quit that evil habit! Christ's will now works in him, and there is a new desire to really become an overcomer. As the sinner continues looking to Christ, a new assurance is developed; now he really knows he has been made whole! There will still be struggles, but angels now come to his rescue. He hears the tender pleadings of the Holy Spirit to be true, and he listens to that voice as he continues to hold out in the conflict. His praying has become more earnest; he seems to touch the very throne of God. Having such access to divine power, he cannot now be overcome by Satan.

There are still other principles for the overcomer to recognize. It is human to procrastinate in the forsaking of sin, but postponing it will merely tend to harden and benumb the already deceived and sin-weakened senses. It is always best to begin the reform immediately, and not tomorrow. Reformation claims no future tense; it is always urgent. The sinner should confess his guilt at once, and then Christ will do what he himself had sought to accomplish by procrastinating—provide the necessary will power! It is now Christ power, and not just will power that attains the victory. The sinner cannot bring about this change by waiting, debating, or struggling against the enemy; his part is to cease his fear, doubting, and trembling, and to believe God's promises.

It is now important for the struggling one to know that Satan will not let him alone. He is a mighty foe, and though he must be outwitted, he is often too powerful for sin-weakened humanity. It may be necessary for the stumbling saint to weep at the feet of Jesus, confessing his shortcomings in the struggle, but the victory is still assured. Again it may mean that confession in prayer must be more fervent, and that he must continue to drink deeper draughts of grace. But he dare not dwell on his past failures, neither must he discourage himself by talking doubt. He should keep fresh in his memory God's tender mercies. This is a daily experience requiring daily consecration. It should be made the first thing in the morning.

As Bible instructors we should help our buffeted readers to see that Christian overcoming is not an empty idealism but rather a great privilege in Christ. The overcomer should keep his Bible with him constantly while he learns to lean more and more on its precious promises. Then when the enemy charges him with his failings, he will find help and comfort in God's Word. It is his chart and compass, and he checks his progress by its precepts. Where once he reached for his pipe or liquor flask, he now reaches for his Bible. The Spirit of prophecy also becomes precious counsel to his hungry soul. His whole bent is to do God's will and to live to His glory. He knows confidently that "sin shall not have dominion" over him.

When Catholics and those who have a background of set creeds for their faith are being studied with, the progressive experiences set forth in *Steps to Christ* meet a real need. An easy method to wean readers away from their catechisms, prayer books, or confessions of faith is not advocated, but it is still sound thinking on the part of the Bible instructor to recognize the usefulness of a little work as explicit on the principles of Christian experience as *Steps to Christ*. It is also a practical help to Seventh-day Adventist young people who must become acquainted with the problem of overcoming sin. Again, this little book ably meets the needs of those deeper Christians with whom advanced light must now be studied in the setting of present truth. It then adds balance to the instruction received when the reader must hear from his relatives and friends that Seventh-day Adventists do not believe in Christ but claim to be saved by the law.

Bible instructors will be able to see the significance of the principles which have been developed in detail in the following outline, "Building Faith for Overcoming." This is not meant to imply that they do not already know these steps, but there is wisdom in mastering them as readers are helped to overcome sin. These principles must be made practical in the lives of their readers. The vocabulary of Bible instructors should be simple. Although it may be important for the reader to know just what is meant by justification, sanctification, and so forth, it is the results of these experiences that should be the chief concern.

Building Faith for Overcoming

(*Steps to Christ*, Pocket Edition)

I. *Sinner to Recognize Sinfulness of His Evil Habits.* (SC 23, 27, 30.)
   1. "To him it is sin." James 4:17.
   2. "Sin is the transgression of the law." 1 John 3:4.
   3. "The wages of sin is death." Rom. 6:23.

II. *Sinner Personally Called by God.*
   "Turn [you] . . . and live." Eze. 18:30-32.

III. *Power to Overcome Provided in Christ.* (SC 21.)
   1. "I can . . . through Christ." Phil. 4:13.

2. I cannot overcome without Christ. John 15:5.
3. "*All* power is given unto Me in heaven and in earth." Matt. 28:18.
4. No temptation is too great. 1 Cor. 10:13.

IV. *Steps Toward Victory.* (SC 49-51.)
1. Claim victory by faith. 1 John 5:4.
2. Pray earnestly for help and confess sin. John 16:23; James 5:16.
3. Flee from evil habit. 1 Cor. 10:14.
4. Plant a good habit for every evil one. Rom. 12:21.
5. Fix eyes on Jesus. Heb. 12:1, 2.
6. Resist "unto blood!" Heb. 12:4.
7. Cause devil to flee. James 4:7, 8.
8. "Resist stedfast in the faith." 1 Peter 5:9.

V. *God's Special Help for Overcoming.*
1. The conscience will be quickened. SC 24.
2. Get a vision of Calvary. SC 31.
3. "He will . . . work in you." SC 47, 48.
4. "God supplies the fact." SC 51.
5. Ministering angels are present. SC 53.
6. The tender pleading of His Spirit entreats the sinner. SC 54.
7. His power is granted. SC 93.
8. He draws near with mercy and forgiveness. SC 55.
9. Satan cannot overcome us. SC 99.

VI. *What the Sinner Must Know About Sin.*
1. Beware of procrastination in the forsaking of sin. SC 32.
2. Neglect to overcome sin hardens and benumbs. SC 33.
3. All confession should be definite. SC 38.
4. Reformation is necessary. SC 39, 59.
5. True repentance will lead a man to bear his guilt. SC 40.
6. "You cannot change your heart." SC 51.
7. Through the "simple act of believing," a new heart is begotten. SC 51, 52.
8. "The true force of the will" needs to be understood. SC 47.
9. The condition to the promise is "Pray according to the will of God." SC 51.
10. God's promises are meant for you. SC 52.
11. "Look up, you that are doubting and trembling." SC 54.
12. Weep over shortcomings and mistakes. SC 64. "The character is revealed, not by occasional good deeds and occasional misdeeds, but by the tendency of the habitual words and acts." SC 57, 58.

13. "Pray more fervently; believe more fully." SC 64.
VII. *How to Treat Doubt.*
  1. "Our faith must rest upon evidence." SC 105.
  2. Do not dwell on past mistakes. SC 116, 117.
  3. Do not talk doubt; pray. SC 119.
  4. Keep fresh in memory God's tender mercies. SC 125.
  5. "Consecrate yourself to God in the morning." SC 70.
  6. "Keep your Bible with you." SC 90.
VIII. *Our Wonderful Saviour.*
  1. He is our High Priest. Heb. 4:14-16; 7:25, 26.
  2. Christ is both advocate and atonement. 1 John 2:1, 2.
  3. "Sin shall not have dominion over you." Rom. 6:12-14, 19.

The following principles are discussed with the readers and each one is given a personal copy of this material.

How to Gain Victory Over the Cigarette Habit
Ena Ferguson

I. *Consider the Sinfulness of the Habit, and Learn to Hate It.*
  1. What are the physical and mental effects? 1 Cor. 3:16, 17.
  2. What would Jesus do? Heb. 1:9.
  3. Then to please Jesus we must overcome. Ps. 66:18.
     "We shall not renounce sin unless we see its sinfulness; until we turn away from it in heart." SC 23.
II. *Have a Sincere Desire to Overcome.* (Matt. 5:6.)
  1. "Hunger" and "thirst" are strong desires.
  2. We "can't" because we do not wish to. DA 466:3.
III. *Make a Firm Decision Now.* (Joshua 24:15; 1 Kings 18:21.)
  1. "Many will be lost while hoping and desiring to be Christians. They do not come to the point of yielding the will to God. They do not now *choose* to be Christians." SC 48.
  2. "Beware of procrastination." SC 32.
IV. *Truly Believe We Shall Overcome, Because He Has Promised.* (John 8:36; 1 John 5:4; Rom. 6:11.)
  1. "Satan cannot overcome him whose heart is . . . stayed upon God." SC 99.
  2. "Look not to self, but to Christ. . . . Then grasp His promise, 'Him that cometh to Me I will in no wise cast out.' Cast yourself at His feet with the cry, 'Lord, I believe; help *Thou* mine

unbelief.' You can never perish while you do this—never." DA 429.

V. *Cease to Make Any Excuse.*
   1. 1 Cor. 10:13. This text shows there is no excuse for sinning—there is "a way to escape."
   2. "All His biddings are enablings." COL 333.
   3. We will offer no excuse in the judgment day.

VI. *Pray Earnestly for Deliverance.* (Mark 14:38.)
   1. "Be as earnest, as persistent, as you would be if your mortal life were at stake." SC 35.
   2. Not only pray earnestly each morning for victory for the day, but instantly, whenever tempted. Rom. 12:12; Prov. 18:10.
   3. The tempter will seek to keep us from prayer. SC 94, 95.

VII. *Be Constantly on Guard.* (Mark 14:38; 1 Cor. 10:12; Matt. 24:43.) We pray for safety, but still we look before crossing a street.

VIII. *Resist Continually and Determinedly, Instead of Yielding.* (James 4:7; Heb. 12:4.)
   1. "The tempter can never compel us to do evil. . . . The will must consent . . . before Satan can exercise his power upon us." DA 125.
   2. Our efforts must not be feeble and intermittent.
   3. "The power of self-restraint strengthens by exercise. That which at first seems difficult, by constant repetition grows easy." MH 491.
   4. Have plenty of oranges and apples on hand. Reach for an orange when tempted, especially just after a meal.

IX. *Meet Temptation With the Word of God, as Jesus Did.* (Ps. 119:11.)
   1. Read promises from the Bible when tempted.
   2. Memorize some good texts to repeat when tempted. Phil. 4:13; Isa. 59:1; Heb. 7:25.

X. *Avoid Exposing Yourselves Unnecessarily to Temptation.* (Matt. 6:13; Ps. 19:13.)

XI. *Speak More Often of Jesus, His Love, and What He Has Done for Us.* (Rev. 12:11.)
Tell the one who offers you a cigarette that you have quit, that you serve Jesus.

XII. *Sense God's Presence.* (Ps. 66:18.) "Whether we choose Him or not, we have a companion. Remember that wherever you are, whatever you do, God is there." MH 490.

XIII. *Reread This Daily.*

Practical Suggestions for Overcoming

1. *Phone Overcomer Daily.*—If possible, the Bible instructor should phone the individual daily while victory over some habit is being established, giving the person an opportunity to testify of his victory. It encourages him to go on another twenty-four hours.

2. *Provide Human Strength as Well as Spiritual.*—To have a brother or a sister in the church, one who has personally conquered the tobacco, liquor, or some other habit, take an interest in the case is a great help. Concentrating on getting the victory for the one who desires to overcome, uniting in prayer and Bible study with him, is a wonderful stabilizer at this stage in overcoming. A buffeted soul now needs to feel the strength of another who has experienced victory. This point must never be overlooked.

3. *Substitute the Good for the Evil.*—The plan to fill the pocket formerly occupied by a pipe or cigarette case with a pocket-edition copy of *Steps to Christ* is of definite psychological advantage. Because of a deep-seated habit, the tempted one will often be reaching for his cigarette case or whisky flask. He must find divine strength for his perverted appetite. In place of sinful indulgence the good habit of tasting the Word must be substituted. New habits will become stronger by practice. This adventure with God against the enemy of souls now becomes an exploit which will mean much to the young Christian. Help the overcomer by showing enthusiasm.

4. *Encourage Expression and Witnessing.*—But these very experiences of victory must be shared with those who know what it is to overcome. The person seeking victory should be given proper opportunities to testify of his victory to date. The prayer meeting, as well as other gatherings of the church, should now be providing these opportunities for expression.

5. *Solidify the Decision With a Pledge.*—Another commendable plan advocated in the Spirit of prophecy is the

signing of the temperance or antitobacco pledge. This personal covenant placed in a small notebook, recording a daily history of answered prayers for victory, may become a "Triumph Diary" for the smoker or drinker. To have him write down briefly each day his little testimony of victory, including perhaps a verse of special significance for that day, appeals to many during their first weeks of victory in overcoming an evil habit. It builds up a new will power or Christ power, and this spiritual exercise is more than a theory for the simplehearted. It suggests a plan for systematic victory until the new habit is well established. The overcomer is encouraged by his successful daily experience in claiming Christ's power.

PART ONE ★ CHAPTER TWENTY-EIGHT

Dress and Other Standards

In presenting the principles of dress reform the Bible instructor would do well to await the guidance of the Holy Spirit. Some readers have a background for good taste and conservatism in dress, and lean toward the cultural side of life. Others have never come under this influence, and display their lack by their very appearance. It would be unwise for the teacher to become concerned immediately about these externals of the Christian life; the problem must be duly dealt with, but from within. New principles will soon control the whole experience of the Christian.

Perhaps some significant question raised by the reader will indicate when there is sufficient interest for introducing the question of dress. God's Spirit always makes its timely impression on the human heart. One soon learns, however, that there is no more delicate problem for the Bible teacher than this problem of dress. To force it into the studies without the reader's having had the proper preparatory work may mean more problems, and often delayed results.

The "Idolatry of Dress"

Introducing dress reform to readers gives one an opportunity to change their appearance. Dress reform is the conspicuous part of denominational evangelism, and that is at least one reason why it must receive emphasis. Though this delicate question must be handled with patience, tact, and good judgment, the Bible instructor will do well to remember the Spirit of prophecy counsel. It is the "idolatry of dress" that must be dealt with today. It is astonishing how many who claim to be Christians persist in dressing and acting like worldlings. Again, how many otherwise sensible people will dress unbecomingly, if not ridiculously. Until one's attention is called to God's better way of dress, many an individual remains unconscious of our modern soul-degrading styles. It pays the teacher to be understandingly sympathetic, and to recognize this deceitfulness of sin. There must be an anointing of the eyes of the reader in order to see one's responsibility as a Christian.

The freaks of fashion play some strange tricks even on Seventh-day Adventists who sense the fact that they should lay aside their ornaments. Under the new appeal of "costume jewelry" for modern ornamentation, some peculiar new trends keep creeping into the church. Because of these strange Satanic devices to destroy God's children, instruction must stress principles rather than things. "All that glitters is not gold," applies to more than the gold of Bible times; neither is propriety in the length of the dress or its sleeves or in the cut of the neckline determined by the yardstick. In presenting the matter of feathers and flowers one does well to take a sensible middle-of-the-road attitude, especially before the

Spirit of prophecy statements are used to help balance extremes and to change unreasonable or corrupting practices.

The Bible instructor's example in dress teaches more positively than all her precepts. It best explains the robe of righteousness that characterizes the true church. Her good taste in style and color harmony offsets any disposition to have the reader feel a "let down" after hearing the subject presented. The pattern of the worker's life must be for copy, but Jesus is the true example. Souls must be taught to look to Him only.

The Standard of Philippians 4:8

Every problem of this type for the truth seeker should be measured by the standard of Philippians 4:8: "Whatsoever things are true, . . . honest, . . . just, . . . pure, . . . lovely, . . . of good report." All doubts are readily settled by asking, "What would Jesus do?"

Neither are our reading habits circumscribed by restrictions of the church. There is no "Index" which bars certain books from the reader. The Holy Spirit's guidance alone is the true index for our reading. And that same principle applies to everything else in the line of recreation or amusement.

Never should the one studying the standards of our church be left in a gloomy or unsettled state of mind as to all that must be given up to be a Seventh-day Adventist. For every seeming pleasure of the world which must be denied, another joy should be substituted. In fact, new delights are already apparent before the step of baptism is taken. The blessing of the regular Bible study now far surpasses the time formerly spent in the cinema, and fellowshiping with new Christian friends at the meetings or in the church answers the social need, provided church members assist the Bible instructor in this way. Where this is left entirely with the worker who has so many others to look after, her busy program makes an extensive social program a burden too great to carry. The Dorcas sisters and deaconesses will here find opportunity to render a helping hand. Where this companionship is not found, the new believer often pines in loneliness, or may be driven to former friends, whose influence will not help in building up the new Christian experience.

Jewelry, Ornamentations, and Make-up

The naturally proud heart clings to its ways irrespective of God's counsel. Vanity and pride of dress characterize this age. Bible instructors must build up sound and appealing argument to meet new and stubborn excuses. Let us here consider a few of the more frequent problems.

I. *Jewelry.*
1. *"God made these beautiful gems, and why can we not wear them?"*

    Vanity and pride originated with Lucifer. They expressed the apostasy working in his heart. While Lucifer wore his gems unconscious of pride, the seeds of rebellion did not germinate in his heart, but when self-glorification arose, then these precious tokens of God's favor became a snare to him. Not because it is actually wrong to wear a few gems today, but because these last days are characterized by the pride of Babylon (Rev. 17:4; 18:12-16), is it better to lend our influence on the side of sobriety and simplicity. This hour calls for abstinence and moderation on many things that might in themselves appear harmless. (Phil. 4:5.)

2. *"Jewelry was worn in Bible times. How do you explain this?"*

    The gems that God made for man's enjoyment sparkled in Eden's sunshine. But gradually man began to appropriate them to deck his person and to display his vanity. Other grosser evils associated with these practices at the time of the Flood had reached such proportions of crime that God found it necessary to destroy mankind and all his works. To safeguard man, these gems were then buried in the earth, and only laborious mining now produces a limited number of jewels. God tried to lift man's eyes from earth's vanities to the Pearl of great price. Gradually, down through the ages, the wearing of jewelry became definitely associated with lust and heathenism. (Eze. 23:38-43; 16:1-17; Judges 8:24; Hosea 2:13.) The Christian must separate himself from temptation and all appearance of evil. (1 John 2:15-17.) Long has God borne with an apostate world. In His Word are recorded other heathen practices which He never sanctioned—polygamy, for instance. There is a complete reform message for today. (Isa. 62:10-12.) Our eyes must not now be on our gems, but on saving souls. (Isa. 13:12; Dan. 12:3.)

3. *"What about other texts that refer to wearing jewelry?"* Gen. 24:30; Isa. 61:10; Jer. 2:32; Eze. 16:11-14; Luke 15:22, etc.

We might question some of these texts for even permitting the use of gems for personal ornamentation, except as we remember they must be balanced with a knowledge of the times to which they applied. We now live in the antitypical day of atonement, when moderation and abstinence are called for on principle because of the ungodly excesses of our day. On the Day of Atonement, Old Testament priests laid aside their royal garments and wore the simple linen dress. (Lev. 16:4, 23; Eze. 44:17-19.) Type, example and principles of health all taught lessons of true holiness. When the work of atonement ceased and sin was reconciled, the royal garments of the priesthood were again worn. In type we too are a priestly people (1 Peter 2:9), and must "lay aside every weight" that we may serve God fully (Heb. 12:1, 2).

4. *"Explain the foundation gems of the New Jerusalem."*

When every vile person and all idolators are destroyed; when every trace of deception, self-glorification, and apostasy is eradicated, then God's children may well feast their eyes on these heavenly gems in the foundation walls of the Holy City. These jewels will again tell their true story—perfection of character! They will be shared as the joint possession of the redeemed, and not to display personal pride. They will not be merely for the rich and the royal, but all will together enjoy the glories of that city. (Ps. 16:11.)

5. *"What about wearing inexpensive jewelry?"*

Since the silver and gold all belong to God, the fact that the article is inexpensive does not change the principle involved. God made man upright, but he sought out his inventions. (Eccl. 7:29.) Because he could not have his own way, man tried to find a substitute plan. Cheap gems cheapen God's creative works. They are an indication that we have become confused in our sense of true values. (Isa. 1:22, 25.)

Dress and Other Standards

6. *"If we are not to wear it, what shall we do with our jewelry?"*

We suggest the example of ancient Israel in Exodus 35:21, 22, 29. Let us lay up for ourselves treasures in heaven by saving souls for God's kingdom. (Isa. 62:3; 61:9, 10.)

II. *Make-up.* *"Should Christians use make-up?"*

The glow and vigor of health is God's finishing touch to our complexions. Here again is the problem that man has sought "inventions" to glorify and beautify self. Early in the history of the world these practices were known among the heathen. (Jer. 4:30; 2 Kings 9:30.) But these were not pleasing to God. The Christian is not conformed to this world. (Rom. 12:1; 1 John 2:15-17.) Let us consider Psalm 34:5 [margin] in the light of Isaiah 3:9. Let us enjoy good health by means of God's reformatory health message, and thereby set the world a pleasing example of true attractiveness.

III. *Feathers, Flowers.*

These millinery accessories are classified in the Spirit of prophecy as artificials. In dealing with this particular problem the Christian considers it in the light of 1 Corinthians 10:31 and Philippians 4:8. Whereas good taste, propriety, and dignified attractiveness should be manifested in all our apparel, the Christian refrains from wearing anything that tends to show and display. This might include frills as well as feathers and flowers, and, incidentally, a hat may not be the only article of offense in dress.

We are today seeking strange excuses for our confused reasoning. It is best to deal with this problem of dress from the angle of our influence. Not every questionable practice affects only the individual; his influence on others is the larger responsibility. A small flower or feather to enhance the hat may be worn without particular harm to the wearer, but that tiny flower or pretty spray might soon become a huge flower garden on some hats if the styles called for it. The wearing of a small chicken feather might set a vogue demanding the killing of precious birds for millinery display. Neither does the point of eye appeal settle the matter with discriminate Christians. Eve was deceived on this very point (Gen. 3:6), and the counsel of the wise man (Prov. 23:31) should also be weighed.

In past decades in our work the tendency was to emphasize thoroughly the dress problem with women; today the pendulum is apt to swing to the other extreme. For obvious reasons many ministers are reluctant even to touch this question of "artificials." Let our sisters save embarrassment to our ministerial brethren by taking themselves in hand. Arguing the point is useless. True faith always decides in favor of obedience. Contemplating the issues that made necessary the thorn-crowned head of our Master should be the best advice to our sisters who may need to take their eyes off the world. (1 John 2:15-17.)

In the use of feathers the Audubon Society has created a strong sentiment in the right direction. Others besides Adventists are happy in being conservative in their dress, and practice these Christian principles. The Christian can well afford to be distinctive in this respect. The advice of Susannah Wesley may also be well pondered:

"Would you judge of the lawfulness or unlawfulness of pleasures? Of the innocence or malignity of actions? Take this rule,—whatever weakens your reason, impairs the tenderness of your conscience, obscures your sense of God, or takes off the relish of spiritual things; in short, whatever increases the strength and authority of your body over your mind, that thing is sin to you, however innocent it may be in itself."—SUSANNAH WESLEY, from *The Sunday School Times,* June 5, 1943, p. 454.

Dress Apostasy in History

1. *Eden's Lesson of Simplicity.*

"In the surroundings of the holy pair was a lesson for all time,—that true happiness is found, not in the indulgence of pride and luxury, but in communion with God through His created works. If men would give less attention to the artificial, and would cultivate greater simplicity, they would come far nearer to answering the purpose of God in their creation. Pride and ambition are never satisfied, but those who are truly wise will find substantial and elevating pleasure in the sources of enjoyment that God has placed within the reach of all."—*Patriarchs and Prophets,* pp. 49, 50.

2. *Self-Glory of Antediluvians.*

"In the days of Noah . . . there were many giants, men of great stature and strength, renowned for wisdom, skillful in devising the most cunning and wonderful works; but their guilt in giving loose rein to iniquity was in proportion to their skill and mental ability.

"God bestowed upon these antediluvians many and rich gifts; but they used His bounties to glorify themselves, and turned them into a curse by fixing their affections upon the gifts instead of the Giver. They employed the gold and silver, the precious stones and the choice wood, in the construction of habitations for themselves, and endeavored to excel one another in beautifying their dwellings with the most skillful workmanship. They sought only to gratify the desires of their own proud hearts."—*Ibid.*, pp. 90, 91.

"The sins that called for vengeance upon the antediluvian world, exist to-day. The fear of God is banished from the hearts of men, and His law is treated with indifference and contempt. The intense worldliness of that generation is equaled by that of the generation now living."—*Ibid.*, p. 101.

3. *Vanity of Abraham's Day.*

"Abraham's neighbors wore brightly colored woolen outer garments. Those of the men were worn toga-fashion, over one shoulder and under the opposite arm, fastened in front with a long pin which might be of gold or silver with a highly ornamented head. Both sexes wore much jewelry, which, against the brunette complexions of the wearers, must have created a very striking appearance. Presumably, the old folks worried then as now because the young women were going 'modern.' The girls plucked their eyebrows, aided nature a bit with a touch of red on the cheeks, and added a dark green shadow under the eyes. When decked out for festive occasions they wore much false hair, fashioned into place with ribbons of pure gold, gold so soft that it would easily wind tight to the head. Surmounting their dusty locks, those that nature gave them and those they had purchased, rose a broad pin of gold, like a Spanish comb, spreading into seven points connected with gold wire. Many of the ladies' 'vanities' recovered still contained the cosmetics that were used to decorate complexions that passed into nothingness over four thousand years ago."—JAMES C. MUIR, *The Spade and the Scriptures*, p. 19.

4. *Jewelry in Isaac's Time.*

"The outstanding passage in Genesis 24 is the twenty-second verse which reads: 'And it came to pass, as the camels had done drinking, that the man took a golden earring of half a shekel weight, and two bracelets for her hands of ten shekels weight of gold.' This offering of gifts is an age-old custom, which even today sometimes proves embarrassing in dealing with the Oriental. The striking feature of the verse, however, is the definite weights given to the articles, and the mention of a single earring, not a pair as we might naturally expect. Both sexes wore much jewelry, but, at that distinct age, it was the custom of the men to wear a single earring. The details of the narrative are correct for the time and location."—*Ibid.*

5. *Pride in the Early Church.*

"Each one was desirous of increasing his estate; and forgetful of what believers had either done before in the times of the apostles, or always ought to do, they, with the insatiable ardor of covetousness, devoted themselves to the increase of their property. Among the priests there was no devotedness of religion; among the ministers there was no sound faith: in their works there was no mercy; in their manners there was no discipline. In men, their beards were defaced; in women, their complexion was dyed: the eyes were falsified from what God's hand had made them; their hair was stained with a falsehood. Crafty frauds were used to deceive the hearts of the simple, subtle meanings for circumventing the brethren. They united in the bond of marriage with unbelievers; they prostituted the members of Christ to the Gentiles. They would swear not only rashly, but even more, would swear falsely; would despise those set over them with haughty swelling, would speak evil of one another with envenomed tongue, would quarrel with one another with obstinate hatred."—Treatise 3, "On the Lapsed," par. 6, in *The Ante-Nicene Fathers,* vol. 5, p. 438.

PART ONE ★ CHAPTER TWENTY-NINE

Preparation for Baptism

Although the directing evangelist in a series of meetings carries the main responsibility for those who present themselves as candidates for baptism, his Bible instructors share this responsibility. They may have done the larger share of the teaching and personal work. During this busy time the evangelist must look to them to thoroughly indoctrinate and prepare these new believers. It falls to the lot of many Bible instructors to work alone, and then the responsibility for the experience of the new believers must concern them most definitely. For this reason the Bible instructor instead of the evangelist is here addressed, but it is recognized, however, that she is his assistant.

The worker who prepares people for the sacred step of baptism must herself have a clear conception of its significance in the Christian life. Most of our workers today have a Seventh-day Adventist background, and have grown up in the message. Such workers at times may not be able to appreciate what baptism means to someone coming out of another denomination into a church whose standards are entirely different from those of the church he is leaving. The struggle is intense, and when the decision to be baptized is finally made, baptism must be a step that will tie the convert firmly to the message.

During an evangelistic campaign baptisms are frequently conducted. The Bible instructor responsible for the souls who take their stand for the Advent message must do everything within her power to make the rite of baptism an impressive occasion. It must be preceded by thorough indoctrination, but this alone does not qualify the candidate for baptism. Baptism is the "answer of a good conscience toward

God," the testimony of a fully surrendered life that the habits of the candidate have been definitely changed. There must be a separation from the world in eating and drinking, reading, amusements, and education generally. In view of the fact that baptism is the planting of a new life, and that the young plant does not have the strength of the mature stock, this step should witness to a godly life in process.

Let us notice a few points worth emphasizing as souls are prepared for baptism. "Idolatry of dress is a moral disease. It must not be taken over into the new life."—*Testimonies,* vol. 6, p. 96. Repentance, faith, and remission of sin must be more than theological terms to the candidate; at the time of baptism these new experiences of grace must be a reality. "There should be no undue haste to receive the ordinance. . . . Before baptism, there should be a thorough inquiry as to the experience of the candidates."—*Ibid.*, pp. 93-95.

Because the tobacco and liquor habits are now so generally practiced, and other denominations have so decidedly dropped their standards on these points, candidates presenting themselves for baptism and admittance into the Seventh-day Adventist church should be thoroughly instructed regarding these evils. But even this is not sufficient. Special help should be given so that a complete transformation will be seen in habits and character. This requires more than a decision, or even the consent of the will. With very few exceptions such habits present a most stubborn battle with the enemy. Too much is likely to be taken for granted, and at almost the first suggestion of surrender to Christ on the part of the struggling soul, baptism is planned. It may be the better part of wisdom to let the candidate wait awhile so that he may live out his conviction and prove his sincerity in the stand which he has taken. But a decision to be baptized must also be based on other evidences of conversion.

How can the candidate be held off and yet not become discouraged in his Christian experience? Again one may ask, Why should he wait to be baptized when he is so fully persuaded to obey and has already taken his stand? At this important time in his Christian experience he would be greatly helped by a progressive series of heart-to-heart talks and Bible studies designed to establish him. Usually a group of people of like need may be gathered for the special purpose of a deeper work of grace through prayer and Bible study. Tobacco and liquor are not the only problems to be dealt with. Every other evil practice will need specific help.

Helping Backsliders

Some study should also be given to the question of reclaiming backsliders. Backsliding is no light malady; too often it is a serious illness of the soul. God abhors sin; and before it can be overcome it must be recognized in all its evil aspects.

Backsliders usually do not need doctrine so much as prayer, which will always bring a new revelation of the need of Christ. The most effective way must be found to help these individuals get onto solid ground, so that their backslidings will cease. They should not be taken all through the regular course of indoctrination, but they must be taught to pray for themselves, so that they may become victorious in their special conflicts. When reclaimed for Christ, these souls are often the most fervent in their love for Him, and they should receive every encouragement on our part.

The Youth of Adventist Homes

How shall the youth of Seventh-day Adventist homes be won? Many are conversant with the teachings of the church, but they still love the world too much to surrender completely to Christ. Baptismal classes should be planned for them in our evangelism. The heart and mind are unconverted. Conscience needs to be awakened. By means of a series of special Bible studies to meet their specific needs, these younger members of the flock should be led step by step to a larger knowledge of our message and its requirements. To the senior youth especially, emphasis should be laid on questions such as amusements, associations, courtship and marriage, employment with Sabbath privileges, and the military problem, which is so important right now.

When our junior youth reach the years of accountability, the church should give special attention to their needs. This is even more necessary where children have not had the background of a church school. It is always inspiring to take in a large group of juniors who may represent the first fruits of an evangelistic series. Children from divided homes must be carefully guarded, and fortified against special tests they will have to meet in the home. A little extra help at the time of baptism will bring courage to the young lad or lassie, and may help him when he needs it most. A too-general preparation for the whole group to be baptized often fails to give the definite help this age level needs.

The challenge of our losses brings every worker face to face with the problem of salvaging our converts for the message. New believers should be welded into our denominational program for soul winning for the finishing of our work. It is imperative that special attention be given to strengthening our plans for indoctrinating and establishing young converts, and providing for each a definite place of service.

Helping Backsliders

(For Bible Instructors' Guidance.)

Text: Hosea 14:4: "I will heal their backsliding, I will love them freely."

I. *Backsliding Man's Common Lot.*
  1. "All we like sheep have gone astray." Isa. 53:6 (Ps. 73:2).
  2. Luke wrote an entire chapter for backsliders. Chap. 15 (lost sheep, coin, son).
     a. "Go after that which is lost." Verse 4.
     b. The shepherd rejoices. Verse 5.
     c. The shepherd's friends rejoice. Verse 6.
     d. All heaven rejoices. Verse 7.
        (More mentioned about rejoicing than searching for lost.)
  3. Jesus' parents lost Him. Luke 2:41-46.

Preparation for Baptism

II. *Turning Back to God.*
   1. "They turned back . . . seeking Him." Luke 2:45.
   2. "They found Him in the temple." Verse 46.
   3. "Turn, O backsliding children!" Jer. 3:14.
   4. "I *will* arise and go to my father." Luke 15:18.

III. *Futility of Human Effort to Return.*
   1. "Without Me ye can do nothing." John 15:5.
   2. Righteousness is as filthy rags. Isa. 64:6.
   3. "If I wash myself with snow water." Job 9:30, 31.
   4. Neither nitre nor much soap erases sin. Jer. 2:22.
   5. We cannot change ourselves. Jer. 13:23.

IV. *Divine Help Promised the Backslider.*
   1. "I can do all things through Christ." Phil. 4:13.
   2. He can do all that we ask, "according to the power that worketh in us." Eph. 3:20.
   3. We are saved, not through our works, but through Christ's power. 2 Tim. 1:9; Col. 1:29.
   4. "Ye *are* complete in Him." Col. 2:10.

V. *Steps Back to God.*
   1. "Come" and "reason." Isa. 1:18.
   2. Acknowledge sin to God. Ps. 32:5.
   3. Confess sin. Verse 5.
   4. Repent and be converted. Acts 3:19; Jer. 24:7.
   5. There must be reconciliation, restoration, reformation. Matt. 5:23, 24; Lev. 6:4, 5; Acts 19:18-20.
   6. Leave one's sinful ways. Eze. 18:30-32; Dan. 4:27; Jer. 4:1, 3.
   7. Washing away iniquity restores soul. Ps. 51:2, 7, 12.
   8. Baptism is outward act of washing. Acts 22:16; 19:1-5.
   9. God's peace is claimed by faith. 1 Peter 3:21; Micah 7:19; Isa. 44:22; 43:25; Zech. 1:16; Mal. 3:7, 18.

VI. *How to Hold the Ground Obtained.*
   1.. Set affection on things above. Col. 3:2-10.
   2. Satan must be resisted. Rev. 12:10, 11; Zech. 3; Job 1; Matt. 4:1-11. (See COL 46-48.)

PART ONE ★ CHAPTER THIRTY

Integrating New Believers

Baptism is frequently referred to as the gateway into the church. Jesus said, "I am the door." Breaking allegiance with the world and joining Christ's spiritual body on earth are most significant steps to the new believers. The Bible compares baptism to a marriage ceremony. Obeying the injunction, "Come out from among them, and be ye separate," makes possible this union with Christ.

The new believer is now following a new master. A whole new code of habits must replace the old habits of sin. We would not limit the power of God to do a quick work of grace in the life of the one who has made the decision to walk in the full light of truth, but good judgment tells us that these changes require more than merely good intentions. Although we certainly do not wish to suggest that the new believer should go through a period of probation, it is necessary, however, for him to have started walking in the path of his new-found faith before he is baptized. There is need for real instruction in habits of diet, dress, and amusement.

Present-day plans for evangelism often require that the evangelist and his associate workers move on to another place before their new converts are really anchored in the church. A church has enough problems without taxing it with new members who are but half instructed in the faith they have accepted. Proper caution and thorough evangelism will save our churches great disappointment. It is unwise to leave these new believers without a worker or two who can continue to help them at this critical stage in their experience. Too many new believers fail in their Christian life, not because they are insincere in accepting new truth, but because they do not receive proper help when they are still weak.

The Master Himself taught that the gospel net would gather both the good and the bad. After being brought into the fold, some will not remain true. With every precaution in evangelism there will still be the weaker elements of human nature to deal with. To wait until every test is made before accepting a person into church membership is not the way of the Master Evangelist. But in these last days too many have a background of careless living, and altogether too few have developed enough spiritual backbone to stand firm when trial and test are brought to bear. It is all the more important, therefore, that strong fortifications be set up against the enemy. Every worker is responsible for developing new believers into strong Seventh-day Adventists. Unless the pastor who establishes these new people in the church is a genuine co-worker with the evangelist and Bible instructors who have preceded him, lack of cooperation and sympathy may add to the problem of membership losses.

The talents of all new converts should be discovered and utilized. Perhaps the Bible instructor is as well fitted as any other worker to give counsel on this point. Her special encouragement will help them to take an interest in the Sabbath school. This department of the church offers them a wonderful field for development. Also the Missionary Volunteer Society may enlist the gifts of youth, and the missionary and Dorcas societies will suggest opportunities for adults.

Christian education is a doctrine of the church. Without a thorough indoctrination on this point of our faith new converts will not be able to save their families for God today. The Bible instructor must not overwhelm them by urging too sudden school changes and too heavy financial obligations, but her failure now to enlist their interest in the church school, academy, or college may close the doors of opportunity to save the youth of these homes for the message. We are not saving individuals alone; we must save families. "Come out from among them" must include all the children of these new converts.

The privilege and need of prayer is a most important lesson for the new believer to learn. He now faces unusual tests, although in this first-love period he may be rejoicing in his tribulations. Drastic changes have come into his life, and these often separate him from his loved ones and former friends. He now greatly needs the communion of the saints and their united prayers. He should be early introduced to the prayer meeting, and perhaps even before his baptism, be invited to take an active part. It may be that he lives a distance from the church and may find it impossible to attend. Arrangements should then be made for believers in his community to form a band for prayer and Bible study. These established Christians can become a tower of strength to him. I know of no other effort that yields such fruitage in establishing the new believer. Too often there is failure to arrange for such prayer groups when these babes in the message need their inspiration.

New believers also need to be introduced to Seventh-day Adventist literature, especially the official organ of the denomination, *The Review and Herald*. Where there are young people in the family, *The Youth's Instructor* will be a great help in building new youth ideals. *Our Little Friend,* which is now generally supplied to the little folk by the Sabbath school, should also find its way into these homes. One should advise the selection of a few of these periodicals in the early experience of new Adventists. Whereas economy might first suggest the wisdom of this course, it is also well not to overwhelm the new believer with too much reading. It is better to guide the reading program until the proper reading habit is established. Here Bible instructors can be a great help to their readers.

The points stressed in the following outline will guide the Bible instructor in establishing those who have more recently embraced our beliefs. Although baptism has sealed the decision to accept Christ, the Christian life must still receive constant nurturing. (Select points helpful to the new believer.)

Daily Christian Living

I. *The Need of a Christian Experience.* (4T 314, 560; 8T 314, 315.)
   1. Christ a reality in the life. 1 John 1:1-3; 3T 543.
   2. Saving and keeping power in the gospel. Rom. 1:16; GW 282, 283.
   3. Jesus' life Christian's example. 1 Peter 2:21, 22; 9T 279; DA 311.
   4. Must now be like Jesus. 1 John 3:1-3; DA 388; 1 John 5:4.

II. *Conversion to Carry Over After Baptism.* (MH 469-482.)
   1. Converted through power of Spirit. John 16:8-13; 14:26.
   2. Walking in newness of life. Rom. 7:18-25.
   3. Putting on new man; putting off old man. Colossians 3; Rom. 13:12.
   4. Consciousness of sin's struggle. Rom. 7:18-25.
   5. Crucified with Christ daily. Gal. 2:20; 1 Cor. 15:31.
   6. Living transformed life in same body. Rom. 12:1, 2.

III. *Daily Spiritual Living.* (MH 483-496.)
   1. Beginning each new day with God. Ps. 130:6; DA 90; E 185; 4T 588.
   Blessing of the early morning devotional hour. Making it a habit.
   Entering into a stillness with God—body, mind, spirit.
   2. Praise and thanksgiving. 5T 317:1.
   Entering into the joy of salvation, being thankful.
   3. Listening to God for counsel and discipline. DA 363:3; FE 391, 442; 3T 72-74.
   God speaks in nature, in His Word, through our common sense, intuition, conscience, friends, and advisers.
   4. Results of God's guidance: Keenness of apprehension, disciplined faculties, full surrender, obedience, and service for God. DA 668.

IV. *Prayer Secret of Spiritual Power.* (*Steps to Christ,* chapter on "Privilege of Prayer"; MH 509-512.)
   1. Definition of prayer.
      a. The breath of the soul. Ps. 42:1; PP 85; GW 52, 254.
      b. Opening heart to God as to a friend. 4T 533.
      c. Comfort for oppressed. Ps. 42:5, 6; Isa. 40:1, 2; 66:13; Ps. 56:8.
      d. Key to heaven's storehouse. 1 John 5:14; James 1:5; E 126.
      e. Christian's power. Mark 11:22, 23.
   2. How to pray.
      a. Believing God is able. Mark 11:24; Heb. 7:25.
      b. Reverently. Ps. 111:9; EW 70:2; 122:1; 1T 410; E 243.
      c. Meekness in request. Ps. 25:9; Matt. 11:29.

       d. Humility of spirit. Psalms 51; 5T 201; 2T 687.
       e. Boldness in asking. Heb. 4:16; DA 668.
       f. Cooperating with God. 1 John 3:22; 7T 239; 4T 259, 538, 539.
   3. Prayer requests.
       a. For Holy Spirit. Luke 11:13; 1T 121; E 258.
       b. To know God's plan. Ps. 119:18.
       c. For power to overcome temptation. 5T 177; MH 70.
       d. For loved ones and friends. Mark 5:19.
       e. That church fulfill its mission. Isa. 60:1-3; 61:4-6; 62:1; 6T 80.
       f. A place in God's service. Ps. 51:12, 13; GW 294.
   4. Results of prayer.
       a. Assurance God reigns in life. Ps. 96:10.
       b. Fitness for life's responsibilities. Ps. 36:7-9; 8T 193.
       c. Casting cares upon God. 1 Peter 5:7; 5T 42, 43.
       d. Increasing spiritual knowledge. Ps. 111:10.
       e. Zeal for God's cause. Isa. 8:17, 18.

V. *The Bible in the Daily Life.* (E 124, 125; GC 593, 594.)
   1. Kept through His Word. Ps. 119:9-11; E 190.
   2. Plan of the ages revealed in Bible. Isa. 46:9, 10.
   3. Learning life of surrender from Bible. Rom. 12:9-21.
   4. Word must convert daily. Ps. 119:30, 32; E 172; PP 460.
   5. Its promises our comfort. 2 Peter 1:4; 1 Peter 4:12; E 126.
   6. How to study God's Word.
       a. Studying daily. Acts 17:11.
       b. Prayer and Bible study. Ps. 119:18; DA 390.
       c. Searching diligently. Isa. 34:16; 8T 157; MB 36.
       d. Witnessing for Bible truth. Acts 5:32, 42; Isa. 43:10; 5T 706.

VI. *Service for Christ.* (GW 295, 296; DA 550; 9T 30.)
   1. Christ's soul-winning example. Luke 19:10; MH 500; GW 292.
   2. Fulfilling gospel commission. Matt. 28:19, 20; 7T 280; 9T 170; GW 294.
   3. Urgency of the gospel. Rev. 14:6-12; 22:17; 9T 47; PK 74.
   4. Reward of service. GW 512-520.
   5. Types of service:
       a. In the home. MH 349-362.
       b. For relatives and friends. 5T 345; 8T 245; 6T 80; 7T 21.
       c. In neighborhood. DA 141; 9T 35, 38; GW 352.
       d. Church campaigns. 7T 19-23; 9T 117.

PART ONE ★ CHAPTER THIRTY-ONE

Teaching Prayer Habits
MARY HARTWELL

For steady Christian growth, prayer habits should be encouraged early in the course of a series of Bible studies. This may be done by a special study or two on the subject of prayer. Or it might be done by emphasis on particular points denoting prayer habits, even though the study is on an entirely different subject.

To illustrate, in the study on Daniel 2 there are at least two factors which can be emphasized in such a way as to lay the foundation for enduring and beneficial prayer habits.

When giving the background for the dream of the image, I like to acquaint my reader with the man Daniel. He was a noble, stalwart youth, true to principle, and desirous of pleasing his God in all his actions. Not only was he mighty in power, but he was mighty in prayer. Even after becoming the prime minister of a flourishing nation he was not too busy to find recourse to prayer three times daily (Dan. 6:10), a habit doubtless established in his youth and practiced by him all through his lifetime.

Incidently, here too is given the correct posture for prayer—"he kneeled upon his knees" while praying. This little side light in Daniel's life, enforced by the words of the psalmist, "O come, let us worship and bow down: let us kneel before the Lord our maker" (Ps. 95:6), can serve readily to acquaint the reader with the proper position in prayer—possibly something foreign to his past thinking.

Coming back to Daniel 2, we read that when the crisis came to Daniel, he immediately thought of prayer. Daniel knew the meaning and efficacy of Matthew 18:20—the presence of divine power, especially when two or three are gathered together. Besides prayer, the *prayer meeting* was undoubtedly an established habit with Daniel and his young friends. Might not we too receive blessings, power, and answers to prayer by emulating Daniel's prayer meeting habit?

Daniel's prayer life did not always consist of asking. He was quick to praise and thank his God for answered prayer. We find Daniel again praying to his heavenly Father before going in to the king with his important message. How many times we make a request of God, and when the request is granted, what do we do? Yes, we ought to follow Daniel's example, and thank our Father for all His blessings to us.

Thus, even in a study on prophecy, principles can be emphasized that should form basic prayer habits for new Seventh-day Adventists. Not only should we pray, but we should kneel in prayer. Not only should we ask in our prayers, but we should be quick to give God the praise and thanksgiving He longs to hear from His children. Not only should we pray, but we should be found at prayer meeting or wherever prayer is wont to be made.

Family Altar for New Believers
Margaret Cosby

Special joy thrills each Bible instructor's heart whenever she has helped a family to accept the truth. Another Christian home has become "an object-lesson, illustrating the excellence of the true principles of life," "to give to the world in their home life, in their customs and practises and order, an evidence of what the gospel can do for those who obey it."—*Ministry of Healing,* pp. 352, 196.

How can the Bible instructor impress this great responsibility upon parents who accept the high standards of gospel truth? How can she help them to mold their homes after the divine pattern? The building and maintaining of a family altar will provide a vitalizing, stabilizing influence that will establish the home in present truth and make it a stanch witness in the community.

Too many of the homes today are prayerless homes. Many times the parents themselves must be taught to pray before they can teach their children. The prayers of the worker in the home serve as object lessons in this respect. Studies on prayer and Christian home life lay the foundation on which the family altar will be built. As the regular Bible studies progress, parents and children should be encouraged to pray audibly. Any problem relative to the devotional program of the home is made the subject of earnest prayer and study.

Personal guidance is invaluable in establishing correct habits of family worship. The worker may at first meet with the family for Sabbath worship, perhaps leading out a few times. These new Christians are helped if the Bible instructor suggests the procedure of worship, encouraging the younger members of the family to pray too. The father should be encouraged to exercise his office as priest of the home.

This can be done even though the mother has not been baptized. And the mother who is alone in the truth cannot afford to lose this opportunity of teaching her children to love God's Word and faithfully obey it. Prayerful planning will bring tact and wisdom to know how to make the family altar a sanctifying influence upon every person in the home, even before the family is united in the faith.

Each family is to be encouraged to plan its own program of worship. We are blessed with a wealth of suitable material, such as pamphlets and books on the Morning Watch texts, the Morning Watch, Sabbath school lessons, devotional articles in our many periodicals, and rich treasures in our denominational books. Let the purpose of the family altar govern every plan and let the basic principles of worship be carefully studied and followed. These principles, which follow, are clearly set forth by God's messenger.

1. Set a fixed, brief, but unhurried time for morning and evening worship.

2. "Let it be understood that into these hours no troubled,

unkind thoughts are to intrude." Rather, they are to be "the sweetest and most helpful of the day," "the most pleasant and enjoyable," "intensely interesting."—*Education,* p. 186; *Testimonies,* vol. 7, p. 43.

3. The program is to be varied and appropriate for everyone, especially the younger children.

4. There must be careful preparation and planning. "To make such a service what it should be, thought should be given to preparation. . . . It will require effort and planning."—*Education,* p. 186.

The purpose of family worship is definitely stated.

1. "To meet with Jesus, and to invite into the home the presence of holy angels."—*Ibid.*

2. To seek pardon for sins committed, to present thanks and praise, and requests for needed blessings. (*Patriarchs and Prophets,* p. 374; *Testimonies,* vol. 7, p. 42.)

3. To consecrate parents and children to God for the day. "Fathers and mothers, each morning and evening gather your children around you, and in humble supplication lift the heart to God for help. Your dear ones are exposed to temptation. . . . Each morning consecrate yourselves and your children to God."—*Testimonies,* vol. 7, p. 44.

4. To "make a hedge about their children . . . that holy angels will guard them."—*Ibid.,* p. 43.

5. To instruct the children how to become followers of the Lamb, to teach respect, reverence for God and divine things, discipline, thoughtfulness. (*Ibid.,* vol. 5, pp. 423, 424.)

The home in which the family altar is established upon these sacred principles, will be a truly Christian home, exerting an influence "far more powerful than any sermon . . . upon human hearts and lives."—*Ministry of Healing,* p. 352. Parents so instructed and established will "work for their households, until with joy they can come to God saying, 'Behold, I and the children whom the Lord hath given me.'"—*Christ's Object Lessons,* pp. 195, 196.

PART ONE ★ CHAPTER THIRTY-TWO

Establishing in the Faith

The responsibility for establishing the new believer in Christ does not rest entirely with the evangelistic workers who made the contact. The convert himself must put forth every effort to become well grounded in his new-found faith. He is a babe in the truth, and will continue to grow into the full stature of Christian manhood only as he avails himself of the means of grace provided for him. The goal ahead is holiness. Spirit, soul, and body must be sanctified, and the added light he has recently received will vitalize his religious experience.

Growth in Christ will come as the new member makes progress in his private devotions and in Bible study. He must learn to exercise his spiritual powers by using his talents for the salvation of souls, and by participating in the various missionary projects promoted by the church. But growth is not merely defined by these acts of grace, or by the things which he should do as a believer. There must also be a daily discipline in overcoming sin. The whole tenure of his life must be decidedly changed, and he must exert a resistance toward the evil habits of the past. He is bound to be a bit confused at times by these drastic changes, and will then need the sympathetic guidance of those who are responsible for establishing him in our message. Living a life entirely dedicated to God is not the accomplishment of a few days; it takes time to make a deep-rooted Christian.

After being introduced to the writings of the Spirit of prophecy, the new convert to the faith usually makes rapid progress. But now he will need more direction if he is to learn to understand the proper relationship of these messages to the Bible itself. Zeal is the by-product of conversion to

Christ, but if misdirected at this stage, it may lead to fanatical tendencies which frequently bring problems to one's family. It is just as much the duty of the Bible instructor to provide wise counsel now as when the believer was facing the Sabbath test. The teacher assumes the role of a counselor, and this requires sound judgment and experience.

Explicit obedience to God brings true soul satisfaction and stimulates the spirit of witnessing for truth. This always stirs up the adversary, and persecution is bound to follow. This is a trial to the young Christian, but it is also a blessing to him. It is his privilege to learn to walk with Christ under all circumstances. If the test is not brought to bear from without, it will come from within. He must learn to keep his eyes fixed on Jesus, and not to expect perfection in the church. To bring home to him the truth that his brethren and sisters in the faith are, like him, just "saints in the making," is sound counsel.

No one is better fitted to give the new believer the tender and important counsel needed at this stage of his experience than the worker who helped to bring him into our message. To leave the new convert without this help, too often causes him to wrestle with the foe when he is not spiritually prepared to do so. When the Bible instructor must be transferred to another community, the pastor who is left in charge may fill the need, provided he is well acquainted with these new people.

Establishing the New Believer
(Pointers for the Bible Instructor)

I. *Acceptance of Special Gift.* (Eph. 4:8, 11-16; 1 Cor. 12:27-31; 14:1-6.)
   1. Place of Spirit of prophecy.
      a. Magnifies Bible truth.
      b. Is the "testimony of Jesus."
   2. Gift encourages study.
      a. Leads into unity of the faith.
      b. Stabilizes in the truth.
      c. Expands vision of service.

3. Abuses of Spirit of prophecy.
   a. Not to take place of Bible.
   b. Narrowed conceptions dangerous.
   c. Radical views unwholesome.
   d. Not to be used as club.

II. *How New Convert May Stand Firm.* (*Steps to Christ,* last three chapters.)
   1. By looking to Jesus.
      a. Ignoring weaknesses of church members.
      b. Even leaders may err.
   2. By leaning on Jesus.
      a. Weaning from spiritual parent.
      b. Standing without props.
   3. By walking with Jesus.
      a. New life "a battle and a march."
      b. Hastening His coming.
   4. By suffering for Jesus.
      a. Bracing for conflicts with Satan.
      b. Facing persecutions bravely.
   5. Always with Jesus.
      a. Fellowshiping in the truth.
      b. "Faithful unto death."

PART ONE ★ CHAPTER THIRTY-THREE

Gaining Friends for the Truth

Truth teaching does not make the same progress in all lives. The fault is not always with the teacher; it is more often with the seeker, who may not be ready to surrender everything for Christ's sake, at least not at that moment. The human teacher cannot hope to do the work that the Holy Spirit Himself is not successful in accomplishing in the inquirer's life because of sin standing in the way. Too often men choose the hard course of disappointment and sorrow before they completely surrender to the demands of Bible truth. We wish it might be otherwise, but the long history of the human race and the examples of Scripture reveal that this is true.

There is, however, an experience in this truth-teaching work which can well afford to be watched—that of avoiding hard climaxes which sever the worker forever from those she has tried to reach, but who have not yet responded to all her appeals. Some workers feel that they have not done their duty for the message unless they have brought about in the inquiring individual's experience an abrupt decision for the message or a sudden turning away from it. When those who study the Bible with them will not accept the points presented at the planned-for time, then these workers feel that they are through with them in every sense of the word. But this is a mistake that should be avoided.

Though the Bible instructor will be greatly saddened by the fact that some people, with whom she may have been carefully studying, do not take their stand, and though she may have tried in every human way possible to impress them with the urgency of such a course, her interest in them must not cease. She may not be able to continue her former studies with the same regularity, because her labors may be needed elsewhere; yet she should make provision to follow up every ray of interest, letting all men know that she is truly interested in their souls. She simply cannot leave them to their condemnation when it is her sole business to save them for Christ.

I can point to a number of very remarkable experiences when souls with whom I had studied and labored years ago eventually took their stand and declared that the truth previously studied had burned its way into their lives. The final decision may have come through another worker's effort, when the gospel net was again cast in their community. The Holy Spirit was calling and calling through the years; and later, circumstances they were not at all conscious of at the time led them to take their full stand. Perhaps no one had recently studied the Bible with them, but this was not necessary. Long ago they had been convinced of the truth. Back of such experiences may be the history of someone's noble Christian effort, or a genuine friendly spirit that would not let them go through those long years until their hearts were won for this message. This is genuine soul winning!

Why is it that some people are truly loved by saints and sinners alike, whereas others do not kindle a spirit of love? Why is it that some workers, without at any time sacrificing one principle of truth, are welcomed even by those who have not yet seen it necessary to accept our message? Such workers seem to vibrate cheer and Christian fellowship, even among those who cannot agree with them on doctrine. They are the ones who cause men everywhere to speak highly of Seventh-day Adventists. It is definitely a talent God lends them to help His church in her difficult and unpopular cause, for it is these very souls that break down the cold walls of prejudice.

The whole question must lead us all to find the more perfect way to the hearts of our fellow men with this truth—the path of Christian love. An unfavorable observer once remarked in my presence that Seventh-day Adventists would never need to face in the judgment their neglect to tell other people what was what! They might, however, be found guilty of not revealing the more gracious way to live with their neighbors after these people could not agree with them in their religious views. This is indeed something to think about! But it is not the usual experience. Someone else remarked to me, "My dearest neighbor is a Seventh-day Adventist. We truly enjoy Christian fellowship together even though we cannot see alike in every point of religion. I believe in my very soul that she will someday win me to her lovely way of life." As instructors in this precious truth, let us learn more and more to present it in the friendly, loving spirit that will win its way not only to the mind but also to the heart.

PART TWO

FEATURING A LARGER BIBLE WORK

Attractive and Impressive Approaches

Everyone connected with the work should keep fresh ideas; . . . and by tact and foresight bring all that is possible into your work to interest your hearers.—Evangelism, p. 178.

Present the truths of God's Word in a fresh, impressive way.—Ibid., p. 195.

There is marrow and fatness in the gospel. Jesus is the living center of everything. Put Christ into every sermon. . . .
Let us gather together that which our own experience has revealed to us of the preciousness of Christ, and present it to others as a precious gem that sparkles and shines.—Ibid., p. 186.

PART TWO ★ CHAPTER ONE

Evangelism for Children and Youth

Suppose that the apostle Paul had been converted at seventy instead of about thirty. Would there have been a history of Paul's life as we read in Acts? There was a Matthew Henry because he was converted at eleven and not at seventy; a Jonathan Edwards because he was converted at eight and not at eighty; a Richard Baxter because he was converted at six and not at sixty. Now bring this reflection into the ranks of the Advent message, and continue supposing what might have been our history had God called Ellen G. White at seventy instead of seventeen. Reflect on others of our pioneers in the same way, and *you* are challenged to labor for youth because of the wonderful possibilities wrapped up in young lives. How much more a soul is worth with a lifetime before it than with the end of life's journey already in sight. Yes, in the realm of souls, lambs are of more worth to God's cause than sheep.

Children's Meetings as an Adjunct
Ernestine Volkers

"Parents who can be approached in no other way are frequently reached through their children. Sabbath-school teachers can instruct the children in the truth, and they will, in turn, take it into the home circle. But few teachers seem to understand the importance of this branch of the work."—*Testimonies,* vol. 4, p. 70.

By analyzing this statement, one may arrive at the following conclusions: (1) One of heaven's appointed methods for reaching souls is to work through non-Adventist children. (2) This means is so effective that through it can be reached individuals who would not otherwise be reached. (3) This work is not being done, because but very few recognize it as an effective means for saving souls.

Those who step out in a God-given plan, after careful preparation and prayer, will be rewarded by Heaven with results comparable to their faith and effort. The fact that the plan is not being followed need not frighten a worker if the plan is Heaven inspired and the worker follows divine leading. The goals one might expect to attain in this work are: 1. The instruction and conversion of children; 2. the instruction of parents by the children; and 3. the use of children as an advertising agent.

Children are able to persuade parents to attend evening meetings when other methods fail. There is something about a child's eager, upturned face, full of expectancy and earnestness, that causes a parent to say yes to his requests. He does not like to see a shadow of disappointment come over the little face because of a firm refusal. Any evangelistic company that does not capitalize on this effective, but inexpensive, means of advertising has certainly failed in utilizing all the means at its disposal for increasing attendance at the evening meetings.

Let us first consider the parents of these children. It is only human to be proud of a child who can explain a thought clearly and tell what he has learned at a lecture or meeting. And what child is there who does not revel in going home and giving to an appreciative listener a glowing, enthusiastic report of what he has learned?

The parent will listen the whole story through, whereas a gospel worker would not get even a respectable start in going over the very same points. Once the interest is aroused by the child, the parent will be more easily persuaded to attend the evening meeting. As for the child, the Saviour Himself said, "Except ye be converted, and become as little children, ye shall not enter into the kingdom of heaven." Thus a child has the advantage of already possessing the qualifications necessary for true conversion. The adult has to reach back to his childhood and somehow gain again the faith, sincerity, and simplicity he lost as he grew up.

The time to convert a person is in his childhood. A large sector of Christendom recognizes the importance of this. But in our evangelistic campaigns the unconverted children and youth are sometimes neglected.

So often we are prone to reverse the order, and convert the grandparents and the parents, fondly hoping that they will bring the children to Sabbath school. Then, later we expect them to send their children to the church school, where they can eventually be converted by having their religious instruction stretched over a period of time, whereas much of this instruction could be given in an intensive campaign in the children's meetings, right along with the effort. Many children rebel at being sent to Sabbath school, or at having their day school changed when they have not been convinced on the idea themselves.

When children reach the age of accountability they should understand the teachings and doctrines of the Bible according to their ability to comprehend—which is greater than we generally give credit for—and should make their own decisions for Christ early. They, in turn, by the example of a steadfast Christian life, and by the knowledge they impart to others, can and will bring both children and adults to Christ. In the time of the Reformation children were used of God to preach Bible truth. In *The Great Controversy* we are told that before Christ's second coming children will again be used to preach the message. The Lord wants us to teach and train the children.

But the teaching of children must be "here a little, and there a little"; otherwise not much will be gained. Instead of giving the instruction as a stereotyped, exhaustive (and exhausting!) study on a doctrinal subject, the youth should be taught in an interesting manner. Object talks, drills, songs and choruses, projector films and slides, charts and diagrams, and other means can be used to cover definite subjects, dropping thoughts here a little and there a little, each point in its proper setting.

For example, on the subject of the good and evil angels, the Biblical account of Lucifer's fall could be illustrated by use of the projector. In this way the children will learn that Satan is a real being and that there are evil angels. The work of the good angels can be shown by telling Biblical and modern stories, showing the real presence and help of the good angels. An object talk, using a magnet, could be given to demonstrate the powers at work in our lives. Selected Bible verses on the subject could be memorized and used as a drill, with flash cards, and the music might well include the learning of a chorus on angels.

The meetings of the whole series should be planned in advance, with the subjects to be taught carefully listed, in order that a comprehensive course in Bible doctrines may be given during the course of the meetings. Consecration services should be a part of the course. Important scriptures selected for memorizing should be included in the plans. The Bible prophecies, with their historical setting, are especially enjoyed by the children. They delight in explaining the 2300 days. The children should be taught to pray, and how to exercise faith without presumption. We should lay such a firm foundation that no one can tear it down.

If earnest, consecrated efforts are put forth to instruct and win the children, many of them, and their parents and friends as well, will be brought to a saving knowledge of this message who might otherwise never have known this truth.

* * * * *

Baptizing Children

Jesus took a special interest in the children, and every Bible instructor should be interested in them. She must know how to guide parents in their training of youth, and be able to advise when the question of baptism is presented. Children who do not have the background of a Christian education in Seventh-day Adventist schools present an entirely different need from that of those who have been carefully instructed over a period of years. As workers we must be well informed on God's plans for the children in our midst. At the proper time they should be encouraged to go forward in baptism, but not before an experience on their part is apparent. The Christian experience of childhood will naturally correspond with the development of the growing child.

Bible instructors should be thoroughly acquainted with divine counsel on this question. Too often church officers hesitate to take children into the church merely because they fear added financial goals. This must never be the deciding factor. Rather the child's personal experience should be weighed in the light of the Word of God and His special instruction to the remnant church.

Youth Problems for the Bible Instructor

1. Conversion of children in evangelism.
2. Present opportunities for child evangelism.
3. Urgency for early conversions.
4. Proper age of baptism.
5. Preparing children for baptism.
6. Responsibility of parents at time of children's baptism.
7. Results to expect in these younger converts.
8. Holding youth in the church.

Spirit of Prophecy Counsel

FEED MY LAMBS.—"The charge given to Peter by Christ just before His ascension was, 'Feed my lambs;' and this charge is given to every minister. . . .

"Very much has been lost to the cause of truth by a lack of attention to the spiritual needs of the young. . . .

"Why should not labor for the youth in our borders be regarded as missionary work of the highest kind? It requires the most delicate tact, the most watchful consideration, the most earnest prayer for heavenly wisdom. The youth are the objects of Satan's special attacks; but kindness, courtesy, and the sympathy which flows from a heart filled with love to

Jesus, will gain their confidence, and save them from many a snare of the enemy."—*Gospel Workers,* p. 207.

OUR FIRST WORK.—"Altogether too little attention has been given our children and youth. . . . The work that lies nearest to our church-members is to become interested in our youth. . . .

"The lambs of the flock must be fed, and the Lord of heaven is looking on to see who is doing the work He desires to have done for the children and youth."—*Testimonies,* vol. 6, pp. 196, 197.

"Only the power of God can save our children from being swept away by the tide of evil. The responsibility resting upon parents, teachers, and church-members, to do their part in co-operation with God, is greater than words can express."—*Counsels to Teachers,* p. 166.

OBJECTIVES OF WORK FOR CHILDREN.—"In our work for the children the object should be not merely to educate and entertain them, but to work for their conversion."—*Testimonies,* vol. 6, p. 105.

"Then let the church carry a burden for the lambs of the flock. Let the children be educated and trained to do service for God; for they are the Lord's heritage."—*Counsels to Teachers,* p. 177.

JESUS' ATTITUDE TOWARD CHILDREN.—"He [Jesus] knew that these children would listen to Him and accept Him as their Redeemer far more readily than would grown-up people, many of whom were the worldly-wise and hard-hearted. In His teaching He came down to their level. He, the Majesty of heaven, did not disdain to answer their questions, and simplify His important lessons to meet their childish understanding. He planted in their minds the seeds of truth, which in after-years would spring up, and bear fruit unto eternal life."—*The Desire of Ages,* pp. 512-515.

CHILDREN MOST SUSCEPTIBLE TO GOSPEL.—"It is still true that children are the most susceptible to the teachings of the gospel; their hearts are open to divine influences, and strong

Evangelism for Children and Youth

to retain the lessons received. The little children may be Christians, having an experience in accordance with their years."—*Ibid.,* p. 515.

EARLY LESSONS AND CHARACTER BUILDING.—"The lessons that the child learns during the first seven years of its life have more to do with the formation of character than all that it learns in future years."—MRS. E. G. WHITE in *Signs of the Times,* April 8, 1903.

"Religious instruction should be given to children from their earliest years. It should be given, not in a condemnatory spirit, but in a cheerful, happy spirit. . . . As the very best friends of these inexperienced ones, they should help them in the work of overcoming, for it means everything to them to be victorious. They should consider that their own dear children who are seeking to do right are younger members of the Lord's family, and they should feel an intense interest in helping them to make straight paths in the King's highway of obedience. With loving interest they should teach them day by day what it means to be children of God and to yield the will in obedience to Him."—*Testimonies,* vol. 6, pp. 93, 94.

"From a child, Timothy knew the Scriptures; and this knowledge was a safeguard to him against the evil influences surrounding him, and the temptation to choose pleasure and selfish gratification before duty. Such a safeguard all our children need; and it should be a part of the work of parents and of Christ's ambassadors to see that the children are properly instructed in the word of God."—*Ibid.,* vol. 4, p. 398.

"Children of eight, ten, or twelve years, are old enough to be addressed on the subject of personal religion. . . . If properly instructed, very young children may have correct views of their state as sinners, and of the way of salvation through Christ."—*Ibid.,* vol. 1, p. 400.

VIOLENT EMOTION NOT ESSENTIAL.—"In working for the conversion of our children, we should not look for violent emotion as the essential evidence of conviction of sin. Nor is it necessary to know the exact time when they are converted. We should teach them to bring their sins to Jesus, asking His forgiveness, and believing that He pardons and receives them as He received the children when He was personally on earth."—*The Desire of Ages,* p. 515.

BAPTISM OF CHILDREN AND RESPONSIBILITY OF PARENTS.—"Baptism is a most sacred and important ordinance, and there should be a thorough understanding as to its meaning. It means repentance for sin, and the entrance upon a new life in Christ Jesus. There should be no undue haste to receive the ordinance. Let both parents and children count the cost. In consenting to the baptism of their children, parents sacredly pledge themselves to be faithful stewards over these children, to guide them in their character-building. . . .

"When the happiest period of their life has come, and they in their hearts love Jesus and wish to be baptized, then deal faithfully with them. Before they receive the ordinance, ask them if it is to be their first purpose in life to work for God. Then tell them how to begin. It is the first lessons that mean so much. In simplicity teach them how to do their first service for God. Make the work as easy to be understood as possible. Explain what it means to give up self to the Lord, to do just as His word directs, under the counsel of Christian parents.

"After faithful labor, if you are satisfied that your children understand the meaning of conversion and baptism, and are truly converted, let them be baptized. . . . If you consent to the baptism of your children and then leave them to do as they choose, feeling no special duty to keep their feet in the straight path, you yourselves are responsible if they lose faith and courage and interest in the truth."—*Testimonies,* vol. 6, pp. 93-95.

Preparing Juniors for Baptism

In the multiplicity of duties which come to the attention of the Bible instructor she may occasionally be called on to prepare a group of juniors for baptism. Some show real aptitude in instructing this age group, and conduct classes for them rather regularly. It is not always teaching experience that qualifies one to handle the particular problems of juniors. A Bible instructor not too far remote from junior thinking often succeeds admirably, especially if she is a trained Master Comrade. Or it may be necessary for a Bible instructor of longer experience and even less preparation to lead juniors, to function as their instructor. In this event it would be well for the worker to approach the responsibility understandingly and not too rigidly. It pays us to modernize our thinking as we deal with these girls and boys, and then to make suitable adjustment to the time in which we live.

Bible instructors usually spend their time with adults, and their thinking, argumentation, and appeal are too often beyond the junior level. Although love for youth is an essential qualification in winning their interest, it is not all that is necessary. There is no reason, however, why any alert worker could not gain skill in dealing with this interesting age. Bible instructors do well to acquaint themselves with this problem, since the youth of Seventh-day Adventist, as well as of non-Adventist, homes comprise our most precious heritage.

Indoctrination and Personal Interest

Since the usual procedure in soul-winning work is through the channel of indoctrination, the Bible instructor is most likely to decide that this must be her sole approach for winning juniors. The fundamentals of the Christian faith and also present truth must be taught, but these doctrines must be exceedingly simplified to be appreciated by the child mind. There should be an emphasis on the principles of kindness, honesty, and virtue. Stories and examples interesting and applicable to this age level will make such instruction a most pleasurable part of the baptismal class. These make their right appeal and provide the proper setting for prayer, which should become a part of each lesson. Such stories reap a rich harvest in years to come.

The Junior Standard of Attainment Course and the *Baptismal Manual for Juniors,* both by the Missionary Volunteer Department, are most suitable for indoctrinating those of junior age. The latter work was prepared by Rose Boose, one of our experienced Bible instructors. One will observe that children who have had the privilege of attending church school, where Bible instruction is a regular part of the daily work, are usually well versed in doctrines. It is then not necessary to spend much time duplicating the efforts of the faithful church school teacher. It will suffice for the Bible instructor to briefly review those points essential for an understanding of conversion.

The Baptismal Class

The room where the class is conducted should be well lighted and ventilated. The Bible instructor should have enough disciplinary and teaching ability to maintain good order. Instruction should always be given in a pleasant tone of voice and in an appealing way. It helps to create an air of expectancy and to vary one's methods of instruction. The class period should not be prolonged, but should have a regular time for beginning and closing. When the lesson has been taught, it is not wise to let the children linger around for the purpose of adding special "preachments" to some who may be needing it. This should be handled with the entire group, or else the teacher should call at the child's home, where matters may be considered privately.

Besides keeping in close touch with the pastor, there should be a thorough understanding with the Missionary Volunteer leader and church school teacher as to plans and the nature of instruction. When the group is ready for baptism, the instructor should share with these associate workers the joy of the combined harvest. She has merely helped them to climax their work for the youth of the church. Such an attitude will show the right spirit on her part and will avoid any unpleasant misunderstandings.

Saving the Youth

The Master Teacher always showed an interest in the youth. He called them into His work. Every young person should especially appeal to those engaged in soul winning. Young people need more than doctrine; most of all they need Jesus. A Bible instructor must know how to help the youth of the families she visits. She should know how to advise them in their personal problems, and wisely guide them in their social instincts.

The appeal should be on the basis of the Master's claims on the young life. These claims should emphasize Christ's fascinating and adventuresome service. With some workers the amusement and dress problems seem to receive all the emphasis. Greater principles are now at stake. Bible instructors do well to master the psychology set forth in *Messages to Young People,* by Mrs. E. G. White. Here are found various youth problems in their proper relationship to the yielding of the heart to Christ.

The average Bible instructor loves young people, but some instructors are naturally a bit too drab to make the right appeal to them. Because of their constant contact with the more mature mind, some are not too well prepared to work for young people when they are considering baptism.

For the Bible instructor who is less experienced in working with young people, a thorough study of the points presented in the following outline will be helpful.

I. *Christ's Call to Youth.* (MYP sec. 6.)
   1. Potentialities of youth. MYP 219-224, 22, 23, 125.
   2. Youth and the last message. AA 414; MYP 23-25.
   3. The ends of the earth waiting for youth. MYP 224, 225, 140, 197.

II. *The Church to Save Its Youth.*
   1. Need of leaders and teachers for youth. CSSW 97-100.
   2. Youth to be trained for church work. MYP 197, 188, 39, 172, 15, 217.
   3. Young people to be used in offices of church. MYP 219, 148, 204, 207.

4. Departments of the church appealing to youth. MYP 226, 409, 302.

III. *Christian Education for the Youth.* (MYP sec. 5; Ed 45-72.)
    1. In the home. MYP 341, 175-180.
    2. Church school for all younger children.
    3. The Christian academy after that. MYP 189-194.
    4. Correspondence courses, lay training courses, etc.

IV. *Guiding Youth in Life Choices.* (MYP 130, 31, 212.)
    1. Education. MYP 171, 172, 189-191, 258.
    2. Employment. MYP 210, 211, 213.
        a. Recognizing bents and skills. CS 210, 211.
        b. Facing the Sabbath test.
        c. Denominational employment. MYP 186, 148, 208 (CS 83, 84).
    3. Military problems.
    4. Marriage. MYP Sec. 15.
        a. Courtship.
        b. Marrying believers. MYP 440.
        c. Results of unequal marriages.

V. *Youth's Social Life.*
    1. The joy of Adventism. AA 344, 563, 564; MYP 383, 384.
    2. The social standards of Adventism. MYP 384, 386.
    3. Social to save! MYP 387-393.

Youth and Recreation

The question of youth's recreation often becomes a vital problem at the time of baptism. Bible instructors should be well informed on our social standards. The young person should see for himself that it is not a matter of our meeting the restrictions of the denomination but rather of our pleasing God. Many don'ts do not give satisfaction, but here is excellent opportunity to teach the youth how to decide such issues for himself. Every young person should be urged to study the book *Messages to Young People.* The Missionary Volunteer Department should be enlisted for further help in supplying suitable literature for more study. Study the following principles in your guidance of youth on the question of recreation.

WHAT TESTS SHALL BE APPLIED TO OUR SOCIAL LIFE? 1 Thess. 5:21.

1. Can you ask God's blessing upon it? CT 337; MYP 386, 398; GC 622.

2. Does it make you less inclined to pray and read God's Word, or does it draw you nearer to Christ? MYP 409, 397; CT 544, 337.

3. Does it make resistance to temptation easier or harder? COL 54, 55.

4. Does engaging in it trouble your conscience? CT 337; 5T 120; MB 139; CT 544.

5. Does engaging in it refresh and strengthen you physically, mentally, and morally, or does it weary and weaken you? MYP 379; CT 333, 334.

6. Does it tend to infatuate and to consume time to no profit? FCE 303; MYP 373, 379; CT 283, 350. Definition: "Anything which tends to absorb the mind and divert it from God assumes the form of an idol." 4T 632.

7. Does it tend toward self-gratification and intemperance, or does it encourage integrity and self-control? MYP 412, 416.

8. Does it better qualify you to perform life's daily duties? CT 336.

9. Does it tend toward pride of dress, frivolity, foolishness, and vulgarity, or does it tend toward refinement, virtue, and purity? MYP 382; PP 460, 461; CT 339, 340, 367.

10. Does engaging in it injure or wound any person or destroy self-respect, or does it tend toward courtesy, generosity, and increased respect for manhood and womanhood? CT 337; CH 295; MYP 421.

11. Does it lead to a love of domination or to brutality? Ed 210.

12. Does it take you into the wrong crowd? MYP 404, 409, 411, 412; PP 453; CT 224. The Christian cannot associate with worldlings in their pursuit of recreation and amusement.

 a. God calls upon the Christian to separate from the world in matters of amusement as in other things. 2 Cor. 6:14-18; CT 321, 336.
 b. He who unites with worldlings in pleasure will be overcome by Satan. MYP 366, 419; PP 459; CT 328.
 c. It is by leading the followers of Christ to associate with the ungodly and unite in their amusements that Satan is most successful in alluring them to sin. PP 458; MYP 395.
 d. We learn the attitudes and practices of our associates, and take their level. MYP 411, 412, 373.
 13. Does it tend to open the door to, or lead on to, some greater evil? MYP 379, 392; PP 452; MB 83; CT 334.

My Prayer

Father, I come to Thee with thankful heart;
I know that Thou art love!
The world is faint and sick with sorrow,
Sin, and woe; and Thou alone canst heal!
But in this sin-sick world I fill a place;
And as I see the needs of those for whom
Christ died, I seek Thy help and claim Thy promises.

I must have strength to share the sorrow
Of the torn and bleeding heart
That sinks beneath the cruel stroke;
Then let my quiet hand relieve the saddened brow.
Let love show me the way to point
The fainting soul to One who understands,
Who heals each wound and fills each vacancy.

O give me tact to gain the confidence
Of those whom I might lead to Thee,
That through my friendship they may find sweet peace,
And rest for aching heart and brain.
All this I pray, dear Lord, for I would be like Thee,
And day by day reflect the love that Thou dost show
A weary, wayward child. For Jesus' sake. Amen.

—JOSEPHINE HOLMES.

PART TWO ★ CHAPTER TWO

A Health Program in Evangelism

Mary Bierly

The evangelistic effort provides an opportunity to teach correct habits of living that if passed by will amount to an irretrievable loss, not of funds alone, but of souls for the kingdom of God. Let us notice a few statements from the Spirit of prophecy relative to combining the health message with our public meetings.

"The gospel and the medical missionary work are to advance together. The gospel is to be bound up with the principles of true health reform."—*Testimonies,* vol. 6, p. 379.

"There are some who think that the question of diet is not of sufficient importance to be included in their evangelistic work. But such make a great mistake.... The subject of temperance, in all its bearings, has an important place in the work of salvation."—*Ibid.,* vol. 9, p. 112.

What better time could be selected to teach health principles to "prospective" church members than the time when their hearts are aflame with the new-found truths of the Bible?

Since there are so many people suffering from the ravages of disease at the present time, this phase of the message will appeal to many in our audiences who otherwise would attend the meetings but rarely, if at all. So one can readily see that a good health program carried on according to the counsel and guidance of God will help build the regular attendance at our meetings, will lay a sturdy foundation for the acceptance of other testing truths, and will contribute much toward making stanch Seventh-day Adventists who will be able to resist the attacks of the enemy and will remain steadfast to the *whole* message of God. We read in volume 3 of the *Testimonies,* "The controlling power of appetite will prove the ruin of thousands, when, if they had conquered on this point, they would have had moral power to gain the victory over every other temptation of Satan."—Pages 491, 492.

With this point established, let us now consider several questions as to how to combine our health program successfully with our evangelistic work. 1. When should such instruction be given, and how much time allotted? 2. What subjects should be studied? 3. What equipment is needed? 4. How should a health class be advertised? 5. What "helps" should be given the people to take home?

1. TIME AND LENGTH.—The time and length of the health class or lecture will vary according to the capabilities of the one who is to present the instruction. If the evangelistic company can obtain the assistance of a local church member who has had medical training and who also has public-speaking ability, or if the Bible instructor will thoroughly acquaint herself with subjects that are not beyond a layman in the medical field, then one evening each week can be profitably given to the subject of health. However, if neither of these is the case, then a brief talk of fifteen minutes by one of the evangelistic group several nights a week, with occasionally a longer period of time for a practical demonstration, would be a good plan. If possible it is well to relieve the evangelist of this responsibility, as his duties are already numerous.

2. SUBJECTS TO STUDY.—The subjects to be considered at these meetings should be those that concern the general public. It would be well to start with the anatomy of the body. The number of people who know nothing of the organs of the body and their functioning is indeed surprising.

This study could be followed with one on the sixteen chemical elements and the need of the various parts of the body for each.

Next nature's remedies might profitably be discussed—sunshine, fresh air, water, rest, and proper food.

After the food question there are unlimited subjects that can be presented—"A Balanced Diet," "The Value of Whole-

A Health Program in Evangelism 209

Grain Foods in Our Diet," "The Body's Need of Protein," "Where Shall We Get Our Protein?" "Acid and Alkaline Foods," "Preparing Foods Healthfully," as well as "Liquor" and "Tobacco."

No series of health messages should close without giving the people a practical demonstration of simple water treatments, including fomentations, foot baths, heating compresses, and so forth. The list of subjects can be drawn out for an extended period, and if a doctor or a nurse is available to give the instruction, many different groups of people can be reached as the medical lecturer presents information on such subjects as "Heart Trouble," "Diabetes," "High Blood Pressure," "Cancer," "Rheumatic Fever," "Arthritis." Since these maladies are so numerous, many who are ailing would be induced to attend.

3. EQUIPMENT NEEDED.—The equipment to carry on this phase of the work can be built up gradually, so no one should feel that he must wait until he has all the material on hand before beginning. Helpful items would include charts showing the organs of the body, charts of fruits and vegetables with their analyses, and those picturing grains and dairy products. These charts can be secured free from food companies, life insurance companies, and other firms.

A blackboard is always useful, and stereopticon pictures also find their place. Some filmstrips can be obtained without cost from certain companies. Eight new filmstrips which present a general summary of our health message are now available from the Mayse Studios. If a cooking school is to be conducted, which is, of course, a most important part of these classes, then cooking utensils, a stove or hot plate, also a table, and dishes will be needed.

The necessary items for the giving of fomentations would include four woolen cloths approximately 18" x 24", a hot plate, two washcloths, a bucket, a foot tub, a basin for cold water or ice, a cot, a blanket, a pillow, three sheets, and six Turkish towels.

4. METHODS OF ADVERTISING.—Different methods of advertising can be employed. The newspaper advertisement would be foremost; then the oral announcement from the rostrum each night. Another good plan is to have blotters made, with the advertisement on the reverse side, to pass out to the people on Sunday nights and to distribute freely in bus stations and places of business.

5. HEALTH HINTS, RECIPES, AND OTHER HELPS.—It is well to give health students some "helps" to take home. If possible, mimeograph your material and duplicate some for each night. Use notebook paper so the sheets can be preserved. If cooking classes are conducted, mimeographed recipes will be helpful in getting the people to start cooking healthfully. (For a set of health lessons write to Medical Department, General Conference or to one of our publishing houses.)

In two series of meetings the following plan was carried out very successfully. One night a week was designated as health night. The subject was advertised in the newspapers and from the desk from night to night. The first part of the evening (or about thirty minutes) was used in the giving of the health talk by the evangelist's wife, a nurse, and then a cooking class or some practical demonstration was given by the Bible instructor.

These meetings proved interesting and helpful, and regardless of the weather, members from three churches within a radius of ten miles, together with our new believers, gathered for the instruction.

After the health talk was given, the meeting was thrown open for questions on the subject presented, and when all questions were answered, the audience was invited into another room, which turned out to be the "kitchen." As each person entered the door, a slip of paper containing a number was handed him. From these numbers one or two were to be selected to receive the prepared dish or dishes of the evening.

Upon entering the room, one observed three tables with attractive covers. One contained health books and cookbooks for sale and some free literature. On the second, health foods were displayed which were sold at the close of the demonstration. The third table set in the center at the front was in readiness for the cooking demonstration. As far as possible all ingredients for the recipe were prepared beforehand.

A few remarks were then made about the dish that was to be prepared, and at the appropriate time quotations from prominent doctors and from the Spirit of prophecy were read, showing the importance of healthful cooking and dealing with the dish that was to be demonstrated. This was an excellent opportunity to mention the nonuse of pepper, vinegar, aged cheese, coffee, tea, and so forth. The mimeographed recipes and health hints were then distributed, and the demonstration followed. (When a stove was not available, the recipe chosen was one that could be prepared during the class and given to a member to take home and bake or cook.) Numbers were then selected, and the dish was given to a different person each night. This procedure eliminated the sampling of food between meals. Near the close of the series of meetings a health supper was prepared by the local church members, and the entire audience was invited to partake. The health class requires some extra work and planning, but it pays large dividends in souls for the kingdom of God, and should be a part of every series of evangelistic meetings.

Evangelistic Cooking School

Mrs. D. E. Jacobs

To teach the people a better way of living, not only spiritually and mentally, but also physically, is the work of the true minister. Evangelists should attempt to correlate these phases in their program as neatly, soundly, and appealingly as possible. In these times there is a larger opportunity than ever for giving our health message to the world.

Through the study of foods and cooking demonstrations people will see and understand that healthful living is a strong Bible teaching and that Seventh-day Adventists have been blessed of God with the most balanced health program of any people on earth. They will come to realize that proper care of the body is vitally connected with care for the soul.

My husband and I opened a Bible and health auditorium in Buckeye, Arizona, where we conducted three nights of Bible lectures and one health lecture weekly for a period of six weeks. It was an opportunity to carry out the teachings of the Spirit of prophecy concerning a program of health reform.

Most of us know what we ought to do. But the thing we want to know is *how*—how to do all the things we should be doing in giving God's message to the world. My husband had been interested in the denominational health program for a long time and had taken every opportunity while in academy and college to acquire a fund of information on the subject.

We were especially favored when the Arizona Conference sent us to take the newly instituted Health Evangelism Course at Loma Linda, given particularly for ministers already in the field. This furnished us with an abundance of inspiration, information, and prestige with the people, for Loma Linda is generally a respected and familiar name in Arizona. While in the Los Angeles area, we interviewed Mrs. R. B. Spear, who for years has successfully conducted a health kitchen in connection with her husband's evangelistic meetings. We gained from her many practical, workable ideas which blend into the evangelistic program.

In Buckeye we chose Tuesday night for our health program, so that we might make full use of both Monday (when there was no meeting) and Tuesday in preparing for it. My husband planned to give a ten-minute health talk preceding the Bible lectures on the other nights, in order to tie the whole program together. But we were forced to dispense with these, as sunset on fast time brought darkness so late. The health message was bound around the cooking school idea, in which we always gave the people a taste of everything that was made. This drew the people and made our crowds on

A Health Program in Evangelism

Tuesday nights almost as large as those on Sunday nights.

If the minister and his wife can be associated in some public way, it helps much in visiting the people later, who then feel acquainted with both workers. So in our health program my husband took the lead, and I was his assistant. He did the major part of the lecturing on principles, and I demonstrated the recipes and talked about them as I worked. Then in our visits to the homes the people had questions to ask of both of us.

As soon as our tent was up, with its sign, "Bible and Health Auditorium," we placed a news article in the local paper concerning the cooking school, which was called the Buckeye Home Builder's Health Kitchen. Before printing the first week's handbills we solicited a local grocery for a donation of food to be used in our school in return for advertising their store. The power company lent an electric range.

The first handbill was a two-color folder with an insert announcing the Home Builder's Health Kitchen, showing our picture with the lecture title "Wartime Foods to Be Demonstrated." On the reverse side was our invitation to the people, telling them that "two delightful hours will be spent in getting acquainted with food that will build strong, healthy bodies. Samples of food will be prepared before the audience and will be given away with a series of savory recipes."

The advertising for the following weeks consisted of a four-page folder, one page being given to the health kitchen. The signboard outside the tent reinforced our printed handbills, as did also posters in the store windows and an occasional notice in the paper.

How We Conducted the Health Kitchen

1. PLATFORM ARRANGEMENTS.—Curved across the back of the platform hung full, green burlap curtains, giving us a rich background for our demonstrations. In the center was a streamlined display of Madison and Loma Linda foods. To the right was the electric range and the long table for food

demonstrations. To the left was the speaker's table, from which he gave his lectures, based on an eight-point program taken from the paragraph in *Ministry of Healing:* "Pure air, sunlight, abstemiousness, rest, exercise, proper diet, the use of water, trust in divine power,—these are the true remedies."—Page 127.

In a room behind the platform other women helped by arranging food to be served, washing dishes, and preparing items that might be needed. Assisting me before the audience was a young woman who supplied my wants from the pantry, and watched the food as it cooked, while I was demonstrating other recipes.

2. PROGRAM ARRANGEMENT.—We planned to vary our program instead of conducting a health lecture or a cooking school only. We made ours a variety program which would appeal to the non-Adventist and provide a little educational entertainment along with our strong health principles, which at first seem extremely strait-laced to the usual person of the world. Here is a sample program, the length of which averaged two hours:

Introduction and words of welcome. Passing out of recipes.—Mr. J.

Demonstration of vitamin broth and gluten steaks.—Mrs. J.

Lecture: "How Little Mistakes in Eating Can Keep You Half Sick."—Mr. J., passing out rusket samples.

Recipe demonstration of carrot bread.—Mrs. J.

Questions and answers. Discussion of "Air."—Mr. J., passing out printed lecture.

Recipe demonstration: asparagus cooked the "waterless way."—Mrs. J.

Colorful salad arrangements demonstrated.—Mr. J.

Recipe demonstration: nut and potato pie.—Mrs. J.

Health pictures (kodachrome slides).—Mr. J.

Remarks concerning a dessert and sandwiches already prepared.—Mrs. J.

A Health Program in Evangelism

Collect premium cards and offering.
Cafeteria service and grace.
Premiums given out. Open forum.—Mr. J.
Good night.

For my running comment during the mixing of recipe ingredients, I discussed the values of the foods I was working with and the methods I was using in mixing and cooking. I talked about everything from vitamins, proteins, and gardens, to wooden spoons, food grinders, and cooking utensils.

I continued to work with the recipes while my husband gave his part of the program. This did not detract attention from him, and it gave me a chance to collect my ingredients and my bearings for the next demonstration. The roasts, pies, cakes, and breads were prepared first, leaving the salads, sauces, gravies, and cookies till later, for they did not require the amount of preparation that the others did.

While the attendance awards were given away, we arranged two rows of food samples on clean sheets of paper along the edge of the platform. After prayer the audience passed around in two cafeteria lines, serving themselves from the steaming dishes, the salad bowls, the sweets, and the sandwiches. We stood by on the platform to help them and answer their questions.

Each dish should be labeled with a sign so that the people may identify it. Music from an electric phonograph will greatly add to the conviviality of this part of the program and help fill in the minutes when nothing can be said.

3. Recipes.—The recipes demonstrated were gleaned from many sources and chosen for their public appeal, as well as for their health virtues. Not until the last two nights did we introduce balanced menus, and then I gave out copies of these. The meals contained dishes we had demonstrated during our health-kitchen nights. We did it this way because, first of all, we wanted to gain the interest of the people without being too technical, and next because we wanted to stress the meatless dishes before we discussed the balanced diet.

No words were spared in giving them the facts concerning the harmful effects of alcohol, tobacco, tea, coffee, meat, spices, and vinegar. We used no baking powder, soda, or vinegar in our recipes, and gave the reasons for omitting them.

There may be some question about serving food samples in the evening, as this violates our principle of avoiding eating between meals. We instruct the people regarding the evils of in-between-meal eating; but inasmuch as it is impossible to go to each individual's home for a food demonstration at mealtime, the audience readily understands why the lecturer must provide food samples at an hour convenient to hundreds of people who could participate in the food demonstration in no other way. Following are some points that will be found helpful.

1. Plan every minute. Avoid pauses by having an abundance of material.

2. To receive names, and to promote interest in health foods, give away several cans and boxes of food to ticket holders with winning numbers.

3. Advertise accasionally the names of the recipes to be demonstrated.

4. Demonstrate several recipes with each lecture.

5. Encourage men to attend by serving them double portions if they wish.

6. Give away pamphlets and samples each night.

7. Display and sell various foods and health books.

8. Lecturer can wear white professional coat; recipe demonstrator, white uniform; ushers, white jackets; waitresses, white uniforms with colorful aprons and caps.

9. Always take an offering, usually before the food is served.

10. Build the platform larger and higher than for the average evangelistic meeting.

11. A stove and refrigerator on the platform help create kitchen atmosphere.

Cooking Lessons by Kodachrome

ELLEN CURRAN

In the presentations of the health reform message, hygienic cooking demonstrations play an important part. How to carry on these cooking lessons in an attractive, impressive, and yet simple way, without too much equipment and volunteer help, has always been a problem to me. For some time, too, I have been perplexed concerning the matter of providing "samples" of the foods demonstrated. This is simple enough for small groups, but when the crowd grows into hundreds, the preparatory work takes too much time out of a busy Bible instructor's crowded program. Another problem has been the advisability of serving food samples, for we teach people that eating between meals is harmful.

In order to overcome these difficulties, I began to use filmstrips especially arranged for lessons on healthful living. The hand coloring of the food pictures was not at first satisfactory. But since "necessity is the mother of invention," I set myself to the task of finding something better. Motion pictures in natural color would be very attractive, but far too expensive. I decided to try the next best thing—kodachrome.

I spoke to two different photographers who were experts in kodachrome work. They said that they had never tried this kind of photography, but if I would arrange the settings just as I wanted them, they would take the pictures. Accordingly I planned the entire procedure of cooking certain health recipes, and each setting in detail. (After the photographer starts working, there is no time to plan, of course.) Some settings are put in just for human interest, and some for a little humor—such things as might actually happen in the kitchen.

A young woman models as housewife, and others form family groups as needed. An attractive kitchen, with a shining stove, a worktable, and a sink, adds greatly to the pictures. Bright kettles, colored mixing bowls, and pyrex cooking utensils enhance the setting. Avoid crowding the picture.

We photograph as close to the setting as possible, in order to show the very texture of the foods. In most cases even the cook is left out of the scene, except her hands (which for photographing should be whitened with face cream and powder, so they will not look red). Often the kettle or mixing bowl containing the foodstuffs is all that is featured in the picture. Many of the settings are taken as close as eighteen, or even fourteen, inches. But to do this requires the best kind of camera and plenty of floodlights concentrated on the objects.

Every step in the process of preparing and cooking the food is thus shown in natural color, and the method is explained by lecture while the pictures are being shown. The finished product is also arranged in an attractive setting, so that it appears delicious and appetizing. Fresh vegetables look especially attractive taken in kodachrome.

Making these slides entails patient effort and some late hours, but the results are gratifying. At the present time one of our doctors in Los Angeles, who makes kodachrome photography a hobby, is helping me, and is doing very good work. I pay him only for the film. With my settings all planned, I go to him once a week with my materials.

Many of our workers are doing their own kodachrome photography these days; those who do not can find experts who do it as a hobby. Thus they can work out their individual ideas. In Portland some nurses took it up with enthusiasm and began to make pictures for their health talks.

Thus far I have developed material for ten lectures, which were well received by my classes at the Radio Reading Room. Some get so hungry as they see the pictures that they go right home and try the recipes. These, of course, are handed out as people arrive for the lecture so that they may be read before the pictures are shown.

Certainly there is a large field for individual development and improvement in the presentation of healthful cookery. I recommend it to our Bible instructors.

PART TWO ★ CHAPTER THREE

Sanitarium Bible Work
BESS NINAJ

Our evangelistic work is carried on at great effort and expense in public meeting places to attract people to come to hear the truth. Our sanitariums have a decided advantage in that a large group of people are assembled in one place, in a favorable contact with our message. Here is an audience divinely brought together. Here two of our most testing truths, the Sabbath and health reform, are lived out before the patients. It was for this very reason that our sanitariums were established.

"To preach the gospel means much more than many realize. It is a broad, far-reaching work. Our sanitariums have been presented to me as most efficient mediums for the promotion of the gospel message."—*Evangelism,* p. 536.

Woven through the many statements related to medical work in the Spirit of prophecy are countless expressions that the spiritual help, the saving of souls, is God's main purpose for the existence of medical work. Among the influences that attract our patients to Christ are the *atmosphere* (as reflected by the institution and by the workers), *prayer, literature,* and the *religious services.* First, let us consider the atmosphere.

ATMOSPHERE OF THE SANITARIUM.—We find among our patients the rich and the poor, the very devout and the skeptical, the open-minded and the bigoted. Many have no faith in God, and have lost their confidence in man. But they all appreciate acts of sympathy and helpfulness. Their hearts are touched as they observe the words and acts of the sanitarium staff and see evidence of unselfish interest on the part of the doctors, the nurses, and other workers. Every worker contributes his part in creating a Christian atmosphere.

"The institution is to be pervaded by *a spiritual atmosphere*. We have a warning message to bear to the world, and our earnestness, our devotion to God's service, is to impress those who come to our sanitariums."—*Counsels on Health,* p. 273. (Italics mine.)

"The religious influence that pervades these institutions inspires the guests with confidence. The assurance that the Lord presides there, and the many prayers offered for the sick, make an impression upon their hearts. Many who have never before thought of the value of the soul are convicted by the Spirit of God, and not a few are led to change their whole course of life."—*Ibid.,* p. 208.

It is interesting to see how prejudice is broken down by the silent influence of Christian living exerted by everyone.

Recently there came to the sanitarium a woman who said, "I was reared by an atheist father, and a mother who had no particular convictions. Personally, I am religiously inclined, but I have never affiliated with any church, because I have disapproved of the denominational divisions. Now I feel that I want to join a church, and I want to know more about your church and its beliefs. You seem to have an inner something, a peace and happiness that radiates in your lives."

Another patient remarked: "The way you *live* your religion puts my church to shame. I have never realized what Seventh-day Adventists were like or what they believed. I'm sorry to say that when they have come to my house in the interest of missions I have given them a donation but have not even accepted their booklet. I shall certainly give them a better reception next time."

This woman and her daughter were given Bible studies. Several weeks after they left, a friend of theirs who came to the sanitarium said, "I wondered how they learned so much from the Bible while they were here." Another day she said, "I've just had a letter from my friends, and they want you to write them immediately and tell them from the Bible why you keep Saturday."

Just a few days ago the sanitarium supervisor, in calling on a patient, was surprised by the question, "Just what is there in the faces of you people that is different? Is there something in your religion?"

"The pleasant disposition, the beautiful character, the Lord will use to bring blessing to the sick."—*Medical Ministry*, p. 173.

"As they exemplify truth in their daily walk and conversation, they will exert a holy influence, and the grace of Christ will coöperate with human effort."—*Ibid.*, p. 195.

The Power of Prayer

Daily association and ministering in things large and small to the patients bring an intimate, personal contact. And of all the influences that draw these souls to Christ and bring a peace and trust, none is greater than prayer. Prayer will usually open up a conversation that will reveal the perplexity, the need, and the longing for hope and understanding. It inspires confidence and trust to know that there is One who is interested in our welfare, who watches over us, and who is directing our steps even in afflictions and trials. It inspires a confidence to know that every doctor, every nurse, and every worker depends on the heavenly Father and wishes the patients to share in His blessings and loving care.

Many are reticent about praying or speaking of spiritual things with others. Perhaps this is because we think of our relationship to God as such a personal one. Then, too, convention has placed a taboo on religion socially, because it is often a controversial matter. Nevertheless, rarely, if ever, does a patient refuse prayer. Most of them look forward to the student nurses' evening prayer for God's watchcare through the night. They tell how impressed they are that a busy physician will take time in their presence to request the Lord for guidance and skill in his work.

In the student nurses' manual for Bible I, Chaplain Moran of Loma Linda mentions the many occasions when it is fitting to have prayer with patients—at bedtime, at mealtime, before surgery (and after), whenever a patient asks for prayer, when the conversation seems to lead up to it, when a heart is touched, when the patient is in great pain, when the patient is discouraged or worried, in times of bereavement or grief, when a relative is deeply concerned over a loved one who is ill, and when patients are discharged, to commit them to God for His continued blessing.

Frequently there are instances when a patient is troubled because he does not know what the outcome of his illness will be. Then there are instances when all medical resources or knowledge produce no change for the better. Here is a real opportunity to accept Christ's invitation to bring all our cares to Him. And "we know that God hears us if we ask according to His will."—*Ministry of Healing,* p. 230. God's power is evident today, and He gives us encouragement in showing His power as we present our patients to Him.

A patient came to the sanitarium with a severe injury to her eye. The physician examined it several days in succession, and told her that in spite of treatment he would have to remove it surgically. She requested the chaplain to come to pray for her. He offered a simple prayer, that if it was God's will, the doctor would not have to operate, and that he would see a change for the better on his next visit. When the doctor again examined it he remarked, "There has been a very marked change in the condition of your eye, and I don't think I will need to operate."

One of our own people recently requested anointing prior to surgery. The following day, as her surgeon examined her, he remarked that the tumor was not evident, but that on the basis of former diagnosis he would operate. Later, on counsel of the chaplain, this patient told her physician that she had been anointed. After some minor treatments she was able to leave the sanitarium without having an operation.

"Behold, I am the Lord, the God of all flesh: is there any thing too hard for Me?" Jer. 32:27. In harmony with His promise, God "sent His word, and healed them." Ps. 107:20. We have the assurance that every sincere prayer is heard in heaven, and that in His providence God grants only those things that are best. Prayer is one of the closest links in our living connection with Heaven, and, without doubt, is one of the strongest evidences that makes ours a living religion.

"We are to offer special prayers for the sick, both when with them and when away from them."—*Medical Ministry,* p. 190.

Literature in Propagation of Gospel

Concerning the use of literature in our sanitariums, we read: "Publications containing the precious truths of the gospel should be in the rooms of the patients, or where they can have easy access to them. There should be a library in every sanitarium, and it should be supplied with books containing the light of the gospel."—*Evangelism,* p. 538.

In each section of the Washington Sanitarium and Hospital there are bookracks filled with our Crisis books. These are available for the taking. Included are spiritual books, as *Thoughts From the Mount of Blessing, Alone With God;* doctrinal books on the home of the saved, the state of the dead, the Sabbath, the judgment; and booklets on health, such as *The Cigarette as the Physician Sees It* and *Better Meals for Less.*

Then there are the various books that cover all our beliefs, such as *Why I Am a Seventh-day Adventist, The Marked Bible,* and *The Bible Made Plain.* The books *Steps to Christ* and *Ministry of Healing* are in each room. In addition, the sanitarium subscribes to a liberal club of the *Signs of the Times* and *Life and Health,* which are distributed freely.

In the chaplain's office there is a lending library, which contains the larger books, as well as the doctrinal tracts and the Pocket Companion Series. The smaller books and pamphlets are especially appreciated by bed patients, who tire quickly both mentally and physically.

Announcements regarding denominational radio programs and Bible correspondence courses are placed in several places in the institution.

The Religious Services

In harmony with divine counsel, vesper services are held every evening. Patients enjoy the old gospel hymns and the simple, earnest talks. These, as suggested in *Evangelism*, should be spiritual and nondoctrinal. (Pages 538, 539.)

Every Sabbath at the Washington Sanitarium a Sabbath school class conducted by the medical director is held especially for the patients. Jewish patients often visit the class from week to week. For many months we have been studying the life of Christ, yet they attend regularly. The weekly church services and the prayer meeting are open to all. The Spirit of prophecy also recommends this as a way by which patients may obtain a knowledge of Bible truths and of our work. (*Evangelism*, p. 539.) At our recent communion service six patients took part with us.

Over the public address system vespers and Sabbath day services are broadcast to all the rooms for the benefit of the patients who are unable to attend. Headphones are provided in each room so that those who are interested may tune in.

Many patients come to us whose hearts are heavy with trials and discouragements. They welcome a friendly call and the spiritual comfort which comes from prayer and encouraging words of Scripture. This interest often leads to further study of God's Word. Gradually questions arise concerning the Sabbath and diet, and as a result a rounded-out series of studies may be given. Some immediately ask about the Sabbath. If all questions are tactfully handled, an interest may be developed that will lead to organized Bible study later on.

Many are impressed by the spiritual atmosphere and the attractiveness of Christian living, and because of this ask about the beliefs of our denomination.

Sanitarium Bible Work

The book *Evangelism* gives this suggestion: "If they [sanitarium patients] ask questions in regard to our faith, it would be proper to state what we believe, in a clear, simple manner."—Page 542.

Does God intend that we tell these people more about His complete message? "Many persons who come to them [sanitariums] are hungering and thirsting for truth, and when it is rightly presented they will receive it with gladness."—*Counsels on Health,* p. 208.

"Why do we establish sanitariums?—That the sick who come to them for treatment may receive relief from physical suffering, and may also receive spiritual help."—*Ibid.,* p. 271.

"It is to save the souls, as well as to cure the bodies, of men and women, that at much expense our sanitariums are established."—*Ibid.,* p. 470.

"Our sanitariums are to be established for one object,— the proclamation of the truth for this time."—*Ibid.,* p. 343.

"We are to do all in our power for the healing of the body; but we are to make the healing of the soul of far greater importance."—*Ibid.,* p. 272.

"The message must go to the whole world. Our sanitariums are to help to make up the number of God's people. We are not to establish a few mammoth institutions; for thus it would be impossible to give the patients the messages that will bring health to the soul. Small sanitariums are to be established in many places."—*Evangelism,* pp. 536, 537.

"The spiritual work of our sanitariums . . . requires thought and tact, and a broad knowledge of the Bible. Ministers possessing these qualifications should be connected with our sanitariums."—*Counsels on Health,* p. 293.

"In our sanitariums, of all places in the world, we need soundly converted physicians and wise workers,—men and women who will not urge their peculiar ideas upon the sick, but who will present the truths of the word of God in a way that will bring comfort and encouragement and blessing to the patients."—*Medical Ministry,* p. 208.

Finding the Interest Among Patients

There are many opportunities for giving regular Bible studies in our sanitariums.

A physician, in his contacts, may notice an interest and refer it to the Bible instructor. Or, as he sees a problem or condition which can be handled through the spiritual approach, he may consult with the chaplain or Bible instructor.

Similarly, while the nurse is giving a treatment or answering a patient's call, she makes an observation, and refers the interest to the chaplain or Bible instructor. The supervisor, the clerk at the desk, or the housekeeper—all contribute in bringing attention to interested ones. Every now and then the patients tell of others who seem receptive, will repeat a conversation, and suggest that something be done.

The Bible instructor herself has ways of finding openings. One of the best ways is to visit the patients, calling on each one. In the conversation she notices the interest or lack of it. Often a book or pamphlet will help to break the barrier. There are certain spiritual, nondoctrinal booklets that seem to be especially enjoyed, and the Bible instructor can make a wise choice in selecting these as various interests develop. In the conversation she can prepare the way for something she would like the patients to read. The Bible and the books *Steps to Christ* and *Ministry of Healing* are in each room, and these are often read and purchased by patients. The Bible instructor on occasion refers to certain chapters or texts that are appropriate for the patient to read.

After taking the admittance medical history of a new patient, an intern stopped by with the comment that this young women needed help spiritually. She was a fashionable young woman whose marriage had thrown her into a social whirl. That, coupled with the standards so different from her own, had taxed her to the limit and brought on a collapse.

At home she had already begun to study the Bible in an unguided way, reading wherever it happened to open. Seeing *Steps to Christ* in her room, she read it through the first day, and later purchased a copy for her personal library. The Bible studies fascinated her, and each day she brought up questions for which she wanted Bible answers. Before leaving, she asked for books on various subjects, and planned to continue her study through the Bible correspondence course. The studies crystallized her convictions on a better life.

One of the desk clerks became acquainted with another patient who had a diagnosis of inoperable cancer. And although the woman showed no interest, I was asked whether I would not try to find an opportunity to study with her. It took at least two months to discover any interest. During those early studies she was cordial but so noncommittal that it hardly seemed worth while. Then one day, after we had to omit a study because of an interruption, she remarked to the housekeeper, "I don't know why that had to happen just as we were about to have a Bible study."

A new patient commented: "This is such a lovely place, and you seem to be such lovely people. I've never known any Seventh-day Adventists, nor why you keep Saturday. I believe, though, that people used to keep it in Old Testament times."

I agreed with her that people had kept Saturday, the Bible Sabbath, in Old Testament times, and that we studied the Bible diligently, and if she wished, I would study with her.

During a Bible study a patient asked, "Do you think that if one prays to the Lord and asks Him the reason for his affliction, He will reveal it?" I replied that He does not always show us the reason for some things, but someday He will.

Her reply was, "Well, I think that He shows us partly at least; for instance, with me, how would I ever have known this truth if I had not been directed here?" This woman, the mother of five children, was afflicted with poliomyelitis five years ago. Her local hospital did not use the Kenny treatment, and the Polio Foundation sent her to the Washington Sanitarium for treatment. She is now ready to be baptized.

These are just a few ways in which opportunities for Bible studies develop. Actually there are a great many opportunities for the sanitarium Bible instructor. The amount of work she can do depends upon the time she can devote to it, her physical limitations, her consecration, and her initiative.

Student Nurses as Assistants

The Bible instructor in sanitarium work participates in the nursing school teaching program for student nurses and in the supervision of their practical experience in giving Bible studies. The student nurses study *Ministry of Healing,* which stresses the example of Christ's correlation of spiritual ministry with the physical, and there are two courses in Bible doctrines taught by the chaplain. In these the key texts on each subject are stressed, so that the nurses will be able to quote from memory if there is an opening for a brief Bible study in the course of a conversation. In the senior year the Bible course of study is "The Life of Jesus," from the book *The Desire of Ages.*

Each student is required to audit four Bible studies and to give four Bible studies. Two of these are of the conversational type, and the other two are organized, planned studies.

It seems more satisfactory, in assigning the planned studies, to have the student give studies to patients who have already had several studies. Then the student is well received, and the patient is receptive. The students thus have better experiences and better impressions, which we hope may inspire them into an interest in the spiritual purpose of Seventh-day Adventist nursing.

How Graduate and Student Nurses Can Help

The nurse, both student and graduate, can cooperate with the Bible instructor and chaplain in the following ways in creating interest:

1. By the example of her own life.
2. By prayer, both with the patient and when away from the patient.
3. By guiding the reading of the patient.

4. By making a special effort to acquaint the patient with our religious services, inviting him to vespers, to the church services, the prayer meeting, and young people's meeting.

5. By reminding the patient about our radio programs, both local and the Voice of Prophecy, and also those in the sanitarium.

6. By referring interested ones, or those who have any particular need, to the chaplain or Bible instructor.

7. By the singing band. The singing band meets and goes through the building singing. In one sanitarium it may be in the morning, in another at sunset Friday and Sabbath, or on Sabbath afternoon.

8. By a health correspondence course.

9. By a Bible correspondence course. Nurses can guide patients into that.

10. By giving Bible studies.

The students have won a place in the hearts of the patients with whom they are studying. The sanitarium Bible instructor selects the patient, paves the way with the beginning studies, and keeps in touch with the patient's spiritual interest and progress.

One of the prevalent problems to consider is the fact that many of the patients leave before a complete series of studies can be given. However, each one is told about the Bible correspondence course, and many begin the course while they are still at the sanitarium. When the reader is agreeable and has a definite interest, the local conference is urged to pursue further personal work.

Only eternity will reveal the true fruitage of sanitarium Bible work. But at least the seed is sown with those who stay only a short time. Even though they may learn no more than God's true purpose in creating us and this world, His plans for our future, an understanding that He brings us all our blessings, and that the author of sorrows is His adversary, a beginning has been made. We have thus opened the way for future contacts with the truth.

PART TWO ★ CHAPTER FOUR

Artistic Bents and Skills
The Projector in Cottage Meetings
IRENE ANDERSON BIRD

In general, people are picture-minded today. Of course, there is nothing that can compare with the study of the Bible, where each person looks up the text for himself, but still there are times when the projector accomplishes great good. I have found that it affords a fine opportunity to gather the whole family together in evening cottage meetings. Men who would not sit down and study the Bible are usually willing to look at the pictures. The children are delighted with the plan, and lessons are deeply impressed upon them. They love to sing gospel songs, and look forward to my coming.

I use the double-frame slides. I find them more satisfactory than the films, for then I can change my studies as I see fit. One of my readers gave me a color camera, and I am able to get some very beautiful pictures in color. I am now working on a set especially for children.

The people soon become interested, and after I have shown the pictures, we open our Bibles and look up some additional texts. Then before leaving, I give them a tract which deals with the subject that has been presented. Many times the father of the family, who feels that the pictures are really for the children and that no one is trying to win him, finally becomes interested, and is won for the truth.

I often use the projector for a review of what has been presented. When studying with interested people, after using our Bibles for two or three studies, I set up the projector and review what we have gone over. I find that the pictures impress the texts more fully on the mind.

The projector has proved to be especially helpful in dealing with Catholics. They are accustomed to pictures, and are more easily interested in this way. I have been studying with a Greek Catholic woman, and although she had come to enjoy the study of the Bible with me, it was really the projector pictures that made the deep impression upon her mind.

When I come into a home with screen and machine, and see how the whole family welcomes me—the older ones setting up the machine and sometimes running it—all anxious to see what is coming, I offer up a prayer of thankfulness that someone devised this effective means of presenting the gospel.

One distinct advantage of the projector is this: When a Bible instructor sometimes has to give six or seven studies a day, if two or three of them are given with the projector, she can accomplish much more in her time, as it does not take so long to give a study with pictures. The pictures help to break down prejudice, put folks at ease, and arouse an interest in the Bible. I feel that my little projector is truly a help in time of need, and I would not be without it.

Value of Chalk-talk Illustrations

JEAN M. CARTER

Confuscius once said, "One seeing is worth a thousand tellings." Or we might put it in a modern version and say, "One picture is worth a thousand words." This is very true. The sense of sight is the quickest and easiest of the routes to the mind. Psychologists agree that 85 per cent of all that is learned is learned visually. Twenty per cent more comes through the sense of sight than through all the other senses.

Drawing with chalk, plain or colored, is one appealing way to take advantage of this sense of sight. The Bible instructor will find many uses for chalk illustrations in her work. One of the most effective ways is that of illustrating the words of a hymn as it is sung in the evangelistic meeting. This will deeply impress the words of the song upon the people's hearts. The picture should always be suited to the words, as the song will have little or no significance if the picture fails to catch the harmony and charm of the words and music. Nothing will have been gained, and a good opportunity to teach others of Christ and His love will have been lost if the picture merely attracts the attention of the people and causes them to admire one's artistic ability.

Because the illustration of hymns can be used to great advantage with the appeals given by the evangelist, both song and picture should be selected in harmony with the subject that has been given and in accordance with the general thought of the appeal. Such a drawing will make a deeper impression than any slide or stereopticon picture that could be flashed on the screen during the appeal.

If the evangelist is holding a series of meetings in a place where he cannot use his slides, a series of prepared charts will be an excellent substitute. When Daniel 2 and Daniel 7 are illustrated with chalk it is best to have the figures drawn ahead of time rather than as the evangelist is speaking.

Chalk illustrations used during the song service before the meeting starts may be a means of encouraging early and prompt attendance. A few words of caution may be in order regarding the use of chalk illustrations in the evangelistic meeting. *Do not overdo.* Illustrations should be used with care and rather sparingly if they are to attain their maximum teaching benefit by providing variety, emphasis, and stimulation.

Aside from the public meetings, the Bible instructor will find many uses for chalk illustrations in her own work as she goes from home to home. For example, when studies on the millennium or the 2300-day prophecy are given, colored chalk or black charcoal may be used on white paper to illustrate the points.

Frequently the Bible instructor has to run competition with the children in a home. If she can tell a Bible story and perhaps illustrate it as she talks, she will find no trouble in keeping the children quiet. In order to hear a story later, they will gladly be quiet during the study the mother is having. When the mother sees that the worker is interested in her children, she will feel at ease and will profit much more from the study.

Bible instructors are often called upon to help take charge of the juniors during the camp meeting session. Nothing will help more to gain the attention, respect, and love of the children than the ability to illustrate the stories graphically and thus indelibly impress spiritual lessons upon their hearts.

Not all Bible instructors should or could use chalk illustrations. We all have individual differences and abilities. However, there are some who should use this God-given talent to tell "the old, old story" again and again with every appeal possible. Let it always be used in such a way that it will draw both young and old closer to God. Our work is not to entertain, but to lead men and women, boys and girls, to a deeper, closer, personal realization of God's love for them.

(See *The Ministry*, April, 1948, for more helpful suggestions by Louise Mattausch.)

PART TWO ★ CHAPTER FIVE

Skills in Meeting People

Differing Religious Backgrounds

Our Advent message finds the honesthearted who are still in Babylon. For this reason the Bible instructor needs a broad acquaintance with the backgrounds of the various religious groups. Although time does not permit her to go too deeply into all their beliefs and practices, she should know the main points of faith of the more prominent groups as well as the outstanding confusions of the main isms and cults.

As a Bible instructor enters a new community she should first become intelligent on the different churches represented, and should manifest a friendly spirit toward their ministers as well as members. Good will may be built up for our message, which, when later presented publicly, is likely to stir up prejudice by those who do not really know us. Wherever Adventism has had an opportunity to prove its good works, our differences of belief are not inclined to be paraded by fair-minded Christians. This point should be well regarded in our careful preparation of any field for evangelism. We cannot federate with other denominations because of our firm stand on Bible truth, but there still remain some open doors of mutual Christian interest, which we would do well to try to keep open as long as possible.

There are a number of reasons why Bible instructors as well as ministers should be intelligent on the various churches of the community in which they labor. Cities, towns, and even villages have their own personalities. The people who group together in a city, large or small, are responsible for its characteristics. We must know the ways of these people as well as the doctrines we are to promote among them. To truly know people means that we become thoroughly acquainted with their cultural, historical, and economic backgrounds, including their religious views. This was the skill of the Master Evangelist (John 2:24, 25), and it must be ours today.

Though we as Adventists must hold to our convictions, we are warned by the messenger of the Lord not to exaggerate our differences of belief, but rather to seek an approach by cooperating with other types of believers in some of their legitimate projects. To find some praiseworthy points in favor of these denominations is the true spirit of Christianity. Such gracious ways make friends for the Bible instructor.

But the need for an intelligent approach to the whole problem of meeting those of other religious affiliations is not merely for good will. We also have the responsibility of enlightening our fellow Christians with the prophetic mes-

Skills in Meeting People

sage for this hour. Various doctrinal teachings and practices of these religious groups suggest that we find the proper approaches in an endeavor to create interest for our own doctrines. To suggest at the proper time the points of one's common faith prepares the way for less prejudice when, for the sake of truth, heresy must be courageously exposed. We should not merely be intelligent on what the other group believes, but should also be able to give recognition for its outstanding contributions.

Public libraries today furnish helpful church census information to make our research rather reliable. The progressive Bible teacher will keep her eyes open for interesting, up-to-date information, which should then be carefully filed. She will also scan the section of church notices in the daily newspapers, keeping in touch with the programs of the churches attended by people with whom she is studying.

What to Know About Another Denomination

1. How the church was founded. When? By whom? Where?
2. How the name of the denomination was received.
3. What doctrinal or ethical teachings led to its organization?
4. What progress was made by the church during its early period?
5. What was its influence on Christianity at large?
6. What is its present standing in Christendom?
7. How large is the denomination today? Where its headquarters? Where its strongest churches and institutions?
8. What are its ritual and polity?
9. Is the denomination Fundamentalist or Modernist?
10. What is its attitude on church federation?
11. Is education for youth stressed? Foreign missions?
12. What is its attitude toward the Advent hope, the Sabbath, dress reform, temperance, and health?
13. How to approach these other religionists.

Bibliography

Ferm, Vergilius. *An Encyclopedia of Religion.* New York: The Philosophical Library.

Perry, George Sessions. *Cities of America.* New York: Whittlesey House, McGraw Hill Co.

Religious Bodies. Washington, D.C.: U.S. Department of Commerce, Bureau of the Census, Superintendent of Documents.

Year Book of American Churches. Lebanon, Pa.: Sowers Printing Co.

(See also articles in *The Ministry,* 1945, 1947, 1948, 1949, on various denominations and beliefs.)

Winning Souls From Other Religions

I. *Religious Thinking of Our Times.*
   1. Catholic interpretation of a mystical return of Christ. Associated errors on the state of the dead and destiny of the wicked.
   2. Dispensationalism founded on Catholic interpretation of prophecy. Associated errors of higher criticism, premillennialism, Antichrist, conversion of Jews, Anglo-Israelism, etc.
   3. Confusions of teachings on spiritual gifts. Pentecostalism with its false holiness teachings.
   4. Spiritism in its many forms, including various types of Oriental mysticism.
   5. Pagan philosophies. The superman and Caesar worship.

II. *Special Problems for Bible Instructors.*
   1. Protestantism at large no longer challenger of un-Biblical teachings.
   2. Protestants adopted many Catholic views on prophecy.
   3. Ignorance of church members regarding Christian fundamentals.
   4. Positive teaching of Ten Commandments lost in Dispensationalism.
   5. Conversion, salvation, and sanctification experienced by only a few.
   6. Skeptics and scoffers in the ranks of the church.

III. *Meeting Protestants With Our Message.*
   1. Restoring the lost Advent hope by means of the prophecies.
   2. Clarifying our Protestant position from the Bible and from history.
   3. Setting forth the arrested Reformation and reforms of the remnant church.
   4. Preparing a people to meet the Lord.

IV. *Meeting Catholics With Our Message.*
   1. Respectful attitude in speaking of the Catholic Church, her priesthood, and her heroes.
   2. Acquaintance with Catholic versions of the Bible and her literature.
   3. Thorough knowledge of the papal system, its rise, progress, and climax.
   4. Ability to trace papal power in Bible prophecy.
   5. Knowledge of important Roman Catholic dogmas and their origin as related to the layman.
   6. Recognition of reverence and a love for Scripture on part of many Catholics.
V. *Strengthening Our Approaches.*
   1. Time-worn attacks replaced with up-to-date knowledge of isms.
   2. Methods of presentation and appeal adapted to the progress of our times.

Reaching the Protestant Mind (Calvinism)

The Bible teacher's approach to Presbyterians, Reformed believers, and others of Calvinistic background should receive careful study. We often refer to Adventism as having much in common with Methodism, but in some ways Presbyterianism comes closer to the spirit of Adventism than Methodism. Presbyterians, even more than Methodists, are church anchored, and therefore the Bible instructor should avoid an impression of trying to change their religion. I have found it helpful to suggest to these groups a mutual study of those fundamental teachings which classify both Calvinists and Adventists with the Reformers.

Beginning with a stimulating reassurance of the Inspired Word from the angle of God's supreme authority, I gradually launch out into deeper channels, presenting the still live issues of popery and antichristian heresy. When Calvinists discover that the Reformation, although exposing the man of sin, was retarded on those points stressed by the Advent message today, then they see a logical reason for a movement other than Calvinism. Our message is not antagonistic to Calvinism, but is rather a challenge for Calvinists to bestir themselves to finish the Reformation. I have discovered that this is the greatest argument to drive them out of their smug complacency—and too often their Presbyterian self-sufficiency.

Calvinistic doctrine is authoritarian even beyond the Bible. The candid student of the Word must discover those philosophical elements of belief which, though often beautifully inspiring, are nevertheless definitely un-Scriptural. This authoritarian element becomes pronounced in the Calvinistic study of the doctrine of predestination, where logic holds out against a careful comparison of Scriptural intent. Again, Calvinistic teachings concerning the doctrine of Christian liberty have led to a dangerous liberalism which reveals the decaying elements of Calvinism as a reform religion. There are some positive, unwholesome elements in Calvinism which must be challenged by a timely reformation.

Hair-splitting exegesis destroys the very spirit of the gospel and merely produces controversy instead of winning souls to the truth. The Bible instructor should guard against an overstressing of minor points which suggest disagreements between denominational beliefs, but rather use the prophecies to reveal to the reader the weaknesses of the Calvinistic system. A search for truth must be the objective of Bible study. Prayer and praise are stressed in Calvinistic ethics, and the Bible instructor should cultivate these elements of Christian fellowship in her work, for they will inspire confidence in both the message and its messenger.

While agreeing with truth and commending its practice, the teacher must still continue to teach accurately, progressively, and forcefully, yet never dogmatically. When the inherent dogmatism of Calvinism is caused to clash with the same characteristic of Adventism, the interest is likely to cool off in argumentation. The aim should be for a blending of spirit and a deepening of the principles of truth. The Bible topics should be built in the setting of Presbyterian thought and terminology. The following series of topics is merely suggestive, and may invite further adaptations.

Appropriate Topics for Presbyterians

1. God's Eternal Purpose in Christ.
2. Man's Fall, and God's Salvation.
3. What Does It Mean to Be Converted? (Stress human will and obedience.)
4. The Imminent Return of Christ.
5. The Hand of God in History (Daniel 2).
6. Final Reward of God's Elect (New Earth).
7. The Atonement in Prophecy (2300 Days).
8. Christ Our Mediator (sanctuary).
9. The Judgment in Session.
10. The Law and the Gospel.
11. God's Sign of Sanctification (Sabbath).
12. Is the Lord's Day the Sabbath? (N. T. Sabbath.)
13. Protestantism or Popery? (Change of Sabbath.)
14. The Test of Christian Living (obedience).
15. Christian Stewardship and Missions.
16. Where Are the Dead?
17. The Doom of the Sinner.
18. The Two Resurrections (millennium).
19. Elijah's Reformatory Message (health reform).
20. What Is Christian Liberty? (Dress, amusements.)
21. The Reformation Completed (Revelation 12).
22. The Call Out of Modern Babylon.
23. Significance of Baptism and the Lord's Supper.
24. Spiritual Gifts for the Church.
25. God's Elect and the Prophetic Gift.

Points to Stress With Calvinists

Calvinists firmly believe in the inspiration of the Old as well as the New Testament, and emphasize its devotional daily reading. Since predestination is embedded in Calvinism, an understanding of God's purpose in creation and redemption is fundamental. The significance of the controversy between Christ and Satan must set forth more than the place of the human will; it must reveal the importance of obedience.

Here the lost chord of Calvinism is struck. Its philosophical teaching regarding Christian liberty has a strong influence on the question of ethics, as affecting diet, dress, amusements, and so forth. The keynote is that the Christian uses the world but does not abuse it. Moderation, not abstinence, is taught in the use of wine and liquor and tobacco. The Christian is regulated by his conscience, which must be built up in Christ. Although we may agree with this in theory in large part, there is here an impractical element which does not relieve the abuses in the ranks of the Christian church today.

Strict observance of the Lord's day (Sunday) is stressed because it is to the glory of God to observe a day of the weekly cycle, and Sunday fits into modern practice. There is strong emphasis on the Ten Commandments in other respects, but the Biblical observance of the seventh day as specified by the commandment is not necessary. On these points the Bible teacher may deepen the idea of the supremacy of God, so prominent in Calvinism, and the superiority of His law.

Peace and prosperity are regarded by Calvinists as visible tokens of God's favor. Providence ordains both prosperity and adversity for an individual. Submission to God's will in this respect glorifies Him. Careful critics charge Calvinism as being at the foundation of some of our modern capitalistic abuses. Calvinists believe and have demonstrated that the church was organized to reign, and is entitled to material power. The setting up of Christ's kingdom here and now is confused with other-world-mindedness. The doctrine of separation of church and state, while never positive in Calvinism, has become more befogged since the war. Calvinism today needs a clear reformatory message.

Calvin was not dogmatic on the question of the state of the dead. He simply was not clear on the subject; nor did he seem to regard it as vital. The interpretation of Scripture to aid in an understanding of the subject is to be left with the individual. On this point the church cannot be dogmatic. One does not meet the arbitrary attitude of Methodism.

Calvinists and Adventists agree well on their joint principles on the doctrine of Christian stewardship. It is the Christian's solemn responsibility to enlighten the depraved heathen mind with the gospel. On infant baptism Calvin shows Scriptural inconsistencies, but there are other emphases on baptism which reveal the strength of Calvinistic practice. The same is true with views on the Lord's supper. The ordinance of preparation should be presented by Bible instructors from the standpoint of reclaiming a lost truth in practice. In John 13, Calvinism can find the solution of the problem that has so often challenged Calvinists on their view that infant baptism does not suffice for the revelation of sin and necessary forgiveness in later life. When the truth of the principle of foot washing is understood as being a miniature baptism, the Presbyterian inquirer quickly sees the beauty and satisfaction of this ceremony.

I have always enjoyed studying the Bible with those of Calvinistic background. One feels a kinship and a fellowship in sharing great fundamental Bible truths. Because of the high ideals mutually upheld, this relationship has frequently grown into the deeper experiences of Adventism.

Meeting Dispensationalists

I. *What Is Dispensationalism?*
   1. Dispensationalism's modern champion is Dr. C. I. Scofield.
   2. Scofield Bible interprets prophecy incorrectly and dangerously.
   3. Scofield received his views from "Plymouth Brethren."
   4. Dispensationalism is modern Antinomianism and Jewish Rabbinism.
   5. Imminent return of Christ is theme of past century's evangelical awakening.
   6. Evangelical awakening at first did not include "dispensational" ideas.
   7. Dispensationalism represents Fundamentalists, not Modernists.
   8. Fundamentalists once refuted Dispensationalism, but now generally accept it.

9. Protestantism surrendered historic interpretation of prophecy.
10. Protestantism accepted Catholic Counter Reformation views on prophecy.
11. The basis of dispensational teachings was the futurism of Ribera and Bellarmine.

II. *What Are Errors of Dispensationalism?*
 1. Scofield enumerates "dispensations."
   a. History of world is arbitrarily divided into seven periods. (See Scofield Bible.)

Innocence	Conscience	Human Government	Promise	Law	Grace	Kingdom
Before sin —Eden	Antediluvian Civilization	Postdiluvian Period	Abraham to Exodus	Levitical Era	Church Period	Eternity

   b. Doctrine produces errors such as antinomianism, false ideas of antichrist, secret rapture, Jews returning to Jerusalem, erroneous teachings regarding Christ's kingdom, false hope of second chance.
   c. The word *dispensation* never correctly refers to a period of time. It usually means a stewardship, an act of dispensing, an administration.
   d. The following texts include "dispensation."
      1 Cor. 9:16. "A stewardship has nevertheless been entrusted to me."—Weymouth.
      Eph. 1:10. Read context carefully. (Acts of dispensing.)
      Col. 1:25. Paul is a minister according to God's administration. 1 Cor. 12:28.
 2. There are two main errors.
   a. One is separation of law and grace; an age of law without grace (O.T.), and an age of grace without law (N.T.). It embraces false ideas regarding two covenants. Protestant champions of Ten Commandments are Dr. Adam Clarke, Dr. Barnes, J. Gresham Machen.
   b. The second is a revival of forlorn hope of Israel in Christian form—the soon-expected Messianic kingdom.
 3. Should we follow Scofield or Bible Truth?
   a. The Bible is not of private interpretation. 2 Peter 1:20, 21.
   b. The Word is its own interpreter. Deut. 29:29; Isa. 28:9, 10; 1 Cor. 2:13, 14.
   c. God's plans are not based on man's thinking. Isa. 55:8, 9.

Skills in Meeting People

    d. The prophets searched to understand God's interpretation. 1 Peter 1:9-12.
    e. Theologians and scholars err by not holding to Scripture. Mark 12:13, 24.
    f. Private interpretation brings confusion and destruction. Deut. 4:2; Prov. 30:6; Rev. 22:18, 19.

III. *What Is Scofield's Antinomian Error?* (See *Secret Rapture,* pp. 85-95.)
    1. Observe Scofield Bible note on Galatians 3:24: "The law is a ministry of condemnation, death, and the divine curse."
    2. Paul's cautions against antinomian teachings. Rom. 3:31; Gal. 3:21; Rom. 7:7.
    3. God's Word teaches law converts souls; not a "ministry of condemnation." Ps. 19:7.
    4. The approach to Antinomianism is to teach soundly *ten commandments, two laws, law and gospel, two covenants.*

IV. *What Are Dispensational Antichrist Misconceptions?*
    1. Observe carefully the development of present-day errors of Dispensationalism's Antichrist. The Reformation had challenged Rome to prove that the pope was not antichrist. The pope enlisted Jesuits to produce Scriptural evidence in favor of Papacy. (Jesuits previously were a militaristic order.) The challenge instigated research by Catholic theologians Bellarmine, Ribera, and Alcazar, and resulted in preterist and futurist interpretations of prophetic antichrist.
    2. Modern Dispensationalism has reversed Protestant historic interpretation of prophecy by accepting antichrist of Futurism. Protestants long held to true interpretation, but today even Fundamentalists teach Rome's views of antichrist.
    3. To approach antichrist misconceptions, teach *historic* interpretation of prophecy.

V. *Did Bellarmine's Confusions Counteract Reformation?*
    1. Cardinal Bellarmine, 1542-1621, Italian, combated Protestant claims that pope was antichrist. Counter Reformation had checked Protestantism in Europe. Bellarmine's chief attack was on year-day principle of prophecy. He paved the way for present futurist teachings, by applying apocalyptic symbols to future.
    2. He used the "Gap Theory"—70th week of Daniel 9 was separated from 69th week and placed just before end of world.

The beginning date for 2300 days was 445 B.C. (See diagrams *Evangelistic Sermons II*, p. 112; also read pages 110-113.)
3. He also taught that antichrist was a Jew of tribe of Dan.
4. The crucifixion date was set by Bellarmine at A.D. 38 instead of A.D. 31.
5. Dan. 9:27. One who confirms covenant is not Christ.
6. Dispensationalists teach that the covenant was confirmed with Jews after "secret rapture" and during 70th week. (A Catholic teaching.)
7. Futurism distorted significant prophetic events, and threw them into future in a meaningless way.

VI. *What Futuristic Teachings of Ribera's Did Bellarmine Accept?*
1. Francisca Ribera was a Jesuit, of Spain, 1537-1591.
2. He taught antichrist was a single individual preceded by reappearance of Enoch and Elijah.
3. Antichrist was a Christ-opposing power to appear shortly before the end.
4. Antichrist was to build the temple at Jerusalem and drive out Christian religion. It was a power that would pretend to be God, be received by Jews, and conquer world. There was involved a future period of "tribulation."

VII. *Was Preterism's Erroneous Interpretation Accepted by Calvin?*
1. Luis de Alcazar, Jesuit of Spain, 1554-1613, applied Preterism to the Apocalypse.
2. The views of Alcazar were:
    a. Revelation 1-11 pertained to Jews.
    b. Revelation 12-19 pertained to Pagan Rome.
    c. The three and one-half years was not a definite time period.
    d. Revelation 20 applied to final persecution and day of judgment.
    e. Revelation 21, 22 pertains to church, the New Jerusalem (originated and taught by Augustine).
    f. Alcazar attacked Ribera and Augustine on millennium and resurrection.
    g. He taught that the church has continual inspiration.
3. Reformer Calvin believed the Little Horn was Julius Caesar. Calvin carried some Catholic errors into Protestant church.

VIII. *Was "Secret Rapture" Fallacy of Futurism Accepted by Protestants?*
1. There would be a silent snatching away of the church before "time of Jacob's trouble." Jer. 30:7.

Skills in Meeting People 245

2. There is a false use of the words *parousia* and *apokalupsis*. Matt. 24:30, 31.

   NOTE: The very word translated "coming" in Matthew 24:27 and in 1 Thessalonians 4:15 is the Greek word *parousia*. The words *lightning, voice,* and *shout,* describe the *parousia*.

IX. *Is There Confusion on Two Phases of the Second Advent, Rapture and Revelation?*
   1. The order of events as taught by dispensationalists is:
      a. The *rapture* is that time when Christ comes in the air and secretly snatches from the earth all true believers to unite them with the great throng of resurrected saints. (Variations of ideas on details.)
      b. The *tribulation* is that time during which evil will rapidly develop and antichrist will appear.
      c. The *revelation* is that time when Christ appears in glory to "ascend the throne of earth, the throne of His father David at Jerusalem."
      d. The thousand-year period is that time during which "mankind will be spiritually quickened," and the Jews will have another opportunity for salvation, and their nation, temple service, and sacrificial system will be restored.
   2. To meet rapture and revelation confusions teach accurately texts on Christ's second coming. Understand sequence of events and manner of His coming. Be acquainted with vocabulary of dispensationalists: rapture, revelation, seven years, tribulation, Jacob's trouble, millennial age, tribulation saints, separation (Matt. 25:31, 32), *parousia, apokalupsis,* epiphany, kingdom versus church, reign of antichrist.
   3. Stress: The Lord descends with a *shout;* the *voice* of the Archangel is heard; the *trump* of God is sounded; the Son of man comes in His *glory; all the angels* come with Him; Jesus sits upon the *throne of His glory;* and *"every eye* shall see Him."

Dispensational Kingdom Teachings

The Scofield Bible teaches the kingdom is an "age to come," and makes the kingdom the possession of natural Jews.

I. *What Bible Teaches About Christ's Kingdom.*
   1. Jesus referred to *"kingdom"* more than 100 times; only twice to *"church."*

2. He preached a kingdom message. Matt. 4:17.
3. John also preached a kingdom message, and prepared men for the kingdom. Matt. 3:2.
4. The twelve and the seventy preached a kingdom message. Matt. 4:17; 10:7; Luke 10:9.
5. The entrance into the kingdom is by new birth, not by racial inheritance. Matt. 3:9; John 3:3, 5.
6. The kingdom of grace belongs to Gentiles as well as Jews. Eph. 2:12-14, 19.
7. Even now we are translated into the kingdom of grace. Col. 1:13.
8. The saints enter the kingdom of glory at Christ's second coming. Dan 7:27.
9. In approaching this subject, teach thoroughly such subjects as Daniel 2, 7, kingdoms of grace and glory, and spiritual Israel.

II. *Return of Jews Illusion.*
1. The illusionary hope of restoration of Jewish nation lures millions.
2. Protestants are more confused than Jews themselves.
3. All God's promises to Jews are based on condition of obedience.
4. The remaining 3½ years of 70th week is declared another special period for the Jews.
5. In the past God did all He could to save Israel; He sent prophets and also His Son. Matt. 21:33-46.
6. The promises made to spiritual Israel are found in Rom. 4:13; 9:6-8; Gal. 3:29; Rom. 4:8-12, 17; Gal. 3:7-9; Hosea 13:9, 10, 11.
7. The hope of all ages for Jews and Gentiles is the resurrection of dead.
8. Our approach should clarify God's promises to true Israel.

III. *"Second Chance" Heresy.*
1. Whitby's Postmillennialism confused modern Protestants.
   a. Daniel Whitby, Salisbury, England (1638-1726), was a Universalist.
   b. He projected elaborate "new hypothesis" on 1,000 years in defense of Anglican Church against dissenters.
   c. He also asserted conversion of world; Holy Spirit's outpouring at time of national establishment of Jews and overthrow of pope and Turk; and denominated it as the "first resurrection"; a resurrection of dead churches (Origen's belief).
   d. Whitby taught the universal reign of paradisiacal righteousness, peace, and victory before Second Advent.

Skills in Meeting People

   e. His theory was built on distorted citations of early Fathers—Origen and Justin.
   f. The condition of Europe—new era of missions, Bible societies, increased interest in Jews—contributed to popularity of new teachings. Eminent divines embraced them.
   g. Whitby was supported by Vitringa (1659-1722), but protested by Bengel, Zinzendorf, and other leading men.
   h. Whitby's erroneous teachings handicapped Advent Movement in England, and became background for many modern isms that feature Christ's temporal kingdom and confusions on resurrection.
2. Whitby's heinous doctrine of a second chance during millennium was capsheaf of error.
3. Bible teaches that there is no hope of another chance beyond the grave. Isa. 38:18.
4. *Now* is the accepted time of salvation. Heb. 3:7-15; 2 Cor. 6:2.
5. The close of probation's hour is before Christ's coming. Matt. 13:38-43; 25:31-46; Rev. 22:11, 12.
6. Our approach should be to teach God's great plan of salvation and show Satan's counterplan. He procrastinates salvation and deceives men regarding its conditions. Emphasize the imminent coming of Jesus. Urge the following of each ray of new light.

Fallacy of the Rapture Theory

(The 70th Week of Daniel 9:24-27)

ALMA DuBois

I. *Claims of the Rapture Theory.*
   1. Second coming of Christ to be secret and invisible.
   2. Angels to take one of elect here and one there to meet Him in the air.
   3. Secret coming to introduce special period of seven years.
   4. At end of seven years Christ to come again.
   5. At beginning of seven years antichrist to appear as a world prince—"Beast-king" (supposed to symbolize composite beast of Revelation 13:1-10).
   6. Claim: At beginning of seven-year period world ruler to enter into league with Jews to protect them.
   7. Jews, persecuted in many countries, to flock to Palestine, believing it to be safe. (Ezekiel 40-47 will be fulfilled.)
   8. Temple to be built on ancient temple site. (Now occupied by

Mohammedan mosque. Ancient Mosaic sanctuary to be resumed.)
9. After three and one-half years antichrist to repudiate his treaty with Jews.
10. This to "cause the sacrifice and oblation to cease" in midst of seven years.
11. Instead of adoration of God by Jews in temple, rapturists say, worship of antichrist, beast-king, to become established religion of world.
12. This event in middle of seven years to mark beginning of great tribulation of Christ's prophecy in Matthew 24:21, 22.
13. Tribulation to be caused by "violation of the covenant" between antichrist and Jewish people.
14. Man worship to be substituted for worship of Jehovah in Jewish temple at Jerusalem.

II. *The Theory Exploded.*
1. Fundamental principle of Scriptural interpretation violated.
2. The seventieth week of the seven-year period of the prophecy of Daniel 9:24-27 source of the seven-year period of rapture theory. "Seventy weeks are determined upon thy people."
3. Each period to follow the other in unbroken succession. Seventy weeks—7 weeks, 62 weeks, and 1 week, or 490 prophetic days or years.
4. A day, or literal year (Moffatt and Goodspeed—70 weeks of years). Eze. 4:6.
5. When 490-year period began—"going forth of the commandment." Dan. 9:25.
6. When Daniel given vision, 70-year desolation of Jerusalem about ended, and now there was to be a restoration. Jer. 25:11; 2 Chron. 36:21.
7. Three decrees by Persian kings—Cyrus (Ezra 1:1-11); Darius (Ezra 6:1); Artaxerxes (Ezra 6:14; Ezra 7).
8. Complete decree by Artaxerxes in seventh year of his reign, or 457 B.C. Four hundred and eighty-three years (69 prophetic weeks) of the 490 years were to reach to Messiah. Dan. 9:24-27. Christ the Messiah. John 1:41.
9. Decrees fully effected in fall of 457 B.C. Ezra 7:9. Four hundred and eighty-three years would reach over into fall of A.D. 27.
10. Jesus anointed by Holy Ghost. Matt. 3:16; Acts 10:38. Baptized by John in A.D. 27. Luke 3:21.
11. Messiah "cut off" (Christ's vicarious atoning death on cross). Dan. 9:26. "In the midst of the week He shall cause the sacrifice and the oblation to cease." Dan. 9:27. Seventieth week reaches

from fall of A.D. 27 to A.D. 34. Halfway between these points Jesus died—spring, A.D. 31.

12. His death caused sacrifice of Mosaic law to cease, because He as "Lamb of God" was antitype of all sacrificial offerings of earthly sanctuary. John 1:29, 36; Heb. 9:8-12; 10:1-9.
13. "Reconciliation for iniquity." Dan. 9:24. Reconciled to God by death of Jesus. Rom. 5:10. Veil of temple rent. Matt. 27:51. Every event of seventieth week of Daniel 9:24 was between A.D. 27 and A.D. 34.
14. Rapturists acknowledge 69 weeks of Daniel 9:25 to be 483 days, or prophetic years, reaching from Persian king to first advent of Christ. Detach seventieth week from 70-week period, which is unit, and carry it over into future and mark it beginning of Rapture. But this, "private interpretation." 2 Peter 1:20. Seventieth week, with all its events, over 1900 years in past. (Some teach antichristian power arose in early century of Christian Era. Need not wait for it in future.)
15. Rapturists concur that "little horn" of Daniel 7:8, 25 is "man of sin" of 2 Thessalonians 2:3-8; composite beast of Revelation 13:1-10, 18 is antichristian power that would oppose true church of God.
16. Daniel saw in vision four beasts arise from sea—lion, bear, leopard, and terrible monster with ten horns. Saw another horn among ten, displacing three. This eleventh horn symbol of antichrist. Angel Gabriel told Daniel that the four horns were four beasts, or four kingdoms. Ten horns were the ten kingdoms. Dan. 7:17, 23, 24. Little horn that arose was antichrist appearing among ten kingdoms which succeeded Roman world power.
17. Ten kingdoms were progenitors of modern nations of Western Europe. Collapse of Roman Empire in A.D. 476. Antichrist power foretold in prophecy arose among them. Since it arose after ten horns came up, must arise after A.D. 476.
18. "Shall wear out the saints of the most High." Dan. 7:25. A persecuting power. This power was Papacy, or Roman power. Arose in past, not future.
19. A resurgence of this power after healing of deadly wound of composite beast in Revelation 13.
    (See *Watchman Magazine,* August, 1945, article by J. C. Stevens, "Is the Rapture Theory True?"; "The Secret Rapture," by Varner Johns; *Prophetic Faith of Our Fathers,* by L. E. Froom, volume 2, chapter 22.)

Bibliography

Exposing Dispensationalism

Allis, Oswald T. *Prophecy and the Church.* Philadelphia: The Presbyterian and Reformed Publishing Company.

Johns, Varner J. *The Secret Rapture and the Antichrist.* Mountain View, Calif.: Pacific Press Publishing Association.

Mauro, Philip. *The Gospel of the Kingdom.* Boston, Mass.: Hamilton Brothers.

———. *The Hope of Israel—What Is It?* Hamilton Brothers.

McGavern, C. G. *Rapture or Resurrection?* Grand Rapids, Mich.: W. B. Eerdmans Publishing Co.

Murray, George L., *Millennial Studies.* Grand Rapids, Mich.: Baker Book House.

Peters, Fred J. *The Present Antichrist.* Hamilton Brothers.

Advocating Dispensationalism

Beckwith, George D. *God's Prophetic Plan.* Grand Rapids, Mich.: Zondervan Publishing House.

Bradbury, John W. (compiler and editor). *The Sure Word of Prophecy.* New York: Fleming H. Revell Company.

Cooper, David L. *The 70 Weeks of Daniel.* Los Angeles, Calif.: Biblical Research Society.

De Haan, M. H. *Revelation* (35 Simple Studies on the Major Themes in Revelation). Zondervan Publishing House.

———. *The Second Coming of Jesus.* Zondervan Publishing House.

Hamilton, Floyd E. *The Basis of Millennial Faith.* W. B. Eerdmans Publishing Company.

Ironside, H. A. *The Great Parenthesis.* Zondervan Publishing House.

———. *Wrongly Dividing the Word of Truth.* New York: Loizeaux Brothers.

Jessop, Harry E. *The Day of Wrath.* Fleming H. Revell Company.

Kromminga, D. H. *The Millennium in the Church.* W. B. Eerdmans Publishing Company.

McClain, Alva J. *Daniel's Prophecy of the Seventy Weeks.* Zondervan Publishing House.

Scofield, C. I. *Rightly Dividing the Word of Truth.* Loizeaux Brothers.

Thiessen, Henry C. *Will the Church Pass Through the Tribulation?* Loizeaux Brothers, Bible Truth Depot.

Working for Catholics

It is not because Roman Catholics are more important to the Advent message than Episcopalians, Presbyterians, Lutherans, or any other group that special attention on how to deal with them is here given. To be sure, Catholicism is an antichristian power, and a great challenge to our cause, but a similar case could be built up for many other religious bodies, Christian and unchristian. It is rather because Catholicism challenges us on our *methods* of approach in bringing Bible truth to this branch of the Christian faith. Therefore Bible instructors and ministers should be made aware of the best way to work for Catholics, for when once won to our message these people make devoted Adventists.

The winning of Catholics to our faith is not growing easier. Quoting Miss Mary Walsh, an experienced Bible instructor in our ranks, and one who grew up in a Catholic environment, we learn:

"Every year the Catholic Church has a great influx of members taken from the ranks of Protestants. This is not accomplished without an effort on the part of the church and its lay members. At intervals missions are held in the various churches, and though these services are primarily for the church's own communicants, she takes advantage of these occasions to gain converts by devoting special services to non-Catholics.

"In these services artful teachers give instruction on subjects that interest curious Protestants. The seeming piety and the dignity with which their services are conducted have an enchanting effect upon those who attend. The liturgical objects, the illuminated altar, the expressive gestures of the officiating priest, the air of scholasticism, the mysticism with which the church's doctrines are clothed—these are all designed to attract and to charm. Then, too, the Catholic Church is leaving nothing undone in promoting her doctrines before the world through the medium of the radio, the press, outdoor meetings, and the Catholic Youth Movement. Thus she is not only gaining accessions from the Protestant world but is steadily growing in prestige.

"What has led the Roman Church to utilize all the resources at her command? A vision—coupled with a firm belief in the bull issued by Pope Boniface VIII, declaring the Catholic Church to be the only true, holy, and apostolic church, and that outside of her, there is neither salvation nor remission of sins."

Miss Walsh then presents a real challenge to our workers in these words: "If the Catholic Church can organize her forces, send them out bearing credentials of this character, and gain converts, how much more should we, as members of the true church, invested with the last message, organize our forces and capitalize on every available means to promote our doctrines among these deluded but precious souls!

"The neglect of reaching Catholics is largely due to a complex that most Protestants have when it comes to dealing with the doctrines of Catholicism. This lack of confidence has kept many from studying with Catholics. The manner in which the doctrine under question is approached from the Bible, as well as the tone of the voice, will have a telling effect upon the hearers. When a Catholic finds a worker who is conversant with Catholic teachings and able to refute them from the Scriptures and even the Catholic Bible, confidence is established, and thus the way is opened for further instruction."

Knowing Catholicism

Workers who have background and experience in dealing with Catholics are best able to help those who are unfamiliar with Catholic thinking and practice. But the Catholic problem is not just an American problem. It has its roots deeply imbedded in European soil, and has flourished in South America as well as in many other lands. Although there are in all these countries some general Catholic problems, it is important that the gospel worker understand that there must still be a difference in our methods when dealing with Catholics in areas where the church predominates and where it has to compete with the strength of Protestantism. On this point Robert Leo Odom, for years a minister in Spain, and a specialist in dealing with Catholics, brings excellent counsel:

"In working for Catholics many blunders are due to a failure to understand their mental attitude toward religious matters. There is a difference, first of all, between Catholics of Protestant lands and those of Catholic countries. The former are no doubt more difficult to approach. They are better educated. They frequently read and cite the Catholic Scriptures. Their teachings are more adapted to resisting Protestant influences and to refuting its arguments. The clergy, as a rule, are gentlemanly and courteous toward non-Catholics. The more sinister doctrines of Romanism are virtually omitted from the catechisms, or so glossed over and tempered down that they do not shock the finer sensibilities.

"Catholics in Protestant lands have an opportunity to observe Protestantism at close hand. The increasing number of sects and conflicting beliefs, the laxity in morals and discipline, the lack of authority, and the modern trend to liberalism, are all evidence to the Catholic that he has nothing to gain by leaving his own church. So Rome holds her own and grows in these lands.

"On the other hand, in Catholic countries the masses are more illiterate. The Bible is scarcely known by the layman. Romish doctrines appear in their more hideous forms, and are practiced more in keeping with their nature. The clergy are more insolent, intolerant, and cruel toward dissident faiths. A great effort for years has been made to stamp out and vilify Protestantism, and the very word is itself odious to Catholic ears. Catholics often believe that Protestants 'protest against God, religion, the church, and everything that is good.'

"Had Protestants been true to the Bible, the name 'Protestant' might be the symbol of something very different from what it is today. To the Catholic it means a religious Bolshevist. But we as a people are distinct from those the world at large denominates 'Protestant.' So I prefer to tell Catholics that I am a Seventh-day Adventist, when it is necessary to identify myself. It will often close their ears if you say you are a Protestant, whereas the word 'Adventist' may raise an inquiry. And Catholics themselves, when once acquainted with us, often consider us a distinct people from Protestants as a body.

"The Catholic is very much prejudiced, and no marvel. Probably born of a devout mother, baptized soon after his birth, perhaps named after the saint on whose day he was born, educated under the care of the religious school, married according to the laws of the church, expecting the last sacrament in the hour of death, burial in consecrated ground, and that he shall be prayed for after his death, he considers the church the custodian of his soul from the cradle to the hereafter.

"The field of religious thought is severely circumscribed by the church. Religious literature must bear the mark of approval by the hierarchy before it is regarded as safe reading for the Catholic layman. He fears to peruse what the church has proscribed. If the Bible is permitted to be read, it must have approved notes (in some versions interpolated words and phrases in the text itself), in order that the reader shall see as the church sees. To him, his is the true and only church, which Christ Himself founded. It would be unreasonable to expect him to go to another communion to worship.

Working Along Tactfully

"Minds which have been kept in spiritual bondage do not appreciate the value of liberty. The ability to draw them out, to lead them to investigate, counts largely in winning this people. Much depends upon the first contact. Eyes that are unaccustomed to the light must not have the full glare of the sun shot into them suddenly. Begin with subjects which

Skills in Meeting People

do not involve controversy, and lead your hearers over common ground to points where there is divergence of belief.

"Christ's regard for the human soul is reason enough for using tact in our work. Tact does not mean deception. It is to understand the mind, and approach it in the best manner. It does not mean that we should master papal theology (few Catholics have done that), though the reading of standard catechisms is useful.

"A positive and explanatory method is better than argument. One may explain his subject so that his hearers will listen and assent, though unconscious at the time that this acceptance is leading them from their own faith; whereas the same theme, taken up in an argumentative manner, may make them conscious of the fact that you are tearing to pieces one of their tenets, and, feeling offended, they will leave to return no more. Catholics learn a great deal by contrast, as did the Jews from the life and teachings of Jesus. Many false doctrines are self-evident without mention when the truth is known. . . .

"As soon as possible try to make a personal contact with the people and visit them. Leave as many of the controverted points as possible for personal visits. Then these subjects may be studied together from the Bible itself. Never raise objections for discussion. Let the people do that. The devil will suggest enough without our help. . . .

"Catholics teach the pre-existence of Christ, the virgin birth, obedience to the ten commandments, tithing, and (in the creed) that Jesus will come again to judge the quick and the dead. They also believe in the resurrection of the body. Of course they differ with us in many points on these subjects, but there is much that can be used as common ground. Almost any of our doctrines may be so presented as to be attractive, without an offensive and antagonizing tone.

"Personal work is very essential in working for Catholics. The public meeting may be a means of drawing them to us, but as soon as possible get them to read or to take Bible studies. They are usually won one at a time rather than by altar appeals. Pray with them and for them, and God's power will be with you to bless. The battle is half won when they can be visited and talked with about their souls. While hundreds may never respond, some will. Never give up, but press on prayerfully and carefully, and win."—*The Ministry,* August, 1932.

Elder Odom's counsel stresses the principle of finding common ground with Catholics. His suggestions apply to both public and personal evangelism, but he strongly advocates an early personal contact with them.

In an attempt to get better acquainted with the problems of Catholicism in evangelism, it was found profitable to give careful attention to the fifteen principles in *Gospel Workers,* pages 325-329. Briefly these are the following:

Principles in Working for Catholics

1. Make allowance for those who do not have the background of Scripture, especially at the outset.

2. Wisely build "precept upon precept; line upon line."

3. Avoid all unkind thrusts and allusions, especially in our literature.

4. Refrain from attacking personalities. It brings a reaction on our own work.

5. Learn Christ's methods and cultivate His spirit.

6. The habit of giving thrusts strengthens with repetition and must be repented of.

7. Every unwise word is treasured up by the prince of darkness, and will bring persecution to God's children.

8. Offense will come, but we must be cautious and restrain all unnecessary statements in defense of truth.

9. Never censure or ridicule Catholics who are deceived and groping their way out of error.

10. Reveal Christ's spirit by exposing error with "pitying tenderness."

11. Never use Satan's weapons. He will turn them upon those who use them.

Skills in Meeting People

12. Walk humbly before God. We grieve Christ by harshness and un-Christlike thrusts.

13. Give the message without apology, but do not thrust, crowd, or condemn.

14. Though in error, many Catholics are still conscientious Christians, and God works for them.

15. Guard against selfish considerations, false reasoning, and false excuses. They bring the worker into a perverse state of mind and heart.

Working for People in Catholic Lands

The majority of people in South America are Catholics or of Catholic extraction, with no interest or background for Christianity. They need to be taught the very rudiments of faith, prayer, and Bible study. The following points of instruction by Walter Schubert may be adapted to people in other Catholic lands.

I. *Teaching Prayer and Exercising Faith.*
   1. The Bible instructor first presents a very simple study on prayer. She suggests how we learn to pray. The reader is then invited to join the worker in prayer. Kneeling is suggested as the proper posture in prayer.
   2. Next the teacher begins her practical lesson by framing a simple sentence petition to be repeated by the learner. Other sentences are then added in the same manner. (Catholics follow the words of their priests in prayer.) The beginning of a prayer should be a simple salutation to God, addressing Him directly in the name of Jesus, not Mary or the saints. This point needs explanation. Prayer is always an act of reverence. Teacher-directed praying continues until the reader gains enough confidence to pray independently.
   3. In a progressive way the Bible instructor continues to explain the wonderful privileges of prayer. The learner soon grasps that he may bring all his problems to God in prayer, his minor as well as greater requests. New-found comfort in prayer now brings added assurance to the learner while he by himself practices praying.
   4. The next step in the art of praying may be family devotions. When family worship becomes established in the home, then the prayer habit is becoming well set.

5. Very soon the new believer's voice is heard in prayer at the weekly prayer meeting, in the Sabbath school, or young people's meeting. Prayer confidence soon brings joy into group praying.
6. Family events as births, birthday dedications, marriages, sicknesses, deaths, and funerals all call for special prayer.
7. As he enlists his unsaved loved ones and friends to pray, the new convert now grows conscious of power in prayer. Often whole communities are made prayer conscious by the influence of some humble Seventh-day Adventist.

II. *Teaching the Use of the Bible.*
1. About 90 per cent of South Americans are said to have no contact with the Bible. Ignorance and superstition are rampant. Many have never seen a Bible. The instructor should provide a brief and very simple history of the Scriptures.
2. Next teach how the Bible should be handled and studied; the meaning of the words *Bible, Old* and *New Testament, chapter,* and *verse.* Show how these chapters and verses are located. Teach the abbreviations for the books of the Bible, chapter, and verse. Provide simple drills to establish these facts.
3. After a short acquaintance with the use of the Bible, begin to teach them how to memorize the books of the Bible and also familiar texts.
4. Instruct how to study the Sabbath school lesson. Demonstrate in a simple way just how the lesson is prepared for a Sabbath school recitation. Bible study can become a habit around the daily lesson study.
5. Soon the memorization of psalms and special chapters of the Bible will provide strength for test and trial.
6. Many have remarkable memory faculties. If the youth are encouraged to memorize doctrinal passages, their elders soon follow their example.

Henry F. Brown has also had a seasoned experience in working for Catholics. Observe how Elder Brown, in the following outline, builds his points on Peter's statements—a valuable technique. His Bible-study sequence is most logical. It will be an excellent guide for Bible instructors who are asked to teach Catholics, perhaps for the first time in their experience.

Topics for Catholics

Refer to the Catholic position on Peter as "The First of the Accepted Popes," and "The Beginner of the Line of Papal Succession."

Refer to Peter's epistles and sermons as infallible and inspired.

1. The State of the Dead. Acts 2:29, 34; 13:36.
2. Forgiveness of Sins. Acts 2:38.
3. Baptism. Acts 2:38.
4. Indwelling of the Holy Spirit. Acts 2:33, 38.
5. Jesus Our Redeemer. Acts 2:32.
6. The Resurrection. Acts 2:27.
7. The New Earth. Acts 3:21; 2 Peter 3:10-12.
8. The Judgment. Acts 10:42.
9. The New Birth. 1 Peter 1:3, 23.
10. Second Coming of Christ. 1 Peter 1:7, 13.
11. Christ the Creator. Acts 4:10.
12. Christ the Soul Mediator. Acts 4:12.
13. Holy Living. 1 Peter 1:16; 2:1, 11.
14. Obedience. 1 Peter 1:22.
15. Religious Liberty. Acts 4:19.
16. Clean and Unclean Meats. Acts 10:14.
17. Rock Christ, Not Peter. 1 Peter 2:4, 6, 7.
18. Peter Not Pope. Acts 10:26.
19. Priesthood of Believers Not Hierarchy. 1 Peter 2:5, 9.
20. God Hears Individual Prayer. 1 Peter 3:12.
21. Christian Witnessing. 1 Peter 3:15.
22. The Nearness of the End. 1 Peter 4:7.
23. Life of Prayer. 1 Peter 4:7.
24. Endurance of Trial. 1 Peter 4:12.
25. Existence of Satan. 1 Peter 5:8.
26. Fallen Angels. 2 Peter 2:4.
27. Rome Is Babylon. 1 Peter 5:13.
28. The Prophecies. 2 Peter 1:19-21.
29. Apostasy of the Early Church. 2 Peter 2:1.
30. Destruction of the Wicked. 2 Peter 3:7.
31. Preparation for Christ's Coming. 2 Peter 3:14.
32. The Sabbath. Peter was present when the Saviour said, "The Son of man is Lord also of the Sabbath." Mark 2:28.
33. Peter puts approval on Paul's writings. 2 Peter 3:15. In Catholic usage this is equivalent to *Nihil Obstat* (there is no objection).

This provides a wide field from which to prove many other truths by using Peter's writings, all on the premise that Saint Peter was the first pope. (*The Ministry,* April, 1947.)

The sound counsel of the late Elder N. H. Kinzer, whose labors in Catholic lands gave him an unusually broad experience in bringing the message to many Catholics, will be helpful to Bible instructors as well as evangelists. He introduces these suggestions with the following remarks: "Tact is an outstanding factor requisite in dealing with any person or group, of whatever religious persuasion. But this is particularly true in winning Roman Catholics to present truth."

Do's and Don'ts in Reaching Catholics

Refrain from putting anything in your advertising matter which might suggest that you are a Protestant, or even a religious worker.

Try always to overcome prejudice by being friendly.

Keep on common ground with them until they are prepared for more difficult matter.

Don't talk about the faults in their religion, or against the clergy of their church.

Don't argue with them.

Respect their sincerity.

Mention the virgin Mary often in your first sermons, even calling her the "blessed among women." Always be respectful in the use of the name.

If you use slides, it is well to show pictures often of the virgin Mary; also of our Lord as a babe.

Mention some Catholic friend or friends you may have.

Speak often of the good things in the Catholic belief (especially in private studies or conversation)—their charity work, their desire and endeavor to maintain world peace, and so forth.

In your first public prayers, make use of the Lord's prayer *according to the Catholic version of the Scriptures.*

Use the term *Holy Scriptures,* and not *Bible.*

Use the Catholic Creed, and make common use of the Catholic version of the Scriptures.

Call Jesus "Our Lord," and Peter "Saint Peter," etc.

Sing and teach songs that do not arouse prejudice.

When quoting from or referring to magazines or newspapers, make use of some of the local Catholic organs. (*The Ministry*, January, 1937.)

Steps in Reaching Catholics

MARY E. WALSH

One of the first steps in dealing with the Catholic is to prove to his satisfaction that the Bible is an inspired book. And by all means use the Catholic Bible in working with them, as it is most important to establish confidence by demonstrating that it is their Bible which is inspired, and not some Protestant book which they have heard about. Catholics, generally, are not familiar with either the Catholic or the Protestant Bible, as they are not permitted to read or study this infallible guide without the church's interpretation.

1. TEACH PROPHECY, TEACHINGS OF JESUS.—One of the best means of convincing a Catholic that the Bible is true and speaks with divine authority is through the study of the prophecies. The prophecies concerning the Messiah are most attractive and interesting, for as the Catholic observes in the New Testament Scriptures the fulfillment of the Old Testament prophecies, his confidence is strengthened. The study of the life and teachings of Jesus appeals to him, and it is essential to place due emphasis on the fact that Jesus is the center of every doctrine we teach. A Catholic has great respect for the very name of Jesus, and we should always mention this name with reverence and respect. When offering prayer, it is always essential to kneel, if we would make a favorable impression, for Catholics kneel reverently during prayer.

The prophecy of Matthew 24 may be presented with good effect, for the fact that this prophecy contains the words of

Jesus Himself will appeal to the Catholic. Thus there is brought to his attention the nearness of the end of this world's history, and the preparation which is necessary in order to meet Jesus when He returns for all who hear His word and obey His voice.

2. APPROACHES TO STATE-OF-THE-DEAD DOCTRINE.—The subject of the sleep of the dead should be carefully explained. This is one of the most important subjects to present to a Catholic, for much depends upon a correct understanding of this truth. His preconceived ideas concerning hell, purgatory, and the invocation of saints are all at stake. If it is explained to his comprehension and satisfaction that the dead are neither in heaven nor in hell, and the condition of the dead is clearly brought to view, then he begins to lose confidence in his preconceived convictions, and becomes more willing to accept light on other themes to be presented according to their relative importance.

3. THE MASS AS RELATED TO PURGATORY.—The mass is a ceremony which involves all Catholic believers, and so great is its power that it holds every individual a helpless captive to its bondage. For anyone to absent himself from mass when physically able to attend, is considered a mortal sin and endangers the soul with eternal destruction. Like every other rite of the Catholic Church, the mass is a means of enlarging the coffers of the church, and in addition to the money paid in for mass in behalf of the individual suppliant, vast sums are exacted from the people to pay for masses for the dead.

As to the manner in which the sanctity of the mass is presented to the people, the following quotation from a standard Catholic work is cited:

"After consecration, God fixes His eyes upon the altar. 'There is My beloved Son,' He says, 'in whom I am well pleased.' To the merits of the offering of that victim He can refuse nothing. You remember the story of the holy priest who prayed for his friend who, as God has apparently made known

Skills in Meeting People

to him, was in purgatory. There came to him the thought that he could do nothing better than offer the holy sacrifice of the Mass for his friend's soul, and at the moment of the consecration he took the host in his hands, and said, 'Holy and eternal Father, let us make an exchange. Thou holdest the soul of my friend, which is in purgatory, and I hold the body of Thy Son, which is in my hands. Well, deliver my friend, and I offer Thee Thy Son with all the merits of His death and passion.' And, indeed, at the moment of the elevation he saw the soul of his friend going up to heaven all radiant with glory."—BLESSED J. M. VIANNEY, *Eucharistic Meditations,* pp. 124, 125.

There is a set price for a requiem and for low mass, yet each year in the month of November there is a *special sale*. At such a time envelopes are passed out, containing a blank upon which the purchaser may write as many names as he desires, and by enclosing the specified sum, he is assured that for each name a special mass will be offered, which will become effective in lessening the penalty in purgatory. These sales of special masses take place the world around, and multiplied thousands of masses are purchased. But according to Rev. R. L. Conway, of the Paulist Fathers, in a book entitled *The Question-Box Answers,* "the Church allows the priest to receive money for only one Mass a day; and if more Masses are asked for than he can say, he is bound to have them said by other priests."—Page 458. Consider the situation: These inducements to purchase special masses are made in every Catholic church throughout the world, so to whom can the devout Catholic go for the additional masses which he pays for? The whole thing is a fraud and a delusion.

The words of the apostle Peter seem fraught with new significance in the light of this actual situation: "Through covetousness shall they [the priests] with feigned words make merchandise of you: whose judgment now of a long time lingereth not, and their damnation slumbereth not," 2 Peter 2:3.

This delusion is carried still further, in that after the required amount of money is paid, and hopes are raised to heights of joy and confidence in the belief that loved ones in purgatory will be benefited thereby, the people are confronted with the uncertainty that "all Masses and prayers for the dead are applied 'by way of suffrage'—that is, are dependent on God's secret mercy and will, who in His infinite justice may apply to another soul altogether the Masses said for a certain individual. . . . The value of each Mass is infinite, but we never know with perfect certainty whether or not God has applied it to the individual soul for whom it has been offered."—R. L. CONWAY, *Question-Box Answers,* pp. 460, 461.

A still further authentic statement on this point is, "No one can be certain with the certainty of faith, that he received a true sacrament, because the sacrament cannot be valid without the intention of the minister, and no one can see another's intention."—CARDINAL BELLARMINE, *Disput, Contooy. De Justific III, V. 115.*

4. TRANSUBSTANTIATION AND THE PRIESTHOOD.—Associated with the mass is the great delusion of transubstantiation, which to the Catholic means that the bread and the wine of the sacrament are changed into the actual body, blood, soul, and divinity of Jesus Christ. This involves the erroneous teaching concerning the power of the priest. The following quotation will give some idea of the doctrine which is taught:

"Behold the power of the priest. The tongue of the priest makes God from a morsel of bread. It is more than creating the world. Some one said, 'Does St. Philomena, then, obey the Cure D'ars? Certainly, she may well obey him, since God obeys him. The blessed Virgin cannot make her divine Son descend into the host. A priest can, however simple he may be. How great is the priest. He will only rightly understand himself in heaven. . . . To understand it on earth would make one die, not of fear, but of love."—*Eucharistic Meditations,* p. 112.

Transubstantiation received its first endorsement at the Fourth Lateran Council, held A.D. 1215. But the final stamp of approval was placed upon it at the Council of Trent, held A.D. 1545-63, and the following decision, as printed in the report of that council, is significant:

"That by the consecration of the bread and wine a change is wrought of the bread's whole substance into the substance of Christ our Lord's Body, and of the wine's whole substance into the substance of His Blood, which change has been by the Holy Catholic Church suitably and properly called Transubstantiation."—*Question-Box Answers,* pp. 416, 417.

5. TEACHING SCRIPTURE.—The remedy for all these gross errors of Catholicism is found in the Word of God. When its flaming searchlight is focused upon these superstitions, darkness is dispelled and the glorious light of the Sun of Righteousness arises with healing in His wings. In the ninth and tenth chapters of Hebrews, the apostle Paul clearly emphasizes that Christ died *"once for all,"* which is exactly contrary to the teaching of the Catholics, "that at the moment of consecration the Lamb of God lies mystically slain upon the altar, for the sacrifice of Calvary and the altar are the same."—*Shall I Be a Priest?* p. 14.

On the altar in every Catholic church there is a compartment which contains the host, known as the "holy place." The apostle Paul states, however, "Christ is not entered into the holy places made with hands." Heb. 9:24. Such texts as Hebrews 10:10-12, 14; Revelation 1:18 prove that Christ died once, and that the sacrifice was complete.

* * * * *

The book *The Wine of Roman Babylon,* by Mary Walsh, is well known to our workers. It is most helpful in dealing with Catholics. It sets forth the various doctrines and practices of the Roman Catholic Church, explaining more in detail the arguments to be employed by the Bible teacher. Mystery of the mass, purgatory, and other Romish teachings should be well understood by every worker.

Approach to the Jewish Problem

RACHEL DZIECIOLSKA

"How then shall they call on Him in whom they have not believed? and how shall they believe in Him of whom they have not heard? and how shall they hear without a preacher?" Rom. 10:14, 15.

The Bible instructor who labors for the Jewish people should be acquainted with their fundamental beliefs, habits, traditions, and history. She should try to explore the soul of the people. She should feel a burden to bring them the light, and she should love them.

For the benefit of those who are not acquainted with the more intimate side of the Jewish life, here is a short summary. It is by no means exhaustive or detailed, but may serve as a basis of study for the Bible instructor who contemplates working among the lost sheep of Israel.

1. MESSIAH.—The word *Christ* always causes the orthodox Jew to become angry. There have been so many cruel things done in the name of Christ, and the Jew has been taught to associate that holy name with all things cruel. At the same time the Jew loves to hear the word Messiah, and loves to talk about Him. The Bible instructor should bear this in mind, and use *Messiah* when speaking of the Son of God.

2. JEWISH CONCEPTION OF JESUS IN NEW TESTAMENT.— Very few Jews have ever held the New Testament in their hands. To the orthodox Jew this is an unclean book and belongs only to the Gentiles. It is a sin for a Jew to touch it. The name of Jesus is not to be pronounced at all. That is why the Jews are not acquainted with the gospel narratives or with the personality of Jesus. They still wait for the Messiah, and this is the only hope that has kept them as a nation until now.

Many of the Jews believe that the so-called coming of the Messiah means the returning of their race to Palestine, and this they determine to hasten. This is the backbone of the modern Zionist movement. To them the settlement of a million Jews in Palestine will solve the problem and end the two-thousand-year dispersion. To this group of Jews, who are on the verge of atheism, the Bible instructor should have a different approach. I believe, however, Reform Jews are more readily approached than the orthodox Jews, for they will discuss, read, and investigate.

3. DIFFICULTIES IN ACCEPTING CHRISTIANITY.—It is difficult to make a Jew understand that to believe in the gospel of the Messiah is to believe in the real and true Judaism. To the ordinary orthodox Jew a person who accepts Jesus as the Messiah has really given up his religion and accepted another belief. The Bible instructor should realize that such a person is having a very serious problem to face. Not only are his people displeased with him but, according to their rabbinical and traditional law, they are forbidden to have anything more to do with him. They will do all in their power to persecute him, even to take his life if necessary.

4. CHURCH ATTENDANCE.— (Do not refer to a house of worship as a "church." Use *synagogue* or *temple*.) Orthodox Jews hold synagogue services three times every day: at six o'clock in the morning (shaharith), at three o'clock in the afternoon (minhah), and at sunset in the evening (maarib). They do not pray from the heart but recite prayers from a prayer book. The prayer kaddish, which is offered at the anniversary of the death of a dear one, can be prayed only in public service in the synagogue. According to the Talmudic teachings, this prayer is of no effect if it is prayed in private.

5. DEATH.—The Jews generally believe that their souls at death go to heaven to stay in the paradise of God. Once a year on the anniversary day the soul returns to the grave to hear the petitions of the family in order to intercede before God in their behalf.

6. THE MEZUZAH.—On the right side of the entrance of his house the Jew has a sign which signifies to everyone that it is a Jewish home. It is a very old sign, and it is called the

mezuzah. The word means "door post." In many homes it is also fastened on the door of every room. The mezuzah, which is a cylindrical case made of olive wood from Palestine, contains a parchment on which the words of Deuteronomy 6:4-9 are written. The Jews believe the mezuzah keeps the evil spirit away and makes the house holy. As they enter the home and on leaving it they kiss the mezuzah.

7. THE TALMUD.—Although the Jews believe in the Old Testament, it is not as important to them as the Talmud and tradition. The Jews are told that Moses received not only the literal law from God on Mount Sinai but also the oral law. This was handed down from generation to generation, until during the second, fourth, and sixth centuries these traditions, ceremonies, rites, customs, and observances were reduced to writing in a book called the Talmud. This book is regarded by the rabbis as a divine book which has to be kept in the same way as the Torah (the five books of Moses). The Talmud is the foundation of the Jewish religion, and that is why the Jews do not know the prophecies relating to the coming of the Messiah.

8. WOMEN.—Judaism is essentially a religion for men. The girls do not get any training in the law. Most of the orthodox Jewish girls and women are, therefore, without any knowledge of the law, and live in the tradition of their parents. In the Jewish synagogue the women do not sit with the men but occupy a gallery especially constructed for them, because a Jewish woman cannot take an active part in any service. Should there be a thousand persons in the synagogue gathered for worship, the service cannot begin until there are at least ten males of thirteen years of age or over. The Talmud states that though men must pray, women may pray. A man must keep 613 precepts daily, but the women are free from these duties. "Women are exempted from the law," says the Talmud. There are only three precepts which a mother in Israel is commanded to keep: (1) lighting the Sabbath candles, (2) offering a small portion of dough, by burning,

when making bread, (3) purification. The following prayer is recited daily by the men: "Blessed art Thou, O Lord our God, King of the universe, who has not made me a woman."

9. BAR MIZVAH, OR CONFIRMATION.—When a boy reaches the age of thirteen he becomes a member of the Jewish synagogue, "a son of the law," or "a son of the commandments." Until then his father bears all his sins, but from then on he is responsible for his conduct. In the daily morning prayer, except on Sabbath and holy days, he now uses the phylacteries, or tephillin. These are long, narrow strips of leather, attached to which are small square boxes, containing verses of Scripture written on parchment: Exodus 13:1-10, 11-16; Deuteronomy 6:4-9; 11:3-21. The Jews take the words in Deuteronomy 6:8 verbally: "And thou shalt bind them for a sign upon thine hand, and they shall be as frontlets between thine eyes." The phylacteries are bound upon the left arm and on the forehead and worn six days of the week during prayers. The Jews do not wear the phylacteries on Sabbath because the Bible says the Sabbath itself is a sign. Inasmuch as the phylacteries are worn daily as a sign, it is not necessary to have two signs at the same time.

10. JEWISH NEW YEAR.—Jews have a different calendar from that of the Gentiles. They also have different names for the months and different names for the days. According to Jewish reckoning we are living now in the year 5709 since the beginning of the world.

The Jews celebrate the New Year in a most solemn manner sometime during September. There is a dread in the heart of every orthodox Jew concerning the judgment day, for this is the day in which God pronounces judgment upon every individual. The Talmud speaks of it as a day in which all the children of men pass for judgment before the Creator as sheep pass examination before the shepherd.

Three books, says the Talmud, are open on the New Year before the Creator, wherein the fate of the wicked, the righteous, and those of an intermediate class are recorded.

The names of the righteous are immediately inscribed for life, and the wicked are at once blotted out of the book of the living and written for death. There is another one, the intermediate class, which is allowed ten days of repentance until the Day of Atonement, to repent and become righteous.

The Jews believe that every New Year, God sits on His throne of judgment with a pair of large scales before Him. The merits of righteous deeds of each individual are put on one side of the scales, and the sins and evil deeds in the other balance. If the good deeds prevail, then, of course, the one judged will be written for life, but if the sins are the heavier, he will be written for death. If the good and evil deeds are even, the judgment for such is suspended until the Day of Atonement. Almost all Jews believe that they belong to this intermediate class, except the rabbis and Talmudic teachers.

Repentance consists, according to the Jewish Talmud, in fasting, praying, almsgiving, and in observing all ceremonies and rituals. All this can avert the decree, but if anyone does not repent in the manner indicated, he will be written unto death. On New Year's day the Jews go to the synagogue early and pray for forgiveness of their sins. In the afternoon it is customary to go to the banks of a river to say the tashlik (the casting away of sins). The words of Micah 7:18-21 are recited. "Thou wilt cast all their sins into the depths of the sea." After the prayer the worshipers shake their garments and empty their pockets with zest over the water, expecting that God will cause their sins to fall into it. The ten days between the New Year and the Day of Atonement are filled with prayers, fasting, and repentance.

11. KAPPARAH (ATONEMENT).—Since the temple of Jerusalem was destroyed, the Jews do not use a lamb for their sacrifices. The rabbis, therefore, have instituted a substitute, a kapparah (atonement).

The evening before the Day of Atonement every Jew is supposed to provide a rooster or a hen, which is swung three times around the head, and the following prayer is recited: "This is my substitute, this is my commutation, this is my atonement, this fowl goes to death; may I be gathered into peace and inherit a long and happy life." The Talmud says, "As soon as one has performed the order of the atonement, he should lay his hands on the fowl as the hand is laid on the sacrifice and immediately give it to the slaughter."

The Day of Atonement is a great and holy day and so dreadful that, "even the fishes in the water tremble." The solemnity with which the minutest details of all the rituals and ceremonies are observed cannot be described. The most remarkable part of the ceremonies at the time of the former sacrifices in the temple was the entrance into the holy of holies. As the Jews no longer have the temple today, the ark of the covenant, which is found in every synagogue today, and which contains the scrolls of the law, is for them the holy of holies now. The whole night and day are spent in the synagogue; and some add to the penance and mortification of the flesh by standing on their feet the whole twenty-four hours. The day ends with the setting sun and a blast from the shofar (ram's horn). This is a signal for every man to return to his inheritance in the hope that God has written his name in the book of life.

When the Jewish unbeliever is approached with the third angel's message, the most fundamental problem to settle is the divinity of Jesus. Once a Jew gets a true understanding of this, the rest will be comparatively easy. Therefore, the studies one should choose for a Jewish listener should be the following:
    1. Does the Old Testament Teach That God Has a Son?
    2. The Passover Lamb and the Lamb of God.
    3. Israel's Mediator—Who Is He?
    4. The Sanctuary.
    5. Zionism, Its Future According to Bible Prophecy.

Understanding Cultism From the Bible
Cultism a Last-Day Evangelism Problem

I. *New Testament Prophecies on Cultism.*
  1. By Jesus. Matt. 24:4, 5, 11, 23, 24; 7:15, 21, 22.
     Deceivers—"deceive many."
     Come in Christ's name.
     Say, "I am Christ."
     "False prophets shall rise."
     "Lo, here is Christ, or there."
     "False Christs, and false prophets."
     "Shew great signs and wonders."
     "If it were possible, . . . deceive the very elect."
     False prophets in sheep's clothing; ravening wolves.
     Say, "Lord, Lord." Prophesy in His name, cast out devils, and do many wonderful works.
  2. By Peter. 2 Peter 2:1-3, 10-15, 17-20; 3:16.
     "False prophets also among the people."
     "False teachers"—bring in damnable heresies.
     "Denying the Lord that bought them."
     "Bring upon themselves swift destruction."
     Many "follow their pernicious ways."
     Because of influence "the way of truth shall be evil spoken of."
     "Through covetousness . . . with feigned words make merchandise of you." (Charge fees.)
     "Walk after the flesh in the lust of uncleanness."
     "Despise government." (Political issues.)
     "Speak evil of the things" they do not understand.
     "Forsaken the right way, and are gone astray."
     "These are wells without water." (Shallow.)
     "Speak great swelling words of vanity."
     "Live in error."
     "Promise . . . liberty" and live in bondage.
     Easily re-entangled in error.
     Wrest the Scriptures to their own destruction.
  3. By Paul. Col. 2:8, 18, 23; Eph. 5:6; 2 Thess. 2:3; 1 Tim. 4:1-3, 8; 2 Thess. 2:9-11.
     "Spoil you through philosophy and vain deceit."
     "After the tradition of men, after the rudiments of the world."
     "Beguile you of your reward."
     "Voluntary humility and worshipping of angels."
     Have a "shew of wisdom in will worship," and humility and punishing of the body. (Hypnotism.)

Skills in Meeting People

"Children of disobedience" and unbelief.
Deceive on the coming of Christ.
In latter days some depart from faith, heeding seducing spirits and doctrines of devils.
Hypocritically speak lies without conscience.
Some forbid to marry.
Some hold to special dietary God never ordered.
"Bodily exercise." Without profit. (Rollers, Shakers, etc.)
With all satanic power and lying wonders.
"With all deceivableness of unrighteousness."
(Law abrogated.)
"Strong delusion."
4. By John. 1 John 4:3.
Deny Jesus Christ has come in flesh. Spirit of Antichrist. 2 John 7.
5. By Jude. Jude 12, 13, 16, 19.
"Spots in your feasts of charity."
"Wandering stars."
"Having men's persons in admiration because of advantage."
"Who separate themselves." (False sanctification.)

II. *Satanic Practices in Old Testament.*

Soothsayers, "replenished from the east." Isa. 2:6.
Familiar spirits, wizards that peep and mutter. Isa. 19:3; 8:19.
"Consulter with familiar spirits," necromancer. Deut. 18:11.
Witchcraft. Ex. 22:18.
Charmers, wizards. Isa. 29:4; 19:3.
"Observers of times." Deut. 18:14.
Diviners, dreamers, enchanters, sorcerers. Jer. 27:9; 2 Kings 17:17.
Human sacrifices. Lev. 18:21.
"These . . . are an abomination unto the Lord." Deut. 18:10-14.

III. *Church Warned of Deceptions.*
1. Outstanding deceptions in cultism.
   a. Based on pagan philosophy.
   b. Patterned after heathen religions.
   c. Seeks righteousness by works.
   d. Denies God's Word, but uses it as convenient. (Astrology uses chance.)
   e. Denies Christ came in the flesh.
   f. Practices spiritism, magic, etc.
2. Church's only safety, adherence to Word.
   "Preach the word," "sound doctrine," "truth." 2 Tim. 4:1-5.
   "Knowledge of the Lord and Saviour Jesus Christ." 2 Peter 2:20.

"Dead with Christ from the rudiments of the world." Col. 2:20.
"Be ye therefore followers of God," children of obedience. Eph. 5:1, 6.
"Sanctification of the Spirit and belief of the truth." 2 Thess. 2:13.
"Believe and know the truth." 1 Tim. 4:3.
"Sanctified by the word of God and prayer." Verse 5.
"Nourished up in the words of faith and of good doctrine." Verse 6.
"Exercise thyself . . . unto godliness." Verse 7.
"Earnestly contend for the faith"—delivered to the saints. Jude 3.
"Keep yourselves in the love of God." Verse 21.
"Looking for the mercy of our Lord Jesus Christ."

IV. *Approaching Cultists With Our Message.*
1. Understand heathen philosophies enough to meet cultists intelligently.
2. Be discerning of "deceiving words." (Cultists talkative.)
3. Learn background of reader's ideas.
4. Do not condemn but rather teach truth.
5. Teach God's purpose, His plan of redemption.
6. Dwell on a personal God, personal Saviour, personal devil.
7. Teach Daniel 2, emphasizing true God reveals Himself in *prophecy,* not *astrology.*
8. Trace erroneous beliefs to heathen sources and expose heresy.
9. Help reader to acknowledge truth.
10. Let prayer help to settle the issue, not argument.
11. Do not hurry cultist into baptism. Teach thoroughly; allow time for adjustment.
12. Urge cultist to accept and walk in new light immediately.
13. As truth is accepted, make sure heresy is cast aside.
14. Tactfully rid home of pictures portraying cultist ideas.
15. Let reader follow scripture in his own Bible.
16. Enjoy light and sunshine in room where you study God's Word.
17. Show no fear of spiritism, but prepare for battle with Satan.
18. Stress art of meditation and prayer on Bible principles.
19. Avoid negative teaching on state of dead, destruction of wicked, etc.
20. Teach sensible sanctification and healthful living.
21. Build new philosophy of worship by teaching sanctuary truth.
22. Cultists "shop" for new religious ideas. Anchor reader into remnant church.

23. Keep new convert busy doing philanthropic deeds rather than "arguing" doctrines.
24. Keep clarifying truth until reader is well established.

Dealing With Bible Skeptics

Kathleen Brownell

There are two main classes of skeptics. First, there are those who have no desire to consider evidence in favor of the Bible, who wish only to cast contempt upon it and to quibble and argue regarding it. This class can rarely be helped to any great extent, because they do not wish to be helped. They must be dealt with kindly but firmly. They must not be permitted to take up a large part of the Bible-study hour in presenting their doubts and in holding the Bible up to ridicule. One method I have found rather effective is to inquire quietly whether they have ever read the Bible through. Usually they will answer no. I then ask whether they consider it fair and consistent to criticize a book they have never read. They will usually see the point.

The other class of skeptics are those who, though honest and sincere in their skepticism, are yet willing to give a fair consideration to evidence in favor of the Bible. In dealing with this class we need to try to understand the underlying causes of their skepticism. A little time spent in becoming acquainted with them in order to find out something of their personal background is time well spent. Some of the factors contributing to their skepticism are the following:

1. Having been reared in a non-Christian home or even in a godless one. This one fact should make us sympathetic toward them, for we can realize what a powerful influence the atmosphere of their home has been away from God.

2. The teachings of advanced education. Evolution and its so-called "evidences" against the Bible.

3. The confusion of teachings in the popular churches.

4. The inconsistencies in the lives of professed Christians.

When we understand all these contributing causes to the skeptic's attitude, we shall feel pity for him and realize his great need of help. This will lead us to manifest great kindness and patience in dealing with him. Usually we shall find that skepticism is particularly applied to certain rather definite fundamental points, some of which are doubts concerning the authenticity of the manuscripts and translations of the Bible, doubts regarding the inspiration of the Bible writers, belief in the existence of contradictions in the Bible, and unwillingness to subscribe to the requirements of the Bible.

In meeting these definite objections we must produce all the evidence and proof we can possibly give to counteract their doubts. We must, for instance, give information regarding the manuscripts and translations, producing dates, facts, and so forth, which will often show that the skeptic has been misinformed regarding this important phase. Clearing up this misapprehension will go a long way toward establishing faith in the genuineness of the Bible.

In meeting doubts regarding the inspiration of Bible writers, I have found that the prophecies are one of our strongest proofs of Bible inspiration. This would include many of the prophecies relating to nations, and their fulfillment, prophecies regarding Christ and His work, and their fulfillment, and of course the important symbolic prophecies. Along with the prophecies it will often be necessary to produce both historical facts and evidence from archaeology, and we shall have to give enough from these sources to show the Bible prophecies and record to be correct. We may even have to bring in enough of astronomy to establish the chronology of the Bible. It is especially necessary to settle the date on which a prophecy was given in order to prove that the prophecy was given many years *before* its fulfillment, and thus show the inspiration of the Bible.

It is desirable to explain thoroughly the fundamental plan of Bible study which we follow. Letting one text explain another and getting complete information on a subject by gathering the Bible texts together is a plan very familiar to us but usually difficult for the skeptic to understand. But if he can be led to accept this plan of Bible study, we shall have gone a long way toward helping him learn the truth. This will enable us to show him the wonderful harmony of Bible teaching through the whole Book and on any one subject. It will also enable us to teach from the positive instead of the negative side of the question. (This is very essential, for most of the skeptic's information has been of the negative type.)

Establishing the Bible-study plan will give us the advantage of putting the whole discussion on the basis of what the Bible says, and off the basis of personal opinion. In fact, the whole aim of presenting all the evidence should be to use it as the authority. This is, of course, the only correct foundation, but with a skeptic it may take some time to establish this fact. Therefore, do not be discouraged if it seems to be slow work, and do not expect to accomplish too much at one time. Perhaps all that can be done is to start a train of thought along right lines in the skeptic's mind during the first study or two. Accept that much cheerfully, and continue working. It may take time and work to lay a foundation upon which we can later build, but it will be well worth the effort if it results in a soul saved.

It is important to adopt a calm, courteous, helpful attitude and to maintain it steadfastly. If we can once convince the skeptic that we are his friend, and that we are sincere in our desire to help him, we have laid another sure foundation in our work of turning him to the truth. If, later, we can lead him to read certain selected texts from the Bible for himself; and most of all, if we can lead him to the Lord Jesus Christ and show him something of God's love for him, we have reached the fulfillment of a carefully and prayerfully planned program of winning another soul, and this soul, it seems to me, will be one over whom the angels of heaven will especially rejoice.

PART TWO ★ CHAPTER SIX

Developing Literary Ability

The Bible Instructor as a Writer

Mable Hinkhouse Towery

One of the most essential needs in life is to know how to speak and write good English. This knowledge is a great advantage in any vocation, and a real asset to anyone. It fosters self-confidence, poise, and assurance, and develops personality and leadership. The master of expression (written or oral) has a good passport to success in social, business, or professional life. This is particularly true of writing. "Skill in writing will get you on in the world faster than almost any other ability."—BOUTWELL.

I. *Gathering Materials for Talk, Study, or Article.*
   1. Sources: Sermons, conversations, interviews, newspapers, magazines, books, encyclopedias, Bible, Bible commentaries, translations and versions, *Source Book* and *Hand Book, Bible Readings, Index to the Writings of E. G. White,* radio talks, note book jottings, lectures, and life.
   2. Filing. (See also pp. 321-323.)
       a. Material may be lost unless classified and indexed.
       b. Clip, collect, analyze, and organize materials.
       c. Gather material around several centers (as doctrinal). Assign subjects to materials, arrange alphabetically and topically.
       d. Buy suitable file and keep material filed. Otherwise clippings become mixed up, torn, and soiled.
       e. Thus you have invaluable collection, available at moment's notice.
       f. "Proper filing is important in business, in any well-organized office, where secretaries are employed to do the work. But it is equally vital in the life of the individual whose time and effort are in many cases his only original capital of success."
       —HALL-QUEST, *Supervised Study,* p. 188.
   3. Marking.
       a. Underscore main word or words.

Developing Literary Ability

  - b. Make vertical line or lines at side of longer passages.
  - c. Use parentheses ( ), brackets [ ], crosses xx, or check marks √ √.
  - d. Have marginal notes—brief summary, new thoughts, suggestions, questions.
  - e. Jot down pages on flyleaves of book, back of magazine, or on separate sheet of paper.
 4. Summarizing.
  - a. Find the topic sentences, or the gist of each paragraph. (Good drill: Select topic sentences of a whole discourse, jot them down in order, and see if they give the skeleton or framework.)
  - b. Make a condensed brief, or review, of the essential thoughts.
  - c. Discriminate between important and incidental features—between the essentials and nonessentials.

II. *The Outline and Its Structure.*
 1. Necessity and use.
  - a. The plight of the unprepared (in giving talk, study, or sermon).
  - b. Careful outlining a great aid to unity. Makes for a closely knit, logical, connected presentation.
  - c. Outline a mechanical device, giving an orderly plan of the material to be used. A map or blueprint of what is to come.
  - d. Indicates the order and manner of presentation.
  - e. Reduces labor of both writer and reader.
  - f. Less essential to brief treatment; more essential to lengthy.
 2. Three main parts of the outline: Introduction, body, conclusion; or starting, developing, accomplishing.
  - a. Introduction, or approach.
    - (1) Arrest attention or arouse curiosity by the introduction. First ten words more important than next thousand. Winning a welcome or losing it.
    - (2) Introduction should reveal the nature or purpose of the article and be suggestive of what is in store. It may state a problem or raise a question for explanation or discussion.
  - b. Body, or development of theme.
    - (1) Divisions and subdivisions, main and secondary lines of thought.
    - (2) Arranged in proper sequence and relative importance by a series of symbols—letters and figures—with proper indention, to express coordination or subordination.
    - (3) Each series of steps related logically, mechanically, causally or chronologically.

c. Conclusion, or appeal.
      (1) Bring to a natural, satisfying close, harmonious with whole.
      (2) Avoid abrupt ending, or one with pessimistic, alarming note.
      (3) End in positive, constructive vein.
      (4) Make a summarizing statement or a brief recapitulation.
      (5) Make application, draw inference, or suggest action.
   d. Do not use words *introduction, body,* or *conclusion* in outline. Substitute contents of these parts of composition for terms mentioned.
   e. The outline in reverse. Build outline backwards. Put each thought on separate sheet or card. Then shuffle, combine, and arrange.
3. The form of the outline.
   a. Vertical or serial (the simplest type).
   b. Topic sentences of paragraphs constitute outline, listed one below the other, all coordinate with each other.
   c. The oblique outline (requires more skill).

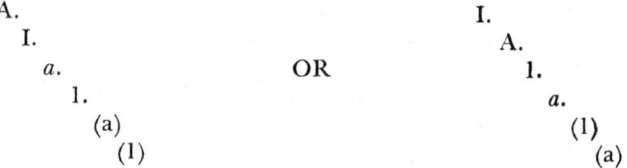

   NOTE.—In the oral presentation of the sermon or Bible study from an organized outline, the eye more readily catches the sequence of figures, both Roman and Arabic, than the letters of the alphabet—especially when they enter the higher brackets. What is therefore desirable outlining style for the printed study, usually yields to the form more easily caught by a glance of the eye. The preferred form for speaking notes is therefore—

        I.
           1.
           2.
              a.
              b.
              c.

4. Rules of outline structure.
   a. Condense the material, arrange, number, and indent in a manner to show the logical relationship of the parts to each

other, with orderly sequence of thought from one topic to the next, and from beginning to end. Use key words and phrases to suggest important ideas.
  b. Main headings (A, B, C, etc., or I, II, III, etc.) represent main divisions, important aspects, or distinct steps in the treatment of a subject. Same indention from left-hand margin.
  c. Indent subordinate headings, covering the treatment of the main headings in detail, under the heading to which they are subordinate, each setting the same distance in from the margin, no matter how many lines. Indent subheads farther than main heads.
  d. When headings or notes run over one or more lines, begin second lines even with the first word of preceding line.
  e. Use parallel symbols to indicate ideas of equal importance.
  f. When outline is completed, glance down the line-up of the various main headings, the subordinate headings, and the subheadings, and see if alignment is correct, and if the headings are coordinate. Also check to see that each group is in balance, equality, and proportion.
  g. A single subheading cannot be justified. Subdivision involves division into at least two parts. No part should stand alone; that is, there should not be an *a* without a *b* following it; nor a 1 without a 2. Join the single item to the preceding item, or omit.
5. "The completed outline . . . gives the writer an opportunity to survey his composition as a whole in small compass, and to make adjustments and alterations that will be likely to save him much laborious revision. It enables him—
   to test the logical relationships between his ideas;
   to discover omissions;
   to secure due proportion and symmetry;
   to omit irrelevant material; and
   to remove or correct apparent inconsistencies or contradictions."—THOMAS, MANCHESTER, AND SCOTT, *Composition for College Students*, p. 42.

III. *Preparation and Appearance of Manuscript.*
  1. First impressions count! Certain time-tried, rudimentary principles to be observed, which we might call the mechanics of a manuscript. However, if an article has intrinsic merit, it is not rejected, no matter how many rules have been disregarded. More concerned over content than form.

2. Rules of writing technique.
    a. Appearance of first page.
        (1) Leave ample space at top (fourth or third of page).
        (2) Assign a suitable title—brief, original, apt.
        (3) Give full name and address.
    b. Kind and size of paper.
        (1) Good grade of white paper, medium weight.
        (2) Standard size (8½ x 11). Convenient for handling, filing, mailing.
        (3) Use full size sheets for all copy, no matter how short.
        (4) Copy handled by at least ten people. Odd size, thin, sleazy paper, or carbon copies puts strain on their patience.
    c. Leave liberal margins.
        (1) An inch or more all around the sheet.
        (2) Six inches the recommended length of typed line.
        (3) Indent paragraphs five to ten spaces, extra space between paragraphs.
        (4) Number each sheet of copy at top of page, and repeat title. Put at right or in middle, never at left.
    d. Typewritten material preferred.
        (1) Change typewriter ribbon and clean keys.
        (2) Handwritten copy acceptable. Make as legible as possible.
    e. Double-spaced typing.
        (1) Always double space, except perhaps in case of poems or outlines.
        (2) Double space correspondence if for possible use as article.
    f. Write on one side only.
        (1) May write on both sides of subject, but not paper.
        (2) Never put inserts on back of sheet. Use separate sheet.
    g. Carbon copies.
        (1) Do not submit. Hard to read, smears, arouses question.
        (2) Keep your own carbon copy, for reference or in case of loss.
    h. Quotations and references.
        (1) Give due credit, and enclose in quotes.
        (2) Avoid excessive quotations.
        (3) Verify, especially if not from standard works.
    i. Length of articles.
        (1) Give editors the lengths they like.
        (2) For the ordinary periodical, short articles of two, three, or four pages. Five to six pages would be the maximum. Longer articles may be divided into a series.
    j. On points of style closely observe magazine for which you are writing.

Developing Literary Ability

Bibliography

Hall-Quest. *Supervised Study*. New York: Macmillan, 1916.
Lomer & Ashmun. *Study and Practice of Writing English*. Boston: Houghton Mifflin, 1914.
Thomas, Manchester, & Scott. *Composition for College Students*. New York: Macmillan, 1928.
Towery, Mable Hinkhouse. *A Word to Writers*. Washington, D.C.: Review and Herald, 1947.
Von Hesse, Elizabeth Ferguson. *So to Speak*. New York: Stokes, 1941.
Woods and Stratton. *Blue Book of Good English*. New York: Doubleday, 1934.
Woolley & Scott. *Handbook of Composition*. Boston: D.C. Heath, 1926.

Topical Suggestions for *Ministry* Articles

1. Techniques in Personal Evangelism.
2. Organizing the Bible Instructor's Daily Program.
3. Meeting Interested People at Our Services.
4. Organizing the Evangelistic Office.
5. Sequence of Bible Reading Subjects.
6. Methods for Meeting New Readers.
7. Teaching Seventh-day Adventist Ideals.
8. Pointers on Gaining Decisions.
9. Bible Instructor's Assistance at Baptism.
10. Winning the Youth for Christ.
11. Methods of Reaching the Aged.
12. Presenting Principles of Health and Dress.
13. Teaching the Spirit of Prophecy.
14. Establishing the New Believer.
15. Guiding the New Convert Into Service.
16. Encouraging Readers to Attend Church Services.
17. Enlisting the Help of Church Deaconesses.
18. Instructing Laymen in Bible Work.
19. Personal Work Methods Used in Other Countries.
20. Training the New Bible Instructor.
21. The Bible Instructor With Musical Ability.
22. The Bible Instructor as a Student.
23. Books for Professional Reading.
24. A Book Review.
25. Using Art in Bible Work.
26. Reporting for the Press.
27. Teaching Classes in Health and Dietetics.
28. Bible Instructor at Camp Meeting.

29. Our Associates in Evangelism.
30. Locating in a New Field.
31. Bible Instructor's Home Needs and Equipment.
32. Making a Vacation Profitable.
33. Bible Instructor's Budget Problems.
34. The Voice of Experience in Bible Work.
35. Reporting Daily Bible Work.

PART TWO ★ CHAPTER SEVEN

Secretarial and Other Skills

The Evangelist's Secretary

The modern evangelist is in great need of secretarial help. This is often best provided by a young woman trained for both secretarial and Bible work. Although some of these young women are interested in some Bible teaching, they still give office work their first preference. There are always those who are better adapted to office routine than personal work, especially that type of personal work which requires force in gaining decisions for our unpopular message.

Such skills are not by chance; God has endowed different individuals with gifts necessary for the furtherance of the gospel in all its various phases. Since there is a need for these individual talents, we do well to recognize where each worker may serve the cause in the best way.

When a young woman spends most of her time in the evangelistic office, her position is that of a minister's secretary. But when her time is mostly taken up with personal work and counseling among those who are making decisions for the message, as well as taking an active part in the evangelistic meetings, she is indeed a Bible instructor. A skilled full-time secretary will probably function in larger efforts only. The combination Bible instructor and secretary is growing in demand. It is becoming evident, however, that unless such a worker has a real burden to visit the people because of an urgent desire to lead them to Christ, the easier course will always be to keep busy about the evangelistic office. Since there is always a great need for office workers, few of the real secretarial type seem to make good as Bible instructors. But we recognize that there is a place for a combination of talent.

Let us guard against calling the full-time evangelistic secretary a Bible instructor merely because the conference is agreeable to providing an added worker. Bible work should always be regarded on the plane of the ministry. All other service in gospel work is equally commendable, but let us choose our Bible instructors with great wisdom, and not confuse them with office secretaries.

Handling the Daily Mail

What are some of the duties of the evangelist's or pastor's secretary? Her responsibility may be varied. First of all, there are tasks requiring meticulous skill in handling office details which are best performed by trained young women. The mail that reaches the modern evangelistic office needs prompt attention. Interested individuals are constantly asking for literature on Bible subjects presented by the evangelist. Many such requests now come through the mail—much more than was customary a few years ago. Associated with radio evangelism there is an expanding correspondence which the evangelist himself does not have the time to look after. Neither would it be profitable for a Bible instructor who is skilled in helping people to decide for the message in their homes to spend a great deal of her time attending to these requests. Such extra duties are far better handled by someone assigned to office work.

Although the pastor's secretary should be a skillful typist, she must also be a person of good judgment. She must know how to regard confidences, for there are many confidential problems which are not to be discussed with others. Again, there will be occasions when the evangelist is not at hand for consultation on some procedure requiring immediate action. She must then be able to act wisely in his behalf, and to the full satisfaction of both the minister and the inquiring or perplexed individual who is seeking help at his hands. Here the right type of worker is a great blessing to the minister, and some of the success of the campaign may be credited to her careful attention to details. She must always be courteous and humble. It is important that she know how to get along with people, and especially, with her associate workers.

The evangelist's wife may need to act as her husband's secretary, helping with the correspondence, radio mail, and requests. She may be qualified to act as treasurer of the campaign, in this way saving an associate worker many hours of time by paying of bills, making out reports, attending to bank deposits, and so forth.

Secretary of Correspondence School

One service which is well rendered by the evangelist's secretary is leadership in the local correspondence school. We have passed the experimental stage in this useful type of evangelism. This excellent method often does much to prepare the way for the Bible instructor's visit and guide workers to souls who are studying themselves into our message.

On this point, however, there is still much question as to the feasibility of employing a large corps of secretaries in an evangelistic office. All the mechanics we can employ will never take the place of real heart-to-heart visiting with interested souls. Whereas lessons by mail now have their place in evangelism, they do not by any means occupy first place. The greatest need is personal work to follow up the interest. Without such personal contacts the results will always be expensive and limited. If the skillful evangelistic secretary senses each case of interest, and detects the psychological moment for making the home contact, she is indispensable as a gospel worker. Cooperative and humble, she works together with the different Bible instructors in the company. Both types of workers share in the soul harvest.

It may be that the campaign's correspondence course is to be of a rather temporary nature. It would not be wise, then, to develop the school into a monstrosity, hard to grip by a smaller force, when the interest should be merged into a conference correspondence school. Too often there is duplication of effort, and this tends to tie up workers in the office who ought to be out in the homes of the people. In our larger cities, however, it may be very profitable to develop a correspondence school that can expand into unentered areas as the evangelist reaches out by means of the radio.

Radio evangelism and correspondence courses go hand in hand. We may need to make constant adaptations so as to fit this plan into the needs of this hour, but we have hardly begun tapping our evangelistic opportunities here. One who directs such a school should keep in close counsel with the conference. Its development will then be by mutual agreement, and will not later appear to be an undue burden, or make it necessary to be suddenly terminated because of a lack of funds or for some other imperative reason. No matter how efficient a correspondence school secretary may be, she should understand that she is to receive constant guidance from her superiors in the development of plans for the correspondence school. This project has too much at stake to be left to the discretion of a lone secretary, especially one who may be very limited in actual soul-winning experience.

As a denomination we have shown definite enthusiasm in the correspondence school. But our zeal has often interfered with its efficiency. Nothing of a slipshod nature should here be tolerated. These correspondence lessons, if not printed, should at least be neatly mimeographed. Stationery should always be of a dignified nature. The markings on the test papers should be neat and thorough, and yet not too detailed.

The corrected papers should always be returned to the student promptly. If any criticism from the public regarding our correspondence school deserves special attention, it is our need for promptness in returning grades to our students who have sent in their test sheets. More people have lost interest on this account than some correspondence school helpers may want to admit. This is a very vital point, and deserves our attention. More and more we are looking to our colleges to foster training in this needful type of evangelism.

Various Helpful Combinations

Frequently the one with secretarial ability also has musical talent. This combination is especially helpful in evangelism, and our growing work should encourage such a blending of skills. We would do well in our college courses to stress this combination. The one who is both a musician and a secretary will need to be extra cautious to avoid criticism. The use of either talent is bound to create some problems on which critical folk will capitalize. One must have a poised and amiable disposition, with much tact, and a not-too-sensitive nature. And yet our larger evangelism needs require just such workers.

There are still other duties in which the efficient pastor's secretary may be helpful. A secretary must be a very adaptable individual. Should she have artistic ability, she will increase her usefulness, for evangelism calls for artistic skill.

We might also enlarge on the talents of the secretary who has an interest in working for children. Such ability is most important in modern evangelism. Attention has already been given to this work for the children. They become a very definite part of our evangelistic endeavor.

The secretary who is a trained nurse or dietitian can also be of special service to the campaign and the local church. In Part II, chapter 2, the services of the nurse and dietitian are given special discussion.

We must admit that there are but few individuals who could claim all these different gifts—and neither should we expect them. The point is well taken, however, that any evangelistic secretary enhances her usefulness by developing various talents for our ever-expanding work.

The evangelist's secretary should not be regarded merely as his errand girl or as a maid for the evangelist's family, to be trained by him for all kinds of personal chores which may include the family's washing and canning, or as a baby-sitter for the children on evenings when the parents must be at meeting. This does not mean, however, that she cannot render those occasional friendly favors merely intended for good will. There is a difference between friendly helpfulness which brings diversion and those regular working policies that must be considered in building our profession.

A secretary should always be treated with office dignity. There must be businesslike regularity to her daily program. The office should be kept in neat condition, and although it may need to be in the basement of the church, it should impress visitors with the importance of this phase of our Father's business. Attention should be given to proper heating and lighting, so that the secretary's health will not be jeopardized. Needless to say, one who serves in this capacity should be a sincere Christian, ever doing her duty when the local church has need of her talents. Although she is not directed by church officers, she should be a loyal church member whose influence will count in the building up of a strong work.

PART TWO ★ CHAPTER EIGHT

Training Personal Workers

The Field Training School

The Bible training school idea is not of modern origin. Several decades ago some denominational leaders sensed a need for this type of training. Elder and Mrs. S. N. Haskell can be pointed to as the first to launch this plan. There is sufficient evidence, however, that Mrs. White herself believed in training workers in this way, and her guidance in this respect is now valuable counsel. (See *Evangelism,* pp. 107-110.) Other leaders have made valuable contributions which still guide us in our training of personal workers.

As the field training school plan grew among us, many efficient personal workers and Bible instructors were developed. In this way men and women were trained especially for gospel work in our larger cities. Earlier in our history few workers were privileged to complete college courses, and this accelerated type of training was instrumental in developing laymen who showed aptitude for gospel service. Again, the field training school helped to start out many a good worker in our home foreign evangelism. In America national, racial, and language problems suggested adaptations of this idea as it was first launched by the Haskells. Many overseas people in our American cities were first introduced to our message by humble workers developed in these local training schools.

With a definite message to give to the world, Seventh-day Adventist evangelism expanded rapidly at the home base as well as throughout the world field. Then more and more the field training school became eclipsed by our rapidly developing ministerial courses in our colleges. Soon a new vision for evangelistic preparation resulted in many youth entering our colleges and completing broader courses of training for the ministry and Bible work.

This was a step in the right direction. Even then, however, it had to be acknowledged that the colleges were handicapped in providing sufficient practice and experience in actual field evangelism. Too often graduates of these courses received their first practical contacts with souls after leaving school, and when thrust out on their own in conference work. As they then engaged in intensive evangelistic campaigns requiring skill and experience in soul winning, these youth keenly felt their inadequacy.

The directing evangelist of a public series of meetings was often too busy to give regular instruction in soul-winning methods to his associate workers, and too many beginners had to find their way through embarrassment and confusion, resulting from a lack of experience. Then again, the pressure of work required that attention be focused on getting decisions, and although the harvest demands this emphasis, the learner must still know the full background of various techniques that lead up to the decision experience. Right here the evangelistic field training school has helped to solve many a practical problem for workers, especially in our city evangelism. The plan, however, is broad enough to be applied to smaller efforts, with adaptation, of course.

Wherever the field training school idea has been successfully tried, our evangelistic workers have shown great enthusiasm. Needless to say, such a training course cannot be made an afterthought of the whole program for the public campaign; the training school should be well planned when evangelism in a city is first given study. It may be that the busy evangelist is not the one to lead out in its instruction. In fact, his well-trained and experienced Bible instructor will more often make a better leader. The purpose of this type of training is not to provide a course in homiletics or apologetics; neither is it to train young interns in the skills of public evangelism. It is to develop *personal workers* and home Bible instructors. A conference may enlist some veteran worker experienced in personal evangelism to be its instructor. There is then wisdom in a plan that will call interns and beginners in Bible work from the entire field into the school. These workers should not merely attend the training school but tie into the public campaign and there apply the methods learned.

Whether the training school during the evangelistic series is to provide daily instruction to the workers would depend on local conditions. Perhaps three instruction periods a week are about all that can be allotted to it, especially when public interest begins to require much visitation. It is well to concentrate on it earlier in the effort so that when decisions must be followed up, there will be no extra responsibilities to absorb the workers' attention. The best time for this instruction is in the morning, when the mind is still fresh. The directing evangelist must be thoroughly behind the plan, making it clear to the company that emergencies only should necessitate a worker's absenting himself.

Instruction for the evangelistic group should be on a progressive basis, fitting into problems as they arise. The teacher should bear in mind the needs of the group as a whole, and not merely concentrate on some workers who may not have had previous training for our work and may be but temporarily employed for the campaign. This work is decidedly ministerial in nature, and the type of instruction given should be a broader training than that given to lay workers. It should more definitely deal with the problems of a public campaign. Helping perplexed and busy mothers to find time for Bible study; leading younger children to Christ; appealing to restless adolescents; building interest in the health phase of our message; making the sickroom call the entering wedge into the home—all these are skills to be developed by an all-round personal worker.

The true results of the evangelistic field training school may best be measured by an increased soul-winning zeal on the part of the entire corps. The school gives occasion for regular counseling, and provides an exchange of better techniques in Bible work. Workers become far more alert as they focus their attention on points of mutual concern for the class. Follow-up plans for public meetings may here be guided so that a soul harvest will be secured, and new converts will be well established in our message. Experienced Bible instructors can help in developing confidence in personal work by guiding younger workers into a more purposeful visitation program and in skills in Bible teaching. The art of securing decisions must be learned by observation as well as practice.

Many a successful Bible instructor today admits that she received the right start in our evangelistic work through the field training school. If this plan were given more attention, especially in our larger city campaigns, with adaptation to various local needs, our evangelism would become far more productive, and better Bible work would materially help toward checking the number of our apostasies.

Training School for Beginners

MARY E. ANDERSON

Our training school in South Africa is not a theological school, but an endeavor is being made to turn out practical Bible instructors. The students are taught how to give personal and family studies and how to conduct cottage meetings.

I give a course of thirty lessons in the doctrines that our denomination teaches. Along with the course in Bible doctrines I give one in theory and methods. Those who accept all these doctrines will be established in the truth and ready for church membership. To my mind it is the business of the Bible instructor to establish people in the faith. I drill the students on these subjects till they are impressed in their own souls, till they thoroughly understand every subject and can answer common inquiries likely to be asked.

I take the outline of studies in the order in which they will be given, beginning with the inspiration of the Book, making sure the reader believes it all as God's word. This gives a foundation upon which to build. The rest of the subjects follow along in the usual order. I first discuss the subject in hand with the class, showing them how to organize the study to bring out a mental picture. I show them the point to stress in each text used. When that point is made, they are to pass on to the next reference instead of rambling along in a prosy fashion, thereby losing the force of the argument. After the discussion of the lesson I present it to one of the class just as I would present it to a stranger who knows nothing about our doctrines. The rest of the class take notes on my procedure as I go along, noticing how I answer inquiries.

After private study each student must then present the lesson to someone in the class as she would present it to a reader. I take notes on the methods of the class members, the expressions, mannerisms, language, and so forth, and show them where they come short and how they could strengthen their argument. These trial readings by the student are for two purposes—that I may be sure they understand the doctrine correctly themselves, and that they may become accustomed to putting the theory and methods into practice before they start out. Thus they are saved from appearing like novices.

After each one has had her trial, the difficult texts are further investigated, and I make sure the students know the application and meaning themselves. Before leaving a doctrine I give the subject again just as I would to a reader, then pass on to the next subject.

Our school hours are from nine in the morning to twelve-thirty, Monday through Friday. Afternoons and evenings are for public readings. I myself carry as many readers as I need to demonstrate the work in actual, practical experience. I take two girls with me to each home where I give studies, taking the same girls each time, so that they may follow the course from start to finish. They observe and take notes on how to put the methods into practice, how to meet inquiries, when to answer directly and when to defer, how to hold the interest, when and how to close the study, and leave the reader anticipating the next visit, how to take one's departure after the study is finished, and how to urge a decision at the opportune time.

When the student goes with me, she merely observes. If it is not clear to her why I did as I did, she asks for an explanation in class the next morning. We discuss then why it was better to follow such a procedure, why I took a different course with that reader, et cetera. I take each student with me to three different homes. Thus they hear me give the lesson under differing circumstances and environments. They learn how to meet various arguments and how to deal with different natures.

Early in the course the girls are sent out to distribute literature systematically in the homes of the people in a certain section. This is to test their ability to make contacts and arouse an interest, as well as to induce the people to take Bible studies. As fast as they find their own readers, they begin studies with them. I review each lesson with them before they give it, so that it will be fresh in their minds and properly organized.

After the students are accustomed to giving Bible readings, they ask their readers whether they will mind if they bring a friend along. I then go as a critic teacher. The reader thinks I am an interested friend of his teacher. I ask for the privilege of taking down the texts. This gives me the opportunity to jot down what I wish to discuss later with the student. I may read texts along with the reader if I am invited to. We have this understanding beforehand. I take no part in the discussion, nor does the student appeal to me. Even if she gets into deep water, she carries on regardless. If a blunder is made, she must rectify it in some future lesson. I discuss all this in class, and the rest benefit by her mistake.

If a public effort is being conducted, the students attend and observe the work of a Bible instructor in the evening meetings. I note her ability to observe who is interested and who comes regularly, how to meet and greet people as they come from evening to evening, how to mingle with the crowd profitably, how to visit the people in their homes, how to get them to begin with further Bible study, how to keep them coming to the meetings.

Each student takes three readers. The studies are begun early in the course, so I will be able to help the students bring souls over the line at the end. Students must have time to study, and they must not be overburdened with readers, for other things also are important to their training. How they carry on their work with the evangelist is left for the evangelist. I teach how to organize and present Bible studies.

By having the benefit of another's experience in this way, the girls learn more quickly how to do efficient work; otherwise they might take years to learn from their own experience.

Training and Selecting Helpers

Mary E. Saxton

The great Master Teacher selected men from various walks of life to be His helpers in the work of saving souls and disseminating the gospel. He could have enlisted angels to be His associates in the ministry, but instead He chose men from the common walks of life. However, He used judgment in selecting the twelve disciples, and no doubt the same discretion was used when He called the seventy and sent them forth to proclaim the first advent of the Messiah.

These chosen disciples were men of latent possibilities, yet they were not prepared for the delicate and important work of representing His name and of teaching the special truths for the time. Christ, after selecting these men, trained them for service. He taught them the truths of the Word of God, so that they became mighty in the Scriptures. By precept and example He instructed them how to meet and deal with the various types of human beings.

They watched with keen interest how Christ adapted Himself to the various situations which arose as He came in contact with those who were characteristically different—the spiritually proud Pharisee, the honest seeker for truth among the wealthy, the poor and illiterate, the cynical, the apparearly in the course, so I will be able to help the students bring wise and kindly approach to the varied personalities.

The disciples had much to learn and more to unlearn, but by close observation and willingness to follow their Master's methods they became qualified, and by the power of the Holy Spirit they were enabled to do the deeds of omnipotence.

Christ is our example in all things; therefore we should copy His methods of labor, especially when it comes to selecting and training helpers. Our Lord, by His Holy Spirit, has given to the church various gifts, and among them is the gift of helps, or helpers, and these are to be found among the lay members of our church. The question may be asked, Do we appreciate this gift? and if so, are we utilizing it as God ordained? The counsel of the Spirit of prophecy is very definite on our responsibility in this matter.

"In every church there is talent, which, with the right kind of labor, might be developed to become a great help in this work [missionary work]. . . . There should be no delay in this well-planned effort to educate the church-members."—*Testimonies*, vol. 9, pp. 117-119.

The training of the laity is of primary importance, and every Bible instructor should consider it a privilege to enter into this field of endeavor during the interim between pressing evangelistic efforts, and before such efforts.

Because of the instruction given in the Spirit of prophecy and the existing need in the local church, as well as the earnest desire on the part of some of the members to get into a definite field of service, and with the encouragement of the local pastor, I felt compelled to conduct a training class for the lay members of the Capital Memorial church in Washington, D.C. Some preliminary work had to be done in order to ensure success. This was accomplished by public announcement, personal contact, and the enlisting of zealous members as publicity agents, who visited a few talented but disinterested members, and aroused their interest to unite with the class.

Although the entire church membership was notified about the class, the primary purpose was to select certain ones who possessed possibilities for development. Included in this select group were young men and young women of talent. These were given special attention and added help. Youthful talent is always needed in the Bible work.

What was our textbook? The inspired Word of God, from which the great Master Teacher taught His colaborers. The fundamental doctrines of the Advent message were studied, also difficult Scriptural passages; thus was the student fortified with knowledge and assurance for the time when he should be obliged to face questions of opponents.

"Every church should be a training-school for Christian workers. Its members should be taught how to give Bible readings. . . . There should not only be teaching, but actual work under experienced instructors. Let the teachers lead the way in working among the people, and others, uniting with them, will learn from their example. One example is worth more than many precepts."—*Ministry of Healing,* p. 149.

In connection with our study of Bible doctrines, instruction was also given on practical methods for presenting them. This included the do's and the don'ts.

Just as Christ demonstrated His methods to His disciples, so I united the practical with the theoretical by having the students give studies to teach others in the presence of the teacher. In addition to this, I had the class participate in actual field experience by accompanying me whenever studies were given and visits made with prospective church members.

Such a Bible training class produces its fruitage both in the spirituality of the church and in the blessing of increased membership. If God's plan for training lay members in our broader Bible work program were faithfully carried out, we would ere this have seen the fulfillment of such endeavors as spoken of by the messenger of the Lord. "In visions of the night representations passed before me of a great reformatory movement among God's people. . . . Hundreds and thousands were seen visiting families, and opening before them the word of God."—*Testimonies,* vol. 9, p. 126.

Is it not the privilege, if not the solemn duty, of the Bible instructor to share in training the church for such a work?

Of course, her pressing schedule allows such a heavy program only occasionally. Joy unspeakable will fill the heart of the worker as she sees this divinely appointed plan entered into by those for whom she has previously labored.

Conducting a Training Class

It is prayer meeting night in a Seventh-day Adventist church. The midweek service begins at eight o'clock, but an hour previous there is assembled at the church the training class for lay Bible instructors, with Mrs. Ena Ferguson, conference Bible instructor, in charge.

This class of twenty is made up of church members who believe God when He says that "many workers are to act their part, doing house-to-house work, and giving Bible readings in families"; also that "consecrated women should engage in Bible work from house to house"; and are therefore seeking a preparation for doing this work acceptably.

Ten members of this class, Sister Ferguson says, are each giving from two to five Bible studies a week, and the other members of the class will very soon be ready to begin practical work. Such a class, averaging from fifty to one hundred Bible studies in the homes of the people each week, points impressively to the fulfillment of that scene which we have been told would take place in the closing period of the proclamation of the third angel's message, when "hundreds and thousands were seen visiting families, and opening before them the Word of God. Hearts were convicted by the power of the Holy Spirit, and a spirit of genuine conversion was manifest."

Believing that the Bible instructors' training class may appropriately serve as a model for the formation of such classes in other churches, we are giving further details, and an outline of the course of study, as furnished by Sister Ferguson, and reported by Grace D. Mace:

"The members of the class provide themselves with looseleaf notebooks, in which they copy from the blackboard the outline of the lesson each week, also outlines of Bible studies.

Ample time is allowed for thorough discussion of the lesson topic and Bible study outline in each class period. We also spend a portion of the time in relating experiences and considering problems which arise, and devote fifteen minutes in each class period to a snappy drill on memory work with texts of Scripture and quotations from the Spirit of prophecy. Each member of the class is given opportunity to go with an experienced instructor, and observe how the Bible study is given in the home, before taking up the work alone."

Suggestions concerning the art of giving Bible studies successfully were placed before the class on a blackboard in the following form:

    I. *Motto.*—"Without a high sense of . . . the exalted character of the work, they cannot succeed."—*Gospel Workers,* p. 365.

   II. *Length of Study.*
      1. A Bible study should not last more than forty-five minutes or one hour.
      2. The mind cannot concentrate for a longer period.
      3. The reader may be inconvenienced in her plans.
      4. It is best to leave the reader eager for more information.

  III. *At Conclusion of Study.*
      1. Leave the house as soon as possible after the lesson is given.
      2. This is recommended in order that the impression made by the lesson may be left unmarred and lead to continued thought and meditation.
      3. If it is necessary to engage in visiting, do so before the lesson is given.

  IV. *The Scripture Reading.*
      1. Permit the individual to whom the study is being given to read the texts of Scripture for himself.
      2. Eye impressions are usually greater than ear impressions.
      3. It helps to establish familiarity with the Bible.
      4. It teaches the reader to form the habit of taking God's word instead of man's word as the basis of belief.
      5. If the individual is not a good reader, the Bible instructor may read, but the individual should follow with the eye.

   V. *Simplicity.*
      1. Make the study simple.
      2. Avoid embarrassing the reader in any way.

Training Personal Workers

3. Seat yourself near by, so as to assist in finding the Scripture texts, if necessary.
4. When giving out the text to be found, suggest where the text is located. For example: "Open your Bible at the middle, and you will have the Psalms. Now, just before the Psalms is the book of Job. Find Job 26:13, 14." If a bookmark is placed between the Old and the New Testament, it often proves of great advantage.

VI. *Terminology.*—Avoid denominational terms which are likely not to be clearly understood, such as "third angel's message."

VII. *Broad-mindedness.*
1. Speak not a word of condemnation of the religious beliefs of others. Be broad-minded.
2. Practice the golden rule.
3. "God sent not His Son into the world to condemn the world" (John 3:17); therefore, He does not send His messengers to condemn.
4. Remember that there are converted people in all churches.

VIII. *Humbleness.*
1. Ever maintain the attitude of being a learner with the reader.
2. Avoid an attitude of superior learning or holiness, even in prayer.
3. "Let *us* see what the Bible says"; NOT, "Let *me* show *you* what the Bible says."

IX. *Regularity and Punctuality.*
1. Regularity in keeping appointments cannot be overestimated. This includes punctuality.
2. Show that you regard business for the King of heaven of paramount importance.
3. Irregularity will produce irregularity on the part of the reader in following the studies, and will result in loss of interest.
4. Failure in being punctual will mean an unwarranted sacrifice of personal convenience or pleasure on the part of the reader.

X. *Preparation.*
1. Be full of your subject, that you may carry inspiration and enthusiasm, and convince people that you have a good thing to give them.
2. It helps to keep the lesson from becoming mechanical.

3. Make fresh preparation.
4. Just before going to the place where the Bible study is to be given, read something inspiring on the subject in hand.

XI. *Subject.*
1. Hold to your subject, for there is great danger of becoming sidetracked, and thus failing to make the desired impression.
2. Do not try to explain the entire verse in the Bible reference, where there is more than one thought conveyed; refer only to those parts of the verse which relate to the subject.
3. Answer irrelevant questions briefly, and bring the mind directly back to the subject. When necessary, promise that another lesson will be given to explain the questions which cannot be answered at the present time.
4. Remember that it is one of Satan's schemes to divert the mind so that truth may lose its force.

XII. *Self-Control.*
1. Be master of yourself. Practice absolute self-control, for sometimes people are purposely exasperating.
2. Let no suggestion of irritation enter into the tone of voice.
3. Be courteous. (Read 1 Peter 3:8; 2:20, and be governed accordingly.)
4. Do not permit sarcasm, discourtesy, or unkindness to influence deportment.

XIII. *Attitude.*—Be considerate. Do not take it for granted that the reader sees in the text all that you do; take occasion to call attention repeatedly to definite words and phrases in the text.

XIV. *Principles of Pedagogy.*
1. Keep the one to whom you are giving the Bible study seriously thinking—thinking for himself and not listening to what you say.
2. Be a Bible teacher, not a lecturer.
3. Always leave reading matter on the subject.
4. Select appropriate quotations, and leave as written or printed slips to be placed in Bible.
5. Occasionally leave with the reader a few pointed questions, written, with Bible references given, asking that the answers to the questions be written on the slips by the time of the next Bible study.
6. If desired, one can use our prepared lesson series and ask the reader to make out test papers.

XV. *Thorough Review.*
  1. The principal points should be gone over again and again.
  2. This is necessary because so much is entirely new to the reader.
  3. Not all which seems clear at the time of the lesson is retained in the memory, and a review of the instruction serves to fix it in the mind.
  4. Careful review reveals how one subject relates to the next, and demonstrates that all truth is one truth.

XVI. *Psychology.*
  1. Study personalities, and adapt the studies to individual needs, as to mental capacity and special points of inquiry.
  2. With one person, the lesson must be made simple; with another person, in order to hold the interest, the study must be of a deeper nature.
  3. Lessons on special subjects will sometimes be necessary.
  4. Keep out of a rut.
  5. Study to find the way to the heart.
  6. Seek to discover the exact nature of difficulties or perplexities which prevent understanding or acceptance of truth.

XVII. *Meeting Opposition.*
  1. While seeking to avoid opposition in every possible way, be prepared to meet it when it comes.
  2. Do not denounce opponents; treat everyone as being honest in heart.
  3. Do not argue; to do so will multiply opposition. 2 Tim. 2:23-26.
  4. Do not repeat opponent's statements; this will only strengthen argument.
  5. Hold to the affirmative—this is Christ's method.
  6. Never get excited, or allow angry feelings to arise.
  7. Avoid discussion, for thereby sacred truth will often be derided. "Let thy words be few."
  8. Follow Nehemiah's example—"We are doing a great work, and cannot come down." (See Neh. 6:3, 7, 9; *Gospel Workers*, p. 376.) If Satan can keep one busy answering the objections of opponents, and thus hinder the most important work, his object is accomplished.

XVIII. *Discouragement.*
  1. Do not become easily discouraged if souls for whom you labor do not respond quickly in obeying the truth.

2. The seed falling on rocky ground is that which quickly springs up, and as quickly withers.
3. Have faith. Remember, "the worker for God needs strong faith."—*Gospel Workers,* p. 262. "Hope and courage are essential to perfect service for God. These are the fruit of faith. Despondency is sinful and unreasonable."—*Prophets and Kings,* p. 164.
4. Never give up a soul as long as there is a gleam of hope, and bear in mind: "We are to present the word of life to those whom we may judge to be as hopeless subjects as if they were in their graves. Though they may seem to be unwilling to hear or to receive the light of truth, without questioning or wavering we are to do our part."—*Testimonies,* vol. 6, p. 442.

XIX. *Fellow Workers.*
1. Guard the reputation of fellow workers. Refrain from saying anything that would cast the slightest reflection upon a fellow worker.
2. "Never speak disparagingly of any man" or woman.—*Gospel Workers,* p. 481.
3. God's ideal for workers is that they "work together, blending in kindly, courteous order."—*Acts of the Apostles,* p. 275.
4. There should be "no unkind criticism, no pulling to pieces of another's work."—*Ibid.*

XX. *One-Soul Audience.*
1. Seek the one-soul audience. Whenever possible, deal with the individual alone when you are going to make an appeal.
2. It permits the effective personal touch.
3. It permits freedom of expression.
4. There is more direct personal appeal.

XXI. *Tact.*
1. Be tactful. Avoid putting the reader on the defensive, or arousing in him an antagonistic spirit.
2. Do not directly contradict any statement; instead, teach the truth on the controverted point at some other time, when there will be no appearance of contradiction, leading up to the point by presenting relative truths in an interesting, convincing manner.
3. Present the least objectionable features first.
4. Win confidence at the start.
5. Convince the reader that you have the love of souls at heart.

6. Do not drive a point so hard as to arouse a combative spirit; lead, do not drive.
7. Use God's Word to bring comfort and hope and joy, not as a whip to bring into line. Luke 4:18.

XXII. *Increased Efficiency.*
1. Seek increased efficiency. It is possible to increase efficiency by diligent cultivation of the talent of speech.
2. Aim to speak clearly, distinctly, impressively. Neh. 8:8.
3. Avoid a shrill tone or a high pitch to the voice.
4. No idle word or slang expression should escape the lips.

XXIII. *Central Theme.*
1. Whatever the doctrinal subject presented, make Christ the central theme.
2. "No sooner is the name of Jesus mentioned in love and tenderness than angels of God draw near."—Mrs. E. G. White, *Manual for Canvassers,* p. 37.
3. Philip "preached Jesus" when he caused the eunuch to understand the need of baptism. Paul said he determined to know nothing but "Jesus Christ, and Him crucified." Acts 8:5; 1 Cor. 2:2.
4. Instead of being thankful to God for this blessed truth as an abstract set of doctrines, thank Him for the truth as it is in the person of Jesus—as it radiates from Him.

XXIV. *Intellectual Assent.*
Do not permit the reader to get the impression that a mere intellectual assent to truth constitutes righteousness. This is not sufficient. Our aim is to be the conversion of men and women. A formal religion is to be avoided. (Read *The Desire of Ages,* pp. 309, 347; *Gospel Workers,* pp. 158, 159.)

XXV. *Essential Qualifications.*
1. Be earnest in prayer.
2. Carry a burden for souls.
3. Be tactful. It is better to lose an argument and win the soul than win the argument and lose the soul. Kindness is akin to tact.
4. There must be consecration. "When every act bears witness that we love God supremely and our neighbor as ourselves, then will the church have power to move the world."
5. The worker should be filled with the Holy Spirit. He is only the *instrument,* like the pencil in the hand of the writer.
6. Have strong confidence in God and recognize the coopera-

tion of holy angels.—*Acts of the Apostles,* p. 154.
7. Be diligently studious.

XXVI. *High Aim.*
1. Seek to attain larger and larger results.
2. "Many whom God has qualified to do excellent work accomplish very little, because they attempt little."—*Christ's Object Lessons,* p. 331.
3. "Future reward will be proportioned to the integrity and earnestness with which they serve the Master."—Mrs. E. G. White in *Review and Herald,* March 1, 1887. (See also Ps. 126:6; Eccl. 11:6.)

XXVII. *Answering Questions.*
1. Let the Bible do the answering.
2. Be sure to have the questioner see and acknowledge that the question is satisfactorily answered.
3. Do not speculate regarding questions of minor importance. 2 Tim. 2:16.
4. It is a true statement that "mysteries not yet revealed, or texts not clearly comprehended by any, might better remain undiscussed."

XXVIII. *Cheerfulness.*
1. Visits in the homes should bring sunshine and cheer.
2. A smiling face is a testimony to the joy of Christian experience.
3. If you don't *feel* happy, refrain from talking about your feelings. Cast no shadow upon the lives of others.
4. Talk of your blessings; talk of God's promises; cultivate thankfulness.

XXIX. *Personal Appearance.*—"Women professing godliness" should give attention to neatness and modesty of apparel, avoiding those things which the Bible condemns. 1 Peter 3:3, 4; 1 Tim. 2:9, 10.

XXX. *Social Relationship.*—Generally speaking, the wise plan is for Bible instructors to seek to help those of their own sex.

XXXI. *Implicit Trust in God.*—Remember that God, not man, is the burden bearer, and lead your readers to this plane of experience.

XXXII. *Friendliness.*—Do not be exclusive; do not seek out the few with whom you delight to associate. Remember, "A man that hath friends must shew himself friendly." Prov. 18:24.

XXXIII. *Prayer With Each Study.*—Offer prayer, either in beginning or in closing the Bible study, for "never should the Bible be studied without prayer. Before opening its pages we should ask for the enlightenment of the Holy Spirit, and it will be given."—*Steps to Christ* (pocket ed.), p. 91. In homes where the voice of prayer is never heard, and people are unaccustomed to the attitude of prayer, it may at times be perplexing to know just how to arrange for audible prayer. The position assumed in prayer, whether kneeling, standing, or bowing the head, should be governed by circumstances, making the matter of prayer as natural and simple as possible. The instruction found in *Testimonies,* volume 9, page 35, should guide the Bible instructor in combining prayer with Bible study.

Lending Library in Bible Work

Mrs. Ena Ferguson has successfully used the lending library in the Bible work. She informs us regarding this method of soul winning.

"The church board having voted on a sum of money to be used in the lending-library project, it is left with me to select the books needed in my work. These books, however, are not to be considered a part of the regular church library, but are for the exclusive use of the newly interested. In the selection of books special attention is given to Mrs. White's works, *Beacon Lights,* books on the sanctuary, Sabbath, state of the dead, et cetera. There is a growing need for booklets on the problems of dress and amusement, and readable literature on health and stewardship. Later on Spirit of prophecy material is greatly in demand.

"It is always difficult for the Bible instructor to break off her regular studies after baptism, and yet the growing interest demands that she help these new believers to learn to stand firm without too much of her personal attention. It is then that these readers begin to feel somewhat lost in our midst, and if kept busy studying and reading by themselves, they are being helped to make a good adjustment during this transition period.

"The Bible instructor should see to it that the lending-library plan does not become too technical. It is possible to develop any good plan into details that will handicap its utility. I do not handle the circulation of these books as a librarian might want to. It is not wise to wait for the reader to ask for a book or to become too rigid about the time for its use; it pays to keep other objectives in mind and to be considerate of the reader's background and opportunities to read. But I make sure that these books move along, and are kept in circulation. I keep a record of all books being lent, but I work the plan to fit into my personal work for these readers. It is surprising, however, how this lending-library plan helps to deepen the experience of these people, and, like all good Seventh-day Adventists, they soon become literature-conscious and reading-minded. When once introduced to the plan, they soon learn to like it, and ask for more literature.

"I consider that the plan of the lending library has many advantages. Not the least of these is the opportunity to bind off our Bible work in a strong way while having a solid plan for checking on the progress of these new believers. On the other hand, it is encouraging to see the missionary possibilities such a plan will afford with those who may be slower in grasping the import of present truth. These silent messengers will continue to speak to the individual conscience, and the Bible instructor's visits are recognized as a service to the family rather than an intrusion with Adventist doctrines.

"The lending library should always be adapted to local needs. One need not begin with a heavy investment in the project, but it will soon be evident that this plan more than pays its way. As the interest at first begins to grow, trained laymen will be able to help in the circulation of our truth-filled books. The Bible instructor should be directing their work, however."

PART THREE

THE BIBLE INSTRUCTOR'S PERSONAL PROBLEMS

Hope Inspires Desire and Faith

In every human being He discerned infinite possibilities. He saw men as they might be, transfigured by His grace,—in "the beauty of the Lord our God." Looking upon them with hope, He inspired hope. Meeting them with confidence, He inspired trust. Revealing in Himself man's true ideal, He awakened, for its attainment, both desire and faith.—Evangelism, p. 487.

PART THREE ★ CHAPTER ONE

Worker's Influence in the Church

When a Bible instructor is transferred to another field of labor, the transfer of her church membership should be promptly attended to. Church membership is the privilege of a conference worker, as well as of the layman. The Bible instructor's work, however, is directed by the conference and not by the church, and her services cannot be monopolized merely to build up the interests of the one church of which she may be a member. It may happen occasionally that, for a limited time at least, a Bible instructor is directed to center her labors upon a church, but usually her services are for those who are not yet of the faith. She is an evangelistic type of worker as truly as the evangelist himself. She is his assistant, directed by him.

Rarely in our work is a minister free to carry on evangelism without having other duties, such as pastoring a church or several churches. He may have an intern to assist him in his many responsibilities, but he is usually the recognized director of the church or district in which he labors, as well as the leader of the series of evangelistic meetings. At times the evangelist and his Bible instructors are called to labor for a church whose departmental machinery is greatly in need of upbuilding. One must then face the question of whether it is wise to use the Bible instructor to lead the young people and perhaps the minister's wife to direct the Sabbath school. It may be necessary to educate a church to carry its responsibility in leading out in these departments, for some may be prone to criticize, feeling that conference-employed workers are being paid to fill these church offices.

Just what is the place of the Bible instructor, and what is her true relationship to the church where she holds membership. Aside from her actual evangelistic duties, such as visitation, the giving of Bible studies, and her work connected with the public meetings, she, with other workers, is recognized as a leader of our church members. Leadership, however, does not necessarily mean that these workers who are set apart to win others to the message must take church offices. They can serve far more effectively when they train and direct those in the church who should be developing for these offices. Experience has taught us that churches always maintain a better spiritual tone when lay members are developed to fill these positions. Conference workers are needed in many places, and it is well for churches to realize that they do not have long-time claims to these workers. A Bible instructor makes the best contribution when she trains others in the church to become soul winners, teachers, young people's leaders, deacons, or deaconesses.

Although it is a recognized fact that evangelism taxes a Bible instructor's strength to the limit, still a worker should not spend all her energy transporting people to church. She belongs in the Sabbath school and church services on the Sabbath day, as well as all other Seventh-day Adventists. When a worker fails to add strength to the church program, when evangelism is divorced from the efforts of the church and its worship, the very plan that should be built up is defeated. We may then expect just what is being experienced in some places—a decided lack of interest in our evangelistic efforts on the part of the church.

Our laymen occasionally express their keen disappointment in the "modern trends" of evangelism, which seem to leave the workers pulling the gospel net by themselves, while the church members wonder what it is all about and often fail to get enthusiastic over our new converts. Our believers, no matter how weary from their week's work, should come to church, because this is an act of devotion and a part of the Sabbath blessing. That same blessing must be claimed by the Bible instructor personally if her efforts to develop new

Sabbathkeepers are not to deteriorate into mere professionalism. Her example counts in this respect, and the believers have a right to interpret her sincerity by her actions.

Some workers toil so hard all week, physically and mentally, that the Sabbath is just an added burden to them instead of a blessing. Surely, this should not be, for those who are definitely responsible for organizing their own labors can change this picture. And they should!

A word regarding our seasonal church soliciting campaigns is also timely. Bible instructors contribute more to the cause of missions by leading others into service than by merely raising large sums themselves. They are leaders of the people in mission projects, and the worker who trains others, perhaps raising a smaller goal herself, is making a better contribution to the cause than the one who leaves the people behind. Too often the motive savors of vainglory.

This same principle holds true in every other church enterprise. The work to which Bible instructors have been set apart is Bible work, and not campaigning. It includes leadership in every worthy project of the church, but Bible instructors should keep their eyes on the objectives of their particular profession, not getting sidetracked in their zeal by competing with leaders whose primary duty is promoting campaigns. Each must know God's program for her work. No organized project should drive her to disregard her mission as the leader of men and women.

Bible Teaching an Art

I. *Teaching a Godly Art.*
  1. "As My Father hath taught Me." John 8:28.
  2. "Thou art a teacher come from God." John 3:2.

II. *Requires Consecration.*
  1. "Be gentle unto all men, apt to teach, patient." 2 Tim. 2:24.
  2. "Lord, teach us to pray." Luke 11:1.
  3. "A teacher . . . in faith and verity." 1 Tim. 2:7.
  4. "Teach them diligently." Deut. 6:7.
  5. "Teach me, and I will hold my tongue." Job 6:24.

III. *Skillful Teaching.*
   1. "Who shall be able to teach others." 2 Tim. 2:2.
   2. "Apt to teach." 2 Tim. 2:24.
   3. "He . . . taught the people knowledge." Eccl. 12:9.
   4. "A teacher of babes." Rom. 2:20.
IV. *Must Be Positive.*
   1. "He taught as one having authority." Matt. 7:29.
   2. "Thou hast taught them the good way." 2 Chron. 6:27.
   3. Teach difference between holy and profane. Eze. 44:23.
   4. "He still taught the people knowledge." Eccl. 12:9.
V. *Teaching, a Gospel Ministry.*
   1. "I am ordained a preacher, and an apostle, . . . a teacher." 1 Tim. 2:7.
   2. "I am appointed a preacher, and an apostle, and a teacher." 2 Tim. 1:11.
   3. "Evangelists; . . . pastors and teachers; for the perfecting of the saints." Eph. 4:11.
VI. *Often Creates Criticism.*
   1. "Dost thou teach us?" John 9:34.
   2. "How shall this man save us?" 1 Sam. 10:27.
VII. *Brings Results.*
   1. "And did as they were taught." Matt. 28:15.
   2. "Great shall be the peace of thy children." Isa. 54:13. L. C. K.

PART THREE ★ CHAPTER TWO

Daily Work Program

The Bible instructor's daily program will now be discussed, and those features which pertain to her own work. Because less experienced evangelism directors sometimes lack training in guiding the work of the team they supervise, the pressure of the daily program too often becomes the only guide to direct her labors from day to day. The evangelist should understand the program of his assistants as well as his own program. Besides following denominational plans for the Bible work, he should plan his week's working schedule with the mutual understanding of the entire evangelistic group. If the evangelist in charge understands what is considered to be an equitable work program for the Bible instructor, there will then be avoided an endeavor to build her program around his own personal plans.

Bible instructors might have a tale to tell as they review the experiences they have had in working with various types of evangelists. One evangelist may be the essence of organization, working its intricacies almost to the point of distraction; another worker may be so entirely opposite that the Bible instructor would come to grief if she could not supply the organization he lacked. After a broad experience a Bible instructor will welcome a leader who is a thorough organizer, but who does not make her machinery jar with the friction of high-pressure organization. A kind, calm, understanding director will receive greater service from his co-workers than a "driver"—one who makes sure they are impressed with how busy a man he is, so that they will keep up with his pace.

The consecrated worker will always find that the needs of the work itself are the driving incentives for each day's duties. But there must be direction, and a Bible instructor is happiest when the director of the effort has definite plans for her work. An understanding of her responsibilities will help her to anticipate what should be done, without requiring frequent and taxing workers' meetings for the purpose of explaining these duties in detail. Workers should be considered mature men and women with insight and interest in each other's work, and after the program of procedure is learned, the weekly workers' meeting will usually be sufficient to keep the machinery running smoothly.

Many inquiries have come regarding the Bible instructor's plan for reporting to the evangelist with whom she labors.

Here are a few suggestions. All such reporting takes time away from personal work the Bible instructor should be doing. The busy evangelistic program never allows for intricate reporting. A totaled report for the weekly workers' meeting in addition to the one the worker sends to the conference should suffice. Evangelists who feel it is necessary for their Bible instructors to render a report explaining how each hour of each day is spent, do not fully understand the pressure of Bible work. There may be an occasional place for such a system, when a group of untrained youth are temporarily employed, but why penalize the usual sensible, conscientious woman?

These are days of tremendous nerve strain and hard application. The hours of service for the Bible instructor are not measured by the dial of the clock. The usual worker is of the conscientious-to-the-last-degree type, who is always sacrificing comfort and sleep. So why should such a worker's lot be made harder by sitting up until the wee hours of the morning working out the day's report? To the director, of course, it is always "such a simple report that doesn't require any time at all," but to young evangelists who may chance to read this, the advice is, Please do not be too sure about what you may regard as simple.

A Bible instructor should be able to plan her own work. She must be an organizer. Good organization does not necessarily leave behind it multitudinous records, for, after all, reporting methods change rapidly. Her records will be best read in the lives of those whom she has influenced for the truth. It is well to bear this point in mind when inclined to build for the campaign a technical reporting system. Let us work for God and under His scrutiny rather than man's.

The working day will not be measured by an eight-hour labor law, but rather by Heaven's system of conscientious service. Bible instructors should not be required to work mornings, afternoons, and evenings, with hasty periods for meals to break the routine of work, holding to a program of continuous visitation until the effort closes. It is up to the director of the evangelistic series and the Bible instructor herself to change such a program. There must be time for rest, meditation, prayer, and study, if lasting results are to be obtained. The art of keeping one's co-workers happy is one that may well be practiced by our workers. Although we should all work diligently and wholeheartedly, we should retain the joy of Christian service which will react in blessings upon us and upon those for whom we labor.

For all workers an occasional holiday which will send them back to their tasks of love with renewed energy is recommended. There is need for these off-duty days if the system is to withstand the strain of Bible work.

During the busy days of an effort there may be little time for frequent assurances by the evangelist that the Bible instructor's services are appreciated. But a word of appreciation never goes amiss, and it helps greatly in lubricating the machinery of service. However, the whimsical Bible instructor is a detriment to the work. That friendly relationship which recognizes true Christian worth in one's co-worker is expressed not merely by means of a periodic eulogy but rather in sympathetic understanding.

PART THREE ★ CHAPTER THREE

Finding Time for Study

The query is often heard, "When in the busy program of the Bible instructor is there any time for personal study?" Judging by the frequency of this question, and because many conscientious Bible instructors are showing no small concern over the matter, it becomes evident that words of counsel on the subject may be timely.

Although the Bible instructor is directed in her work by the evangelist or the pastor with whom she is associated, her daily program is largely regulated by herself. She is duty bound to render the best service of which she is capable, but it is to be expected that she herself will become the real manager of her daily work. Inasmuch as Bible work needs more preparation and planning than some other types of service, she should not be required to be out in the field from early morning until midnight. Her work requires frequent seasons of relaxed and unhurried meditation, as well as proper time for study. Without this private preparation she would soon become uninspirational, if not inefficient or mechanical.

During a season of intensive evangelism any worker's study routine is seriously affected by interruptions necessitated by the many new contacts that must be developed. One may wish to arrange and plan for some time during each day for quiet study, but alas! it simply does not work out that way. The more experienced worker has made the discovery that this pressure for study time will not always remain acute, but the young worker may become exceedingly perplexed over it, if not depressed or annoyed.

Therefore, it becomes necessary to regard our Bible work at long range, and by taking heart from the experiences of those who have traveled the way before, the Bible instructor may hope for a more elastic schedule in the days to come. However, when a worker once enters the field of evangelism she will need to learn that her own program must constantly be subjected to adjustments, in order that the needs of the souls for whom she labors may be met.

Somewhere during the busy week's routine every worker must still be able to find time for inspirational study and unmolested meditation. Our habits of life vary so in this modern age that it would be useless to suggest the same schedule for all workers. This may necessitate the reshaping of some plans, but one is always able to find a way to do those things he enjoys doing or considers essential.

Finding Time for Study

Here is a question that each should weigh carefully: Have I learned to use God's gift of time to the best advantage? The busiest folk are the ones most frequently called on when real tasks must be accomplished. They, without outward worry or strain, can still find time to take on added responsibility. Tactfully and courteously they have the ability to turn down some minor tasks others may be able to do just as well as they, and they also seem to know on which problems they should personally concentrate. Some jealously guard every spare moment they can find for a little extra reading for self-improvement; others have not learned to improve these odd moments. Some Bible instructors may find a half hour's relaxation by stopping off at the library on the way to the other end of the city to meet an appointment.

Surely it is not commendable for Seventh-day Adventist workers to be constantly telling each other or their readers that they simply cannot find time for personal study. Such a serious admission is most regrettable. It is high time such took stock of their objectives, and used the same wisdom of organization they display in other matters. This is not so much a denominational problem as a personal responsibility.

But where must the worker begin to bring about a change? First of all, she should calmly make at least a mental list of the scope of each day's duties. Next she must eliminate some of her responsibilities, assigning them to helpers who can handle them perhaps even better than she can under such pressing circumstances. Too many times she is carrying church responsibilities which greatly add to her work load. To be associated with the youth and to counsel them in their work is one thing, but to be in leadership in their organization is quite another. This is equally true of the Sabbath school or any other department of the church. Often Bible instructors would save themselves much time and effort, if not embarrassment and disappointment, were they not involved in some department of the church, officiating where a willing layman could be doing just as acceptable service, if they had perhaps taken the time at the start to help him or her learn how. There is still too much of the deaconess type of service by our Bible instructors. Let them hold to the Bible work and guard against serving tables.

Responsible sisters in the church should be trained to help with the new Sabbathkeepers. Much time-consuming attention that these new believers require could be nicely met by such sympathetic helpers. Therefore, every Bible instructor should be on the lookout for understanding, tactful, kind layhelpers who would be greatly blessed themselves while ministering to others. The excellent help that many talented laymen could render in evangelism has not been taken advantage of. Workers must first learn to let go of some of their duties, and then be willing to train helpers. Such effort will amply repay in good will in the church, as well as provide more time for personal study.

An attitude of defeatism on the problem of not finding sufficient time for personal study dare not be assumed, and no worker need give up trying if she will intelligently and resolutely work on the following suggestions:

Pointers for Self-improvement

1. Learn to know your own study needs.
2. Counsel with your associates how to meet these needs.
3. Work out a feasible weekly study program.
4. Allow for emergencies, and plan an alternative study program.
5. Master your study time to fit your personal needs, not another's.
6. Improve days between intensive visitation or seasonal campaigns.
7. Plan to read our leading denominational journals.
8. Read the *Review* and study *The Ministry* magazine.
9. Visit local library about once a month to scan some religious journals of other denominations.
10. Determinedly pursue the Ministerial Reading Course.
11. Read books to broaden out in your profession.
12. Occasionally take a Home Study Institute course.

PART THREE ★ CHAPTER FOUR

Filing Notes and Materials

An alert Bible instructor will always appreciate helpful suggestions for professional tools and equipment. Ministers, Bible teachers, and departmental workers have occasionally discussed their personal filing systems in the columns of *The Ministry,* but for the Bible instructor's use, these would have to be adapted. Usually my domicile is in small quarters, and the very suggestion of a filing cabinet brings an added problem to my cramped home conditions. This need not, however, be made an excuse for me to be disorganized in my notes and materials. It is decidedly to my advantage and efficiency to have and use system and order. The extra effort it takes to install and utilize a convenient filing system is well repaid by the lessened strain on one's nerves and time.

The need of economy for one in Bible work is recognized, especially when she first enters the profession, but nevertheless some instructors have used an ingeniously devised file made of carton boxes or orange crates, covered with attractive, inexpensive cretonne. But for the worker who has graduated from such primitive ways, a few types of files seen on display in office-furniture supply houses and in almost any city department store are suggested.

A very practical and suitable type of file for Bible instructors is one that appears to be an attractive end table. It serves a double purpose, because it is a convenient article of furniture as well. It is made of metal, in tones of green or brown blends, and also in finishes of oak, cherry, or mahogany woods, and contains an $8\frac{1}{2}''$ x $11''$ standard-size filing drawer. It is a standard file in every respect.

Another type, standing a little higher than the end-table type, resembles a small chest. One kind opens on the front, and another type has a lid that opens at the top. Of course, there are also the smaller office files resembling a large book, and made of either strong cardboard or metal.

It is possible that even better suggestions for filing needs will be on the market in the near future. For the beginner who wishes something simple and inexpensive to start with, the telescope type of file can be purchased at dime, stationery, or department stores at a very nominal sum.

Catalogs show files that can be built up in units of two or more sections, or a combination file and storage cabinet suitable for many purposes. The Bible instructor who is interested in buying a file would do well to get it through the General Conference Department of Purchase and Supply.

Using the File

Every Bible instructor should have a file of some sort in which to keep her notations, observations, clippings, illustrations, quotations and references. This material should be classified and cross-indexed.

The order of procedure will be, first, clipping and collecting, then analyzing and organizing. Gather the materials around several large centers, and assign tentative subjects, such as Sabbath, Christ's Return, Prayer, Youth, and so forth.

The filing method should be simple and practical, neat and orderly, efficient and logical. If the standard-size business file is chosen a supply of Manila file folders should be purchased. These hold papers of size $8\frac{1}{2}''$ x $11''$ and afford room for small clippings. Use one folder for each classification.

The names of the subjects can be typed or written on the tab of the file folders, to make a temporary index. The various subjects arranged in alphabetical order allow one quickly to pick out the desired folder. The folders may be obtained with the projecting tab showing in various graduated positions—1, 2, 3 (left, middle, right), or a five-way position. Those desiring to know more details regarding filing are referred to *A Word to Writers*, Review and Herald Publishing

Association, 50c. This most helpful work includes a very practical section on filing.

An index on a separate sheet, listing all the subjects in order, is most helpful. Allied subjects or cross references may be typed at the bottom of the sheet, or on a separate sheet with a reference notation. For example, one may have a little material on "Armageddon" which she decides to include under "Last Plagues," and in the cross index it is listed "Armageddon—See Last Plagues."

Because time is so precious in home evangelism, a Bible instructor should not be tempted with the clipping mania. Her skill should include more than deftness with the scissors. It is better to make the wastebasket a fitting receptacle for unimportant clippings rather than clutter up an otherwise necessary file. The wise Bible instructor does not try to compete with the evangelist in gathering much introductory, interest-catching material. She usually steps into the picture after the evangelist has already gripped the initial interest, and it is then up to her to supply pointed Scriptural facts to hold that interest. And yet she too is a specialist, and should have adequate equipment for her work. She should have at her command those necessary facts and aids that will mark her as an intelligent teacher and an all-round professional success.

A Method of Biblical Research

Lillian A. Woodyard

OBJECTIVE.—To compile the Biblical evidence bearing on one subject, letting the weight of the evidence determine the conclusion.

"Search the Scriptures . . . until link after link is searched out, and united in a perfect chain." 2T 692.

METHOD.—Preconceived ideas are not followed. The Bible is the only source, and the Holy Spirit the sole teacher.

"The Bible is its own expositor. Scripture is to be compared with scripture." Ed 190.

KEY WORDS.—"One passage of Scripture will prove a key to unlock other passages." CT 437.

To secure key words make a list of all words having any connection with the subject. Example: Some key words for the second coming of Christ might be: come, appear, clouds, angels, descend, reveal. Then with the aid of a complete concordance each text containing a key word which bears on the subject should be carefully analyzed.

CARDS.—"Let the student take one verse, and concentrate the mind on ascertaining the thought that God has put into that verse for him." Ed 189.

Each text should be carefully analyzed as to how it relates itself to the subject. From this analysis there are four essential features to be placed on the card: subject, key thought, brief quotation, and reference. Example:

SECOND COMING   VISIBLE

"He cometh; . . . and every eye shall see him." Rev. 1:7.

A separate card should be made for each thought in the text. The importance of being extremely careful in heading the cards cannot be overemphasized, as it facilitates matters in the final compilation.

COMPILATION.—After all the key words have been looked up and all the cards have been made out, the next step is to separate the cards into groups bearing the same heading. Each group of cards should then be placed in its logical sequence in the study. The study is then ready to be copied from the cards, which have now completed their purpose.

APPLICATION.—It should be understood that this final form is primarily for reference. From this material a detailed study may be derived or, if so desired, just the outstanding points may be taken. This type of studying teaches the student to draw from the primary source of divine truth rather than to be satisfied with secondary material.

"The study of the Bible demands our most diligent effort and persevering thought. As the miner digs for the golden treasure in the earth, so earnestly, persistently, must we seek for the treasure of God's word."—*Education,* p. 189.

PART THREE ★ CHAPTER FIVE

Dress of the Bible Instructor

Grace Cox Ochs

The minister is first judged by his ability to preach. The Bible instructor is usually first judged by her appearance, and then by her conduct and speech. If she is slovenly or overdressed—and both are extremes—then the effect on her work is bound to be detrimental.

On the one extreme are those who are careless and untidy, who have unpolished, run-down shoes, crooked seams, dresses of absurd length, garments that need pressing, hair that strings around the neck and ears, loose powder on the collar and about the neckline, and runners in the hose. Why do they allow these conditions? Perhaps they think that to appear otherwise would be considered worldly. Thus poor taste is confused with humbleness. Untidiness that results from saving on shoe repair, dry cleaning, et cetera, is mistaken economy. Odd fashions and drab, toneless colors are misconceived for simplicity and piety! This is one extreme.

At the other extreme are those who overdress. Their whims lead them to choose unnecessary furbelows, gaudy colors, and the modern fads. Balanced simplicity disappears to satisfy an innate desire for many things rather than a well-chosen few. And why do they do it? Because others do it? Because they are really worldly? Not necessarily, although the outward appearance is a good index to the status of the heart. "The dress and its arrangement upon the person is generally found to be the index of the man or the woman."—Mrs. E. G. White in *Review and Herald,* Jan. 30, 1900.

The reason for overdressing, as well as for incorrect dressing, may be a lack of education or of good taste. It may be but a careless choice. Whatever may be the cause, the one who overdresses or dresses carelessly is a poor commentary on the Advent message. Both extremes should be avoided. It is the "middle road," dressing sensibly, that should be followed. This can be done wisely only as the principles and laws underlying proper dress are understood and followed.

From a practical viewpoint let us consider a few underlying principles which may help in choosing sensible attire. People differ in size, shape, features, height, and so forth. One may have a short, fat neck, another a long, thin neck. One may have a big nose and a receding chin, another a small nose and a prominent chin. One may be tall and thin, another short and fat. All these individual characteristics must be taken into consideration when a sensible dress is chosen.

Adapt Clothing to Physical Characteristics

Since individuals differ so widely, the garment that is sensible for one woman may not be sensible for another. A round collar may be just the thing for a long-faced woman, but not becoming at all for a round, fat-faced person. The sensible dress and accessories are those that do not attract attention to the wearer (other than that of seeing the individual as a harmonious whole), nor are they so intricate in detail, design, or color as to attract notice to themselves.

"The well-dressed woman may be said to wear inconspicuous clothing; her dress and hat are simple in design, yet they have an individual note that expresses her personality; . . .

and while not calling attention to themselves, they serve to make the wearer and the costume a perfect unit."—GOLDSTEIN, *Art in Everyday Life.*

Any garment or accessory which emphasizes some disturbing feature of the person, such as a big nose, a double chin, or a large head, to the point where these features are so exaggerated as to be conspicuous or comical to the observer, is neither becoming nor sensible, no matter how simple and unassuming the garb may be while hanging in the closet.

A study of lines in relation to clothes and personality will reveal the facts that parallel lines and contradictory lines emphasize individual characteristics. Therefore a round or square neckline, or collar, will emphasize a round or square face; a V neckline will exaggerate a thin, long face and neck. Horizontal lines, whether in design of material or cut of dress, increase the width of a figure, and vertical lines tend to increase the height.

It has been said that perhaps no part of the attire can be so detrimental or so helpful in personal appearance as a hat. A good hat should form a background or frame for the face, but it should never be so intricate in detail that it draws attention instead. Neither should the details of the hat be such as to center attention on some particular feature of the face. A dominant line in the face, if repeated in the hat or its trimming, will be emphasied. Therefore, a feature which is irregular, as an oversized nose or a drooping line about the mouth, should not have that line repeated in the hat. There are many types of hats, but most of them can be classified in specific groups.

Generally speaking, a hat should follow the natural contour of the head, and should appear as though it will stay on the head without being fastened. When a hat is to be purchased, plenty of time should be taken. The lines in the face, particularly around the mouth, the double chin, and the high forehead, are points to be examined as well as the design of the hat.

In thinking of sensible attire as a whole, one should go deeper than merely criticizing a specific decoration, a color, or the length of a dress. These, as well as numerous other phases, must be considered, but they must be thought of as a unified whole. In other words, sensible dress is an individual matter. Attire will be sensible, becoming, and unworldly when the principles laid down in the writings of the Spirit of prophecy and the laws of good taste in dress are followed.

Harmony and Design in Dress

The selection of proper clothes is a challenge to any woman's artistic ability—a challenge to her sense of what is appropriate under her immediate environment. This is particularly true of the Bible instructor and the minister's wife. Simplicity and good taste are synonymous terms to be used in the selection of any wardrobe. They are the very nucleus of all that it takes to be well dressed.

There are scores of simply styled garments on the market. But it is not so much what is on the market as what one chooses to buy from the market. For instance, one finds a simple, unobtrusive hat. It is bought! Down the street is a lovely, modest dress. It is bought. Shoes are purchased at another place. A coat is still good from last year's buying. The new selections are put together—and they just do not harmonize! The modest hat becomes conspicuous because of poor color or material. The dress seems out of harmony with the hat. The style chosen, though a simple one, has the wrong lines for the wearer. The result is that instead of a simple, harmonious unit, the purchaser has an overdone, conspicuous combination.

How can one know just what goes with which, and vice versa? There are many factors to be considered. Some of these factors are age, size, and complexion, as well as the color, design, and texture of the material, the design of the dress, the hat, the shoes, and so forth. All details of a costume should be related in idea as well as in color and texture.

For example, let us consider *texture*. Stiff fabrics should be worn with tailored accessories. Soft fabrics should be worn with the dressier type of hat and shoes. A stout woman would find a hard, shiny surface unbecoming, as it catches light and makes the figure appear larger. This type of material also accentuates hard lines, sharp angles, and irregular features of the body and face. Therefore a softer fabric would give the opposite effect, and is more becoming to the older woman. It is true that textures can be combined, such as using a wool, sergelike material with taffeta or satin as a trim. There are no special rules for such combinations. An understanding of harmony is the best guide.

Materials with conspicuous patterns soon become tiresome to look at. It is more desirable to select designs in which the figures are not so noticeable. All colors should be becoming to the wearer. The choice depends on the person's age, size, coloring, and personality. Any good authority on color will give color scales and harmony charts for various types of individuals. (See *Art in Everyday Life,* by Harriet and Vetta Goldstein, pp. 289-308, Macmillan, New York City, 1940.)

The matter of the selection of a *design* for a dress seems to be a difficult thing for most people. Older women prefer something simple and dignified, and yet because of cheap trimmings or perhaps exaggerated trimmings, the dignity and the simplicity of material or design are lost. Self trimmings (tucks, cording, bands of the same material) usually add more dignity to a garment than a quantity of cheap lace or much beading.

Again, one must consider her age, size, and build when selecting any design. A dress should bear resemblance to the figure, as shape harmony is very important in considering a beautiful design. If some part of the figure is exaggerated by the style of the dress, then a comical or even slovenly appearance may be the result. The waist length should be so proportioned as to make a harmonious unit. Such a length should not cut the figure in two. Too short dresses are likely to throw the spacing of length of skirt and waist out of harmony. The figure should appear to be balanced whether standing, sitting, or walking. The authors of the aforesaid *Art in Everyday Life* summarize these thoughts as follows:

"The well-dressed woman wears simple clothes, having an individual note which expresses her personality, and distinguishes her from all those around her; her shoes, hose, gloves, bag, are fitting accessories, and while not calling undue attention to themselves, they serve to make the wearer and the costume a perfect unit."—Page 275.

Relation of Dress to Influence

Some say it is wrong to spend much time talking about clothes. That is true! It is a waste of time to spend too much time on clothes—but since custom, modesty, and climate demand clothes, and since they play such an important part in how we look, and our influence upon others, then surely *enough* time should be used to choose that which is correct. "A refined taste, a cultivated mind, will be revealed in the choice of a simple, appropriate attire."—*Messages to Young People,* p. 353. Does it not take forethought to get this result? Ideals and standards underlying all true modesty and godliness are revealed in the choice of what we wear, as well as in our conduct. Should not enough study and thought be applied to clothes to bring about the right revelation of what we really are?

The Scriptures tell us we are spectacles to the "world, and to angels, and to men." 1 Cor. 4:9. If our clothes, because of being ill-chosen, attract so much attention that the world cannot see Christian character in the individual, then we help to defeat a purpose God has for us. It is the Christian's duty to avoid extremes and to keep balanced in judgment and thinking. Christian ideals should shine forth in every costume that is worn. If at any time the fashions of the world so swing to the extreme that the Christian woman cannot find clothes in keeping with such ideals and standards as she may have, then, regardless of how she may appear to others, she "should humbly pursue a straight-forward course, irrespective of applause or of censure, and should cling to the right because of its own merits."—*Ibid.*, p. 350.

Heavenly Representatives

REATHEL JENKINS

Tidiness should mark the costume of the Bible instructor, her hair, her face, and her fingernails. Her clothes and her person should be clean. A Bible instructor should be an example of the Book she teaches, and adorned in modest apparel. Her life fragrant with the breath of heaven, her hands clean, her heart pure, she is to glorify God. Her manner and her bearing should be dignified, with her message more prominent than her dress. Her dress is at all times to be appropriate for the time and the place. She is an ambassador from heaven, and in Christ's stead is reconciling men to Him. If we recognize that the seal of God will not be placed upon a proud, self-loving person, it makes us realize the magnitude of our task in setting a right example, for we are trying to prepare people to meet the approval of God.

PART THREE ★ CHAPTER SIX

Home and Personal Problems

Selecting a home is no simple matter for the Bible instructor, for there are some vital factors to be taken into consideration if she is to have the necessary comforts and conveniences, and also to live where her work will be carried on to the best advantage. Usually she is one of the type of workers who know no permanent dwelling place; yet her life should not be a gypsylike existence. Our attitudes influence our work, and although one's stay in a certain place may be of short duration, the time spent there should be happily spent and influential in every respect.

The Bible instructor must develop the knack of settling herself in a new place without making a whole community aware of her arrival. It is recommended, for the sake of the work, that she have but few possessions. Every article should be necessary for a small apartment; the majority have to live in just one room, with limited housekeeping facilities. This is hardly from choice, for these plans do not appeal to the average woman; but they are truly sacrifices made for the work. Some become experts in working out their home furniture and equipment problems on the next to "blessed-be-nothing" scale, as far as ownership is concerned; but this causes one to keep on replacing items at financial loss, or be forced to borrow or rent those articles which others own as standard essentials.

The Bible instructor of experience has learned some pointers she might well pass on to others. When locating in a new place, she makes but temporary arrangements at the start. If she then lives with a Seventh-day Adventist family until more permanent plans are worked out, there is no disappointment later when changes must be made. A Bible instructor should not be asked to live with a struggling Seventh-day Adventist family, merely to help them work out their financial problem. Experience is a hard teacher, and she can save herself much embarrassment by being more cautious beforehand than sorry afterward. She needs a telephone and some utilities which poverty cannot provide.

There may be some definite advantages when a Bible instructor lives with those of like faith, but a worker must also weigh those problems which present disadvantages. It is always difficult for one not in this type of work to understand the reasons for the irregularity of the Bible instructor's daily program. Forced to be busy about her work until late in the night, she must, for health reasons, sleep in a little longer in the morning. Again, a Bible instructor has many confidences to guard, and her telephone conversations and the visitors she receives at her home must be private matters. When living with church members, she would be expected to be more than just casually friendly with the family, but such a relationship would be likely to be misunderstood by others in the church. Many other problems which often present embarrassment when the Bible instructor makes her home with our believers need not be elaborated on. These few suggestions will suffice to help the beginner to use the necessary precaution before avoidable complications arise. There is, however, no denominational ruling against living in Seventh-day Adventist homes. Many workers have demonstrated that it can be done with profit, especially when an apartment furnishes the necessary privacy. After having weighed this issue from every angle, the Bible instructor herself must use her best judgment.

The Bible instructor's living quarters may be a bit cramped, but her little home can still be neatly organized. Cleanliness and neatness should not be affected by congested conditions, for these are personality traits of the worker. To stress Sabbathkeeping and health reform to those not of our faith, when our own little home is a scene of disorder and confusion, destroys the very message we teach.

When making arrangements for a place to rent, the worker should ask whether it includes facilities to wash and press one's clothes. We are judged by our appearance. The Bible instructor's work is visiting. Good taste suggests that she dress, not as a housewife, but as a caller, and not as a neighborly visitor, but as a professional gospel worker.

Another question that enters into the Bible instructor's home problems is that of the amount of money she should pay for rent. She should live in a good neighborhood of the middle class of people. However for this privilege she may have to pay a little higher rent than is ordinarily the case.

Bible instructors should be good managers. Bills should be paid promptly. A budget and a record of one's daily expenditures are important, especially when an itemized laborer's report showing the expenses for each day must be filed with the conference every month. Some workers detest keeping accounts, but since this is a part of a Bible instructor's life, one should adjust her likes and dislikes and fall into line. To humor one's idiosyncrasies is foolishness, but to take oneself in hand is Christian wisdom.

We who claim to be experts of Bible mathematics and of the finance of the church should be masters of our own finances. It is to be regretted when poor management necessitates enlisting the help of the conference treasurer. True, illness can come to anyone, and emergencies will bring pressure to our personal budget, but there are always ways by which the conference can handle these items. As Christian workers we should manage our own affairs so judiciously that we will give to those who are watching us no cause for the slightest suspicion of imposition or ill management on our part.

After a few years of frequent transfers to other cities or fields, some workers develop a restive spirit, which grows on them to the extent of becoming a real problem to conference administrators. Let us believe that an all-wise Providence is shaping our future and that we must eventually give an account of the time and money conferences have to spend to settle us again and again. On the other hand, some fields would never provide the proper development for some workers, and it is a sign of alertness and good judgment for them to help bring about transfers that will make them more useful to the cause. Although it is not wrong for us to have an occasional conviction that the Lord is leading us elsewhere, we should maintain our confidence in God's leadership and in the brethren who plan for His work at large.

Pointers on Locating a Home

1. Seek counsel from those well acquainted with workers' locating problems.

2. Study needs of field to be worked as well as proximity to meeting hall.

3. It is important to locate in residential section of better middle class.

4. Make sure that your location is convenient to main transportation lines. (For quiet, avoid closeness to stations and terminals.)

5. Select a well-lighted neighborhood. (Bible instructor's program requires much evening work, and protection and safety are important.)

6. When working without a car, make sure stores are conveniently near.

7. A private entrance to your apartment is not only more convenient but also most desirable.

8. Kitchenette and bathroom for private use are preferable.

9. Where there is joint occupancy, have a definite understanding about heat, light, use of kitchen, bathroom, laundry, phone, et cetera.

10. Leasing is hardly practical for Bible instructor, but assure yourself reasonable permanency.

11. Pay rent promptly. Refrain from requests for extra favors.

12. Have understanding with conference on personal budget and rent arrangements.

13. Renting from nonmembers is often advisable.

14. Living with non-Seventh-day Adventist relatives usually hinders one's efficiency.

15. When sharing rent with an associate, mutually count the cost.

16. It is preferable not to live in home of evangelist or pastor.

The Rock by the Side of the Road

"Come, sit on the rock by the side of the road,"
    Said the Master to me one day.
So He led me away from the jam in the road
    To where that hard rock lay.

I sat on the rock by the side of the road,
    But I cried with anguished tone,
"Must I leave my work in the broad highway
    To tarry here alone?

"Just look at the folk on the crowded road,
    And, Master, so much to be done.
Souls may be lost as I linger here;
    'Tis not long till setting sun!"

My Jesus smiled as He looked at me,
That wondrous smile I love to see,
"My child, I know that the work is great,
I know full well that the hour is late.

"But earnestly pray for the busy throng;
    Thus you will hasten My work along,
While your life and message will sweeter be
    Because you paused and learned of Me."

Here on the rock by the side of the road,
    Sweet visions of home I see,
More of the beauties of heaven beyond,
    As my Lord is speaking to me.

There will be no rock by the side of the road
    In the place He has gone to prepare;
The lessons of life must be learned right here,
    And not in the mansions there.

So we'll sit on the rock by the side of the road—
    We'll sit, when the twilight is dim—
But our lives and message will sweeter be
    For having paused and learned of Him.

—GRACE FOLKENBERG.

PART THREE ★ CHAPTER SEVEN

Preserving the Worker's Health

Elva R. Heald, R.N.

"Since the mind and the soul find expression through the body, both mental and spiritual vigor are in great degree dependent upon physical strength and activity; whatever promotes physical health, promotes the development of a strong mind and a well-balanced character. Without health, no one can as distinctly understand or as completely fulfil his obligations to himself, to his fellow-beings, or to his Creator. Therefore the health should be as faithfully guarded as the character."—*Education,* p. 195.

All are familiar with the principles of healthful living and with nature's remedies; thus it is not necessary to review them here. However, there is one which I wish to stress, which in this day and age seems most neglected.

We are told that one in five persons has one of the degenerative diseases which are taking such a heavy toll of human life. Your doctor will tell you that one of the predisposing causes is the tempo of the times. Speed, speed, speed, the race for money, lands, fame, and brilliant records is wearing down the delicate machinery and nerve energy of our physical organism.

"The laws of nature are the laws of God."—*Ibid.,* p. 196. Jesus taught from nature, and there are so many beautiful lessons to learn from it. Let us see what there is for us about *rest.*

In Isaiah 61:3 we are called "trees of righteousness, the planting of the Lord." Who does not thrill to the beauty of a fruit tree in bloom, or the coolness of a stately pine, or the majesty of a stalwart oak, and lift his heart in praise to a loving and thoughtful Creator? I like to think of workers as fruit trees. With fruit trees we observe that there is a period of activity and a period of rest. They have been planted, pruned, and nurtured, and in spring put forth their blossoms —a promise of fruit. Spring and summer are a period of activity in nature's factory. In the autumn the harvest of fruit is accomplished to the joy of all. Then comes winter—a period of rest and quietness.

When there is normal balance in nature, we see an abundant harvest. Sometimes we observe an imbalance, due to untoward circumstances. In northern climes it may be a "January thaw," the ice and snow disappear, and it becomes so warm that the buds and even blossoms burst forth on the trees. But soon frost and snow come again; the buds freeze and drop off. The tree may try again in spring to produce more blossoms, but with poor results. The rest period has been interrupted, and at best there will be only a partial crop.

Surely Bible instructors are of the Lord's planting, and He rightly expects a harvest. He will tenderly care for and nourish us by His grace.

Jesus invited His disciples to "come . . . apart . . . and rest a while." "I sat down under His shadow with great delight." Song of Solomon 2:3. If we will sit down and rest quietly in His promises, we will gain strength for the conflict, learn how to lessen toil and worry, and how to speak to the glory of God. "All who are under the training of God need the quiet hour for communion with their own hearts, with nature, and with God. In them is to be revealed a life that is not in harmony with the world, its customs, or its practises; and they need to have a personal experience in obtaining a knowledge of the will of God. We must individually hear Him speaking to the heart."—*Ministry of Healing*, p. 58.

"The Saviour offers to share with us the work God has given us to do."—*The Desire of Ages*, p. 523.

Be one with Him and see men and women accept Him. (John 17:21.) Let us avoid the frost and blight of weariness.

Are you chronically tired? Do you have indefinite aches and pains? It may be your diet needs balancing or alkalinizing, but what is more probable, you need nature's sovereign remedy—rest and relaxation. Chronic fatigue changes the body chemistry and produces acid poisons, which are cumulative and are contributing agents to disease.

Do you apologize or feel condemned for taking a midday or eventide nap, or twenty minutes of relaxation? Don't; for if you will acquire this habit, it will mark you as a person who plans and arranges his program with a desire to be in harmony with God's laws and commands.

Take your vacation daily as you do your food, and as you observe other health principles—a noonday rest, early evening relaxation, and eight hours of sound sleep. Do not crowd it into two short weeks a year.

The out-of-doors is quite conducive to rest. Find some quiet retreat where you can completely relax. Watch the little creatures around you, breathe in the life-giving oxygen and the sweet fragrance of growing things. Lift your eyes to the blue canopy of heaven, and watch the clouds sail by. Stretch out every muscle, and then relax them. You will be refreshed and more able to impart to others the story of the Creator and of a soon-coming Saviour.

Relaxation is an antidote for tension—today's number one enemy of health. Learn to relax while working; cultivate a serene, cheerful attitude of mind. Refuse to worry about what might happen, or what has happened and cannot be undone. Rest in God's glorious promises. Trust Him more fully.

"Let us turn from the dusty, heated thoroughfares of life to rest in the shadow of Christ's love."

Balancing Activity and Rest

Health a Personal Duty. *Testimonies,* vol. 6, p. 369; *Gospel Workers,* p. 513.

Need for Sleep, Rest, and Exercise. *Testimonies,* vol. 7, p. 247.

Poise and Health Through Prayer. *Education,* pp. 270, 261; *Gospel Workers,* p. 255.

Recreation Essential. *Ibid.,* vol. 4, p. 653; *Education,* p. 206.

PART THREE ★ CHAPTER EIGHT

Hints by a Minister's Wife

ETHEL N. COON

From the viewpoint of an evangelist's wife I should like to discuss a few items which, if recognized and corrected, would make the work of the Bible instructor more valuable to the evangelist.

First, be willing to adapt your own personal plans to fit those of the evangelist with whom you are working. There are methods, and there are methods. We do not all use exactly the same procedure. When I took my first position as a stenographer I had just finished my course and naturally thought I knew the right form for turning out a finished letter. And, of course, I felt that my way was the only right way. My employer taught me a lesson I have never forgotten. He had his own style, and he expected me to follow that style as long as I was working for him.

So, although you may feel—and at times rightfully so—that your method is superior to that of the evangelist, you must be willing to give up your wishes at times and fit right into the method of the man at the head of the company. This will go a long way in making the machinery run smoothly, and the more smoothly the machinery can be made to run, the better will be the finished product. Remember, *cooperation* is of more value than *method*.

By this I do not in any way mean to infer that a co-worker should not be free to express herself concerning her ideas of ways in which the work might be improved. This is one of the objects of the workers' meetings held during the campaign. Be free to counsel together and express your own mind. But if your plan is not followed, be willing to follow the plan of your leader without irritation. Ever be on the alert to see anything you can do to make the work of the evangelist easier, but be careful not to go to the extreme of making yourself officious. In your eagerness to help, do not appear bossy and overbearing. Most men are allergic to being bossed by the feminine sex. This is just as true in an evangelistic company as it is in the home or office.

Be loyal to the evangelist. Although you may not see eye to eye in everything, uphold each other before the people. A spirit of unity seen among the workers by those in attendance is very helpful in aiding them to make favorable decisions.

My husband and I once had an experience which perhaps is unusual, but it illustrates the point in question. We had a very capable Bible instructor working with us. No one could give a better Bible study than she; neither could we find anyone who could give a more helpful Sabbath school lesson review. But she was so sympathetic with the people when visiting in their homes that instead of helping them to decide for the truth, she actually made it seem very reasonable for them to reject it. We could not determine for a long time what the trouble was, but finally it came to light. And years later we found also, by her own confession, that this same worker talked against the evangelist as she visited among the people. Then, of course, it was plain why greater and more enduring results were not seen. "If a house be divided against itself, that house cannot stand." Mark 3:25.

When reporting work done and visits made, be as brief as consistent. An evangelist does not appreciate being burdened with unnecessary details. If he felt capable of carrying all details in his mind and caring for them, he would not need your help. Always remember that when it comes down to the last analysis, the burden of the whole campaign is resting on his shoulders. He has to care for the larger matters. Most evangelists now have card reporting systems by which they can determine at a glance the degree of interest of each person. If he has to listen to a long, detailed account, he might save time if he made the visit himself. So in reporting, be brief, concise, and to the point.

Be wide-awake, alert, farsighted. During a public effort keep close watch of your people. Make it a point to know the new faces from night to night, as far as lies within your power. If you can help it, don't let the newcomers get away without a hearty handshake and a friendly smile. Show a personal interest in them that will make them want to return. The evangelist appreciates such cooperation.

In giving Bible studies don't talk too much. You will be a greater asset to your evangelistic company. Leave your people wanting more rather than being worn out. And be careful not to go ahead of the evangelist in doctrinal studies. This is appreciated by all leaders.

I suppose there is no characteristic of a Bible instructor that is more valued by an evangelist than dependability. This is true in any branch of work. The dependable person is the one in demand. What a load is lifted from the shoulders of the evangelist when he is able to outline some particular work, turn it over to his Bible instructor, and *know* that the work will be done faithfully! If he takes time to give it to another, then has to check to see whether it has been done, and then, perhaps, in the end do it himself, it would be much easier for him to do the work in the beginning. Rare are the individuals who are absolutely dependable—so very rare that when one joins our company it is as refreshing as an oasis in the desert. As Bible instructors, would it not be well to develop on this point till you can be rated as A-1?

Effective Working Relationship

Don't force your own methods. Be willing to submit to your leader, but still be yourself.

Don't speak of the failings of the evangelist—be loyal.

Don't wear out the evangelist with details—make your reporting brief, concise, and to the point.

Don't talk too much—just enough.

DO be dependable. Carry your responsibility faithfully.

PART THREE ★ CHAPTER NINE

Professional Relationships
What Should the Evangelist Expect of the Bible Instructor?
J. H. BAYLESS

1. *Spiritual Relationship to the Work.*

The Bible instructor should be conscious of a definite, direct, inward call from God to her work.

Her service for humanity should be prompted by the presence of an indwelling Christ and His love.

She is not expected to have attained to the acme of perfection, but to foster a progressive Christian experience.

She should be firmly grounded in Adventist teaching and practice, and unwavering to the cause she represents.

2. *Relationship to the Evangelist.*

She should recognize herself as the evangelist's co-worker, cooperator, counselor, and Christian friend.

She should, therefore, feel free to offer intelligent, constructive criticism and helpful suggestions relative to: (*a*) Methods of evangelistic labor. (*b*) The evangelist's pulpit deportment, postures, gestures, mannerisms, preaching, and sermon substance.

At the same time she should be prepared to accept kindly reciprocal guidance, for, if it is an eternal truth that two cannot "walk together, except they be agreed," it is certainly a pertinent question in evangelistic labor: Can two work together, except there be agreement?

3. *Relationship to Her Evangelistic Duties.*

The Bible instructor should plan her work prayerfully and methodically at the beginning of each week, so that time is allotted to the workers' meeting, visiting, giving Bible studies to the interested people, and conducting prayer services, the Sabbath school class, children's and young people's services when required, assisting in the activities of the Missionary Volunteer Society, Ingathering, and other church campaigns. Time should also be set aside for personal devotion, preparation for personal Bible studies and other services, relaxation, and rest. It is imperative that she meet all her appointments on time.

In every case she should give priority of attention to potential Adventists.

She should keep a prayer list of all the interested people, and pray through the list every day, considering this, to say the least, a vital part of her daily routine duties. For, the work that grows out of persistent intercession is easy, and the results are enduring.

She should be prepared for any emergency, such as the unavoidable absence of the evangelist and should always carry her Bible and notes on several subjects.

4. *Personal Attention.*

She should give study to her apparel, by dressing modernly and neatly, without employing any of the exaggerated fashions of the day. She should not use colorful cosmetics.

She should pay attention to her health by spending her free time profitably in legitimate recreation and exercise, by proper diet, regular meals, and sufficient sleep.

To qualify as an alert and progressive worker, the Bible instructor must give attention to study and reading. She cannot grow in grace and knowledge and technical training without a program for self-improvement. This time must be closely guarded and individually regulated.

What Should a Bible Instructor Expect of the Evangelist?

Bessie Cleary

Expectation is the state of anticipation of future benefits or excellence—the prospect of future good. So the dictionary has it, and so the Bible instructor hopes, as she is invited to take up work with the evangelist.

For the sake of clarity and speed I have divided the subject into four sections:
1. The Evangelist in the Workers' Meeting.
2. The Evangelist in Campaign Work.
3. The Evangelist in the Homes of the People.
4. The Evangelist as a Man.

1. *The Evangelist in the Workers' Meeting.*

The Lord designs that His work shall be carried solidly. It was the Saviour's purpose that the messengers of the gospel should be associated together to be mutually helpful, the defects in one being partially covered by the virtues in the other. It is the workers' meeting that provides time and opportunity to study together not only the problems of the work in your particular district, but also lessons from the Word as a means of counsel and help. In all the Lord's arrangements there is nothing more beautiful than His plan of giving to men and women a diversity of gifts. The Lord desires His chosen servants to learn how to unite together in harmonious effort. The workers' meeting can be a consulting room where evangelist and Bible instructor may talk together, offer kindly criticism, suggest, adapt, encourage, sympathize. It should not be allowed to develop into a situation where a very important evangelist raps out orders and issues commands.

The evangelist should begin his workers' meeting on time. When his Bible instructor arrives at his home at ten o'clock on a lovely spring morning, he should never tell her that she has a bad conscience and can't sleep! But he should be ready, with his breakfast eaten and his shoes laced up, and he will find a Bible instructor who respects him and who will work faithfully with him.

The evangelist should explain his methods of work and the keeping of records to his Bible instructor. If she has any better suggestion for doing things, even though she has learned it from her previous evangelist, he shouldn't throw it out untried with a "You're not with So-and-so now!" If that is his attitude, she will have tumbled to the fact already.

As the names and problems of the interested are discussed, the evangelist and Bible instructor must pray. I do feel that much more success would be manifested if the workers could pray together in peace and quiet, without the disturbing knowledge that the baby's bath was in progress, or some such evidence of domestic bliss. Let us not become so familiar with holy things that we fail to give the work of God the respect and reverence it demands. Let us have order and system as we plan the work of God. Let us seek the Lord together. God intends that we shall be a help and blessing to each other. Let the workers' meeting fulfill that purpose.

2. *The Evangelist in Campaign Work.*

The Bible instructor understands that the evangelist bears the brunt of responsibility for the planning of the campaign. She does not wish to usurp his place. But she does expect to be informed of the plans in operation for the campaign, and is willing to share in the tasks of preparation. She wants to feel that this is a united effort to win souls.

The Bible instructor should be made acquainted with the order of service. She is just as avid to see things done successfully as the evangelist is, so he should let her make suggestions where necessary. A woman can often see where a man is blind.

The evangelist should introduce his Bible instructor to the people. His words will help her tremendously to find an entrance into homes. He should remember that she will be the first to make personal contact with the individual. She will get to know his problems and worries more intimately, perhaps, than the evangelist. She will have more opportunity to get nearer to him. Therefore, she stands or falls by the evangelist's representation of her to the people. He should encourage them to have confidence in her. She will do the same for him as she talks with them privately. If they know she is a graduate from the same missionary college which he attended, she will at once be given a standing, and the people will not think of her merely as the woman who gives out the hymnbooks, or tidies up afterward.

Important events sometimes occur to call the evangelist away right in the crisis of the interest. If he has backed up his Bible instructor and created confidence in her, then she can hold the fort until his return, with no slackening of the interest. He should recognize that in many respects she is just as capable as he is.

If it is at all possible, the Bible instructor should be free from playing for meetings, so as to be able to greet the people and get to know them. Many a contact has been made as the interested ones come and go. Therefore the Bible instructor ought to have this opportunity.

While the effort meetings are in progress I don't think it advisable for the Bible instructor to be outside the hall or in some anteroom, caring for the evangelist's child. She expects to be allowed to remain in the meeting, to watch the effect of the message on the hearers and generally to do the work for which she has been trained. Many of the hearers are devout worshipers in the established churches, and judge us by the dignity and reverence of their own assemblies.

The Bible instructor expects the evangelist to preach the Word. That is his task. The truth-seeking public are not interested in his family affairs and whether he thinks he is underpaid or not. He should keep these things out of his sermons. The Bible instructor feels ashamed when she has to face the suggestion from several dear old ladies that they should take up an offering for the evangelist, as he is so poor! The things he says in the pulpit reflect on the organized work and on the message of truth we preach. He should see to it that that reflection always shows the beauty of the truth in Christ, and loyalty to the movement he represents.

There is a welcome idea growing in our ranks that the Bible instructor can be more profitably employed than in giving out handbills week by week. No Bible instructor will refuse to do her reasonable share of this work, if the evangelist's budget cannot provide release. But she should not have the burden of seeing to the distribution of all the bills, taking a major share herself. She expects, therefore, that the evangelist will see to these things, and so allow her to concentrate on the visiting, with energies fresh and unimpaired.

Studying the truth with people and pleading for souls takes time. The Bible instructor expects the evangelist to be reasonable in his demands and not expect her to be in and out of the home in twenty minutes. He should trust his worker; advise her, by all means; but trust her. She has, as he has, a sense of responsibility to God for the way she spends her time in the homes of the people. The evangelist should remember that sometimes she is doing some service in the home to help the aged or infirm, or to break down prejudice. He should let her know he trusts her common sense not to outwear her welcome.

3. *The Evangelist in the Homes of the People.*

In the course of time, then, as a result of her visiting, she will arrange for the evangelist to call on the people in their homes. Here the Bible instructor expects to take a back seat. She likes the evangelist to bring his own Bible, not to borrow hers, and to live up to the reputation she has been building up for him over the weeks. She is wise enough to know that the wind and the weather must form part of the conversation, but she rejoices as he turns to spiritual themes and establishes the eager soul in present truth. Her heart warms as he forges another link in the chain that anchors the soul to the Rock of Salvation.

The Bible instructor expects the evangelist to follow up the work he begins in the pulpit. She is dismayed when he spends so much time in his own house that he has no time to visit or engage in any part of the work except preaching. She expects him to be free of home duties during the hours of a normal working day. No minister should be measured simply by his ability as a speaker. The harder part comes after he leaves the pulpit. If but half the sermonizing were done, and double the labor given to souls in their own homes, a result would be seen that would be surprising.

4. *The Evangelist in His Personal Relationships.*

Finally, what does the Bible instructor expect of the evangelist in his personal relationships to her?

She expects him to be a Christian gentleman. She is thrown much into his association, and learns to read him as an open book. She expects friendliness, but not familiarity; authority, but not dictatorship; appreciation, but not flattery; an understanding that she is human and a woman.

There is a danger that the women connected with the work will be required to labor too hard, without proper periods of rest. Such severe taxation should not be brought upon the workers. Periods of rest are necessary for all, especially women. Because she is a woman, she is prepared to be faithful and loyal to the evangelist, to prove herself capable and willing in service. She may not be able to sing like Melba, or play like Paderewski, or preach like Paul. But if he remembers she is not a machine, and is prepared to regard her as a colaborer with himself and God, their joint labors will issue in success and fruitfulness for the cause to which all evangelists and Bible instructors have dedicated themselves.

PART THREE ★ CHAPTER TEN

Greater Power and More Efficiency

Retrospect and Prospect

LeRoy E. Froom

The unfolding of the majestic mission of the great Second Advent Movement, in the minds of our leaders, and the gradual grasp of the means God designed to employ for the finishing of His work on earth, form a fascinating story. Just as truly as the great phases, or departments, of our work were slowly perceived and set in motion—publishing, educational, health, youth, lay missionary, and so forth—just so truly did God lead in the prior development of special groups or categories of workers. One of the earliest of these was the faithful helper and associate of the ordained minister—the Bible worker, as formerly called.

PLAN BEARS INSIGNE OF HEAVEN.—Let us first take a retrospective view of the profession and its development to date. Heaven-indicted instruction encouraging this very work came to this people back in the nineties. It is therefore not merely of man's devising. It was specifically called for by the Spirit of prophecy, and bore the insigne of heaven. Launched by the Haskells in connection with the staggering task of reaching the great metropolitan masses, it has gone on from those humble beginnings until now it has its established place among us as one of the great soul-winning means destined to play an increasingly important part in the closing work.

The plan of Bible readings was launched back in 1883, in California, our then far western outpost, by S. N. Haskell. He had just returned from Europe, where he had been impressed by the method of Bible instruction used by the Waldenses. He conceived the idea at the Nebraska Conference, on the way West, by observing how colporteurs followed up interests through explaining the Bible in the homes of the people. To this was added Mrs. White's personal urge that we should be able to explain the great lines of Bible prophecy to others. "Fireside Preaching" was one of the earliest terms used to designate the plan.

But it was apparently at the Lemoore, California, camp meeting in May that the name Bible Readings, or Bible Classes, was first used to describe the plan. In fact, that was the burden of the camp. The same plan was stressed in Los Angeles, next in the Upper Columbia camp meeting, then back in San Francisco and Healdsburg. Finally, at the San Jose camp meeting, the California Conference passed the first formal resolution recommending the plan of Bible Readings, and urged those who could to attend a special course of Bible instruction at Healdsburg College—"especially designed to fit men and women for active duty in the field, especially the work of holding Bible readings."

The same plans and recommendations were carried to the Michigan and Indiana camp meetings in October. And an "Institute for Instruction in Bible Readings" was begun at Battle Creek on October 30. Three hundred joined the class under the leadership of S. N. Haskell. The attendance increased until it passed the thousand mark. Some of these workers were early called "helps." (1 Cor. 12:28.) From this developed the monthly *Bible Reading Gazette* in 1884, the first one of which, "On the Sanctuary," had 149 questions. Such is the fascinating story of the beginnings of this heaven-born Bible-readings plan, in 1883. (See "Origin of Our Bible Work," *The Ministry*, Oct., 1948-March, 1949.)

SPECIAL COLLEGE TRAINING COURSES DEVELOPED.—Slowly the vision of professionally trained Bible instructors has come into focus, and this plan is now operating in connection with many of our colleges. A number of years ago our training schools came to sense the need of offering special training courses, and their further development seems bright with promise. Plans are also being perfected that will result in more adequately prepared and experienced Bible instructors, as they go forth to serve in personal and public evangelism.

The early plan was to select mature sisters of consecration, who possessed the knack of teaching and had the love of souls in their hearts. These were associated with evangelists of ability and allowed to develop by experience. That was also the way that many of our earlier ministers began their work, and some marvelous preachers developed out of the process. But it gradually dawned on the consciousness of our leaders that a thorough preparatory training in our colleges would produce better preachers, and more uniformly and quickly. Courses for this purpose were developed, and the years have amply justified this opinion. And that training process is still being perfected.

We have been slower, however, in sensing and applying the same principle to Bible instructor training. For years some young women took the regular ministerial training, homiletics and all, and accepted that as their prescribed training for Bible work. But now, for several years, specific personal work courses, developed to meet the distinctive needs of the Bible instructor, have been increasingly brought into operation by most of our colleges. The process of development is still under way, but real strides have been made, and improvements are being added with each passing year. So the prospect is bright with hope.

NAME, BADGE, AND CREDENTIALS ESTABLISHED.—A more adequate and accurate name for the profession was chosen in 1942, after wide consultation with the field. And *Bible instructor* is now the permanent and honored name. A neat and attractive Bible instructor badge, shaped somewhat like a shield, is provided for identification in public meeting. And for our sisters, a distinct Bible instructor garb with cape has also been designed.

Appropriate and adequate conference papers are provided. No longer is the former missionary license or credential used. Distinctive Bible Instructor Credentials, are given to the experienced regular Bible instructors devoting their energies and life to this work. And a Bible Instructor License is provided for beginners in Bible instructor work, and for those of lesser experience. This parallels precisely the ministerial credentials and licenses—the license being preparatory to the credentials, and issued only to those preparing to continue in the Bible work.

ADVANCED COURSES IN THEOLOGICAL SEMINARY AVAILABLE.—Another major advance in the training and perfection of the Bible instructor was the introduction of the special courses in our Theological Seminary, at Washington, D.C., for Bible instructors. These have proved a godsend in the form of practical help and in the development of areas of study and guidance in advanced Bible instructor training.

These have served as a proving ground for many of the methods and techniques that appear in this manual. They have also proved to be an invaluable bridge, spanning the gulf between that large group of faithful, experienced, and successful Bible instructors who have not had the advantage of the later, more formal training now offered in our colleges, and the more recent products of our schools. That made the functioning of these Seminary courses a little more difficult, as they had to meet the needs of both groups. But now the problem becomes increasingly simpler.

BIBLE INSTRUCTOR MANUAL BECOMES ACTUALITY.—Then came the development of this manual—the result of seven years of planning, observation, and coordination, superimposed upon a background of many years of Bible work and teaching. Field experience, close contact with worker groups and institutes, college visitation, and participation in actual evangelistic efforts, as well as teaching in the Seminary, have all played their part. The result is before you, and is destined to have a cumulative effect for good in the field and in our schools. The purpose has been sixfold: (1) To lift the Bible work into a profession; (2) to chart a course for the profession; (3) to provide a guide for Bible and personal work methods; (4) to preserve valuable techniques developed by the field; (5) to develop greater efficiency in the Bible work; and (6) to unify the plans and methods of Bible work.

HOME STUDY INSTITUTE COURSE PLANNED.—A further course of instruction is now available—a set of advanced lessons is offered as a special help through the Home Study Institute. This will be not for laymen or for beginners, but for regular Bible instructors who perhaps cannot come to the Seminary, but who have the desire to study under supervision, and to perfect their gifts and increase their soul-winning efficiency. This, too, should prove a godsend.

VITAL PLACE FOR MALE BIBLE INSTRUCTOR.—And now, as we face the future, the broadened vision of a great company of Bible instructors, embracing men as well as women, comes before us. Of the place filled by our faithful sisters, nothing further need be said. But there is an honored and vital place for male Bible instructors that has not yet been capitalized upon, except in a few lands overseas. Not all men have the gift of preaching—that of holding and molding large concourses of people. But many have the distinctive gift of teaching and persuasion, and would make outstanding personal soul winners and evangelistic Bible teachers. Infinitely better would it be to be a highly successful personal worker than a poor public preacher. At the end of the year, under such a plan, they would win far more souls to this blessed message than through the public platform. Here are real possibilities.

EMBODIED IN OUR GREAT EXEMPLAR.—Christ combined in Himself, as the perfect one, all the various phases and forms of service He designed His entire church to have and to perfect. He is the great exemplar, the complete and perfect example of all aspects of spiritual service. And Christ spent the greater portion of His time and effort with the single soul and the small group. He gained more adherents that way than through His mighty discourses to the multitudes. That very fact gives us the clue to His emphasis, and His plan for His church—many giving themselves to personal and group work, just as others are called primarily to public preaching in the desk. Beyond contradiction, one is as important and as indispensable as the other.

INCLUDED IN THE DIVINE PROGRAM.—Indeed, this whole principle is written right into the constitution of the church by the pen of Inspiration, in Ephesians 4:11-13, where, in addition to apostles, prophets, evangelists, and pastors, the Spirit gave to the church the gift of "teachers," for the perfecting of the saints, the work of the ministry, and the edifying of the church, until all are brought into the unity and fellowship of the faith. And this provision appears even more specifically in 1 Corinthians 12:28, where the same first two categories of apostles and prophets are listed, and then follows, "thirdly teachers"—and after that gifts of helps, healings, governments, and the like. Surely the Bible instructor is divinely designated in the plan and provision of God. These diversities of gifts are given to utilize every talent in the church, one having the spiritual enduement of wisdom, another of knowledge, and another of faith, but "all these worketh that one and the selfsame Spirit, dividing to every man severally as He will." (Verses 4-11.)

NEEDED TILL THE WORK IS FINISHED.—Now let us take a glimpse into the future. God expects the entire church to witness for Him in the closing phase of its pilgrimage here on earth. The laymen form a distinct part of the over-all picture. But to the end of probationary time God designs that the ordained minister and the specially called and trained Bible instructor shall give themselves wholly to the high calling of public and personal evangelism in the church.

Both will have certain responsibilities in training and leading the laity in soul-winning work, some as lay preachers and many as personal workers. But just as specially trained and recognized physicians and nurses will ever be needed to minister to the body, quite apart from the active witness of our faithful people to the principles of healthful living and temperance, so, as long as time lasts, ministers, and Bible instructors will likewise function in their heaven-designated capacities. They will never be superseded.

The Bible instructor will therefore be increasingly needed, wanted, and utilized as long as the church has a work to do on earth. And in the light of the great soul-winning advances designed by God for the last phase of the church's witness, Bible instructors in all lands and embracing all nationalities will fill an increasingly important and destined place in these latter days. So, Bible instructors of the Advent Movement, be of good cheer. Much is expected of you, both by God and by man. Rise to the full height of your high calling and your marvelous possibilities. Yours is one of the most delicate, the most sacred, the most important tasks on earth. It calls for high intelligence, deep consecration, broad sympathies, and full understanding. It calls for a mastery of the Word of life, the gift of teaching, the knowledge of the operation of the human mind, the principles of salesmanship, the gift of persuasion, the art of personal counseling, the love of souls, and an understanding of human frailties and possibilities. It calls for strong faith in God and man.

INFINITE POWER AWAITS YOUR RECEPTION.—You must bear upon your heart the souls entrusted to your care, just as the skilled nurse watches his or her patient with a trained eye and ministers with skilled hand—only yours is a far more delicate and exacting mission. You deal with sinsick souls, desperately ill with every sort of ailment and every type of spiritual disease. You must stoop down and lift up fallen humanity. To do this, you must first of all know Christ and the fullness of His wondrous grace and salvation. Then you must know how to lead others to that Saviour, and the full acceptance of His forgiveness, His transforming grace, and the undivided reign of His will in the life.

Infinite power and limitless help await your demand and reception. Therein lies your source of power and the secret of effectiveness in your appointed work. You are front-line shock troops in the army of the Lord, indispensable in the battle against sin and departure from God. All honor to the Bible instructors of the Advent Movement.

He Will Finish

God's work has grown
With passing year;
The gospel's close
Is drawing near!

For task so great,
I lack much power;
With grave concern
I face the hour!

This joyous truth
Has come to bless,
"He will finish . . .
In righteousness!"

So let it be!
Complete your plan;
Use me, wise God,
As best you can!

L. C. K.

PART FOUR

BIBLE READINGS
by Our
Bible Instructors

Ye Bible Teachers

Go forth, ye Bible teachers;
  Search out His wand'ring sheep,
Deep down in lonely valley
  Or on the mountain steep!
Go in the lanes and byways,
  Seek in the cities till
Each honest soul is gathered
  To serve the Master's will!

Go carry ye the Bible
  To souls whose hearts are sore.
Bring them the Saviour's promise;
  Bid them to weep no more!
Find hungry souls inquiring
  For light upon their path;
Warn sin-cursed men and women,
  Of God's impending wrath!

PART FOUR ★ CHAPTER ONE

Introductory Subjects

The following outline Bible readings by Bible instructors of experience will be helpful to beginners. Mature and trained workers will appreciate observing techniques of their associates.

These Bible readings vary from the simplest type of outline to more detailed notes. Just as there are various types and temperaments, so each worker may have her own ideas about outlines. Some prefer more brevity, and others an outline that conveys ideas quite fully. Some use fewer texts, whereas others appreciate having available the background of textual investigation. A number of the conversational type of studies —those suggesting a vocabulary of appeal—have been purposely included in this series.

Because these Bible readings represent a broad area of our world-wide work, an endeavor has been made to hold to the original plan of each. The question-form Bible study is still recognized as more practical than lecture-method presentation. Bible instructors would do well to develop skill in transforming constructed textual outlines into question-and-answer-type Bible readings. The desire for brevity will explain why the majority of studies in the manual appear in outline form.

These selected Bible readings are intended to preserve for our evangelism our methods for doctrinal argumentation and logical appeal. Techniques of directness and force in enlisting obedience to God's commandments should continue to characterize our present truth teaching. Seventh-day Adventists have a special message to present to the world, and our Bible readings should bring a real awareness of Christ's return. Their approaches, build-ups, and appeals should definitely emphasize preparation for this imminent and glorious event.

Human nature is so diversified that it requires tact and skill to enlist interest and to develop it, and then to secure a full decision for the gospel. The introduction to a Bible study is one of the crisis points of the interest, and without a successful beginning there can be no developing.

Some people whom the Bible instructor meets, present no special difficulties, for just a little pleasant visiting soon results in at least a mutual acquaintance. Improving the opportunity to present some Bible proof to an inquiring mind may readily open the way for a series of Bible studies. But not all are Bible-minded, even though they may be sincere. Too often souls are burdened down with life's perplexities or sorrows, and comfort may need to be applied before doctrinal instruction can be affective. Some are inquisitive, but not deep. They need to be caught in the net of curiosity. Others are prejudiced, yet open-minded. These usually respond to the guile of the gospel worker. Many are uninterested until the study of the prophecies of the Bible awakens a spark of enthusiasm. A Bible instructor is challenged by these different types, but even at an early stage in the study she may use the Word effectively if she knows how.

God's Wonderful Book

I. *Introduction.*

Why is the Bible the most wonderful book ever written?
1. Sixty-six distinct sections, yet combined, form complete book.
2. Forty men had part in its writing over a period of 1,500 years, all unified as to its message.
3. It reveals the only way of salvation.
4. Teaches man how to please God.
5. Converts head-hunters into civilized people.

II. *The Bible God's Book for Man's Study.*
1. What are its evidences of inspiration?
    a. 2 Peter 1:20. Not private interpretation.
    b. 2 Sam. 23:2. Holy Spirit spoke through men.
    c. Heb. 1:1. God spoke unto prophets.

Introductory Subjects 363

    d. 2 Tim. 3:15, 16. All scripture God inspired.
  2. Why is it so important to study the Scriptures?
    a. Ps. 119:105; 2 Peter 1:19. God's Word gives light; reveals future.
    b. Ps. 33:6-9; 1 Peter 1:23. Instrumental in producing new birth.
    c. 1 Peter 2:2. Produces spiritual growth.
    d. Ps. 119:9, 11. Hiding in heart, as safeguard against sin.
    e. 2 Tim. 3:15. Makes men wise unto salvation.
  3. What should be our attitude toward God's Word?
    a. Acts 17:11. Study diligently.
    b. 1 Cor. 2:13; Isa. 28:9, 10. Compare scripture with scripture.

III. *Conclusion.*
  1. God speaks in the Bible. He helps and comforts us.
  2. It contains the way of salvation.
  3. Its teachings have power to recreate us in Christ.
  4. To neglect Bible study is perilous.

ETHELINE VAN NOCKAY PORTER.

History's Coming Climax (Daniel 12)

How will God's kingdom be established? Who will belong to it?

I. *Importance of Daniel's Prophecies.*
  (Introduction when first study of series.)
  1. Recommendation of Christ to understand Daniel's prophecies. Matt. 24:15.
  2. Prophecies for time of the end. Dan. 12:4, 9, 10; 2:28; 8:17; 12:13.
  3. Important to know about events of the end. Luke 21:31, 36.
  4. Revelation of God's kingdom to the prophets. Amos 3:7; 2 Peter 1:19, 21.
  5. In dreams and visions. Num. 12:6; Dan. 1:17.

II. *Nebuchadnezzar's Dream Foretold Future.*
  (Narrate verses 1-30; read verses 31-43.)
  1. King's dream left his memory. Dan. 2:1-5.
  2. Wise men were unable to reveal it. Verses 4-11.
  3. Decree to kill the wise men called attention to Daniel. Verses 12-16.
  4. God revealed dream to Daniel. Verses 17-23.
  5. Daniel revealed forgotten dream to king. Verses 24-35.
  6. He interprets king's dream. Verses 36-43.

III. *Establishing God's Kingdom.*
  1. The stone that filled the whole earth. Dan. 2:35, 44, 45.
  2. Christ's kingdom represented by this stone. Isa. 28:16; 1 Cor. 10:4; Rev. 11:15.
  3. His kingdom established at His appearing. 2 Tim. 4:1.

IV. *Prophecy Fulfilled and in Fulfillment.*
  1. Babylon, the golden kingdom, was to pass away. Dan. 2:37-39. The Medo-Persian kingdom followed the Babylonians in 538 B.C.
  2. Medo-Persia, the silver kingdom, was to pass away. Dan. 2:39. The Grecian kingdom overthrew the Medo-Persian in 331 B.C. at the decisive Battle of Arbela.
  3. Grecia, the brass kingdom, was to be displaced by Rome. Dan. 2:40. The kingdom of Rome followed the kingdom of Greece. Battle of Pydna, 168 B.C.
  4. Rome, the iron kingdom, was to be divided. Dan. 2:41. Rome ruled for about six hundred years. Then it began to disintegrate, and was finally torn apart by the invasion of barbarian tribes. The ten main ones, corresponding to the ten toes of the image, were Alamanni (Germans), Franks (French), Burgundians (Swiss), Suevi (Portuguese), Saxons (English), Visigoths (Spanish), Lombards (Italians), Heruli, Vandals, Ostrogoths. Rome's fall is generally dated A.D. 476.
  5. Rulers and nationals would intermarry. Dan. 2:43. At the outbreak of World War I many of the ruling heads of Europe were related by blood or ties of marriage. Intermarriage among the citizens is, of course, widely prevalent.
  6. Nations of Europe would never permanently unite. Dan. 2:43. Various forms of union and federation have been attempted. Charles the Great, Charles V, Louis XIV, Napoleon Bonaparte, Kaiser Wilhelm, and Adolph Hitler have tried it. The Holy Alliance and the League of Nations tried it. Also the United Nations. Men can never achieve permanent unity in this world.
  7. God's kingdom would follow the break-up of earthly governments. Dan. 2:44.
     a. This is God's literal kingdom of glory. It has a throne. Matt. 25:31.
     b. The King reigns forever. Rev. 11:15.
     c. It is future. Dan. 2:44, 45.

V. *Preparing for Christ's Kingdom.*
  1. "Be ye ... ready!" Matt. 24:42, 44.
  2. Our prayer: "Thy kingdom come!" Luke 11:2.
  3. Consequences of unpreparedness. Matt. 21:44.

Introductory Subjects

VI. *Additional Points of Emphasis.*
1. Daniel is granted time, but not the wise men. Dan. 2:16, 8.
2. Prayer reveals God's secrets to His servants. Verses 17-23.
3. The destiny of kings and kingdoms is in God's hands. Verse 21.
4. Truth exposes error. Verse 27.
5. The certainty of prophecy is emphasized. Verse 45.
6. Dream has significance for time of the end. Verse 28.
7. Prophecy reveals the true God. Verse 47.
8. A heathen king was converted. Verses 46-49.

God's Eternal Purpose

I. *God's Purpose.*
1. Does God have an end to which He is working? Eph. 3:11.
2. Has God declared to man His eternal purpose? Isa. 46:10.
3. What does God say concerning His counsel? Verse 10.
4. Where may we read God's declaration of His eternal purpose?
   a. "Remember the *former things of old:* for I am God." Verse 9.
   b. For the "former things of old" we turn to Genesis 1.
5. What is God's declaration of His eternal counsel? (See Isa. 45:18; 43:21.) A perfect people, in the image of God, having dominion over a perfect world—this is God's eternal purpose. It included the Eden home, with its spacious gardens providing nuts, fruits, grains, and vegetables, a perfect diet for a perfect people; the tree of life. The holy couple were privileged to talk with God. God's eternal purpose will be carried out in detail.

II. *The Entrance of Sin.*
1. What delayed God's plan? Rev. 12:7-9; Rom. 5:12.
2. Whose servant did man then become? Rom. 6:16.
   When Adam and Eve became servants of the devil, he usurped their kingdom. He said in his rebellion, "I will exalt my throne above the stars of God." Isa. 14:13. Now he had territory, the lovely earth; and subjects, Adam and his wife. But God had a great surprise for Satan. God's eternal purpose included the plan of salvation. Satan was not permitted to bind the human race in hopeless, helpless slavery. God walked in the garden, and revealed His plan to redeem sinners and destroy Satan.

III. *The Plan of Salvation.*
1. What promise was made in the hearing of Adam and Eve on day of their sin? Gen. 3:15.
   The plan of salvation went into immediate operation. All who

wish may be enemies, and not friends and servants, of the devil. The blood of Jesus was paid for our redemption. Isa. 52:3.
2. What were some results of Adam's sin? Gen. 3:17, 19, 24.
Man lost his image of God, his Eden home, tree of life, dominion of earth, and life itself. God's eternal purpose includes restoration of all things lost by sin.

IV. *The Seed Promised.*
1. How was the promise of complete restoration repeated to Abraham? Gen. 12:7.
2. How much was included in the term "land"? Rom. 4:13.
3. Who is this "Seed" to whom the world was promised? Gal. 3:16.
   a. Christ is the seed of the woman. Gal. 4:4.
   b. He is also the seed of David, the seed of Abraham. Matt. 1:1. Promise also repeated to David. 2 Sam. 7:12, 16.
   c. Through Christ are all the precious promises of redemption and restoration. Col. 1:13, 14.

V. *The Second Adam Restores.*
1. Who is the first Adam? The second Adam? Read 1 Cor. 15:45, 47.
By sin of first Adam sin and death reigned in earth; by sinless life of second Adam, by His death and His intercession, He saves "to the uttermost" those "that come unto God by Him."
2. How does God describe the renewed earth? Isa. 51:3.
3. How can we share in the full inheritance of the second Adam? See Dan. 7:14.
   a. By belonging to Christ. John 1:12; Gal. 3:29.
   b. By cooperating with Him in restoring the divine nature. 2 Peter 1:4.
   When God created the world He said, "Let there be light," etc. The mighty Christ is saying today: "Let this mind be in you." Phil. 2:5. When we forsake sin and yield the will to Christ, the nature and mind of Christ are restored in us. God's eternal purpose is moving on to glorious consummation. A perfect people, with Christ their King, will dwell in a perfect world. For appeal read assuringly Jude 24 and 25.

GRACE STEWART.

Signs of Our Times

Text: Matt. 24:1-12.
I. *What Conditions Do We Find at the Close of World War II?*
   1. The fall of dictators and war lords.
   2. Atomic bomb surprised nations.

Introductory Subjects

3. Sufferings of displaced civilians.
4. Cold, hunger, and famine problems.
5. Diseases and epidemics; many deaths.
6. Punishment of war criminals; mysterious suicides.
7. Lack of agreement among nations on war adjustments.
8. Churches persecuted and reorganized.
9. Industrial and economic problems in many lands.
10. Juvenile delinquency; the liquor problem.

II. *What Does the Bible Prophesy Regarding Wars?*
1. Growing warfare. Matt. 24:6, 7.
2. Judgments on nations. Eze. 7:1-6.
3. Vast and sudden desolations. Jer. 4:19, 20.
4. Destruction of cities. Zeph. 1:14-18.
5. Loftiness of man brought low. Isa. 2:2, 9-22; Jer. 9:21-24.

III. *What Lessons May Be Learned From Recent Destructions?*
1. Sinners and hypocrites to receive surprise. Isa. 33:14.
2. God musters His hosts. Isa. 13:3-9.
3. Statesmen fearful. Luke 21:25-27.
4. Bloody crimes increase. Eze. 7:15, 23-25.
5. Omens of coming destruction. 2 Peter 3:7, 9-12; Jer. 4:23-29.

IV. *How Will These Modern Nations Seek Help? Results?*
1. Church and state seek each other's help. Micah 4:1-5.
2. Leaders desperately confused. Isa. 29:9-16.
3. Nominal church to teach God's law to nations. Isa. 2:2-5.
4. Worldliness of the church. 2 Tim. 3:1-5.
5. Fear of end produces revivals. Isa. 26:5, 9.
6. Lawlessness still continues. Isa. 30:8-10.
7. Followed by famine for Word. Amos 8:11, 12.

V. *What Comforting Message Is for Us Today?*
1. "Take heed." "Watch, . . . and pray." Luke 21:28-36.
2. Kept in perfect peace. Isa. 26:3, 4 (48:18, 22).

Labor and Management in Conflict

(To interest business and laboring men.)

Text: Job 22:21.

I. *How Does the Bible Picture Our Last-Day Unemployment Condition.*
1. Isa. 8:21, 22. Confusion, darkness, and trouble on earth.
2. 2 Tim. 3:2. Perils of the last days. Men lovers of self, proud, disobedient, unholy, etc.

II. *What Does the Bible Teach About the Last-Day Economic Problems?*
   1. Deut. 8:18. God gives power to obtain wealth.
   2. James 5:1-8. Treasures heaped in last days. Corruption of riches, capitalists and laborers in conflict.
   3. Isa. 8:9, 10. Men's plans all fail: unions, strikes, boycott.

III. *What Is God's Counsel for These Distressing Times?*
   1. Matt. 7:12. God's solution the golden rule.
   2. Matt. 22:39. Love neighbor as self.
   3. Phil. 2:4. Prefer fellow man.
   4. Luke 3:14. "Be content with your wages."
   5. James 5:7, 8. "Be patient.... Stablish your hearts."

IV. *What Will Be the End of All This Confusion?*
   1. Matt. 6:10; 2 Tim. 4:1. Return of Jesus to this earth.
   2. Isa. 32:1. His reign of righteousness.

ARTHELIA WATLINGTON DAVIS.

Why Do Christians Have Trouble?

I. *Our Relationship to God.*
   1. We are the sons of God. Gal. 4:5-7.
   2. The Lord invites us to call on Him. Matt. 7:7-11.
   3. God delivers from all trouble. Ps. 34:4, 6.

II. *God's Purpose in Sending Trials.*
   1. God directs in all things for our good.
      a. "All things work together" for our good. Rom. 8:28.
      b. God directed Joseph in order to save life. Gen. 45:7, 8.
      c. We suffer so we may learn to comfort others. 2 Cor. 1:3, 4.
   2. God expresses His love by chastening.
      a. "Whom the Lord loveth He chasteneth." Heb. 12:5-8.
      b. Despise not chastening. Prov. 3:11, 12.
   3. God tests and purifies us with trials.
      a. Physical affliction kept Paul humble. 2 Cor. 12:7-10.
      b. Abraham tested and strengthened. Gen. 22:12.
   4. God's assurance to the tempted.
      a. God furnishes strength proportionate to trial. 1 Cor. 10:13.
      b. Can do all things through Christ who strengthens. Phil. 4:13.

III. *The Christian's Privilege.*
   "Casting all your care upon Him." 1 Peter 5:7.

MRS. SADIE WALLEKER.

Introductory Subjects 369

"Thou Leadest Me"

(Scriptural uplift for troubled and nervous. Select texts.)

I. *Introduction.*
"Tossings" and fears man's lot. Isa. 54:11, 12; Ps. 55:3-6; Job 7:4; Eph. 4:14.

II. *Trusting in Divine Leadership.*
  1. "He leadeth me." Ps. 23:2.
  2. "I am with you alway." Matt. 28:20.

III. *Man's Helplessness Requires God's Guidance.*
  1. Guidance in daily problems.
     a. "Get thee out . . . unto a land that I will shew thee." Gen. 12:1.
     b. "Return; . . . I will be with thee." Gen. 31:3.
     c. "The Lord went before them; . . . to give them light." Ex. 13:21.
     d. "Moses . . . is dead; . . . arise, go over this Jordan." Joshua 1:2.
     e. "I will doubtless deliver . . . into thine hand." 2 Sam. 5:19.
     f. "I have commanded the ravens to feed thee." 1 Kings 17:3, 4.
  2. Guidance in judgment.
     a. "Thou shalt guide me with Thy counsel." Ps. 73:24.
     b. "Thine ears shall hear a word, . . . This is the way." Isa. 30:21.
  3. Guidance in religion.
     a. "He will guide you into all truth." John 16:13.
     b. "Lead me in Thy truth." Ps. 25:5 (John 17:17).
     c. "Teach me Thy way, O Lord." Ps. 27:11.
     d. "Teach me to do Thy will." Ps. 143:10.

IV. *Looking Back Upon God's Leadership.*
  1. "Thou shalt remember all the way which the Lord . . . led thee." Deut. 8:2.
  2. "So the Lord alone did lead him." Deut. 32:12.
  3. "The Lord . . . saved . . . out of all . . . troubles." Ps. 34:6.
  4. "All things work together for good." Rom. 8:28.
  5. "I will . . . lay me down in peace, and sleep." Ps. 4:8.

Comfort for Burden Bearers

I. *The Outward Look.*
"Bear ye one another's burdens." Gal. 6:2.
  1. Burden of bereavement.

a. God pities like a tender father. Ps. 103:13-18.
  b. Comfort in hope of resurrection. 1 Thess. 4:13-18.
  c. God Himself shall remove all traces of sorrow. Rev. 21:4.
 2. Burden of sickness or misfortune.
  a. Hope for blind, deaf, and maimed. Isa. 35:5, 6.
  b. Creator of universe knows each detail of our lives. Isa. 40:28-31.
   (1) Even a sparrow noticed when it falls. Luke 12:6.
   (2) Hairs of our head numbered. Verse 7.
   (3) Environment in which we live known. Ps. 87:4-6.
   (4) Even the street we live on known, and just what we are doing. Acts 9:11.

II. *The Inward Look.*
 Bear your own burdens. Gal. 6:5.
 Purpose and value of trials.
 1. Trials necessary to perfect us. Job 23:10; 1 Peter 5:10.
 2. The Lord chastens those He loves. Heb. 12:6.
 3. These trials yield precious aftermath. Verse 10; 2 Cor. 4:17.
 4. Trials allowed that we may be able to comfort others. 2 Cor. 1:4.
 5. God's grace sufficient for every trial. 2 Cor. 12:9.

III. *The Upward Look.*
 "Cast thy burden upon the Lord." Ps. 55:22.
 1. Cast thy burden of anxiety on Him. Phil. 4:6, 7; Psalms 46.
 2. Cast thy burden of sin on Him. Ps. 38:4, 15, 18.
 3. The believer's relationship to God in trouble.
  a. We must *love* Him; then all things work together for good. Rom. 8:28.
  b. We must *submit* humbly to His will. Luke 22:42.
  c. We must *trust* Him where we cannot define His leading. Job 13:15; Ps. 37:5.
 4. The blessed provision of the divine Burden Bearer. 1 Peter 5:7.

MRS. MARGARET REEVES.

PART FOUR ★ CHAPTER TWO

Christ's Coming Kingdom

Heaven has been preparing the way for the gospel worker to present the theme of Christ's imminent return, and those related subjects which cluster around this glorious event. Conditions in our world have made many conscious of the signs of the times; there is a general awareness of the end of all things. But though this present spirit of inquiry concerning what the Bible teaches is most encouraging to the worker, too often the enemy of truth has preceded us by sowing the seeds of his fallacious doctrines, with their strange interpretations of prophecy. The Bible teacher must know what phases of the coming of Christ need special emphasis. General facts on the subject are not sufficient proof to meet the present barrage of error. A discerning mind is necessary on the part of the instructor. During the early stage of the interest Bible lessons must be speedily guided toward our ultimate objective —preparing a people to meet the Lord!

The Return of Jesus

I. *Does the Bible Reveal Jesus Will Come Again?*
   1. Jesus' own promise to return. John 14:1-3.
   2. Angels testified of His return. Acts 1:9-11.
   3. Apostle Paul taught second coming of Jesus. Heb. 9:28.

II. *What Will Be the Manner of Jesus' Second Coming?*
   1. Jesus will not come secretly. Matt. 24:23-26.
   2. He will come in the sky. Verse 27.
   3. His coming will be visible. Rev. 1:7.
   4. It will be audible. 1 Thess. 4:16, 17.
   5. Jesus will return to earth as He left. Acts 1:9-11.
      (He will come in the flesh. Luke 24:33-43.)
   6. Jesus will come in the clouds. Rev. 14:14.
   7. He will come with the angels. Matt. 24:31.
   8. Jesus will come with power and glory. Matt. 24:30.

III. *What Is the Purpose of Jesus' Return to Earth?*
  1. For the righteous.
     a. Raise the dead. 1 Thess. 4:16, 17.
     b. Change these vile bodies. Phil. 3:21.
     c. Give immortality. 1 Cor. 15:51-53.
     d. Give reward to righteous. 2 Tim. 4:8.
  2. For wicked.
     a. Character as deeds. Rev. 22:11, 12.
     b. God's indignation. Isa. 26:20, 21.
     c. Wicked destroyed. 2 Thess. 2:8.
IV. *What Will Be the Attitude of People When He Comes Again?*
  1. Fear and despair of wicked. Rev. 6:15-17.
  2. Rejoicing of righteous. Isa. 25:9.
V. *How Should We Be Preparing to Meet Jesus?* (1 John 3:2.)

LORAINE H. BAUM.

Millennium—One Thousand Years

I. *Introduction.*
  1. "Millennium" does not occur in Bible.
  2. Comes from two Latin words: *mille,* 1,000; *annum,* a year.
  3. Expression "a thousand years," as found in Revelation 20, is equivalent to the word *millennium.*
II. *What Events Mark the Beginning of the Millennium?*
  1. Heb. 9:28. Jesus comes without sin unto salvation.
  2. 1 Thess. 4:16, 17. Righteous dead are raised.
  3. 2 Thess. 2:8. Wicked destroyed with brightness of His coming. (Jer. 25:33. No funeral, no burial.)
  4. 1 Thess. 4:17. Righteous translated. John 14:1-3 promise fulfilled.
  5. Rev. 20:1-3. Satan bound, no one to tempt or deceive.
III. *Where Is Satan During the Millennium?*
  1. Isa. 24:1-6. Earth utterly empty. Why? Verse 5.
  2. Jer. 4:23-27. No man, no bird, no tree.
  3. Earth in chaotic condition Satan's abode.
IV. *Where Are the Saints During the Millennium?*
  1. Rev. 20:4. They reign with Christ.
  2. Rev. 19:9. Attending marriage supper of Lamb.
  3. 1 Cor. 6:2-4. Judging wicked and angels.
V. *What Events Mark the Close of the Millennium?*
  1. Jude 14. Christ and saints appear.
  2. Rev. 21:2. Holy city comes down from heaven.

Christ's Coming Kingdom

3. Zech. 14:4. City rests on former site of Olivet.
4. Rev. 20:5. Second resurrection that of the wicked.
5. Rev. 20:3, 7, last clause. Satan loosed.
6. Rev. 20:9. Wicked destroyed by fire as Satan makes last great attack upon God's people.
7. 2 Peter 3:10. Earth utterly burned. Same fire purifies earth.
8. Rev. 21:1. New heaven and new earth appears.

VI. *Appeal.*
1. Where will you be at beginning of millennium?
2. Where will you be at close of millennium?

ALMA DUBOIS.

The Bible Millennium

I. *Introduction.*
1. Millennium means 1,000 years. Derived from two Latin words.
   a. *Mille* meaning thousand.
   b. *Annus* meaning years.
2. Some beliefs regarding millennium. Which correct? (Use when confusions must be clarified.)
   a. Righteous go to heaven at second coming of Christ and remain there for 1,000 years; wicked are dead.
   b. Millennium preceded by seven-year reign of antichrist. Righteous caught up during this period.
   c. Millennium preceded by Christ's secret coming.
   d. Christ came in 1914. Wicked will be resurrected and given second chance.
   e. Jews given opportunity of repentance in millennial period.

II. *Millennium Begins With Second Coming of Christ.*
1. How many resurrections were taught by Jesus? John 5:28, 29.
   a. Righteous in first resurrection at second coming. Rev. 20:6. A first resurrection logically implies a second.
   b. Wicked in second resurrection at close of 1,000 years. Rev. 20:5.
2. What about the righteous at His second coming?
   a. Dead raised. 1 Thess. 4:16.
   b. Living caught up with them. Verse 17.
   c. Taken to New Jerusalem for 1,000 years. John 14:1-3; Rev. 20:6.
   d. Judge wicked during millennium. Rev. 20:4; 1 Cor. 6:1-3.
3. What about wicked at second coming?
   a. Drop dead at brightness of His coming. 2 Thess. 1:6-9; 2:8; Rev. 6:15-17.

Cannot stand brightness of Christ with millions of angels. Matt. 25:31; Rev. 5:11.
    b. Righteous all in heaven and wicked all dead. Jer. 25:30-33.
    c. Remain dead for 1,000 years. Rev. 20:5, first part (last sentence belongs to verse 6).
4. What about the earth?
    a. Great earthquake. Rev. 6:14.
    b. Earth becomes desolate. Jer. 4:23-27.
        (1) Notice *no man* on earth.
        (2) Not a full end of the earth. Why?
5. What about Satan?
    a. Bound 1,000 years. Rev. 20:1, 2.
    b. Cast into bottomless pit. Verse 3. (Explain.)
    c. Bound with chain of circumstances.
        (1) Satan's work for 6,000 years to deceive.
        (2) None to deceive during 1,000 years.

III. *Christ's Third Coming Closes Millennium.*
1. When will Christ return with New Jerusalem? Rev. 21:1, 2. Holy City descends where old Jerusalem now stands. Zech. 14:1, 4, 5.
2. What about the resurrection of the wicked? Rev. 20:5, 7, 8.
3. How will it affect Satan? Verse 7.
Deceives wicked that the city can be taken.
4. When will Satan and the wicked finally be destroyed? Verse 9.
5. What about fire that burns wicked? 2 Peter 3:10; Mal. 4:1, 3.

IV. *Appeal: Will You Inherit Christ's Kingdom?*
1. Christ and saints possess earth. 2 Peter 3:13; Matt. 5:5.
2. If Christ's, promise is yours. Gal. 3:29.
Requires complete surrender to Christ, not mere profession.
3. Illustration: Poor child in London looking into toy shop through glass window. Longed to grasp toy. Run over by auto. Toy soldier brought to him at hospital. He cried, "No glass between!" (1 Cor. 13:12.)
God's promises are real. Let us prepare to possess them.

RACHEL MAE LEMON.

The Home of the Saved

I. *Introduction.*
1. There will be a new earth. Rev. 21:1, 5.
2. Location: present earth. Matt. 5:5; Prov. 11:31.
3. To endure forever. Dan. 7:18, 27.

II. *How Is the Capital of the New Earth Described?*
   1. Capital: New Jerusalem. Rev. 21:2.
      a. City of gold. Verse 18.
      b. Walls of jasper. Verse 18.
      c. Foundation of precious stones. Verses 19, 20.
      d. Gates of pearl. Verse 21.
      e. Street of gold. Verse 21.
      f. River of life. Rev. 22:1.
      g. Tree of life. Verse 2.
      h. No night there—Lamb is the light. Rev. 21:23.
   2. What is said of its beauties?
      a. Like Eden. Isa. 51:3.
      b. Desert like rose. Isa. 35:2.
      c. Eye not seen, nor ear heard. 1 Cor. 2:9.
   3. Of its inhabitants?
      a. Meek people. Matt. 5:5.
      b. Pure people. Rev. 21:27.
      c. Forgiven people. Isa. 33:24.
      d. Healthy people. Verse 24; Isa. 35:5, 6.
      e. Happy people. Rev. 21:4; Isa. 35:10.
      f. Some will be children. Isa. 11:6, 8.
      g. Real people—like Him. 1 John 3:2.
         (1) Will know each other. 1 Cor. 13:12.
         (2) Recognized by form and figure. John 20:27, 28.
         (3) Recognized by voice. Verse 16.
         (4) Recognized by peculiarities of manner. Luke 24:30, 31.
   4. How will the saved occupy their time? Isa. 65:21, 22.
   5. Will animals be changed as well as man? Isa. 11:6-8; 65:25.
   6. What does the Bible teach about worship on the New Earth?
      a. Regular seasons. Isa. 66:22, 23.
      b. "They shall see His face." Rev. 22:4.
   7. How enduring is its life? Dan. 7:18, 27.
   8. Will sin ever re-enter the realms of the redeemed? Nahum 1:9.

III. *Conclusion.*
   How may we be assured of a home there? Acts 4:12; Isa. 1:19, 20; Rev. 22:14; 2 Peter 3:14.

Mrs. Ethel N. Coon.

Is Heaven a Real Place?

(For one who doubts heaven will be real. Select texts.)

I. *What Does the Bible Teach Concerning Our Reward?*
   1. We may know what our reward will be. Matt. 19:27, 28.
   2. The Holy Spirit has revealed it in God's Word. 1 Cor. 2:9, 10.

3. Signs now show the time of reward at hand. Rev. 11:18.
4. Jesus will soon bring our reward. Rev. 22:12.

II. *What Will Eternal Life Embrace?*
1. A place of reward; Jesus preparing mansions. John 14:1-3.
2. A heavenly country and a "city." Heb. 11:10, 16.

III. *How Does Our Present World Become the New Earth?*
1. Jesus promised this earth as reward. Matt. 5:5.
2. Present earth cleansed by fire. 2 Peter 3:7, 12, 13.
3. Sin and wickedness destroyed. Ps. 37:34, 9-11.
4. Earth returns to Edenic condition. Isa. 51:3.
5. Jesus restores Adam's lost kingdom. Micah 4:8; 1 Cor. 15:22-24; Gen. 1:26.

IV. *How Are the New Earth and Its Capital Described?*
1. Called a "new earth." Rev. 21:1; Isa. 65:17.
2. New Jerusalem center of joy. Rev. 21:2, 10; Isa. 65:17-19; 35:10.
3. City has jeweled foundations, pearly gates, wall of jasper. Rev. 21:12-21.
4. Natural beauty and fertility. Isa. 35:1, 2, 7, 8.
5. Animals tame and friendly. Isa. 65:25; 35:9.
6. Satisfying occupation and education. Isa. 65:21-23; Ps. 16:11.
7. Communion with God. Rev. 21:3; 22:4.
8. Sabbath joy and peace. Isa. 66:22, 23.
9. No curse, disappointment, pain, sorrow. Rev. 22:3; 21:27, 4.
10. Family and friendship ties restored. Zech. 8:5; Isa. 65:23; Matt. 8:11.

V. *What About Our Right to the New Earth?*
1. Tree of life; eternal life. Rev. 22:14.
2. Heavenly kingdom prepared at creation. Matt. 25:34.
3. Lord's prayer then fulfilled. Matt. 6:10.

VI. *Appeal.*
Heaven is a real place. Its joys are eternal. Jesus will soon bring our reward. Are you planning to be there?

The New Earth and Its Subjects

I. *Prophetic Assurance of Fifth Universal Empire.* (Dan. 2:44.)
1. Not a mere putting together again of parts of any former empire. .... Dan. 2:43.
2. Present heavens and the earth to be burned up. 2 Peter 3:10-13.
3. The new will entirely eclipse the old. .... Isa. 65:17.

II. *Two Phases to Christ's Kingdom.*
 1. Kingdom of *grace* already in existence.
    a. Not of this world. .... John 18:36.
    b. Set up in our hearts. .... Luke 17:20, 21.
 2. Kingdom of *glory* to be ushered in.
    a. Earthly kingdoms to pass into His control. .... Rev. 11:15.
    b. Christ as King of kings then occupies the throne. Matt. 25:31.

III. *Nature of Christ's Kingdom of Glory.*
 1. Government.
    a. He is King of kings. .... Rev. 17:14.
    b. Throne of Father will be with men. .... Rev. 21:3; 22: 3, 4.
    c. Victorious man to have active part. .... Rev. 3:21.
 2. Capital city.
    a. Location. .... Zech. 14:4.
    b. Made in heaven—comes to this earth. .... Rev. 21:2, 10-21.
       (1) Size—1,500 miles in circumference.
       (2) Walls—jasper—375 miles long.
       (3) Gates—12—names of patriarchs.
       (4) Foundations—12—names of apostles.
       (5) Tree of life—12 manner of fruits.
       (6) River of life—out of God's throne.
       (7) Mansions of the saints. .... John 14:2.
 3. Citizens.
    a. Real beings—like Christ. .... 1 John 3:2, 3; Luke 24:36-43.
    b. No sickness, pain, or death. .... Rev. 22:4; Isa. 35:5, 6; 33:24.
 4. Country.
    a. Eden restored. .... Isa. 35:1, 2.
       With our mental and physical powers restored to perfection, unbounded opportunities open before us to realize dreams unfulfilled on this earth, with ever fresh vistas ahead.
    b. Privileged to build our homes and plant our gardens. .... Isa. 65:21, 22.
 5. Worship.
    a. Assemble at Jerusalem each Sabbath. .... Isa. 66:22, 23.
    b. Assemble each new moon (perhaps to partake of the tree of life). .... Rev. 22:2.

IV. *Citizenship Requirements.*
 1. Citizens of new earth are *chosen*. .... 2 Peter 1:10.
 2. What must I do? .... Matt. 19:16, 17; Eccl. 12:13; Micah 6:8.
 3. Above all else, I must be "in Him." .... Eph. 1:3, 4.

DOROTHY WHITNEY CONKLIN,

PART FOUR ★ CHAPTER THREE

Conversion Studies

Bible instructors become increasingly conscious that the reader's heart needs first attention, and often much more than his intellect. To plan a series of informative studies on our doctrines without first emphasizing the need of conversion and revival is useless effort. To take conversion for granted is another mistake. Neither does church membership in some group preclude the need of conversion. Our times are perilous because church members share in the sins of the worldly. Our only recourse must now be to help all with whom we study the Word to know its central Person. Christ-appeal and prayer must mark the very beginning of our instruction and personal work.

What Is Bible Conversion?

I. *How Is Man's Lost Condition Described in the Bible?*
   1. All have sinned. Rom. 3:10, 12, 23.
   2. Under death sentence. Rom. 5:12; 6:23.
   3. Righteousnesses as filthy rags. Isa. 64:6.
   4. Helpless to change. Jer. 13:23.

II. *How Is Sin Defined in God's Word?*
   1. God's law His standard. Rom. 7:12.
   2. Transgression of law sin. 1 John 3:4.
   3. All unrighteousness sin. 1 John 5:17.
   4. Disobedience. Rom. 5:19.
   5. Sin is rebellion. Dan. 9:5.

III. *How Must Man Cooperate With God for Salvation?*
   1. God's Part.
      a. Gave His Son. John 3:16.
      b. Died for our sins. 1 Cor. 15:3.
      c. Wounded for our transgressions. Isa. 53:5, 6.
      d. Bore our sins. 1 Peter 2:22, 24.
      e. Death paid penalty for sin and purchased life. Rom. 5:17-21.

2. Man's Part.
   a. Conviction of sin. John 8:9.
   b. Contrition, sorrow for sin. Ps. 51:17.
   c. Repentance. Acts 5:31.
   d. Belief in Christ. Confess and receive forgiveness. 1 John 1:9.
   e. Forsaking sin. Isa. 55:7.
   f. Being converted. Acts 3:19.
   g. Accepting Christ as Saviour and turning away from sin is new birth. John 3:3-7. Baptism outward sign of inward experience. 1 Peter 1:22, 23.

IV. *What Experience Follows the New Life in Christ?*
   1. Past sins covered by Christ's righteousness. Rom. 3:24, 25.
   2. Righteousness of law to be fulfilled in life. Rom. 8:3, 4.
   3. Dead to sin, alive to righteousness. Rom. 6:3-8, 12-18.
   4. Christ dwells in heart, living His life again in human flesh. Eph. 3:17; Gal. 2:20.
   5. Can do all things *through Christ*. Phil. 4:13.
   6. Faith the victory that overcomes. 1 John 5:4.
   7. Christ our Advocate in sin's emergency. 1 John 2:1.

V. *Conclusion and Appeal.*
   Christ delivers from the *penalty* and from the *power* of sin. He is an all-sufficient Saviour! Have you accepted Him and do you know that you are saved?
   Additional references: Rom. 7:18, 19, 24, 7; 2:4; 2 Cor. 7:10, 11; John 3:16; Heb. 11:6; Ps. 51:3, 4; 32:5; Prov. 28:13; Eze. 18:31, 32; Rom. 6:3; 4:6-8; Jer. 31:33; Col. 1:27.   BESSIE MOUNT.

Steps to Conversion

I. *Introduction.*
Seven significant steps mark the experience of our conversion. The Christian should know these steps and how to take them.

II. *Steps to Conversion.*
   1. What is the first step in the life of the sinner?
      Conviction.
      a. "He came to himself." Luke 15:17.
      b. "They were pricked in their heart." Acts 2:37.
   2. What experience must follow conviction?
      Contrition.
      a. "What shall we do?" Acts 2:37.
      b. Peter wept bitterly. Matt. 26:75.
   3. How and to whom must sin be confessed?

Confession.
    a. David acknowledged his sin. Ps. 51:3-7.
    b. If we confess, He is faithful to forgive. 1 John 1:9.
4. How is man's complete surrender to God described?
Renunciation.
    a. "Let us reason together." Isa. 1:18.
    b. "Let him return unto the Lord." Isa. 55:7.
5. What is necessary for the sinner to find peace of mind?
Restitution.
    a. Promise of forgiveness. Eze. 33:15.
    b. Zacchaeus. "Restore . . . fourfold." Luke 19:8.
6. How is the new life made a reality?
Reformation.
    a. "Let every one . . . depart from iniquity." 2 Tim. 2:19.
    b. "Bring forth . . . fruits meet for repentance." Matt. 3:8.
7. What other experience reveals a complete separation from sin?
Transformation.
"In Christ, he is a new creature." 2 Cor. 5:17.

III. *How May We Summarize These Realities of Conversion?*
1. *Admit* our lost, helpless condition. Luke 15:17.
2. *Submit* our will to God's will. Verse 18.
3. *Commit* our life into His hands. Verse 19.
4. *Permit* Him to reveal His righteousness in us. Phil. 1:6; Jude 24.

ALMA DuBois.

Evidences of Conversion

I. *Has God a Standard of Living for His Children?*
1. Man was made in the image of God. Gen. 1:26, 27; Eccl. 7:29.
2. "Be ye . . . perfect." Matt. 5:48.
3. Holy, without blemish, no spot or wrinkle. Eph. 5:27.

II. *Is It Natural for Man to Meet God's Holy Standard?*
1. By nature the children of wrath. Eph. 2:3.
2. All are sinners, condemned to die. Rom. 3:23; 6:23; 1 John 3:4.
3. Man's righteousness is as filthy rags. Isa. 64:6.
4. Aliens. Eph. 2:12.
5. Manifest works of flesh. Gal. 5:19-21.

III. *Can Money or Works Help Us to Reach God's Standard?*
1. Cannot do good when accustomed to do evil. Jer. 13:23.
2. Saved by grace, a gift of God; not by works. Eph. 2:8, 9.
3. Gift of God not purchased with money. Acts 8:9-24.

IV. *What Experience Is Necessary for the Natural Man to Be Saved?*
   1. "Except ye . . . become as little children." Matt. 18:3.
   2. "Ye must be born again." John 3:3, 5, 7.
   3. Daily death to sin. Gal. 2:20; 1 Cor. 15:31.
   4. Flesh must be crucified. Gal. 5:24.

V. *How May We Know That We Are Truly Converted?*
   1. Sorrow for sin. 2 Cor. 7:9-11.
   2. Confession of sin. Ps. 51:3-7; 1 John 1:9.
   3. Forsaking sin. Eze. 18:30-32; Prov. 28:13.
   4. Restitution. Luke 19:8; Eze. 33:15.
   5. Fruit of Spirit instead of flesh. Gal. 5:22, 23.
   6. New creature in Christ. 2 Cor. 5:17; Rom. 6:5, 6.
   (Appeal and prayer.)   MARY HARTWELL.

Conversion Essential to Salvation

I. *How Does the Bible Teach Man's Complete Ruin in Sin?* (Rom. 3:23.)
   1. Man's condition by nature is carnal. Rom. 7:14; 1 Cor. 2:14.
   2. Death passed upon all men. Rom. 5:12.
   3. Man doomed unless saved. Rom. 6:23.
   4. Conversion necessary for moral man as well as sinner.
      a. Paul needed it despite his zeal and religious education. Acts 9.
      b. Nicodemus was a noble man but needed new birth. John 3:3.
      c. Peter knew teachings of Jesus but needed conversion. Luke 22:32.
   5. The human heart is morally bankrupt. Rom. 8:7, 8.
      a. If our righteousness is as filthy rags, what must our sins look like? Isa. 1:5, 6.
      b. Paul cried out for deliverance from dead body of sin. Rom. 7:24.
      Illustration: In this age of miracles one of the most wonderful discoveries is penicillin, the miracle-healing drug developed from plain green mold. But a greater miracle takes place when God can make a new creation from sin-wrecked human lives. 2 Cor. 5:17.

II. *God's Perfect Remedy in Christ—How Is It Provided?* (John 1:29; Isa. 45:22.)
   1. Our salvation lies in leaving one family and being born into the other.

       a. Those who are led by the Spirit become the sons of God. Rom. 8:14.
       b. Impossible to educate anyone into it. We must be born of God. 1 Peter 1:23.
       c. Not by works, but according to His mercy He saves. Titus 3:5.
  2. Necessary steps in conversion.
       a. Belief. John 1:12.
       b. Repentance. Acts 3:19.
       c. Confession. 1 John 1:9.
       d. Assurance. Gal. 3:26.
       e. Obedience. Heb. 5:9.
  3. Fruits of conversion. Matt. 3:8.
       a. Living the Christian life daily. 1 John 2:2-6; 5:2, 3.
       b. Dying with Christ daily. Gal. 2:20; 1 Cor. 15:31.
       c. New heart given. Eze. 36:26, 27; 1 Sam. 10:6.
  4. A complete salvation consists of:
       a. Justification—saved from sin's penalty at conversion. 1 John 4:10.
       b. Sanctification—saved from sin's power. 1 John 1:7.
       c. Glorification—saved from sin's presence at Second Advent. Heb. 9:28.

Mrs. Margaret Reeves.

Conversion and Predestination
(For Calvinists.)

I. *Bible Predestination.*
  1. What does the Bible teach regarding predestination?
       a. We are predestinated in Him. Eph. 1:11.
       b. "Predestinated us unto the adoption of children." Verse 5.
  2. How does God's plan help us to understand predestination?
       a. Earth created to be inhabited by obedient. Isa. 45:18; 1:19.
       b. Man to replenish the earth. Gen. 1:26-28.
  3. How was God's purpose thwarted by sin?
       a. Entrance of sin brought confusion. Gen. 3:1-15.
       b. Result of sin is death. Rom. 5:12.
       c. In Adam all have sinned. Rom. 3:23.
  4. How was man rescued from the fate of sin?
       a. Christ tasted death for every man. Heb. 2:9.
       b. To everyone that believeth. John 3:16; 1 Tim. 2:3-6.

II. *Restoration in Christ.*
  1. How was God's eternal purpose to be realized?
     To gather together all things in Christ. Eph. 1:9, 10.

2. How many are predestinated to eternal life?
    a. "Unto the adoption of children by Jesus Christ." Verses 4, 5.
    b. "Made nigh" through the blood of Christ. Eph. 2:11-13.
    c. Complete salvation provided for all who accept. Rom. 8:29, 30.
3. How did God provide for sin's emergency?
    a. God is love. 1 John 4:8.
    b. Righteous and holy. Ps. 145:17.
    c. God is full of compassion. Ps. 86:15.
    d. In Christ love, justice, and power to save complete. Isa. 33:22.

III. *God Calls All Men to Be Saved.*
  1. Do all men accept God's offer of free salvation?
      a. Jesus teaches there are two classes. Matt. 25:32, 34, 41.
      b. The majority are heedless of God's call. Rev. 20:8, 9.
      c. God's plan still goes into effect. Isa. 46:10; Rev. 21:1, 7.
  2. To how many is God's call of mercy now extended?
      a. Christ stands at the door of each heart. Rev. 3:20.
      b. Whosoever will may accept Christ. Rev. 22:17.
      NOTE.—God calls man by His Spirit, by nature, and by the Bible. God wants our love, but it cannot be forced, just as the child cannot be forced to love its parents by whipping it.

MRS. MARIE SCHMIDT.

How May We Become Righteous?

I. *God's Standard of Righteousness.*
  1. What standard of righteousness does Jesus set for us? Matt. 5:48.
  2. What word picture is given of the human heart? Rom. 3:10-18.
  3. What the Bible teaches about man's righteousness. Isa. 64:6.
  4. If we try hard to make ourselves righteous, will that make us perfect? Jer. 13:23.

II. *Christ's Righteousness Imputed to Us for Past Sins.*
  1. "Be perfect." Since our efforts are of no avail, what then must we do? Isa. 1:18.
  2. What first step must we take? Then what does God do? Acts 2:37; 1 John 1:9.
  3. What change now takes place in the old heart of stone? Eze. 36:26.
  4. Forgiveness of sins and a new heart is a wonderful experience. But God does even more. What additional gift is provided? Rom. 3:22-26.

NOTE.—His righteousness is available to us through faith. It is a gift just as forgiveness of sins is a gift. Note verse 25. He *declares* His righteousness for sins that are past. Our righteousness is as filthy rags, but His righteousness is perfect. When He declares His righteousness in place of our past sins, instead of a record of sins forgiven, we have a record of *Christ's righteousness*.

5. When we have accepted Christ's righteousness do we stand condemned or accepted? Rom. 8:1, first part.
6. If we are "in Christ" we are accepted, but what must we do to remain accepted? Verse 1, last part. God's part is to supply righteousness; our part is to walk after the Spirit.
7. What besides the death of Jesus is necessary for our salvation? Rom. 5:10. We have not lived a perfect life, but Jesus did; so the record of His perfect life goes down as our record. This is called *imputed righteousness.* The word *impute* means "counted as though it were so."

III. *Christ's Righteousness Imparted for Daily Living.*
1. Now we stand perfect in His sight. We do not plan to sin, but if we do, what then? 1 John 2:1.
   Confess, be forgiven, accept His righteousness, and walk in the light. Each moment He supplies His righteousness. This is *imparted righteousness.* The imputed righteousness of Christ makes the past a perfect record. His imparted righteousness keeps present records perfect as we walk after the Spirit.
2. Although Paul counted himself not to have apprehended, what did he do? Phil. 3:13, 14.
3. Paul did not look perfect to himself, but as he pressed forward, how did God regard him? Phil. 3:14.
   Illustration: A small green apple may be perfect, but as it grows and develops, it will be more useful and more beautiful. So with the Christian.
4. Does acceptance of Christ's righteousness make any change in our lives? 2 Cor. 3:18.
   As we behold Jesus and realize *He* is the perfect One, a work of grace takes place in heart and life. We will put forth every effort to choose right and shun wrong—not to be saved, but because we *are* saved. Grace to live right is imparted as freely as grace was imputed to change the records of our sinful past.

IV. *God's Righteousness Is Ours by Faith.*
   May a Christian know he is accepted? 1 John 5:11-13.
   Let us remember that this precious provision of Christ's right-

eousness is available to us only as we do our part. What is our part? 1 John 1:6, 7. God helps us to walk in the light as He lets its shine upon our pathway, that we may be perfect in Him. Additional references: Zech. 3:1-4; Gen. 7:1; 1 Kings 9:4; Job 1:1; compare 9:15, 20, 21; Luke 1:5, 6.

Mrs. Marguerite Williamson.

Confession and Forgiveness
(For Catholics.)

Emphasis must be placed on godly sorrow for sin, not penance. There must be a thorough understanding of justification by faith, not works. Christ is our only Mediator. Intercession by Mary and the saints is not taught in the inspired canon. The Indulgence also belongs to Rome.

I. *Man's Only Saviour Is Christ.*
  1. Gulf of sin spanned by Christ's sacrifice. John 12:32.
  2. His righteousness alone atones for sin. Rom. 3:25; Isa. 64:6.
  3. Sinner may come to God direct. Isa. 1:18.
  4. No other mediator than Christ. 1 Tim. 2:5; 1 John 2:1.

II. *The Way to God.*
  1. Repentance, not penance. Acts 2:38.
     a. Repentance precedes forgiveness of sin. Acts 5:31.
     b. Must always be sincere. Luke 18:13.
     c. God's love leads to repentance. Rom. 2:4.
     d. Necessary for removal of sin. Acts 3:19.
  2. Confession to God.
     a. Confess to God direct. Ps. 32:5.
     b. Through Christ—not Mary, saints, or priests. Heb. 4:15, 16.
     c. Faults to be confessed one to another. James 5:16.
     d. Forgiveness promised on confession. 1 John 1:9.
  3. Justification necessary for forgiveness.
     a. Justification is God's gift. 1 Peter 1:18, 19.
     b. By faith in Christ. Rom. 5:1.
     c. Justification for sins that are past. Rom. 3:23-26.
     d. Christ's atoning sacrifice offered once. Heb. 9:28.

III. *Conversion and Freedom From Sin.*
  1. True conversion results in transformation of life. Ps. 32:1, 2; 51:1-14.
  2. Works of Satan destroyed by Christ. 1 John 3:8.

3. Walking after the Spirit. Rom. 8:1, 2.
4. Restored to God without works of penance. Ps. 51:16, 17.

IV. *Points of Truth Summarized.*
1. Conviction comes through God's Spirit.
2. Repentance is godly sorrow for sin, without penance.
3. Intercession through Christ, not Mary or saints.
4. Confession to God direct, not to priest.
5. Forgiveness pronounced by Christ, not priest.
6. Justification by God; no place for penance or indulgence.
7. Continual daily confession of sin.

V. *Appeal.* (Heb. 10:22, 23.)
Additional references: Heb. 10:19-22; 2 Cor. 5:21; Rom. 4:6-8; Gal. 2:16.

AMELDA GUSTAVSEN.

Baptism and the New Life
(For Protestants.)

I. *Introduction.*
1. Greatest facts of gospel.
   a. Christ died for our sins.
   b. He was buried and rose again.
2. These facts represented in true form of baptism taught in the Bible.

II. *Is Baptism Necessary to Salvation?*
1. "He that believeth and is baptized shall be saved." Mark 16:16; 1 Peter 3:21.
2. Part of Christ's commission. Matt. 28:19.
3. He set the example for us. Mark 1:9.

III. *What Are the Requisites for Baptism?*
1. Repentance. Acts 2:38.
2. Belief based on instruction. Mark 16:15, 16.
3. "If thou believest with all thine heart." Acts 8:34-37.
(These requisites would exclude infant baptism and baptism for the dead or for any others who are not in a condition to understand what is being done.)

IV. *What Is the Meaning of Baptism?*
1. Sins washed away. Acts 22:16.
2. Buried with Christ into His death, raised with Him to walk in newness of life. Rom. 6:3-5.
(Baptism God's divinely appointed memorial of the resurrection of Christ.)

Conversion Studies

3. Baptism a public profession of faith in the Saviour. Gal. 3:27.
4. United with the body of Christ. 1 Cor. 12:12, 13.

V. *The Bible Mode of Baptism?*
   1. One baptism. Eph. 4:5.
   2. Baptism meaning immersion. (See *Source Book*, pp. 75-77.)
      a. *Luther:* "Baptism is a Greek word; in Latin it can be translated immersion, as when we plunge something into the water that it may be completely covered with water."
      b. *Calvin:* "The very word 'baptize,' however, signifies to immerse; and it is certain that immersion was observed by the ancient church."
      c. *Neander:* "In respect to the form of baptizing, it was in conformity with the original institution and the original import of the symbol, performed by immersion."
   3. After His baptism Christ came up out of the water. Mark 1:9-11.
   4. John baptized where there was much water. John 3:23.
   5. Philip and eunuch both went down into water. Acts 8:38.
   6. Father, Son, and Holy Ghost associate in converting sinner. Matt. 28:19.

VI. *What Experience Should Follow Baptism?*
   1. "Walk in newness of life." Rom. 6:4, last part.
   2. No longer live to sin, but to the will of God. 1 Peter 4:2.
   3. Grow in grace. 2 Peter 1:5-11.   Mrs. Marjorie Vansickle.

The Experience of Baptism

I. *What Is Baptism?*
   1. "Apart from Christ, baptism is a worthless form." DA 181.
   2. Having read, heard, and believed God's Word to repentant sinners (Matt. 28:19; Mark 16:16), you now desire to witness publicly to your acceptance of the "everlasting gospel" (Rev. 14:6), because it is "the faith which was once delivered unto the saints" (Jude 3), and now held by the faithful remnant acclaimed by Christ at His second appearing (Rev. 14:12; 2 Thess. 1:10).
   3. In all things you covenant to walk as He walked! 1 John 2:6.
   4. Jesus was baptized (Matt. 3:13-16), though He "knew no sin" (2 Cor. 5:21). Therefore He had no sins to "wash away." Acts 22:16; John 15:10.
   5. Now we know that baptism is that outward symbol of the washing away of our sins in the blood of Jesus. Rev. 1:5; 1 John 5:6; Matt. 26:28; Mark 1:4.

II. *What Are the Bible Examples of True Baptism?*
 1. The full righteousness of God would not have been met had Jesus not suffered Himself to be baptized. Matt. 3:13-15; 1 Peter 2:21; 1 John 2:6.
 2. He was baptized *in* the river Jordan. Mark 1:9-11.
 3. The divine relationship existing between Father and Son, it will be noted, was *not* attested to until *after* the public baptism of Jesus.
 The Son of God *must* "fulfil all righteousness."
 "Suffer it to be so now." Matt. 3:15-17. "His time had come!" DA 109.
 4. John led the Saviour down into the Jordan, and buried Him beneath the water. " 'And straightway coming up out of the water,' Jesus 'saw the heavens opened, and the Spirit like a dove descending upon Him.' " DA 111.
 Hundreds of years before (Isa. 61:1), this very occasion had been foretold by the prophet. Later Jesus claims His authority in His personal fulfillment of and as the Word. Luke 4:14-21; John 1:14.
 5. In our immersion we acknowledge Jesus' death and resurrection for us! Rom. 6:3, 4.
 6. We have assurance that "if we have been planted together in the likeness of His death, we shall be also in the likeness of His resurrection." Rom. 6:5.
 7. Apostles also taught and administered rebaptism. Acts. 19:1-5.

III. *Repentance Before Baptism—How Important?*
 1. True sorrow for sin precedes conversion, baptism, and the reception of the Holy Ghost. Acts 3:19; 2:38.
 2. The Ethiopian eunuch was immersed in a pool "toward the south unto the way that goeth down from Jerusalem unto Gaza, which is desert" (Acts 8:26), at his own request, and upon his full statement of belief in the Son of God. (Acts 8:36-39.)

IV. *Appeal.*
 1. In compliance with the command of Jesus in Mark 16:15, you have had "the gospel" preached (or taught) to you. Do you now accept the challenge He gives you in verse 16? "He that believeth and is baptized shall be saved; but he that believeth not shall be damned."
 2. "And now why tarriest thou? arise, and be baptized, and wash away thy sins, calling on the name of the Lord." Acts 22:16.

Mrs. Lucia H. Lee.

Is Infant Baptism Scriptural?
(For Catholics.)

I. *Christians Must Follow the Scriptures.*
   1. "Believeth . . . as the scripture hath said." John 7:38; 10:35.
   2. "In vain . . . commandments of men." Matt. 15:9, 3; 22:29.
   3. Significance of Scriptural baptism.
      a. Washing away of sin. Acts 22:16.
      b. Dying, being buried, resurrected in Christ. Rom. 6:3-6.
      c. Witnessing for Christ publicly. 1 Peter 3:21.

II. *Infant Baptism Unscriptural.*
   1. Steps necessary for baptism.
      a. Instruction. Mark 16:15.
      b. Understanding leading to contrition. Acts 2:37, 38.
      c. Sorrow unto repentance. 2 Cor. 7:9, 10.
      d. "Believest with all thine heart." Acts 8:37.
      e. Joining Christ's church on earth. 1 Cor. 12:12, 13.
   2. Why infant does not need baptism.
      a. Infant does not know right from wrong. Deut. 1:39.
      b. God's law and sin unknown to child. Rom. 7:7; 1 John 3:4.
      c. Sin not imputed where no law. Rom. 5:13.
      d. Sinner must choose new master; child cannot choose. Rom. 6:6-18.
   3. Problem of "inherited sin."
      a. Master's teaching regarding children. Luke 18:15-17; Matt. 18:1-6.
      b. Consciousness of sin with child's growth. Rom. 7:9, 10.
      c. Parents must train child's conscience. Prov. 22:6.
      d. With manhood, new responsibility to God. Luke 3:21, 23; 1 Cor. 13:11.
      e. Jesus paid for all sin (original sin included). Rom. 5:8, 9.
      f. "Every one according to *his* ways," not Adam's sin. Eze. 18:20, 30.

III. *Scriptural Mode of Baptism.*
   1. "One *Lord,* one *faith,* one *baptism.*" Eph. 4:5.
   2. Symbols: death, burial, resurrection. Col. 2:12, 13; Rom. 6:3-6.
   3. Candidate and administrator both enter and leave water. Acts 8:38, 39.
   4. Example of Jesus' baptism. 1 Peter 2:21; Matt. 3:13-17; John 3:23.

PART FOUR ★ CHAPTER FOUR

The Sanctuary and the Law

The problem of sin and atonement in Christ is best presented to the reader through a study of the sanctuary. Here the way to Christ may be beautifully taught by means of the Bible's illuminating types and shadows. God's plan and purpose is clearly revealed in these lessons to ancient Israel. The teacher has the opportunity to keep building truth on the atoning sacrifice of Christ. Sin is seen in its proper relationship to it, and conversion becomes a need. To "make an end of sin" (Dan. 9:24) is the objective. The foundation principles of the gospel—confession, atonement, consecration, sanctification, and glorification—here have their proper setting. The significance of the investigative judgment, a new truth, will be understood in the light of the typical Day of Atonement. It reveals God's immutable law even before the Sabbath message is studied. The sanctuary truth is basic in an understanding of the three messages. It is the very heart of our complete message and should not be left for a later presentation in the series.

Verbatim Study on the Sanctuary Service

The sanctuary service reveals to us the wonderful love of our Saviour, the love of One who died that all may have salvation. Turning to Acts 4, verse 12, we read that "there is none other name under heaven given among men, whereby we must be saved." In spite of this, many people, rich and poor, think they can buy salvation; but salvation is a gift. It is free. Peter says in his first epistle, the first chapter, verses 18 and 19, that we are not "redeemed with corruptible things, as silver and gold; . . . but with the precious blood of Christ, as of a lamb without blemish and without spot."

In the beginning God made a perfect world; He planned that it should continue as such, but sin came and marred that which God had made perfect. Now the great plan of salvation came into operation.

The Sanctuary and the Law

John 3:16 tells us, "God so loved the world, that He gave His only begotten Son, that whosoever believeth in Him should not perish, but have everlasting life." This plan of salvation introduced the great sacrificial service, for we are not redeemed with silver or gold, but by the precious blood of the Lamb.

Wherever the people of God built an altar and sacrificed a lamb thereon, God met with the sinner. As Moses led the children of God out of Egypt to the land of Canaan, God spoke to him about the matter of worship. In Exodus 25:8 we read that God told Moses to have the people make Him a sanctuary where He could meet with them and commune with them, and He told Moses to make it after the pattern shown him in the mount. (Verse 40.) What kind of pattern was this? Hebrews 8:5 tells us that it was a shadow of the heavenly, a miniature of the heavenly sanctuary.

This sanctuary was divided into two apartments. (Ex. 26:33.) [Draw a sketch.] It was a large room divided by a beautiful, hand-embroidered curtain, separating the holy from the most holy place.

What kind of furniture was placed in the sanctuary? First of all, we read in Exodus 26:34 that the ark of the testimony, with the two cherubim above the mercy seat, was placed in the most holy apartment. Hebrews 9:3-5 mentions that the ark of the covenant held the golden pot that contained manna, and Aaron's rod that budded, also the tables of the covenant. [Indicate on sketch.] The Lord met with His people between the two cherubim above the mercy seat.

In the holy place we find several articles. (Note Exodus 40:22-33.) Verse 22 says that the table of shewbread was placed on the north side. [Indicate on sketch.] Jesus says, "I am the bread of life." John 6:35.

Between the tent of the congregation and the altar the laver was placed, where the priests could wash daily before entering the tabernacle. Christ has promised to wash away our sins if we come in faith, and to present us before His Father in heaven. We now have before us a sketch of the sanctuary.

This sanctuary was made so that it could be taken down and folded up neatly, and easily carried when the children of God moved. The high priest went into the holy place every day to burn incense before the Lord while the offering was burning on the altar in the court where the morning and evening sacrifice was made. (Num. 28:3, 4; Ex. 29:38-46.) A double offering was made on the Sabbath. (Num. 28:9.)

Besides this the people daily brought sacrifices—sin offerings (Lev. 4:27-30), peace offerings, thank offerings, et cetera. The sinner would lay his hand on the offering, transferring in type his sin to the lamb. Then he himself would slay it, and the priest would take the blood and sprinkle it, or take part of the flesh and eat it. Thus was the sin transferred in type to the priesthood and the sanctuary. (Lev. 4; 6:24-30; 1 Peter 2:24.) Yes, it does make one shudder at the thought of slaying a lamb, but God wanted to impress upon the sinner the awfulness of sin, and how Christ, the true Lamb, would suffer for us.

The greatest day of all came once a year—the Day of Atonement. (Ex. 30:10.) This day ended the year's rites and sacrifices. Before this great Day of Atonement all were to prepare themselves spiritually. (Lev. 16:29, 30.) Just picture this great day—all the congregation before the tabernacle in fear and trembling, pleading in their hearts that God would accept their sacrifice and cleanse them from all sin. The priest, after offering a sacrifice for the priesthood, would take two goats and cast lots at the gate of the tabernacle, one goat for the Lord and the other for Azazel, or the devil. The Lord's goat was offered as a sacrifice. (Lev. 16:15, 16.) The blood was taken by the high priest into the most holy place and sprinkled before the mercy seat. [Indicate.]

As the high priest came out of the most holy place he would linger awhile in the first apartment, then proceed to the gate of the tabernacle, and place his hands on the head of the live goat (Azazel). This goat typified Satan, the instigator of all sin. Just as Satan will perish for his sin at the end of the millennium, so the live goat in type was left to perish in the wilderness. (Lev. 16:20-22.) Notice that the goat representing Christ was slain as an offering for sin, but the live goat representing Satan was not sacrificed but perished. The final responsibility for all sin must eventually revert back to its originator, Satan. All unforgiven sinners will then perish with him. Only then are the works of Satan completely destroyed. (1 John 3:8.) What a significant lesson!

The candlestick was placed on the south. [Indicate.] Jesus says, "I am the light of the world." John 8:12. Right before the veil the golden altar of incense was placed [indicate], whereon sweet incense was burned and ascended up before God, just as the prayers of the saints ascend as sweet incense before the throne of God. The altar of burnt offering was placed by the door of the tabernacle of the congregation. On it the lamb was offered as a burnt offering unto the Lord. This reminded the people of the promise of a Saviour, Jesus the true Lamb, who would one day be slain for their salvation.

All this was a "figure for the time" (Heb. 9:9, 10), and pointed forward to the sacrifice of Christ, the true Lamb. [Stand a book up on the table and draw attention to its shadow.] When the people offered the lamb, they lived in the shadow of the cross; then when type met antitype, it all came to an end. (Matt. 27:50, 51.) Christ, the true Lamb, was slain.

Now, this side of the cross, we partake of the communion service, thus showing the Lord's death till He comes. (1 Cor. 11:26.) Baptism is evidence of believing in the cleansing and resurrecting power of Christ. We also have the privilege of evening and morning worship. We now have a High Priest, Jesus Christ the righteous; He is pleading for us before the throne of God in the heavenly sanctuary. (Heb. 9:23-26.) When He lays down His priestly robes and dons His kingly robes, probation will have closed; it will then be too late to be saved. Now is the day of our salvation.

Mrs. Brown, Christ is pleading for you before the heavenly Father. Will you respond to His pleading call? We know when Christ entered the most holy place, but we do not know when He will come out. Not even the angels in heaven know. (Matt. 24:36.) But this we do know, that when probation closes, the plagues will fall; then it will be too late for salvation to be sought.

In the end sin and sinners will be destroyed, just as the live goat was taken into the wilderness to die. Let us live faithfully day by day so that when Christ comes to our names in the book of life, He will be able to confess us before the Father. Always remember that "in such an hour as ye think not the Son of man cometh." Matt. 24:44.

Next week we shall find out when Christ entered the most holy place in the heavenly sanctuary. LILLIAN G. BRADLEY.

Lessons From the Sanctuary

Text: Ps. 77:13. Where is God's plan of atonement revealed to us?

I. *The Earthly Sanctuary.*
   1. Apartments and furniture.
      a. What did God command Israel to build? Ex. 25:8, 9.
      b. How many apartments did it have? Ex. 26:33.
      c. What furniture? Heb. 9:1-5.
   2. Daily service.
      a. What service in holy place in behalf of sinner? Lev. 4:27-31. Why was this necessary?
      b. What is sin? 1 John 3:4.
      c. What is the penalty for sin? Rom. 6:23.
      d. What is the only hope for the sinner? Heb. 9:22.
   3. The typical Day of Atonement.
      a. How often was atonement made in the most holy place? Heb. 9:7.
      b. Purpose of service on Day of Atonement (At-one-ment). Lev. 16:29, 30.

  c. Describe cleansing of sanctuary. Lev. 16:5, 7-9, 15-21.
  d. What kind of day was this? (Day of judgment.) Lev. 23:27-29.
 4. Only a shadow of good things to come.
  a. Of what was work of Levitical priests an example and shadow? Heb. 8:4, 5.
  b. Did this service actually remove sin? Heb. 10:1-4.
  c. What, then, was its object? Heb. 9:9-12.
  d. What sign showed that services in earthly sanctuary should end? Matt. 27:50, 51.

II. *The Heavenly Sanctuary.*
 1. Atonement in first apartment.
  a. Of what was the earthly sanctuary a type? Heb. 9:23, 24.
  b. How is the heavenly sanctuary described? Heb. 8:2.
  c. When door of holy place opened, what was seen before throne in heaven? Rev. 4:1, 2, 5.
  d. How is the altar of incense described? Rev. 8:2, 3.
  e. What was seen in most holy place? Rev. 11:19.
 2. Christ our high priest in heaven.
  a. Who is our high priest? Heb. 4:14.
  b. Who ministers in heavenly sanctuary? Heb. 8:1-4.
  c. What is Christ doing in heaven? Heb. 9:24.
  d. How do we receive forgiveness? Heb. 9:12-14; 1 John 1:9.
 3. Atonement in second apartment.
  a. How is record of sin blotted out? Heb. 9:23-26; Acts 3:19, 20.
  b. When did this cleansing begin? Dan. 8:14.
  c. How was this event revealed to Daniel? Dan. 7:9, 10.

III. *Significance of Judgment Hour.*
 1. Message to prepare men for event. Rev. 14:7.
 2. Will man have another chance after this cleansing is finished? Rev. 22:11, 12.
 3. What should we now do with our sins? 1 Tim. 5:24.
 4. For whom only does Christ's blood atone? Heb. 7:25.

Mrs. Sadie Walleker.

Meaning of Types and Antitypes

I. *Introduction.*

 Review and tie in with 2300 days of preceding study. Suggest we will learn today what the cleansing of the sanctuary involves.
 1. What was the purpose of tabernacle in the wilderness? Ex. 25:1, 8.
 2. Who provided its pattern?

The Sanctuary and the Law 395

  a. Ex. 25:9, 40. The pattern provided by God.
  b. Heb. 9:2-5. The furnishings.
  c. Heb. 9:6-10. Order of service.
II. *What Was the Meaning of the Sin Offering?*
  1. Lev. 4:3, 4, 22-24, 13-15, 27-29. Brought a sin offering without blemish, confessed sin over it, killed it.
  2. Lev. 4:5, 6, 16, 17; 10:17, 18. Priest ministered for sinner. Figuratively carried sin into sanctuary.
  3. Lev. 4:20, 26, 31. Sin forgiven; sinner reconciled to God.
III. *What Disposal Was Made of Sin on Day of Atonement?*
  Lev. 16:5, 7-10, 15, 16, 20-22. Cleansing of the sanctuary.
IV. *How Did the Cross Affect This System of Offerings?*
  1. What happened when type met antitype?
    a. Dan. 9:27. "Cause the sacrifice and the oblation to cease."
    b. Matt. 27:50, 51. The veil of the temple rent.
    c. Col. 2:17. "A shadow of things to come."
  2. What is meant by the new-covenant relationship?
    a. Heb. 8:1, 2. Christ a minister of the true and heavenly sanctuary.
    b. Heb. 9:20, 23, 24. The earthly sanctuary was a type, figure, pattern, or shadow of the heavenly, "now to appear in the presence of God for us."
V. *What Is the Antitypical Day of Atonement?*
  1. Who is our great High Priest? Heb. 8:1, 2.
    a. Col. 1:12-14. "In whom we have redemption through His blood."
    b. Acts 3:19, 20; Dan. 7:9, 10. Sin blotted out; investigative judgment.
    c. Heb. 9:28. Christ shall appear second time without sin unto salvation.
    d. Dan. 8:14; Rev. 22:12. When will atonement for sin be completed?
VI. *Appeal.*
  1. 1 John 1:9. God's faithful promise is to forgive and cleanse.
  2. Zechariah 3. The Lord is our righteousness.
  3. 1 Tim. 5:24. Make sure our sins are now under the blood.

Sanctuary and the Atonement

I. *Location.*
  1. Where is God's true sanctuary? Heb. 8:2; Ps. 102:19.
  2. To whom was its pattern given? Heb. 8:5; Ex. 25:8, 9.

II. *How Is the Earthly Sanctuary Described?* Heb. 9:1-5.
III. *What About Its Daily Service?* Ex. 29:38-42; Num. 28:1-10.
There were daily burnt offerings for the nation. Also burnt offerings for individuals. See Leviticus 1-4.
  1. In type.
      a. What took place in the court of the earthly sanctuary?
          (1) Sacrifice slain by sinner at brazen altar.
          (2) Sinner confessed his sin.
          (3) Blood sprinkled "round about the altar." Lev. 1:4, 5; 4:25-30.
      b. What was the significance of its service?
          (1) Priest administered shed blood at brazen altar.
          (2) Sinner forgiven.
          (3) In type record of sin remained in holy place.
          (4) Holy place entire sanctuary enclosure—court and tent.
  2. In antitype.
      a. What lessons are taught by the court of the sanctuary?
          (1) Christ slain here on earth. John 1:29.
          (2) We must confess before His sacrifice can help us. 1 John 1:7-9.
IV. *What Lessons Are Taught by the Heavenly Holy Place?*
  1. Christ is our high priest. Heb. 3:1; 8:1, 2; 9:11.
  2. Glimpse of heavenly service. Rev. 8:3, 4.
  3. Forgiveness promised. Heb. 8:12.
  Christ began His heavenly ministry when He ascended into heaven. John saw Him in the first apartment of the heavenly sanctuary. (Rev. 1:13.) Even though Calvary was a finished work, "Christ ever liveth to make intercession." Heb. 7:25. Until every blot and remembrance of sin is eradicated, He is our great high priest.
V. *What Was the Meaning of the Yearly Service?* (Lev. 16; 23:26-32.)
  1. Its significance in the most holy place on earth (type).
      a. Service conducted before ark.
      b. High priest offered bullock for his sins first.
      c. He offered goat for cleansing of people.
      d. Both sanctuary and people cleansed.
      e. Sins thus removed placed on head of scapegoat to be separated forever from camp of Israel (Azazel).
      f. Leaving the most holy signal for great rejoicing of those whose sins were blotted out; mourning for those who had neglected opportunities to put away sin.
      g. Complete cleansing from sin typified.

The Sanctuary and the Law

2. What is Christ now doing in the most holy in heaven (antitype)?
   a. Service conducted before throne of God.
   b. Christ offers Himself as sin-bearer. Heb. 7:26, 27.
   c. Christ presents Himself as sinless one. Heb. 9:25, 26.
   d. Heavenly things must be purified. Heb. 9:23.
   e. God's people made clean. Rev. 7:14; 1 Tim. 5:24.
   f. Sins forever removed; Satan bears his share. Rev. 20:2, 3.
   g. Christ returns for His people. Heb. 9:28.
   h. Too late for repentance. Rev. 22:11, 12.

VI. *What Is the Lesson of the Most Holy Place?*
Now, while our High Priest is officiating in the inner apartment, within the second veil, let us accept His invitation and enter in with Him to the victorious experience of having made an end of sinning. Heb. 6:19, 20; 10:19, 20.   Mrs. Dorothy Conklin.

The 2300-Day Prophecy
(To meet the b.c. to a.d. problem.)

I. *Introduction.*
   1. Jews had fulfilled about 68 of their 70 allotted years of captivity.
   2. Eighth chapter of Daniel was written during the rule of Babylon.
   3. In the ninth chapter Medo-Persia is ruling, but Daniel is still in the employ of the government.
   4. Daniel, an old man, has his vision by the banks of the river Ulai.

II. *Daniel Saw Four Symbols.*
   1. Ram: Medo-Persia. Dan. 8:3, 4, 20.
      a. "Two horns."
         (1) Media.
         (2) Persia.
      b. "Higher came up last." Persian side came into power last and was the stronger.
      c. "Became *great*." Became a world empire.
   2. He goat: Grecia. Dan. 8:5-8, 21.
      a. Feet "touched not the ground." Conquered so swiftly.
      b. "Notable horn between his eyes." Represented Alexander, the first king.
      c. "Waxed *very great*." Greece conquered Persia at the Battle of Arbela 331 b.c., and became even stronger than Persia.
      d. "Horn was broken."
      e. Four horns came up. Twenty-two years after Alexander's death his four leading generals divided the empire into four parts—north, south, east, west.

3. Little horn: Rome. Dan. 8:9, 10, 22-25.
   a. "Waxed *exceeding great.*" Through Macedonia came Rome in 168 B.C., in which empire the Papacy developed. Papal Rome became exceeding great.
   b. "Cause craft to prosper." Under papal Rome selling of indulgences, etc. introduced.
4. 2300 days to the cleansing of the sanctuary. Dan. 8:14, 26, 27.
   a. Daniel fainted before Gabriel could explain this symbol.
   b. Astonished at the terrible deeds of the little horn.

III. *Daniel Prayed for Explanation of 2300 Days.*
   1. Seventy years' captivity was the result of Israel's sins.
      a. Daniel evidently thought sanctuary mentioned was one at Jerusalem, and that God would extend their captivity.
      b. He confesses his sins and the sins of his people. Dan. 9:3-5, 19, 20.
   2. Gabriel tells him to consider the vision where he had left off explaining. Dan. 9:21-23. (At the 2300 days.)

IV. *2300 Days Explained.*
   1. A prophetic day is a literal year. Num. 14:34; Eze. 4:6. 2300 days=2300 years.
   (Cite authority. See *Source Book,* p. 609.)

70 weeks—490 years—Cut off for Jewish nation				
		3½ 3½		
7 wks.	62 wks.	1 wk.		1810 yrs.
	69 wks.—483 yrs.—Messiah	7 yrs.		

   2. 70 weeks of 2300-day period allotted to the Jews. Dan. 9:24.
      a. Daniel's people the Jews.
      b. *Determined* means "cut off." *Source Book,* p. 554.
      c. Jews given 70 prophetic weeks.
      d. 70 weeks=490 years.
   3. 69 weeks to the Messiah. Dan. 9:25.
      a. *Messiah* means "anointed." John 1:41, margin.
      b. Christ anointed at His baptism. Acts 10:38.

c. Therefore this dates to His *baptism,* not His *birth* or *crucifixion.*
d. 69 weeks=483 years.
e. The first seven prophetic weeks of this time to rebuild Jerusalem after the captivity.
4. Messiah cut off. Dan. 9:26. Crucified after His baptism.
5. Crucified in the midst of the week. Dan. 9:27, first part.
   a. The "sacrifices" typified the crucifixion of Christ.
   b. God showed these were to "cease" at the death of the true Lamb. Dan. 9:27; Matt. 27:51.
   c. 70 weeks cut off for the Jews; 69 weeks to reach the baptism of Christ.
   d. One week, seven literal years, between these events.
   e. "Confirm the covenant with many for one week." Christ and apostles (Heb. 2:3) directed their ministry to the Jews.
   f. Christ's crucifixion in the "midst of the week." His ministry, 3½ years.
6. 2300 years to cleansing of sanctuary.
   a. 490 years to cutting off of Jews.
   b. 1810 years from cutting off of Jews to cleansing of sanctuary.
7. Prophecy begins with decree to restore Jerusalem, 457 B.C. Dan. 9:25; Ezra 7:12, 13.
   a. Decrees were made by three kings, but only the decree of Artaxerxes granted all called for in the prophecy and went into effect. Ezra 6:14. (*Source Book,* pp. 554, 555.)
   (Begin here to fill in dates on diagram.)
   b. Work began about one-half year later. Ezra 7:9.
   c. It would be 456½ B.C. (*Source Book,* p. 435.)
   d. Jewish year begins in the spring. (Ex. 12:2.) Brings prophecy to the fall of the year.
8. Christ baptized A.D. 27. Matt. 3:16, 17.
   a. 483 years to Messiah. 456½ B.C. the decree went forth. A.D. 26½, which is literally the fall of A.D. 27.
   b. Proof: A child born in the fall of 3 B.C. would be 6 years of age in the fall of A.D. 4, and not in A.D. 3, as one would think. (Each section represents a year.)

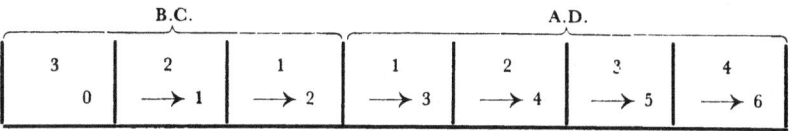

c. Another illustration:

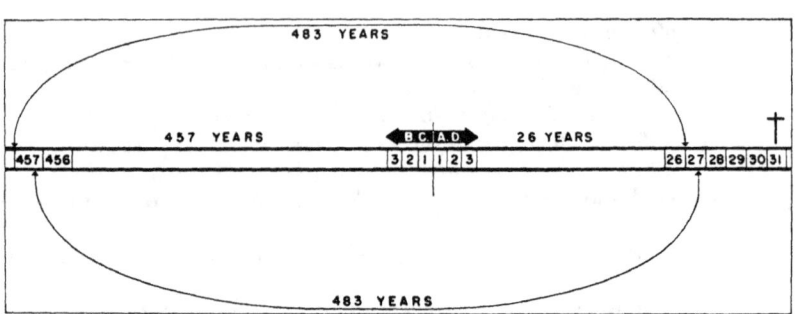

If the decree had gone forth January 1, 457 B.C., it would have ended December 21, A.D. 26. But it was in the fall of the year that the decree went forth. Therefore the 457 and 26 must each be pushed ahead three fourths of a year, making it run into the fall of A.D. 27.

"In the Christian era the years are simply distinguished by the cardinal numbers; those before Christ being marked B.C. (Before Christ), . . . and those after Christ A.D. (Anno Domini). . . . Chronologers, in conformity with common notions, call the year preceding the [first of our] era 1 B.C., the previous year 2 B.C., and so on."—*Encyclopaedia Britannica* (11th ed.), vol. 6, p. 313b, art. "Chronology."

9. Christ's ministry exactly 3½ years.
   a. Four passovers from baptism to crucifixion. John 2:13; 5:1; 6:4; 13:1.
   b. Passover came in the spring.
      First passover spring A.D. 28—preached ½ year.
      Second   "   "   29—   "   1   "
      Third   "   "   30—   "   1   "
      Fourth   "   "   31—   "   1   "

                                          ─────────
                                          3½ years.
   c. Baptized in the fall.
10. Jews "cut off" A.D. 34. Acts 8:1-5; 13:46.
    a. Christ baptized A.D. 27.
       One week   7 years
                        ─────────
                        A.D. 34

The Sanctuary and the Law

   b. Four events marked cutting off of Jews.
      (1) Stoning of Stephen.
      (2) Persecution of Christians.
      (3) Conversion of eunuch.
      (4) Apostles turned to Gentiles.
11. Sanctuary cleansed fall of 1844.
    Jews cut off A.D. 34.

    1810 years
    ___
    1844

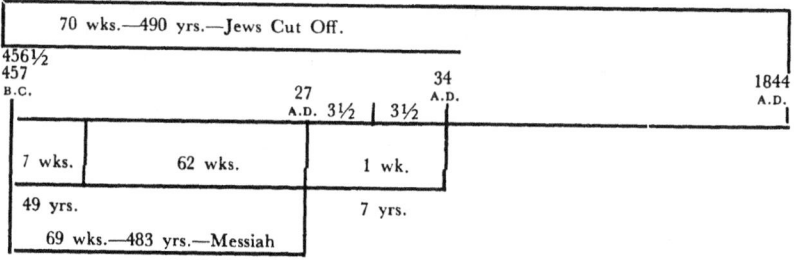

V. *1844 Disappointment.*
   1. People mistakenly thought earth was sanctuary.
   2. Could be cleansed only with fire.
   3. Christ must come October 22, 1844, to take the righteous home.
   4. When Christ did not come, thousands ridiculed Advent hope.
   5. Some searched for the meaning of the "cleansing." Found consolation in Revelation 10.
   6. After bitter experience to "prophesy again." Rev. 10:11.
   (In our next lesson we will learn the great truth they discovered.)

RACHEL MAE LEMON.

You Have an Appointment With God!

I. *Introduction.*
   God has appointed a day to judge the world. Acts 17:31. Before an earthly court convenes, its session is announced. God made a similar provision. Important that we understand its significance.
II. *What Does the Bible Teach Regarding the Time of the Judgment?*
   1. Time foretold about 600 years before Christ. Dan. 8:14. [Review briefly.]

2. Judgment still future in Paul's day. Acts 24:25.
   3. Message announced judgment hour had come. Rev. 14:6, 7.
   4. It began at the house of God. 1 Peter 4:17.
III. *How Is the Judgment Described?*
   1. Daniel in vision foresaw the judgment. Dan. 7:9, 10.
   2. All must appear before the judgment seat of Christ. 2 Cor. 5:10.
   3. We are judged from the books. Dan. 7:10.
      a. Book of remembrance. Mal. 3:16.
      b. Book of life. Rev. 20:12, 15; 3:5; Acts 3:19; Ex. 32:33.
      c. Book of death. Ps. 69:28.
IV. *How Is God's Justice Then Revealed?*
   1. His holy law the basis of the judgment. Eccl. 12:13, 14.
   2. Jesus our substitute and mediator. Rom. 5:8, 9; 1 John 2:1.
   3. Each judged according to his opportunities. Luke 12:47, 48.
   4. God recognizes our environment. Ps. 87:4-6.
   5. More tolerable for Tyre than unfaithful believers. Luke 10:13-15.
   6. He judges the very secrets of men's hearts. 1 Cor. 4:5.
V. *How May We Prepare for This Solemn Event?*
   1. Accepting God's provision for sinners. 1 John 1:7, 9.
   2. Sending our sins beforehand into judgment. 1 Tim. 5:24.
   3. Placing our case in Jesus' hands. Luke 12:8, 9.
VI. *Appeal.*
   1. We individually have the most urgent appointment with God.
   2. None can dodge its responsibility.
   3. The hour of this appointment is now!
   4. Are you making the proper provision for it?
   [Close with earnest prayer.]

The Investigative Judgment

I. *The Judgment in Session.*
   1. Is there a judgment day? Heb. 9:27.
   2. Who is to be judged? 2 Cor. 5:10; 1 Peter 4:17.
   3. When will the judgment take place?
      a. God has made an appointment to judge this world. Acts 17:30, 31.
      b. Judgment was still future in Paul's day. Acts 24:25.
      c. God announced its beginning with a message. Rev. 14:6, 7.
      d. At close of 2300 days. [Review using diagram.]
   4. Where will the judgment be held? Dan. 7:9, 10.
      a. In Father's presence. Ps. 50:6; Heb. 12:23.
      b. At judgment seat of Christ. 2 Cor. 5:10.

The Sanctuary and the Law

5. Who will be man's mediator?
   a. Jesus saves, justifies, and mediates. Rom. 3:23-26.
   b. He confesses our names before the Father. Matt. 10:32, 33.

II. *The Judgment Determined.*
   1. How will each case be decided? Dan. 7:10; Rev. 20:10, 15.
      a. Book of remembrance—records man's good deeds. Mal. 3:16.
      b. Book of life—names of forgiven sinners. Luke 10:20.
      c. Sin or name of sinner blotted out. Acts 3:19; Rev. 3:5.
      d. Names of unforgiven sinners not in "book of living." Ps. 69:28; Job 14:17.
   2. What standard is used in the judgment? Eccl. 12:13, 14; James 2:8-12.
   Deeds compared with God's law. Rom. 2:6.
   NOTE.—God awaits the harvest of man's deeds. He judges every thought and motive. Jer. 17:10; 1 Cor. 4:5.

III. *Close of the Judgment.*
   What takes place at the end of the investigative judgment? Rev. 19:11-16.
   NOTE.—Jesus has then declared each case eternally sealed. Rev. 22:11, 12.

IV. *Appeal.*
   Ps. 32:1, 2, 5; 1 Tim. 5:24, 25. This is a most solemn study. Close with earnest prayer to prepare for the judgment, that our sins may then be covered with Christ's blood.

Is the Law Still Binding?

(Use suitable excerpts showing stand of Protestants and Catholics on God's law. See *Source Book*, pp. 300-307.)

I. *Relation of Law to Salvation.*
   1. For what purpose did Jesus come into this world? Matt. 1:21.
   2. What is sin? 1 John 3:4.

II. *The Law Given at Sinai Immutable.*
   1. What great manifestation attended the giving of this law at Sinai? Ex. 20:18-22.
   2. Who spoke and wrote the law? Ex. 20:1; Deut. 4:12, 13.
   3. What did Moses say concerning God's speaking directly to Israel? Deut. 4:32, 33.
   4. Did God add anything to the Ten Commandments? Deut. 5:22.
   5. Can man now change the law of God? Deut. 4:2.
   6. Would God Himself change it? Ps. 89:34.

III. *The Perfect Law of God.*
  1. Law is spiritual.
      a. What is the nature of God's law? Rom. 7:12; Ps. 19:7.
         NOTE.—The law converts the soul, or turns it rightabout-face from the wrong direction to the right direction.
      b. To what is the law compared? James 1:23-25.
      c. What is its purpose? Rom. 7:7; 3:20.
      d. How is it possible for an unconverted person to keep God's law? Rom. 8:6, 7, 9.
  2. Law is comprehensive.
      a. Can we disregard one of the commandments and still be guiltless? James 2:10.
      b. How much of our duty is comprised in the law? Eccl. 12:13, 14.
      c. Of what is the keeping of the law an expression? 1 John 5:2, 3.
      d. What will be the reward of true commandment keeping? Rev. 22:14.

IV. *Christ and the Law.*
  1. Jesus kept the law.
      a. Why was the law a delight to Christ? Ps. 40:7, 8.
      b. What does He promise to do for those who desire to keep His law? Heb. 8:10.
         To seek to keep the law in our own strength is merely bondage, for our nature is against His law. Only when the Lord changes our natures to conform to His nature do we find pleasure indeed in keeping His commandments.
  2. Law kept by us through Christ.
      a. We are saved by faith in Christ. He justifies the sinner, imputing to him His own righteousness. Christ then provides grace to do God's will. His righteousness is now our title to heaven. Luke 18:13, 14; Ps. 40:7-9; John 15:4, 5, 10.
      b. We are fitted for heaven by the writing of His commandments in the heart. In this way His righteousness is imparted to us. Heb. 8:10.
      c. Two sets of tables. God wrote His commandments on first tables of stone. Later these were broken by Moses to symbolize man's inability to keep law. On the second set of tables God again wrote His law, the same as at first. We must today bring our hearts to the Lord, if we would again have the law written therein. Ex. 34:1.
         ILLUSTRATION: A music-loving little boy desired to attend a musical to be held in his neighborhood. His mother, a widow, assured him it would be impossible, since the price of the

The Sanctuary and the Law

ticket was far beyond their meager earnings. He went out to play, and soon was disheveled and dirty in appearance. A neighbor heard of his desire to attend the musical, and presented the mother with a ticket for him. She called him, and in his joy he seized the ticket and started to hurry to the concert hall, for the hour was late. His mother with difficulty impressed him that not only must he have a ticket to get into the hall, but he must also be made presentable. So she cleaned him up, and sent him on his way. However, in his pride of appearance he forgot his ticket, and at the door of the concert hall discovered that appearance alone would not admit him; he must be clean and have his ticket. So we must not only have God's law written in the heart as our preparation for heaven, but we must accept His perfect obedience to the law as our title to heaven. Righteousness imputed and imparted are both necessary.   MRS. EDITH A. SAWYER.

Should Christians Keep the Law?

The gospel consists of two parts: faith and obedience. The law of God and the gospel should be studied together. Sin—the transgression of the law—made the gospel necessary. The gospel is the good news of salvation from sin through Jesus Christ.

I. *How Is the Importance of God's Law Taught for All Times?*
  1. Spoken by God and written by Him on two tables of stone. Ex. 20:1-17; Deut. 4:12, 13.
  2. Jesus the author. Neh. 9:12-14; 1 Cor. 10:1-4.
  3. God does not change; His law is unchangeable. Mal. 3:6; Ps. 89:34.
  4. All God's commandments stand fast forever. Eccl. 3:14; Ps. 111:7, 8.
  5. Keeping commandments sums up our duty to God. Eccl. 12:13.

II. *Is It Necessary Today to Keep the Law?*
  1. Jesus did not change God's law. Matt. 5:17-19; Heb. 13:8.
  2. Jesus Himself kept God's commandments. John 15:10.
  3. He magnified the law and made it honorable. Isa. 42:21.
  4. Obedience to the law marks our love for God. John 14:15; 1 John 5:3.
  5. Disobedience to God's law a denial of our faith. 1 John 2:4.
  6. Obedience an act of faith. "Faith without works is dead." James 2:24-26.

III. *What Is the Relationship of the Law and the Gospel?*
   1. Jesus had to die to meet claims of law. John 3:16; Rom. 6:23.
   2. "Sin is the transgression of the law." 1 John 3:4.
   3. Jesus came to save us *from* sin, not *in* sin. Matt. 1:21.
   4. He had the law in His heart. Ps. 40:8.
   5. He writes the law in our hearts. Heb. 8:10.
   6. Entrance into Christ's kingdom requires obedience to God's commandments. Isa. 1:19; Rev. 14:12; 22:14.

RUBY M. CREELMAN.

Under the Law, or Under Grace?

I. *Introduction.*
   1. Some people believe that law and gospel are enemies, and that the two cannot work together. They quote Galatians 5:4. Now we want to find out just what relationship exists between the law and the gospel. Are they friends, or enemies, and can we have one without the other?
   2. In order to understand this let us define law and gospel.
   Law: a divine command or revelation. God's will.
   Gospel: "the power of God unto salvation." Rom. 1:16.
   3. Establish fact that we believe in grace for the sinner. Explain that grace is provided through Christ. The gospel reveals His grace. Eph. 2:5, 8.

II. *Christ Came to Save From Sin.*
   1. Saves "His people from their sins." Matt. 1:21.
   2. What is sin? 1 John 3:4.

III. *The Law and Grace.*
   1. There can be no sin without a law to break. Rom. 4:15; 7:7. No law, no sin. If no sin, no need of a Saviour—no need of grace.
   2. Law established by faith. Rom. 3:31. God established the law in the universe. Faith in human heart is a law-abiding life.
   3. Blending of law and grace in Old Testament, and grace and law in New Testament. Ps. 19:7; Gen. 6:8; Rom. 6:14-18; Rev. 22:14, 21.
   4. Law and sin make grace a necessity. Rom. 6:1, 2; 3:20, 21.
   5. Christ came to take away sin, not law. John 1:29; Matt. 5:17.
   6. Close relationship between sin and law. James 1:22-25. The law is our mirror. I look into law, and it tells me I am a sinner, but it cannot save. It only points me to grace.
   7. What does it mean not to be "under the law" but "under grace?" Read Romans 6:14, but we must also read verse 15. [Explain

what it means to be under condemnation of the law. Illustration: Man who has broken law. After paying the penalty is free until he breaks the law another time.]

IV. *Conclusion.*
   1. People whom God calls saints will be keeping commandments and have faith of Jesus (the gospel). Rev. 14:12.
   2. Remnant church will keep commandments. Rev. 12:17.

The Two Laws and the Gospel

I. *Introduction.*
   1. Basis of government—law, a rule of action established by authority.
   2. Laws are established to ensure peace, harmony, order, liberty.
   3. Broken law brings a penalty: suffering, sorrow, bondage, death.

II. *God's Basic Ten-Commandment Law.*
   1. Eccl. 12:13, 14. Government of God founded upon law by which we shall be judged.
   2. James 2:12. Called "law of liberty"; also called "moral law."
   3. Ex. 31:18. Written by God Himself.
   4. Rom. 7:10; Prov. 29:18. Commandments ordained to life and for happiness.
   5. 1 John 3:4. Breaking or transgressing the law called sin.
   6. Rom. 6:23, first part. Penalty of sin is death.
   7. Ps. 111:7, 8. This law stands forever.

III. *The Sinner's Hopeless Condition.*
   Rom. 3:23. All have sinned, broken God's law, and are therefore worthy of death.

IV. *Christ the Atoning Gift of God.*
   1. Rom. 6:23, last part. Eternal life through Jesus Christ.
   2. Gen. 3:15. After Adam and Eve sinned, first promise of plan of salvation.
   3. Luke 2:10, 11. Jesus is our Saviour.
   4. Matt. 1:21. Saves "His people from their sins."
   5. Acts 4:12. Our only hope of salvation.
   6. Eph. 1:7. "In whom we have redemption through His blood."

V. *Purpose of the Ceremonial Law.*
   1. Heb. 10:4-10; Gal. 3:19. Ceremonial law added to teach atonement work of Christ.
   2. Heb. 10:1. Ceremonial law was "shadow of good things to come."
   3. Heb. 9:11, 12. Christ our true sacrifice.

4. Eph. 2:15; Col. 2:14 (Matt. 27:51). Ceremonial law done away with at Christ's death. He paid penalty required for man's breaking the law.

VI. *Conclusion.*
 1. John 3:16. Whosoever believeth in Him has everlasting life.
 2. Eph. 2:8. "By grace are ye saved through faith."
 3. Rom. 5:1. "Being justified by faith, we have peace with God through our Lord Jesus Christ." MRS. MARJORIE VANSICKLE.

God's Two Laws

I. *The Moral Law.*
 1. The royal law. James 2:8.
 2. Spoken by God to the people. Deut. 4:12, 13.
 3. Written by God's finger on tables of stone. Ex. 24:12; 31:18.
 4. Placed in ark. Ex. 40:20; 1 Kings 8:9; Heb. 9:4.
 5. Perfect. Ps. 19:7.
 6. Not destroyed but magnified by Christ. Matt. 5:17; Isa. 42:21.
 7. Stands fast forever. Ps. 111:7, 8.
 8. Gives knowledge of sin. Rom. 3:20; 7:7; 1 John 3:4.
 9. Standard in the judgment. James 2:10-12.

II. *The Ceremonial Law.*
 1. Law contained in ordinances. Eph. 2:15.
 2. Spoken by God to Moses, who gave it to the people. Lev. 1:1-3.
 3. Written by Moses in a book. Deut. 31:24; 2 Chron. 35:12.
 4. Placed in the side of the ark. Deut. 31:26.
 5. Made nothing perfect. Heb. 7:19.
 6. Abolished by Christ. Eph. 2:15.
 7. Nailed to cross; taken out of way by Christ. Col. 2:14.
 8. Was instituted in consequence of sin. Lev. 3-7.
 9. Not the standard in the judgment. Col. 2:16.
  NOTE.—By the moral law we know sin. By the ceremonial law we recognize Christ as the remedy for sin.

III. *Man's Relation to Moral Law.*
 1. Natural man cannot keep it. Rom. 8:7.
 2. Man needs new birth to keep it. Eze. 36:26, 27.
 3. A Christian lives the law. Ps. 119:34.
 4. A Christian loves the law. 1 John 5:2, 3; Ps. 40:8.
 5. A Christian meditates upon it. Ps. 1:2.
 6. Obedience to it brings happiness. Prov. 29:18.

IV. *Conclusion.*
 Let us pray for better understanding of God's law. Ps. 119:18.

MRS. DOROTHY BATCHELDER.

Does Grace Dispense With Law?
Which diagram is correct?

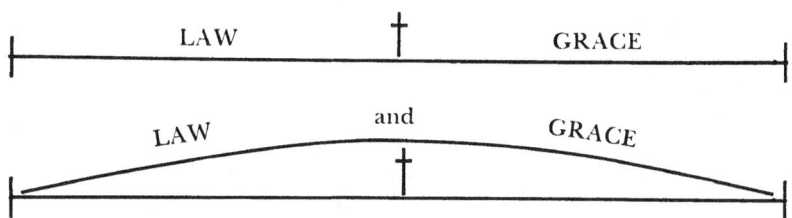

I. *Salvation Is by Grace.*
   1. *Grace* means mercy, pardon, love, kindness. Eph. 2:4-8.
   2. God has always been gracious. Ex. 34:6; Titus 2:11.
   3. Men before the cross received the grace of God. Gen. 6:8; Rom. 4:1-4; Ex. 33:12, 16.
   4. All men before the cross would have been lost if that period had been a dispensation of law with no grace. Rom. 3:23.
   5. No need of grace since the cross, if there is no law. 1 John 3:4; Rom. 4:15.
   6. So from Adam until the present we have law, and sin, and grace. Rom. 5:20.

II. *What It Means to Be "Under Grace."*
   1. Wrath of God comes upon the disobedient. Eph. 5:6.
   2. It is when a man is disobedient to the law that he is "under the law." Rom. 3:19.
   3. Grace (mercy) is promised only to those who turn from disobedience to obedience. Ex. 20:6; Rom. 2:13; Ps. 103:17, 18; Rev. 22:14.
   4. Grace frees a man from the condemnation of the law but not from its jurisdiction. Rom. 6:23; 8:1; 6:1, 2.
   5. Read Romans 6:14-16. Reread, substituting the definition of sin (1 John 3:4) for the word *sin*.

III. *Conclusion.*
   1. We should be *thankful* for the grace of God. Rom. 6:17.
   2. Let us yield ourselves servants to obey. Rom. 6:16.
   3. Then the grace of God will not be in vain for us personally. 2 Cor. 6:1.

MRS. ENA FERGUSON.

Is the Moral Law Abolished?
(When specific texts need to be clarified.)

Text: "Do we then make void the law through faith?" Rom. 3:31.

I. *How to Understand Difficult Texts.*
  1. Peter recognized difficulty in understanding Paul's writing. 2 Peter 3:16.
  2. We may know meaning of any doctrine. John 7:17.
  3. Prayer first essential for spiritual understanding. Ps. 119:18.
  4. Ascertain God's thoughts in texts. Matt. 22:29; Prov. 14:12.
  5. Always compare scriptures. 1 Cor. 2:13, 14.
  6. Separate man's opinions from God's. Matt. 15:9.

II. *Puzzling Texts Examined.*
  1. *Rom. 6:14, 15.* Are we now under law, or grace? Gal. 5:4.
     a. Man's bondage state by nature. Rom. 3:19; Gal. 3:22; 1 John 3:4.
     b. Law condemns man to death. Rom. 6:23; Gal. 3:10.
     c. Man redeemed from curse of law. Gal. 3:13; Heb. 2:14, 15.
     d. Saved man no longer condemned. Rom. 6:11-14.
     e. Grace forgives past sins. Rom. 3:25.
     f. Faith accepts forgiveness and justifies sinner. Gal. 3:23, 24.
     g. Justified man under grace obeys law. Rom. 6:15, 17, 18; 8:4.
     h. *Conclusion No. 1:* The law and gospel agree. Gal. 3:21. Grace demands we observe law.
  2. *Col. 2:14-17.* What was "nailed to the cross"?
     a. The "handwriting of ordinances." Col. 2:14; Deut. 31:26.
     b. To what did these ordinances refer? Col. 2:16.
        (To "meats" and "drinks," and ceremonial sabbaths. See Lev. 23:37, 38.)
     c. Why were these against us? Heb. 10:1; Col. 2:17.
     d. How were these taken away? Heb. 10:8, 9; Eph. 2:15, 16; Matt. 27:51.
     e. *Conclusion No. 2:* Ceremonial law abolished at cross. Sabbath of moral law still binding.
  3. *Rom. 10:4.* Does text state Christ brought an end to obeying ten-commandment law?
     a. Ten Commandments endure forever. Ps. 119:44; Eccl. 12:13, 14.
     b. To lead to faith in Christ. Gal. 3:24.

The Sanctuary and the Law

   c. Faith is the purpose of law. Gal. 3:25, 26.
   d. *Conclusion No. 3:* "Christ is the end [aim, objective, purpose, fulfillment] of the law." Faith leads to better observance of God's law.

III. *Summary of Conclusions.* Rom. 3:31; Rev. 14:12; 22:14; John 15:10.
   1. Law teaches need of gospel.
   2. Gospel brings obedience to Ten Commandments.
   3. Ten Commandments still binding.
   4. Jesus' followers keep Father's commandments.
   5. Redeemed will be commandment keepers.

Two Laws and Two Priesthoods
(Explaining what was changed at the cross.)

I. *God's Two Laws.*
   1. Laws defined.
      a. God's Ten Commandments.
      b. Moses' precepts, statutes, and laws.
         2 Kings 21:8; Deut. 4:13, 14; Neh. 9:13, 14.
   2. *The Law of God* (also known as "Law of Moses").
      a. Ten Commandments written by God on stone. Deut. 4:12, 13.
      b. Kept in the ark. Deut. 10:5.
      c. Perfect, holy, just, good. Ps. 19:7; Rom. 7:12.
      d. To continue forever. Ps. 111:7, 8; Luke 16:17.
   3. *The Law of Moses* (also called the "law of God").
      a. Consisted of "carnal" ordinances." Heb. 9:10.
      b. Written by Moses in a book. Deut. 31:24.
      c. Kept "in the side of the ark." Deut. 31:26.
      d. Had its limitations. Eze. 20:24, 25.
      e. To pass away at the cross. Heb. 9:9-11; Col. 2:14, 15.

II. *The Two Priesthoods.* (Heb. 7:11.)
   1. Priesthood of Aaron ("Levitical," "Mosaic").
      a. Regulated offerings and sacrifices for sin. Heb. 5:1; 8:3, 4.
      b. Could not bring perfection. Heb. 7:11.
      c. Could not take away sin. Heb. 10:1, 4, 11; 7:19; 1 John 3:4.
      d. Served as an object lesson. Heb. 9:9, 10.
      e. Christ was its objective, aim, and "end." Rom. 10:4; 1 Peter 1:9.
   2. *Priesthood of Christ* (Melchisedec).
      a. Change of the priesthood from Aaron to Christ. Heb. 7:11-16.
      b. Christ understood His relationship to this change. Ps. 40:6.

c. Christ the perfect sacrifice; "separate from sinners." Heb. 7:24-27.
d. His priesthood triumphed over Aaron's. Col. 2:14, 15.

III. *Conclusion.*
   1. Christ's ministry ended sacrificial system. Heb. 7:17-19.
   2. But Ten Commandments still effective under Christ's priesthood. Matt. 5:17-19; Ps. 40:7, 8; 111:7-9.
   3. Christians still obligated to keep the whole law. James 2:8-12.
   APPEAL: Rev. 22:12, 14.   MRS. JESSIE HESLIP.

Are Christians Under the Old Covenant?
Should They Keep the Law?

I. *What Is a Covenant?*
   An agreement between two or more people.
II. *What Was the Old, or First, Covenant?*
   1. God's covenant with Israel.
      a. Basis of covenant the Ten Commandments. Deut. 4:13.
      b. God's proposition with Israel is covenant or contract. "If ye will obey . . . ye shall be . . . an holy nation." People responded, "All that the Lord hath spoken we will do." Ex. 19:5-8.
      c. Moses prepared the people to hear God's voice. Ex. 19:9.
      God gave commandments one by one. People in great fear. Ex. 20:3-17, 20.
      d. Moses rehearsed commandments to the people. Ex. 24:3. God's proposition given: "If ye will obey . . . ye shall be . . . an holy nation." Ex. 19:5, 6.
      e. People again responded, "All the words which the Lord hath said will we do." Ex. 24:3.
      f. God also gave Moses judgments. Moses explained them. (Written in a book.) Ex. 24:3-8.
      g. Moses read proposition to people in detail from book. Again the people said, "All that the Lord hath said will we do." Ex. 24:7.
   2. How was the old covenant ratified?
      a. After Israel's repeated promise, ratification by sprinkling blood of animal upon people. (This covenant is built upon promises of the people.) Ex. 24:8.
      b. Moses in righteous anger broke the tables of stone when Israel broke the covenant by worshiping a calf. (First two commandments broken.) Ex. 32:1, 7-9, 19.

The Sanctuary and the Law

III. *What Is the New, or Second, Covenant?*
  1. Covenant of grace with all God's children. God next made new covenant; wrote law in hearts. John 17:3. Forgave their iniquity and forgot their sins. Gives eternal life. Jer. 31:31-34. Law is no longer on tables of stone, but in fleshy tables of heart. Heb. 8:6-13.
  2. How was the new covenant ratified?
    a. Ratified by the blood of Jesus Himself. Heb. 9:14; Matt. 26:26-28.
    b. *Law* and *will* the same. Will is also a legal declaration concerning disposal of property after death. Ps. 40:8; Rom. 2:18.
    c. "My covenant will I not break, nor alter the thing that is gone out of My lips." Ps. 89:34.
    d. New covenant upon better promises; Jesus' promises. Heb. 8:6-13; Jer. 13:23; John 15:5.

IV. *Summary.*
  1. Covenants contrasted.

Old Covenant	New Covenant
Concerning law of God.	Concerning law of God in heart.
Made with the people of God.	Made with all people, not Jews only.
Established upon their promises.	
Ratified with blood of sacrifices.	
Experience of human efforts.	Established on Jesus' promises.
	Ratified with His blood.
	Experiences of those in Christ.

  2. Allegorical record explains difference between old and new covenant. Gal. 4:22-26.
    a. Abraham's two wives represent the two covenants. Hagar, bond woman and her son—child of the flesh. Sarah, free woman and her son—child of promise.
    b. Ishmael, Hagar's son of natural birth, represents old covenant; people who try to save themselves by works.
    c. Isaac, Sarah's son of miraculous birth represents new covenant; people who are converted.
  3. We are saved by grace only, through faith, "born again." Eph. 2:8, 9; John 3:3-7.

V. *Conditions of Inheritance Under New Covenant.*
  1. "Ye must be born again." John 3:7.
  2. To love God with the whole heart. Matt. 22:35-40.
  3. Keep His commandments. Matt. 19:17.

ALMA DUBOIS

God's Covenant With Israel

THE EXODUS

Deut. 6:20-25. The Lord brought Israel out of Egypt that they might keep His laws.

Deut. 7:6-11. This fulfilled His promise to their fathers.

Deut. 9:4, 5. The Lord drove the wicked nations out of the land.

Deut. 10:12-25. He asked only that they love Him and keep His laws.

Deut. 28:1, 13. If they trusted and obeyed the Lord, they should be the head of the nations.

God permitted Israel to be brought into bondage that they might realize the difference between His service and laws and the service and laws of the heathen. Their awful experience as slaves for a century or more should have given them such an aversion to idolatry that they could never have been tempted even to think of a false god.

They were delivered from Egypt that they might trust God and keep His holy law. During their bondage the law which their fathers had known so well and obeyed grew dim in their minds. They mingled with it many false principles which they had learned from the heathen. So God in awful majesty came down on Mount Sinai and repeated His law in its purity and perfection. Then He wrote it on tables of stone that it might be preserved forever unchanged.

The government of Israel was a theocracy. A theocracy is a government in which God is the ruler. He made the laws, and the penalties for breaking the laws. Thus Israel was different from all other nations. God planned that Israel should demonstrate the principles of His kingdom—love, truth, justice, mercy, purity, righteousness, holiness. In these attributes they were to stand far above all other nations. They were to be a light in the world and give the knowledge of God to all people.

THE OLD COVENANT

Ex. 19:4-6. Promises to Israel if they would keep the covenant.

Deut. 4:12, 13. They were commanded to keep the Ten Commandments.

Ex. 24:3, 4, 7. Israel promised to keep the law.

Heb. 9:16-19. Covenant to be ratified by blood.

Ex. 24:5-8. This covenant was ratified by the blood of animals.

After Israel heard the law, they made a covenant, or promise, to obey it. In chorus they said: "All the words which the Lord hath said will we do." This covenant, to be valid, must be ratified, or made sure, by the shedding of blood. It was ratified by the blood of animals sprinkled on the people and on the book in which the law and the covenant were written.

Israel Broke This Covenant

Ex. 32:1-8. Israel made and worshiped a calf-god.
Ex. 32:30-34. Moses asked God to forgive Israel.
Ex. 33:1-3. The Lord withdrew His presence.

But, alas, in a very short time Israel broke this covenant. They made a golden calf and worshiped it. They said, "These be thy gods, O Israel, which brought thee up out of the land of Egypt." We wonder why they should fail so soon and so completely, until we remember how we too fail to keep our good resolutions, however sincerely made. It is by these experiences that we learn how weak we are and that we cannot keep God's law by our own strength. We need a Saviour who gives power to overcome all evil. This is what Israel learned.

When Moses learned of Israel's sin, he threw down the tables of stone upon which the law was written, and they were broken to pieces. This was a symbol of how Israel had broken the law and the covenant they had made.

Moses also removed their place of worship, the tent of the congregation, outside the camp of Israel.

The New Covenant

Ex. 33:4-6. The people repented.
Ex. 33:7. Each one sought the Lord alone.
Ex. 33:8-14. He forgave and accepted Israel again as His people.
Jer. 31:31-34. Under new covenant God writes law in the heart.
Heb. 8:6-13. Jesus is the mediator of the new covenant.

Each individual repented of his sin. Then he was directed to go out to the tent of the tabernacle. He did not now make vain promises, but confessed his sin and offered a sacrifice that represented the Saviour. He asked God to forgive and keep him from sin. Ancient Israel was saved under the covenant ratified by the blood of animals until the new covenant was ratified on the cross by the blood of Jesus.

In doing this, they became once more the children of God under the new, or everlasting, covenant—the covenant that was made with man in the Garden of Eden. This covenant does not depend upon the promises of man, which are like "ropes of sand." It is "established upon better promises," even the word of God, who by His Spirit writes the law upon the heart. This covenant was ratified by the blood of Christ.

Additional References

Eze. 20:9-11	Heb. 10:15-17	Deut. 4:5-9; 15:6
Deut. 27:26	Eph. 2:11, 12	Rom. 9:4
Jer. 32:40	Ps. 105:8-10	Gal. 4:24-31

Alma E. McKibbin.

PART FOUR ★ CHAPTER FIVE

The Sabbath Reform

The Sabbath truth requires a build-up. It is important to teach God's law in contrast with tradition. The subject, being new to many, bears emphasis and repetition before its importance is well established. Queries will arise, and these will need to be met in a kindly, yet positive way. Christ is the central figure of the Sabbath. His obedience and example are our strongest argument. The everlasting gospel allows for no change in the day of which He is lord. Instruction from the Old Testament must reveal the Sabbath perpetuity of the New. The faith of Jesus includes the keeping of all His commandments. Indeed, it is more than the keeping of a day; the Sabbath is God's eternal plan for sanctifying His children. From Eden lost to Eden restored, the Sabbath must remain!

Memorial of Creation and Re-creation

I. *How Does the Bible Record the Existence of All Things?*
   1. In the beginning God created heaven and earth. Gen. 1:1.
   2. Through faith we understand worlds framed by word of God. Heb. 11:3.
   3. "He spake, and it was done." Ps. 33:6, 9.

II. *Who Was Associated With God in the Work of Creation?*
   1. God created all things by Jesus. Eph. 3:9.
   2. "By Him [Son, verse 13] were all things created." Col. 1:16.

III. *How Is the True God Distinguished From Other Gods? His Memorial?*
   1. "The gods that have not made . . . shall perish. . . . He hath made the earth." Jer. 10:11, 12.
   2. "Ask Me . . . concerning the work of My hands." "God Himself that formed the earth." Isa. 45:11, 12, 18.
   3. The Sabbath is God's memorial of creation. God *rested, blessed,* and *sanctified* the seventh day for man. Gen. 2:1-3; Ps. 111:4.

The Sabbath Reform

IV. *What Did Paul Teach About Creation?*
  1. Men forgot, denied God's creative power. Rom. 1:21, 22.
  2. God's creative glory debased by human reasoning. Rom. 1:23.
  3. "Truth of God into a lie." (Moderns taught evolution.) Rom. 1:25.

V. *What Conditions Exist Today Destroying Faith in Creation?*
  1. Men deny creation was by God's word. 2 Peter 3:3-5.
  2. God's last-day call warns all to worship Him. Rev. 14:6, 7.
  3. The Sabbath is still God's memorial of creation. Ps. 111:7-9.
  4. Man to remember to keep it holy. Ex. 20:8-11.

VI. *When Will God Again Manifest His Creative Power?*
  1. "I create new heavens and a new earth." Isa. 65:17.
  2. Regenerated people will inhabit new earth. 2 Cor. 5:17; Isa. 35:10; Rev. 21:24.
  3. Sabbath to be kept on this earth. Isa. 56:1, 2.
  4. Sabbath worship continues in new earth. Isa. 66:23.

Margaret Cosby.

Old and New Testament Sabbath

I. *When and by Whom Was the Sabbath Instituted?*
  1. Instituted by God through Son. Gen. 2:3; John 1:1-3, 14.
  2. A memorial of creation. Gen. 2:2, 3; Ex. 20:11.
  3. God blessed Sabbath. Gen. 2:3.
  4. God rested on Sabbath. Heb. 4:4.
  5. God hallowed the Sabbath. Ex. 20:11.
  6. Command to keep Sabbath part of God's law. Ex. 20:8-11.

II. *What Does the Bible Teach About God's Sabbath?*
  1. Abraham kept God's law. Gen. 26:5.
  2. Israel observed Sabbath. Ex. 16:16-26.
  3. Sabbath kept in Isaiah's time. Isa. 56:1, 2.
  4. In Ezekiel's day. Eze. 20:12, 20.
  5. Jeremiah preached observance of Sabbath. Jer. 17:22, 27.
  6. Jesus kept Sabbath. Luke 4:16.
  7. Christ's followers kept Sabbath. Luke 23:55, 56.
  8. Paul kept Sabbath. Acts 17:1, 2; 18:1-4.

III. *Did Jesus Here on Earth Keep the Sabbath?*
  1. Christ is Lord of Sabbath. Mark 2:28.
  2. Jesus regularly kept Sabbath. Luke 4:16.
  3. He healed on Sabbath. John 5:5-9.
  4. Taught lawful to do good on Sabbath. Mark 3:1-5.

IV. *What Should Be Our Relationship to God's Sabbath?*
   1. Sabbath made for man. Mark 2:27.
   2. Sign between God and His people. Ex. 31:17.
   3. Only commandment keepers will enter gates of heaven. Rev. 22:14.
   4. Sabbath throughout eternity. Isa. 66:22, 23.

LUCILLE PFLAUMER.

Restoring God's Rest Day
Sunday or Sabbath?

Text: Luke 6:46-49. (Building without a foundation.)

I. *What Is the Sure Foundation of All Doctrinal Faith?*
   1. Doctrine must be grounded on God's Word. Ps. 19:7 (margin); 2 Tim. 3:16.
   2. Not *any* foundation; Christ *the* foundation. 1 Cor. 3:11.
   3. Christians must make certain of foundations. Ps. 11:3.
   4. Commandments of men no substitute for Sabbath. Matt. 15:3, 9, 13.

II. *How Does Prophecy Reveal the Origin of Sunday Observance?*
   [Review briefly.]
   1. Dan. 7:25. Rise of blasphemous, lawless, persecuting power.
   2. The little horn.
   3. "*Think* to change times and laws."
   4. Obscured truth 1260 years.
   [Read Catholic assertions to verify prophecy. See *Bible Readings*, pp. 222, 223. Observe *The Ministry* for more recent authorities.]

III. *What Prophecies Foretell a Last-Day Sabbath Reform?*
   1. Not a general reform.
      a. Priests to teach God's Sabbath. Compare Eze. 44:23, 24; 31:16, 17.
      b. Sabbath will be kept in new earth. Isa. 66:22, 23.
      c. Sabbath reform before Christ returns. Isa. 56:1, 2; 58:1-3, 12, 13.
   2. May we look to ministers to lead out in restoring God's true Sabbath?
      a. Shepherds spiritually confused. Isa. 56:10-12.
      b. Priests hide eyes from Sabbath. Eze. 22:26.
      c. Leaders substitute spurious commands. Eze. 13:2, 3, 10, 14.
      d. Cause "many to stumble at the law." Mal. 2:7-9.

The Sabbath Reform

   3. Who will restore God's rest day?
      a. A commandment-keeping remnant. Rev. 12:17; 14:12.
      b. Reform associated with world-wide gospel. Rev. 14:6-11; Matt. 24:14.
IV. *Is the Keeping of the True Sabbath Important?*
   1. "Blessed is the man that . . . keepeth the Sabbath." Isa. 56:2; James 2:10-12.
   2. Binding upon Jews and Gentiles. Isa. 56:6-8; Mark 2:27.
   3. New Testament as well as Old Testament institution. Heb. 4:4, 9, 10.
   Typical of soul rest, eternal rest.
V. *Appeal.*
   Redeemed keep commandments. John 14:15; 15:10; Luke 4:16-18. Isa. 58:13, 14; Rev. 22:14. Let us not lose God's promised Sabbath blessing for this life and the life to come.

Will the Sabbath Be Reformed?

[The following study provides conversational argument helpful to the beginner in Bible work. Its direct, positive presentation should be guarded by less experienced workers. This study well meets the needs of the confused mind, for truth today requires action, and many need to be aroused on the Sunday issue. While being specific, the teacher should find a kindly approach.]

The Lord has given in His Word unmistakable evidence of His deep regard for the Sabbath-reform message that is to prepare the inhabitants of the earth for the second coming of Christ. Through metaphors and other figures He shows His disapproval of those who, while claiming to be expositors of His Word, teach and act contrary to its commands.

The seventh-day Sabbath will be the battleground of the last and final struggle between truth and error. The clergy of all denominations will be compelled by circumstances to take their stand for the Sabbath of the fourth commandment or the false sabbath as commanded and taught by the Catholic Church.

The Lord devotes many portions of His Word to entreaties, warnings, and denunciations of those who are entrusted with souls. In the thirteenth chapter of Ezekiel we have a graphic picture of how the clergy of today regards the binding claims of the fourth commandment. Let us proceed to examine each text.

   I. *False Prophets Fail to Uphold God's Law.*
      1. Eze. 13:1, 2. Preacher to "hear . . . the word of the Lord." When Bible is laid aside, a man preaches out of his own heart. Listeners not nourished with faith and good doctrine.

2. Jer. 5:13. In absence of the "word," "wind" (inflation) evident.
3. Eph. 4:14. Those deceived by the "wind of doctrine" not established. Prey to false shepherd's un-Scriptural teaching.
4. Jer. 23:21, 22. Ministry a sacred calling. Some not called of God don clerical robes.
5. Jer. 23:31-33. Teaching "lies" causes people to err. No "profit" from man-made doctrines. Isa. 9:16; 29:13.
6. Matt. 15:9. "Vain . . . worship." A travesty upon would-be follower of truth!
7. Mal. 2:1, 7-9. Priests and ministers "caused many to stumble at the law." Taught a "partial" law instead of *entire Ten Commandments*.
8. Compare Ezekiel 13:3 with Matthew 23. "Woe upon religious teachers of Ezekiel's day. Same condemnation today. Clergy refuse to teach a complete law.

II. Like *"Foxes in the Deserts."* Eze. 13:4.

Why clergy like "foxes in the deserts"—subtle, crafty, sly. Characteristics of prairie fox: appears out of one of many holes, sits on hind legs and barks. When stone thrown at him, ducks down in hole and springs up from another and barks some more. Repeats procedure when more stones are thrown.

Ministers confronted with Bible texts supporting seventh-day Sabbath, take refuge in many alibis Protestants have devised in defense of spurious, un-Scriptural Sunday observance:

1. *"Christ rose on first day of week,* and therefore we observe it in honor of His resurrection." Scriptural truth used showing our Lord "rested" in grave on Sabbath, and holy women kept it according to the commandment. Luke 23:51-56. Fact He arose on first day did not make it holy. If Christ intended it be kept to commemorate His resurrection, He would have given command. Metaphorical fox now resorts to many subterfuges, such as *"Christ always met with His disciples on the first day."* Emerges and appears until all alibis exhausted. Here are a few:
2. *"We cannot keep the seventh-day Sabbath on a round world." "We are not under law but under grace." "We are now under the new covenant." "The Sabbath was nailed to the cross with the law."*
3. All such holes of security of little worth in day of God's wrath. Isa. 28:15, last part.

The Sabbath Reform

III. *The Gap in the Hedge.*
 1. Eze. 13:5. "Gaps" in the "hedge." Hedge is God's law, an impregnable fortress. Protects the flock from wandering into forbidden paths, keeps the enemy from entering.
 The gap—one of Ten Commandments, the second, taken out, allowing flock to wander and devourer to invade. Result of tampering with the law and abridging the fourth commandment. People not prepared to "stand in the day of the Lord." When probation ends no protection from seven last plagues.
 2. Eze. 13:6. Ministers teaching falsehood not recognized by God. "Others" confirm their doctrine. Hosea 4:6-9.
 3. Eze. 13:7. "Foxes" misquote His Word. While tempting Christ, Satan misquoted Scripture. Omitting portion of text artfully conveyed wrong construction to lead Christ into sin. Matt. 4:5, 6; Ps. 91:11, 12.
 4. Eze. 13:8. Deceitfully using Holy Writ to support false doctrine displeases God.
 5. Eze. 13:9. What an indictment! Names not in writing of house of Israel. Eze. 34:1-10.
 6. Eze. 13:10. Text reveals shallowness of peace based upon false premise.

IV. *The Built-up Wall.*
 1. The "wall" refers to man's efforts to fill in the gap made in hedge. Removing true Sabbath by papal church, substituting Sunday as day of worship, constitutes "wall" that was "built up." "Others daubed it with untempered morter." Protestant clergy defending Sunday, keeping and plastering it with Bible texts misapplied. Coating will not adhere. Lacks a "Thus saith the Lord." Bible says, "Seventh day is the Sabbath." Catholic Church says, "No." Claims divine authority for making holy first day of the week. Does not support Sunday from Bible; admits that cannot be done. Protestantism does the daubing, with unsatisfactory mortar.
 2. Eze. 13:11. The wall—Sunday keeping—will fall when seventh-plague hailstones fall upon inhabitants of earth. What a day of reckoning!
 3. Eze. 13:12. Unanswerable question from countless lips of long-deceived people. Discover "foxes" have misled them by fraudulent means.
 4. Eze. 13:13-15. Lord has borne long with counterfeit sabbath and false teachers. Forbearance comes to an end. The hand *mighty to save* then *mighty to destroy.*

      5. Eze. 22:25. "Conspiracy" of prophets (ministers) against the Sabbath. Secretly designing plan to overthrow law of God.
      6. Eze. 22:26. "Have hid their eyes from My sabbaths," reveals conspiracy by those who claimed to teach people.
      7. Eze. 22:27. Destroying souls for "dishonest gain." Guilty of blood of souls.

V. *Daubing the False Wall.*
      1. Eze. 22:28. Subtlety of *daubers:* "Thus saith the Lord God, when the Lord hath not spoken."
      2. Eze. 22:30. Not finding a man to restore fourth commandment, the Lord raised up separate and distinct people to reveal God's Sabbath and build up the "gap" broken down by Catholic Church. God finds "repairers of the breach!"

VI. *Repairers of the Gap.*
      1. Isa. 58:1. A message for both professing and nonprofessing Christians. "My people" are guilty of "transgression." Reveals one of God's commandments broken. People must be shown, regardless of church affiliation or piety. "Spare not" is the command.
      "Shew . . . the house of Jacob their sins." Jacob stands for unconverted. Gen. 32:28. Nonconformist guilty of breaking more than *one.* They must be shown their "sins" by calling attention to law of God. Points out sin and points to the Lamb of God.
      2. Isa. 58:12. Those who give message called builders, "The repairer of the breach, The restorer of paths to dwell in." The "gap," or breach, in the law of God now being repaired. Attention directed to the fourth commandment.
      3. Isa. 58:13. Appeal to "take" our feet off Sabbath shows it has been trampled underfoot. Seventh day still holy. Moses asked by God to remove shoes. "Holy ground." Ex. 3:5.
      We honor the Lord by taking our feet off His Sabbath and observing day as sacred. Tells us how to keep it—not following our own *ways,* finding our own *pleasure,* speaking our own *words.*

VII. *The Promised Blessing of Jacob.*
    Isa. 58:14. To meet God's standard in proper observance of His day, we must give the heart fully to Christ.
    Such surrender brings its reward. Jacob, homeless and penniless, fleeing as a refugee, made vow to God to ever be true to Him. The Lord provided for his needs and blessed his labors. He will

sustain and bless us as we take our stand for His downtrodden Sabbath. Some may have to lose their position, but the promise is, "He will feed thee with the heritage of Jacob." All heaven will work with us as we carry out His command.

VIII. *Urgency to Return to True Sabbath.*
1. Isa. 56:1. "My salvation is near to come." Refers to Christ's second coming. Heb. 9:28.
"Righteousness to be revealed"—revelation of God's commandments. Ps. 119:172.
"Revealed" indicates commandments kept in obscurity brought to light.
Teaching of return of Christ and revelation of God's law closely related.
Not prepared to meet our Lord unless our lives conform to Ten Commandments.
2. Isa. 56:2. A blessing upon the doer and keeper of the Sabbath!
3. Isa. 56:3-7. Note promises to all who receive light on the Sabbath.

IX. *Warning Against Unfaithful Shepherds.*
1. Isa. 56:10. "Watchmen [clergy] are blind." "Hid their eyes" from God's Sabbath. Eze. 22:26. Refuse to teach binding claims of fourth commandment, guilty of supporting the day instituted by Rome. Not alarmed over prevailing iniquity ripening the world for destruction. "Sleeping" and slumbering in carnal security. Parishioners lulled into stupor of death.
2. Isa. 56:11. Position, social standing, and salary prevent leaders from understanding. John 10:12, 13.
3. Isa. 56:12. The "wine" of these false shepherds taken from intoxicating cup of Catholic doctrines. World sipping beverage which benumbs and beclouds sensibilities.
God calls us to fountain of life and truth, the Holy Bible. Taking stand for revealed truth clears mind. Discern divine character of His holy law. Prepared for second coming of Christ.

X. *Appeal.*
Ask pupil to surrender his will to God's divine will by taking his feet off the Sabbath. Much is now accomplished by prayer. On bended knees, by faith place his trembling hand in the hand of God. He will lead, strengthen, and uphold those who seek His help.
MARY E. WALSH.

The Sabbath God's Sign Today

(Origin of Sabbath and New Testament Sabbath combined.)

I. *What Day of the Week Did Christ Recognize as His Holy Day?*
   1. There is one certain day in the week which Jesus Christ claims as His day. Rev. 1:10.
   2. What day has Christ especially claimed as His holy day? Mark 2:28.

II. *In What Way Is the Sabbath a Sign of God's Creatorship.* Ex. 31:14, 17.
   1. The complete Godhead, or Trinity, worked together in creation. Gen. 1:1, 26; Eph. 3:9; Gen. 1:2.
   2. Creation distinguishes the true God from false gods. Jer. 10:10-12, 16.
   3. Creatorship gives God the right to rule. Ps. 95:6; Rev. 4:11.

III. *How Does God's Rest Day Meet Man's Need in All Ages?* Gen. 2:1-3; Ex. 20:10.
   1. The Sabbath was made for man. Mark 2:27.
   2. It was made for Adam as the first man. Gen. 2:1-3.
   3. For Abraham who knew and obeyed God's laws. Gen. 26:5.
   4. For men in Moses' time. Ex. 5:4, 5; Ps. 105:43-45; Deut. 5:7-22.
   5. For men in Isaiah's time. Isa. 56:1-7; 58:12-14.
   6. For men in Jeremiah's time. Jer. 17:21-25.
   7. For Jesus, the Son of man, and men in His time. Luke 4:16; John 15:10; Luke 23:52-54.
   8. For Paul and men in his time. Acts 13:14, 42-44; 15:19-21; 16:12, 13; 17:1, 2; 18: 1-4, 11; 24:14; 25:8.

IV. *What Proves That the Seventh-Day Sabbath Was to Continue?*
   1. Jesus recognized seventh day would continue to be the Sabbath after His resurrection and in the new earth. Matt. 24:20; Isa. 66:22, 23; Rev. 22:14.
   2. Christ gave no permission to substitute a rest day in place of seventh day which He had blessed and sanctified. Matt. 5:17, 18; Deut. 4:2.

V. *Why Is the Sabbath a Twofold Sign for the Christian?*
   1. Sabbath commemorates redemption as well as creation. Eze. 20:12.
   2. Seventh-day Sabbath restored under special last-day message. Rev. 14:6-14.

3. What day would Jesus keep if living on earth today? He kept the seventh when He was here. Luke 4:16; John 15:10. He has not changed. Heb. 13:8.

Mrs. Marjorie Harder.

The Seal of God and the Mark of the Beast

I. *Introduction.*

This study reveals the great apostate power of God's government in the final conflict of the church. Just before the return of Jesus to this world the preaching of the gospel will emphasize the judgment hour, the worship of the Creator, and the fall of spiritual Babylon. Associated with these events is the most solemn message in the entire Bible—the warning against worshiping the beast and his image, and receiving his mark in the forehead or hand. It is most important that we understand what these warning messages mean.

1. Warning against mark of beast. Rev. 14:9-11.
2. Sealing message simultaneous with receiving mark of beast. Rev. 7:1-4.
3. Meaning of "seal" and "mark." (Seal, sign, and mark used interchangeably.) Rom. 4:11; Eze. 9:4; Rev. 7:2, 3.

II. *What Is the Seal of God? Significance of the Sealing Work?*

1. How God seals His servants.
   a. Sealed with the Holy Spirit. Eph. 1:13.
   b. "Sealed unto the day of redemption." Eph. 4:30.
2. Seal is connected with God's law. "Seal the law among My disciples." Isa. 8:16.
3. God's seal is in the fourth commandment—the Sabbath.
   Note.—The three essentials of a seal must include name of person issuing seal, official title of person, jurisdiction or dominion over which official rules.
   a. Name—"The Lord thy God."
      Title—Maker or Creator.
      Dominion—heaven and earth. Ex. 20:8-11.
   b. Sabbath a perpetual sign of His lordship. Ex. 31:17, 13; Eze. 20:20.

III. *What Does the Bible Teach Concerning the Mark of the Beast?*

1. "Mark" sign of opposition to God's "seal." Rev. 13:16, 17; 14:9, 10.
2. Roman Catholic Church claims having changed the Sabbath to Sunday as the sign of her power. (Furnish proofs of Catholic Church's claims.)

3. "Number" of beast. "It is the number of a man;" his number 666. Rev. 13:18. Explain *Vicarius Filii Dei.*
4. All the world to worship beast. Rev. 13:7, 8.
5. Fate of those who worship beast.
    a. Receive the seven last plagues. Rev. 16:1, 2, 10, 11.
    b. Destroyed by God's wrath. Rev. 14:9-11.

IV. *Conclusion.*
1. Those who refuse homage to the beast and his image will be victors on the sea of glass. Rev. 15:1-4.
2. They keep the commandments of God and the faith of Jesus. Rev. 14:12.
3. God is now calling His people out of Babylon; not to partake of her sins. Rev. 18:4, 5.   JEAN MEYER CARTER.

How to Observe the Sabbath

I. *Why Is the Keeping of God's Sabbath a Test of Our Loyalty to God?*

Since creation observance of the Sabbath a great *test* of loyalty to the Creator. GC 605.
1. "*Remember* the Sabbath day, to keep it holy." Ex. 20:8.
2. "All through the week we are to have the Sabbath in mind, and be making preparation to keep it according to the commandment. . . . All who regard the Sabbath as a sign between them and God, showing that He is the God who sanctifies them, will represent principles of His government. They will bring into daily practice the laws of His kingdom." 6T 353.
3. The Sabbath to be kept from sunset Friday to sunset Saturday. Lev. 23:32; Mark 1:32. "We should jealously guard the edges of the Sabbath. Remember that every moment is consecrated, holy time." 6T 356. Begin and close the Sabbath with prayer and praise.
4. A day of fellowship and worship. Luke 4:16; Heb. 10:25.
5. No secular work to be done on Sabbath. Ex. 20:8-11; Lev. 23:3.
6. Even in harvesttime we should rest. Ex. 34:21.
7. Not to buy or sell on the Sabbath. Neh. 13:15-19.
8. The preparation day. Also for spiritual preparation. Mark 15:42; Luke 23:55, 56; Matt. 11:28.
9. A threefold miracle marked the Sabbath for forty years. We should prepare our food on sixth day, Friday. Ex. 16:22-30.
10. Not even to plan our work on Sabbath. Amos 8:5.
11. Not to do our own pleasure or talk business on Sabbath. To guard our thoughts, reading, music. Isa. 58:13, 14.

12. Those within our gates should rest. No duty pertaining to the six working days is to be left for Sabbath. Ex. 20:10.

II. *How May the Sabbath Become a Day of Holy Joy to Us?*
 1. He who made the Sabbath said, "It is lawful to do well on the sabbath days." Jesus healed the sick, went about doing good, and made Sabbath a day of joy and happiness. Matt. 12:10-12.
 2. Sabbath to be a delight to us and to our children. To view beauties of nature. For meditation and prayer. For our spiritual and physical well-being. Isa. 58:13, 14; Ps. 16:11.

III. *Appeal.*
Let us show our loyalty to God by observing His true Sabbath as a delight and blessing to our family. Isa. 58:13, 14.

Mrs. Edith Cross.

PART FOUR ★ CHAPTER SIX

Healthful Living

Seventh-day Adventists are not unique in stressing healthful living. But with all the many and various helps to health and longevity, our instruction must not be of a general nature; we owe the world God's health message. Health teaching is a part of the everlasting gospel and must be included in the gospel worker's program.

Whether the subject of health is presented as the entering wedge to a series of Bible studies, or imbedded in its progressive instruction, no feature of present truth is more important than health. This subject should always be presented tactfully and at the proper time. Where our health work is well known, we may lead out with health instruction, but where it is just beginning we should first build up confidence. We should also guard against a negative approach by presenting health in an appealing, buoyant way.

God's Health Message

I. *What Does God's Word Reveal About a Health Message for Our Day?*
   1. God has health message for today. Ps. 67:2.
   2. This message found in His Word. Ps. 107:20.
   3. Warned not to be indifferent. Deut. 12:8, 28.

II. *What Should Be Our Attitude Toward This Message?*
   1. Good food should be enjoyed. Eccl. 3:13.
   2. Purpose to follow God's ways of health. Dan. 1:8; Deut. 30:19, 20.

III. *What General Health Principles Are Taught in the Bible?*
   1. God's requirements based on reason. Rom. 12:1; Isa. 1:18.
      a. Good health is to His glory. 1 Cor. 6:19, 20.
      b. Eating and drinking a part of our religion. 3 John 2; 1 Cor. 10:31; Matt. 15:11.
      c. Moderation today important. Phil. 4:5.
      d. The Christian avoids fanaticism. Rom. 14:17.
   2. Diet for man.
      a. God's original diet fruits, grains, nuts, vegetables. Gen. 1:29; 2:16; 3:18, 19.
      b. Man's diet changed after Flood. Gen. 9:4, 5; 7:1-3.
      c. Israel's diet. Ps. 78:24, 25.
         (1) Manna supplied daily. Ex. 16:15, 16; Deut. 2:7.
         (2) Restrictions on flesh foods. Lev. 11; Deut. 14.
         (3) Lusted for flesh food. Num. 11:4-7; Ps. 106:14, 15.
         (4) Israel warned against other heathen practices. Deut. 29:17-20.
         (5) Priests not to use strong drink. Lev. 10:9, 10.
         (6) Diet as related to holiness. Lev. 11:43-47.

IV. *How Is Modern Israel Challenged on Living Healthfully?*
   1. We must not fail today. 1 Cor. 10:5-7; Heb. 4:1, 2.
   2. Modern Israel called unto soberness. 1 Thess. 5:6, 7.
   3. Surfeiting and drunkenness of last days. Luke 21:34, 35.
   4. Moderation now to be made known. Phil. 4:5; 1 Cor. 9:25.

V. *Why Should We Be Concerned About This Health Message?*
   1. God's children called unto sanctification. 1 Peter 2:9; 1 Thess. 5:23.
   2. Sanctification of flesh as well as spirit. 2 Cor. 6:17, 18; 7:1; Lev. 11:43-47.
   3. God's messengers must lead out in holiness. Isa. 52:11.

Healthful Living

4. Mastery over intemperance. 1 Cor. 9:25.
    a. Swine's flesh. Isa. 66:15-18; 65:4-6.
    b. Intoxicating drinks. Prov. 20:1; 23:29-35.
    c. Stimulants and narcotics. Deut. 29:17-20. (See margin, verse 18.)
    d. Overeating. Ps. 78:27-31; CDF 47, 244, 101-103, 131-142.
5. What victory is assured all who accept God's health message?
    a. A people sanctified in body, soul, spirit. Rev. 14:12, 1-5.
    b. Cleansed by the Word. Eph. 5:25-27.

VI. *Appeal.*
Present to God a living sacrifice. Rom. 12:1.

Health Reform Principles
(For S.D.A. indoctrination class.)

Text: 3 John 2.

I. *Has God an Interest in Our Personal Health?*
  1. God desires physical as well as spiritual prosperity. 3 John 2. In the beginning God created man in His own image. Gen. 1:26-28. He was given good health and had access to the tree of life, which was essential to never-ending life. Sin brought the curse of sickness, disease, suffering, and death. Even though these conditions prevail, much can be done to prevent sickness and suffering, and so prolong life.
  2. Christ did much to relieve suffering. Matt. 4:23, 24.
  3. Christian's duty to observe health.

II. *What Inspired Principles of Health Are for Our Instruction Today?*
  1. Our bodies are "the temple of the Holy Ghost." 1 Cor. 6:19, 20; 3:16, 17.
  2. Do all things "to the glory of God." 1 Cor. 10:31.
  3. Be "temperate in all things." 1 Cor. 9:24-27.
  4. "Let it ever be kept before the mind that the great object of hygienic reform is to secure the highest possible development of mind and soul and body." CH 386.
  5. "Pure air, sunlight, abstemiousness, rest, exercise, proper diet, the use of water, trust in divine power,—these are the true remedies." MH 127.

III. *What Further Instruction on Healthful Diet Is Important to the Christian?*
  1. God's original diet for man is the best. Gen. 1:29; 3:18.
  2. After Flood, Noah was permitted to eat flesh. Gen. 9:3-5.

3. Noah distinguished clean from unclean animals. Gen. 7:2.
   4. In Moses' day this distinction was put in writing. Lev. 11.
   5. Flesh not the best food. Num. 11:4, 18-20, 31-33.
   6. God will soon destroy eaters of swine's flesh. Isa. 66:15-18. Soul-destroying habits will affect man's whole being before end. His thoughts and aspirations entirely unholy. Man has disobeyed God physically and morally. Rev. 18:1-5.
   7. Strong drink a deceiver. Prov. 20:1; 23:29-32.
   8. Christians should discard all filthy habits. 2 Cor. 7:1.
   9. Eat for strength and not for drunkenness. Eccl. 10:17.
   10. "Fruits, grains, and vegetables, prepared in a simple way, free from spice and grease of all kinds, make, with milk or cream, the most healthful diet. They impart nourishment to the body, and give a power of endurance and a vigor of intellect that are not produced by a stimulating diet." CH 115.
   McCollum, of Johns Hopkins University, says, "I have not the slightest hesitation in saying that a vegetarian diet, supplemented with fairly liberal amounts of milk, is the most satisfactory diet that man can take." (See *Essentials of Nutrition,* Sherman and Lanford, the Macmillan Company.)

IV. *Conclusion.*
   1. Why were these warnings given? 1 Cor. 10:6, 10, 11.
   2. Warning to the people in the last days. Luke 21:34.
   3. Being fully prepared for the coming of the Lord. 1 Thess. 5:23.

Mrs. Laurice A. Klein.

Health and Religion
(Bible and Spirit of Prophecy Approach.)

I. *God the Creator and Upholder of Man.*
   1. His interest in our physical being.
      a. God great caretaker of human machinery. CH 586, 587.
      b. "All life-giving power is from Him. When one recovers from disease, it is God who restores him." MH 113.
      c. His desire for us. 3 John 2.
      d. His purpose for our health. Ps. 67:2.
      e. His written Word and book of nature reveal laws of life.
      f. God's Word teaches the way to health. Prov. 16:24; 4:20, 22; Jer. 30:17; Ps. 103:3-5.
      g. God's constant interest in man. Ps. 139:13-18.
   2. Instruction to Israel regarding health habits.
      a. Distinction between clean and unclean. Lev. 15:4-12.

b. Thorough instruction. Lev. 13:46-52.
c. Cleanliness. MH 279.
d. Diet. Lev. 20:23-25; MH 280.
3. Jesus, the Great Physician.
  a. "The Saviour in His miracles revealed the power that is continually at work in man's behalf, to sustain and to heal him." MH 112.
  b. Teaching, preaching, healing. Matt. 9:35, 36.
  c. Christ the burden bearer. Matt. 11:28.
  d. Sun of Righteousness with healing in wings. Mal. 4:2.
  e. Saviour of the world: Jesus the Majesty of heaven. 4T 225.
II. *Health Results When God's Conditions Are Met.*
"The laws of nature are the laws of God,—as truly divine as are the precepts of the decalogue. The laws that govern our physical organism, God has written upon every nerve, muscle, and fiber of the body. Every careless or wilful violation of these laws is a sin against our Creator." Ed 196, 197.
1. Relation of health to obedience.
  a. Health the reward of obedience. Deut. 7:12, 15; Ex. 15:26; Deut. 32:46, 47.
  b. Health based on definite conditions according to Jesus. John 5:14; Luke 8:48; Matt. 9:2.
  c. Jesus brings spiritual healing. Isa. 53:5.
  d. Promise to each individual—"not one feeble person." Ps. 105:37; PP 429; MH 283.
2. Results of disobedience. Ps. 106:15.
  a. Leanness. Isa. 10:6.
  b. Slew fattest; smote chosen. Ps. 78:24-31.
  c. Disobedient fell in wilderness. Heb. 3:17.
  d. Fate of those who indulged themselves in Noah's day. Matt. 24:37-39.
  e. For our examples. 1 Cor. 10:6, 11.
  f. Glorify Him not—heart darkened. Rom. 1:21.
3. God's promises and His desire for us.
  a. His promises are to us individually. Received, they give strength and health—vital energy. He gives grace and power.
  b. His commands for our good. Deut. 6:24, 25.
  c. Sickness taken away. Ex. 23:25.
  d. "Healeth all thy diseases." Ps. 103:3-5.
  e. God gives grace and glory. No good thing withheld. Ps. 84:11.
  f. "Ye shall eat the good of the land." Isa. 1:19.
  g. "Thine health shall spring forth speedily." Isa. 58:8.

ELVA R. HEALD, R.N.

Flesh Food From Eden to Eden

Creation to Flood	After the Flood	Wilderness Experience to Christ	Days of Christ	Last Days—Spiritual Israel	Eden Restored
4004 B.C.	2348 B.C.	1491-1451 B.C.	A.D. 31	1844-End	Eternity
Gen. 1:29. Gen. 5:5, 8, 11, 14, 17, 20. As long as man lived on original diet he lived 900 years or more. He had vigor of body, mind, and soul. CDF 81, 313.	Flesh foods added as an emergency measure. Gen. 9:3-5. Lev. 20:25, 26. Lev. 3:17; 11. Deut. 14:2, 3, 7, 8-10. Gen. 11:10-12, 24, 25. No blood or fat to be used. After blood of animals used for food, man's life shortened. Life span cut from 500 to 205 years. Gen. 11:10-12, 32. Today average length of man's life is 50 years. Permission has never been granted to eat unclean animals, blood, or fat. Deuteronomy 14 in force before Mosaic law (Gen. 7:2); still in force at second coming, Rev. 18:2; Isa. 66:15-17.	Ps. 105:1-45. Israel tested on two points as they came out of Egypt: Sabbath and diet. Some were rebellious and only half converted. God may let us go our own way, but we suffer the consequences. His laws are immutable. CDF 374 ff. Ex. 15:26. Ex. 16:7-14. Num. 11:4-6; 16-33. Ps. 78:17, 18, 24-32. 1 Cor. 10:6, 11. Heb. 3:17. Ps. 106:15. Dan. 1:1-15. CDF 29 ff. Daniel followed health principles.	Same restrictions as 2d period and same results. CDF 375. Deut. 12:16, 20. Leviticus 11. Matt. 3:4. John's diet restricted. CDF 70, 71. Acts 15:19, 20. (First general council prohibited.) Isa. 7:14, 15. (Jesus' diet.) Ps. 106:15. MH 311, 312.	Today God is calling out those who will be obedient to all His laws. To spiritual Israel the call comes: "Be ye separate, . . . touch not the unclean thing." God testing us on the Sabbath and appetite. God is preparing a people for the heavenly Canaan. CDF 378-382. 1 Cor. 10:6, 11, 31. Isa. 22:12-14. Isa. 66:15-17. Phil. 3:18, 19. 2 Cor. 6:17. Luke 21:34. 1 Kings 19:6, 8. Elijah a prototype of remnant. CDF 71. God is bringing us back to original diet. CH 473, 573; 9T 153, 154.	As we enjoy the companionship of heavenly angels we will eat of the "bread from heaven." Isaiah speaks of planting vineyards in the new earth, and eating fruit of them. John mentions the tree of life with "twelve manner of fruits," whose leaves are for the "healing of the nations." Rev. 22:2. Isa. 11:5-9. Isa. 65:25. Isa. 33:24. Tree of life lost in Genesis; restored in Revelation.

E.R.H.

Healthful Living

Are Unclean Meats Prohibited Today?
(A follow-up lesson explaining difficult texts.)

I. *"Clean" Dietary Taught in New Testament.*
  1. God's instruction: "Touch not the unclean thing." 2 Cor. 6:16-18.
  2. Separation from unclean practices a New Testament doctrine. 2 Cor. 6:17.
  3. Holiness includes cleansing from *"all* filthiness." 2 Cor. 7:1.
  4. Flesh cleansed as well as spirit. 2 Cor. 7:1.

II. *Unclean Meats of Old Testament Still Unclean.*
  1. All God's prohibitions based on reason. Rom. 12:1-3; Isa. 1:18, 19.
  2. Eating affects thinking and actions. Prov. 23:6-8.
  3. God's people a holy people in every age. Lev. 11:43-47; Rev. 22:11.
  4. Disregard for unclean things results in general carelessness. Eze. 22:26. (Observe that Sabbathbreaking is mentioned with unclean practices.)
  5. Swine's flesh still unclean when the Lord returns. Isa. 66:15-18.
  6. Last generation's unclean thoughts and deeds. Isa. 66:18.
  7. In last days some who claim holiness eat swine's flesh. Isa. 65:1-5.
  8. Heaven's record of these unclean practices. Isa. 65:6.
  9. What God calls unclean man cannot call clean. Job 14:4.

III. *A Holy People Enter a Holy City.*
  1. "Abomination" and "curse" cannot enter New Jerusalem. Rev. 21:27; 22:3.
  2. Unclean not found on the way of holiness. Isa. 35:8.
  3. Swine's flesh remains an "abomination." Lev. 11:42, 43, 46, 47.
  4. Overcoming on all points necessary. Rev. 21:7, 8; 14:1-5.
  5. True church must restore a clean dietary. Matt. 28:20; Acts 3:19-21.

IV. *Explaining Difficult Texts.*
  1. *Acts 10:9-16.* Peter's vision had a deeper significance than the eating of food. Peter, a Jew, regarded all Gentiles as "unclean." It required a special command from God for Peter to enter the home of Cornelius, a Gentile. But Peter's vision clearly revealed to him God's plan to save even the Gentiles. "God hath shewed me that I should not call any *man* [not "any *animal"*] common or unclean." Acts 10:28. Issue involved was salvation of a Gentile, and not eating of unclean animals. Every conscientious Jew was careful of his dietary.

2. *Col. 2:14-17.* The cross brought no change to meats God had stated were unclean. Christ's blood was shed for sinners, not for animals that never sinned. 1 John 1:9. The tendency of some was to overemphasize asceticism. Study Romans 14 and 1 Corinthians 8:4-13.
3. *1 Tim. 4:1-5.* "Meat" here means food generally. God expected man to "refuse" unclean animals for food. "Meats" to be "received with thanksgiving" are those which God provided for man's diet. Gen. 1:29; 2:16; 3:18. Flesh foods of any kind were only a temporary provision after the Flood. At that time Noah's family already knew which animals were clean or unclean. Gen. 8:20. Some who now argue the text's true meaning might be brought into a real predicament should they not refuse *any* creature as food. This is evident from the Scriptures that list "abominable" creatures, including rodents and vultures. Leviticus 11; Deuteronomy 14; Isa. 66:17. The setting of 1 Timothy 4:1-5 proves that there is here no allusion to Seventh-day Adventist dietary practices.

(Appeal: Rev. 21:7, 8.)

PART FOUR ★ CHAPTER SEVEN

Life in Christ (State of Dead)

No subject can become more negative in its teaching than the state of the dead, but this is not at all necessary. Though the nonimmortality subject requires caution and build-up equally as much as the Sabbath truth (*Evangelism,* pages 246-249), it is not here suggested that it should always follow the presentation of the Sabbath. Where the Bible teacher detects no special conflict on the part of the reader, and because of providing background for other doctrines, the state of the dead may be presented rather early in the series. But where there is confusion or prejudice, it is important that solid foundation teaching on God's purpose in Christ should precede this study. More is gained by a cheerful, friendly approach to the subject than by a combative spirit. Reinforcing our points on the state of the dead in its relationship to other doctrines, is more effective than an intensive, exhaustive, and dogmatic study of the subject.

The Hope of the Resurrection
(Introduce after death in family.)

God in His wisdom terminates life with its problems and sorrows by permitting the enemy, death, to enter our homes.

I. *Introduction.*
It pays us in the hour of sorrow to seek to understand its mysteries, and to learn what the Bible teaches.
  1. The living know that they must die. Eccl. 9:5; Heb. 9:27.
  2. The Spirit goes back to God. Eccl. 12:7.
  3. Death is the result of sin. Gen. 2:17; 3:22, 24.
  NOTE.—After the wonderful work of creation, God saw that everything He had made was good. Man also had been created a perfect being, but subjected to the law of obedience from the very beginning, for God had made one request of man: not to eat of the tree in the midst of the garden lest he die. Gen. 3:3. When man did eat of that tree, the result was death. The spirit of life (breath) by which man lives and which is only lent to man by God, at death goes back to the Author of life.

II. *What Change Takes Place at Death?*
  1. Life's functions then cease. Eccl. 9:5, 6.
  2. Thoughts perish that very day. Ps. 146:4.
  3. The living can praise the Lord. Ps. 146:2.
  4. The dead cannot praise the Lord. Ps. 115:17.
  5. "Death can not celebrate Thee." Isa. 38:18, 19.

III. *Why Is Death Called a Sleep?*
  1. The psalmist calls death a sleep. Ps. 13:3.
  2. Jesus calls death a sleep. John 11:11, 14.
  3. They sleep in their graves. Matt. 27:52.
  4. Paul said the dead are asleep. 1 Thess. 4:15.
  5. The righteous dead sleep in Jesus. 1 Thess. 4:14.
  NOTE.—More than twenty-five times the expression, "slept with his fathers," is used when recording the death of the kings of the Old Testament.

IV. *Will the Dead Be Raised Again?*
   1. The dead in Christ shall rise first. 1 Thess. 4:14, 16, 17.
   2. Christ will call forth the dead. Isa. 26:19; John 5:28, 29.
   3. He will call, and the saints will answer. Job 14:14, 15.
   4. The dead will come from their graves. 1 Cor. 15:35-38.
   5. Christ was the "firstfruits" of the dead. 1 Cor. 15:20.
   6. At the call of Christ man will again live. John 5:25.
   7. He will ransom man from death. Eze. 37:13, 14; Hosea 13:14.

ILLUSTRATION: When training a little canary to sing, the bird fancier places its cage near a canary that is already a good singer. The cage is then covered so that the bird in training will learn to concentrate on the song of his little fellow singer. He is now learning in the darkness the mastery of notes he could never have achieved in the sunshine. So God is helping us in these sorrowful experiences to learn the sweeter notes of our song to be sung at the sea of glass. Shall we submit to His kind wisdom and allow Him to teach us in the gloom some of the most precious lessons of His love? Someday, and soon, we shall see God's wisdom in permitting this sorrow in our lives.   ETHEL M. NELL.

What Happens to Man at Death?

I. *The Origin of Man.*
   1. How did man come into being? Gen. 5:1, 2.
   2. What three parts make up the entire man? 1 Thess. 5:23.
   3. Of what is the material body composed? What was breathed into his nostrils at creation? Gen. 2:7.
   4. When God added the breath to the body, what did the man instantly become? Gen. 2:7. Body plus breath equals living soul.
   5. Then what is the living soul? Answer: Living, intelligent being.
   6. What activities are attributed to human souls?
      a. Thirst. Prov. 25:25.
      b. Hunger. Prov. 27:7.
      c. Eat, drink, make merry. Luke 12:19.
      d. Souls smitten with sword cease to breathe. Joshua 11:11.
   7. Can the soul die? Eze. 18:4.

II. *The Breath.*
   1. Are the breath and the spirit the same thing? Job 27:3; James 2:26, margin.
   2. Is man's breath the same as that of the beast's? Gen. 6:17; 7:15, 21, 22, margin.
   3. Does mankind die differently from the beast? Eccl. 3:19.
   4. In death what becomes of the physical body? Gen. 3:19.

Life in Christ

5. What becomes of the breath of life? Ps. 146:4.
6. What becomes of the intelligence produced by brain activity? Ps. 146:4.
7. Do the dead know anything? Eccl. 9:5, 6.
8. Are they engaged in praising the Lord? Ps. 115:17.
9. Can they know more about truth than the living? Isa. 38:18.
10. Can they come back and visit their earthly homes? Job 7:9, 10.

III. *State of the Dead.*
1. What did Jesus say of Lazarus when he was dead? John 11:11-14.
2. Where is the waiting place for those sleeping in death? Job 17:13-16.
3. Till what time will the dead sleep? Job 14:10-12; John 5:28, 29.

IV. *The Resurrection Time.*
1. When will the resurrection of the righteous take place? 1 Thess. 4:16, 17.
2. The resurrection of the wicked? Rev. 20:5, first part.
3. What awaits the raised wicked? Rev. 20:14, 15.
4. How does this second death differ from the first death?
Answer: The first is followed by a resurrection. The second death is everlasting—the punishment which is eternal.

V. *Appeal.*

How comforting for the Christian to know that the sleep of death is not eternal, that there will be a resurrection and a translation. Even now he may live in the hope of dying in Jesus and "sleeping" in His loving arms. Christianity sees through the portals of the tomb. We may commit our deceased loved ones to Him who said, "I am the resurrection, and the life." MYRTIS BEAMAN.

The State of the Dead

I. *Introduction.*

What actually becomes of us when we die? There are many theories concerning death, but there can be but one fact. No human being knows what is beyond death; only God knows. If we wish to know the truth about where people go after death, we must turn to God's Word. God knows where the dead are and what their state is, and He tells us plainly.

Some say that people go to heaven at death; others say to purgatory, to the grave, to a great career, or into some animal. It is not what people say but what God says. To arrive at truth, we must consider the questions:

1. What is death?
2. Are we mortal or immortal now?
3. What is the soul?
4. What is the spirit?

II. *Death the Result of Sin.*
What declaration is made in Hebrews 9:27? Because of sin the human family must die.

III. *Death a Sleep in the Grave.*
1. By what figure is death represented? 1 Thess. 4:13; John 11:11-14.
2. Why the figure "sleep"? John 5:28, 29. Because all that are in the grave shall awake again.
3. Where do the dead sleep? Dan. 12:2. "In the dust of the earth" —grave. Ecclesiastes 3:20 says *all*, both righteous and wicked, go to the same place.
4. How long do they sleep there? 1 Thess. 4:16, 17. Till Jesus comes in the clouds of heaven. Both the righteous living and the righteous dead go together.
5. What did Job say he would do? Job 14:14, 15. Wait. Where? Job 17:13.

IV. *Man Unconscious in Death.*
1. How much does one know about his family when he is dead? Job 14:21; Eccl. 9:10.
2. What becomes of the thoughts? Ps. 146:4. He is unconscious.
3. How much does one know when he is dead? Eccl. 9:5, 6. Man knows he shall die. God says that when he is dead he knows nothing.
4. Does not engage in worship. Ps. 115:17. Why? Ps. 6:5.

V. *Awaiting the Heavenly Reward.*
1. Why are not the righteous dead in heaven? Heb. 11:39, 40.
2. When did David say he would be satisfied? Ps. 17:15.
3. When only do we receive that likeness? 1 Cor. 15:51-55; Phil. 3:20, 21. We are mortal till the trumpet sounds and the dead come forth from the graves.
4. Death is the last enemy to be destroyed. 1 Cor. 15:26. Death does not transport us into heaven. To be dead does not mean we keep right on living.

VI. *The Reward of Immortality.*
1. Soon we shall see God in body, soul, and spirit. Job 19:25-27; 1 Thess. 5:23.
2. When do we receive our reward? Rev. 22:12; 2 Tim. 4:7, 8.

VII. *Appeal.*
"Blessed are the dead which die in the Lord." Rev. 14:13. We cannot afford not to BE ready. We must be prepared continually, for life is very uncertain. We need not fear death. To the righteous it will be as a sweet night's sleep.

In our next study we will discuss, *What is the soul? What is the Spirit?* (With some both lessons can be given as one study.)

Mrs. Mary E. Anderson.

"Spirit" and "Soul" Defined

I. *Introduction.*
Spirit and *soul* are not the same thing, nor can the terms be used interchangeably. The Bible says when man is dead he knows *"not any thing."* Eccl. 9:5. This is a clear and positive statement. God also says, through the same writer, that when man dies "the spirit shall return unto God who gave it." Eccl. 12:7. These statements are in perfect accord when we understand the text. Notice, not the *soul*, but the *spirit* returns to God when our body returns to earth.

II. *Man Created as a Living Soul.*
1. What made man a living soul? Gen. 2:7.
Man was made of the dust of the ground. A perfect, complete, inanimate human body was formed; all the vital organs were in their place. The brain, the seat of intelligence, was in place but did not function. The ears were there, but gave no heed. The tongue was there, but uttered no sound. The lungs were in place, but made no response. He was perfectly formed but lifeless. One thing was still lacking—only one thing—the breath. Then God breathed into man's nostrils the breath of life. Man was no longer a lifeless form, but a living soul. We exclaim with the psalmist, "I am fearfully and wonderfully made: marvellous are Thy works." Ps. 139:14.
2. Man consists of three parts: body, soul, spirit. 1 Thess. 5:23. (Greek, *Pneuma.*) Body, thoughts, breath. Ps. 146:4. (Hebrew, *Ruah.*)

III. *The Spirit.*
Ps. 104:29; Job 27:3 (margin, "breath"). Spirit and breath are here used interchangeably. (Also James 2:26, margin, says "breath.") The Greek word for *spirit* is *pneuma.* The same identical word is used for both breath and spirit. It was breath, or spirit, which God breathed into man's nostrils that made him a living soul. When man dies, it is his breath, or spirit, *only* that goes out of him. God says the spirit is the breath of life. The Hebrew for *spirit* is *ruah.*

IV. *The Soul.*
  1. Body, breath, and thoughts, or intelligence, make a living soul. Each is dependent on the other in order to function. Without the breath man is but a lifeless form, as we find him in death. The soul cannot function without a living body, for it is part of the body; the body is useless without life and intelligence.
  Does the breath have eyes to see, or ears to hear, or a tongue with which to speak, or nerves with which to feel, or legs with which to move? No, the body contains these. What good is the breath apart from the body? It takes the body, breath, and spirit to make the living soul, the man who was made in the image of God.
  2. "In my flesh shall I see God." Job 19:26. If we stand before God blameless at His coming, it will be in the whole, complete person as God made us. 1 Thess. 5:23. Not in soul alone, not in spirit alone, but the whole man, complete as God made him.
  3. What returns to God at death—the spirit or breath of life? Eccl. 12:7.
  It is God who gives life. No one can take it from us except He permits it.
  4. When breath goes forth, man is just a lifeless form. The soul remains in that lifeless body. Isa. 38:17, 18; Ps. 30:3. It is dead, and remains so until God puts breath back into the body on the resurrection morning. Ps. 104:29, 30; Eze. 37:5, 6, 12-14. When man dies, he sleeps until he is called, a period of time which to him is only a night's rest. No one knows what death is like any more than he knows when he goes to sleep. God is merciful!

MRS. MARY E. ANDERSON.

Where Will the Wicked Spend Eternity?

I. *Introduction.*
  1. What will eventually happen to the wicked?
  This is not the most appealing Bible topic, but it must be well understood by all Christians. Punishment seems contrary to God's nature, and yet it is definitely a part of His love and justice. Sin has involved more than the individual who sinned. All who are influenced by his sins must be considered in God's dealing with the sinner. The Bible clearly teaches that unrepentant sinners will be destroyed. How literal is this destruction? Is there a hell-fire? Will hell burn forever? These important questions should be answered by the Bible. Let us carefully investigate its instruction.

Life in Christ

2. Popular teaching concerning hell-fire substantiates Satan's doctrine to Eve: "Ye shall not surely die." Gen. 3:4.

II. *Are the Wicked Now in Punishment?*
   1. Wicked are reserved unto the day of punishment. 2 Peter 2:9.
      a. Wicked are to be resurrected for their destruction. John 5: 28, 29. Sinners awake to everlasting contempt. Dan. 12:2.
      b. Resurrection necessary; the sinner must suffer punishment. Matt. 5:29, 30.
      c. This punishment set for the end of the world. Matt. 13:40-42.
   2. Will the sinner burn throughout eternity?
      a. Fire that destroys wicked unquenchable. Matt. 3:12.
         Jerusalem destroyed with this type of fire. Jer. 17:27.
      b. Torment of the wicked described as lasting forever. Rev. 14:10, 11.
         Bible examples of "for ever." 1 Sam. 1:22, 28; Jonah 2:6; Ex. 21:6.
      c. Wages of sinner must be death. Rom. 6:23.
      d. Wicked must die a second time. Rev. 21:8.
   3. Will the lake of fire accomplish utter destruction?
      a. Not only wicked but earth also reserved unto fire. 2 Peter 3:7, 10.
         (1) This earth to be a lake of fire. 2 Peter 3:10.
         (2) All things present are to be dissolved by fire. 2 Peter 3: 11, 12.
      b. God's example of the destruction of wicked. Jude 7.
         (1) This type of destruction reduced Sodom and Gomorrah to ashes. 2 Peter 2:6.
         (2) Likewise the wicked will be ashes under righteous' feet. Mal. 4:1, 3.

III. *Has God Provided an Escape From This Destruction?*
   1. Destruction is prepared for devil and his angels. Matt. 25:41.
   2. Heavenly mansions are prepared for righteous. John 14:2, 3.
   3. God reasons with sinner. Offers life for obedience. Isa. 1:18, 19; John 3:16.

IV. *Appeal.*
Since God has instructed man regarding the final consequences of sin, and has given us the choice of eternal life or eternal death, let us choose wisely.
Close with reading Ezekiel 18:30-32. Have earnest prayer for help to respond to God's offer of eternal life. John 3:16.

ETHELINE V. PORTER,

What Happens to the Wicked?

(A follow-up study to clarify doubt.)

I. *God's Dealing With Unrepentant Sinners.*
  1. Wages of sin is death. Rom. 6:23.
  "The day . . . thou eatest thereof thou shalt . . . *die*." Gen. 2:17.
  "The soul that sinneth, it shall *die*." .... Eze. 18:4.
  Deut. 30:15, 19; Rom. 5:12; 6:21; 8:13; James 1:15; Rev. 20:15; 21:8; 2 Chron. 25:4; Prov. 8:36.
  2. Wicked to be destroyed.
  "All the wicked will He *destroy*." .... Ps. 145:20.
  "Shall be punished with everlasting *destruction*." 2 Thess. 1:9.
  Ps. 37:28; 92:7; Prov. 13:13; Isa. 1:28; Matt. 7:13; Rom. 9:22; Phil. 3:19; 1 Cor. 3:17.
  3. The wicked shall perish.
  "Into smoke shall they *consume* away." ..... Ps. 37:20; Job 20:5-9.
  "Yet he shall *perish* for ever." .... Job 20:5-9.
  "With all deceivableness of unrighteousness in them that *perish*." .... 2 Thess. 2:10.
  "Shall *utterly perish* in their own corruption." 2 Peter 2:12.
  "So let the wicked *perish* at the presence of God." ...... Ps. 68:2.
  "He that speaketh lies shall *perish*." .... Prov. 19:9.
  "They that strive with Thee shall *perish*." ...... Isa. 41:11.
  4. Wicked to go to perdition.
  "Reserved unto fire against the day of judgment and *perdition* of ungodly men." .... 2 Peter 3:7.
  "None of them is lost, but the son of *perdition*." .... John 17:12.
  "That man of sin be revealed, the son of *perdition*." 2 Thess. 2:3.
  "Drown men in destruction and *perdition*." ...... 1 Tim. 6:9.
  "Not of them who draw back unto *perdition*." .... Heb. 10:39.
  5. The Lord will slay wicked.
  "Surely Thou wilt *slay* the wicked, O God." ...... Ps. 139:19.
  "*Slay* them before Me." .... Luke 19:27.
  "Ye shall be *slain* all of you." .... Ps. 62:3.
  "With the breath of His lips shall He *slay* the wicked." Isa. 11:4.
  6. Sinners will be cut off.
  "They that war against Thee shall be as *nothing*." Isa. 41:12.
  "Seed of the wicked shall be *cut off*." .... Ps. 37:28.
  "Transgressors shall be *rooted out* of it." .... Prov. 2:22.
  "*Chased out* of the world." .... Job 18:18.
  "Shall *cut them off* in their own wickedness." .... Ps. 94:23.
  7. Burning, fate of the wicked.
  "Day cometh, that shall *burn* as an oven." .... Mal. 4:1.

"Utterly *burned with fire.*" .... Rev. 18:8.
"Will *burn* up the chaff with unquenchable fire." Matt. 3:12.
"Shalt cast them into a *furnace of fire.*" .... Matt. 13:41, 42.

II. *Man May Choose to Live Forever.*
"Man may eat thereof [heavenly bread], and *not die.*" John 6:50.
"He shall *never see death.*" .... John 8:51.
"Whosoever liveth and believeth in Me shall *never die.*" John 11:26.

III. *Appeal.*
"Believest thou this?" .... John 11:26.

BETTY CANNON.

Where Does the Soul Go at Death?
(For Catholics.)

It is assumed that the reader has been receiving studies and is ready for doctrine based only on Scripture. Doctrines of the Catholic Church are compared with God's Word.

I. *Teachings of Catholic Church.*
(Quoted from *Christian Doctrine,* by Rev. Jos. Deharbe, published by Fr. Pustet and Co., N.Y., 1901, pp. 18, 19.)

"107. What happens in man at the moment of his death?
At the moment of death, man's soul separates itself from his body, and the body is returned to the earth.

"108. How long shall the body remain in the earth?
The body shall remain in the earth till the day of the last judgment, when God will raise it again to life and reunite it to the soul forever.

"109. Shall all men rise again?
All men, whether good or wicked, shall rise again.

"110. Will the risen bodies be all alike?
The bodies of the wicked shall be wretched and hideous, while the bodies of the good shall be glorious.

"111. What happens to the soul, when it has separated from the body?
It appears at once before the judgment-seat of God.

"112. What do we call this judgment?
We call it the Particular Judgment.

"113. What are the things of which the soul shall be judged?
The soul shall be judged of all its thoughts, words, actions, and omissions.

"114. Whither does the soul go immediately after the Particular Judgment?

The soul goes either to Heaven, to Hell, or to Purgatory.
"115. What souls go to Purgatory?
   The souls of the just, who have departed this life in the state of venial sin or have yet to expiate the temporal punishment due to their sins.
"116. Will Purgatory remain in existence after the General Judgment?
   No; after the General Judgment only Heaven and Hell shall remain.
"117. What souls shall be cast into Hell?
   The souls of those who die in the state of mortal sin.
"118. What souls will go to Heaven?
   The souls of those who die in the friendship of God and are free from all sins and all punishment due to sin.
"119. Which are the four last ends of man?
   The four last ends of man are: Death, Judgment, Heaven and Hell."

II. *Teachings of Scripture.*
   1. Mortal man is subject to death. 1 Cor. 15:53.
      a. God only has immortality. 1 Tim. 6:15, 16.
      b. We are admonished to seek immortality. Rom. 2:6, 7.
      (If we possessed it we would not have to seek for it.)
   2. Man composed of body, soul, spirit.
      a. Soul and spirit distinct parts. Heb. 4:12.
      b. Spirit is the breath. Job 27:3; James 2:26, margin.
   3. What happens to man at death?
      a. To the body.
         (1) Returns to dust. Eccl. 3:20; Gen. 3:19.
         (2) Sleeps in the grave. Matt. 27:52; 1 Thess. 4:15.
      b. To the soul or person.
         (1) Dies. Eze. 18:4; Ps. 78:50.
         (2) Goes into the grave. Ps. 89:48; 30:3.
         (3) Loses memory, emotions, knowledge. Eccl. 9:5, 6, 10; Ps. 146:4.
         (4) Cannot return to earthly home. Job 7:9, 10.
      c. To the spirit, breath.
         (1) Breath goes forth. Ps. 146:4.
         (2) Spirit goes back to God. Eccl. 12:7.
         (3) Beasts have same breath. Eccl. 3:19.
   4. Scriptural examples.
      a. David is buried; not in heaven. Acts 2:29, 34.
      b. Lazarus came *forth,* not down from heaven. John 11:39-44.
      c. Jesus did not go to heaven while in the grave. John 20:17.

5. No hope of salvation after death.
   a. Dead know nothing. How can they be saved? Eccl. 9:5, 6.
   b. Dead cannot hope for truth. Isa. 38:18.
   c. *(Purgatory* is not mentioned in the Bible. Not introduced until close of sixth century. Not made article of Catholic faith until 1439. Comforting to know our dead loved ones are not burning in purgatory but are peacefully sleeping in grave. If fire could purge sin, Christ would not have had to die for our sins. John 3:16. The blood of God's Son, not the fires of purgatory, cleanses us from sin. 1 John 1:7. We must come to Him, confess our sins (1 John 1:9), and be free of sin (Isa. 1:18).
6. The Christian's hope for life.
   a. Shall be raised at second coming. 1 Thess. 4:16, 17.
   b. Righteous dead raised immortal. 1 Cor. 15:51-54.
   c. Eternal life then given man by Christ. 1 John 5:11, 12.
   d. Righteous will live with Christ. John 14:3.
   e. *Now* is the time to accept Christ. 2 Cor. 6:2.

III. *Scripture, or Tradition?* John 7:38; Matt. 15:3, 9.

MRS. LUCILLE PFLAUMER.

Is Purgatory Scriptural?
(For Catholics.)

I. *Introduction.*
   1. Prov. 18:13. A doctrine or practice must not be condemned without fair investigation.
   2. John 17:17. True Christians earnestly seek truth and accept it.
   3. Isa. 8:20. Only one safe course: Compare teaching with Bible.

II. *Purgatory Doctrine According to Its Teachers.*
   Charles A. Martin, *Catholic Religion*, p. 288: "Christian revelation teaches us that besides heaven into which no imperfection can enter, and hell from which there is no redemption, there is a state in which the souls of the just who in this life were not perfectly cleansed, shall undergo purifying suffering before being admitted into heaven. This state of purgation is properly called purgatory. The defined teaching of the church is expressed in the words of the Council of Trent: 'That there is a purgatory and that the souls detained there are benefitted by the prayers of the faithful and especially by the acceptable sacrifice of the altar.' "
   The Jesuit Seminary News, vol. 3, no. 9. (Nov. 15, 1928), p. 70: "By prayer we temper the agonies of the souls in purgatory. We hasten their liberation by sacrifice."

III. *Purgatory Doctrine in the Light of Scripture.*
  1. Do souls burn in purgatory after death?
      a. Teaching of church: Cardinal Robert Bellarmine, prominent Catholic theologian, quoted by Abbé Cloquet, *The Mouth of the Dead*, p. 64: "There are souls condemned to burn in Purgatory till the day of Judgment."
      The Jesuit Seminary News, vol. 3, no. 9 (Nov. 15, 1928), p. 70: "Could we see these dear souls in purgatory we would not forget them. They cry out in thirst while we sit and drink. They are weary with restlessness while we are sleeping. They are sore with grievous pain while we are playing. They are eaten up with burning fire while we are feasting. They cry out for help from those who once held them dear. They plead that you have the pity, the prayers, the sacrifices that you promised."
      b. Teaching of Bible:
          (1) 1 Kings 2:10; 22:40. Death is a sleep for good and bad alike.
          (2) Eccl. 9:5, 6, 10. The dead know nothing, are silent and and inactive, all peacefully resting (sleeping) in graves.
  2. Do prayers of faithful and the mass liberate from purgatory? (Eze. 14:14; Rev. 22:12; 2 Cor. 5:10.)
  3. Prayers and masses are performed on payment of money.
      a. A well-known fact.
      b. Teaching of Bible:
          (1) Matt. 19:23, 24. Riches do not give anyone a premium on heaven, or eternal life.
          (2) Rom. 6:23. Eternal life is a gift of God.
          (3) Acts 8:20, 23. It is dangerous to try to purchase God's favor. It was not allowed in the Apostolic church.
  4. Are souls purged by fire in preparation for heaven?
      a. Teaching of church: W. E. Addis and Thomas Arnold, *A Catholic Dictionary*, p. 766, art. "Purgatory": "All the souls in Purgatory have died in the love of God, and are certain to enter heaven. But as yet they are not pure and holy enough to see God, and God's mercy allots them a place and a time for cleansing and preparation."
      Cardinal Robert Bellarmine, quoted by Abbé Cloquet, *The Mouth of the Dead*, p. 64: "There are souls condemned to burn in Purgatory till the day of Judgment."
      Charles A. Martin, *Catholic Religion*, pp. 228-290: "In purgatory the souls can themselves wipe out their debt by suffering."
      b. Teaching of Bible: Jer. 2:22; 1 John 1:9, 7.

Life in Christ

5. Uncertainty of masses and prayers for dead.
    a. Teaching of Church: Bertrand L. Conway, *The Question Box* (old ed.), p. 325: "All Masses and prayers for the dead are applied 'by way of suffrage'—that is, are dependent on God's secret mercy and will, who in His infinite justice may apply to another soul altogether the Masses said for a certain individual. Non-Catholics generally think that five hundred Masses have five hundred times the efficacy of one. This is not the case. The value of each Mass is infinite, but we never know with perfect certainty whether or not God has applied it to the individual soul for whom it has been offered, although we do know He answers all our prayers."
    Cardinal Robert Bellarmine, *De Justificatione*, book 3, chap. 8: In his *Disputations de Controversiis Christiane Fidei adversus Heyies Temporis Haereticos*, vol. 4, p. 442, col. 2: "No one can be certain, with the certainty of faith, that he receives a true sacrament, because the sacrament cannot be valid without the intention of the minister, and no man can see another's intention."
    b. The Bible teaches a sure way of salvation. John 6:37; Heb. 7:25.

IV. *Time for Salvation Now, Not After Death.*
    Eccl. 11:9; Isa. 38:18; 2 Cor. 6:2.

V. *Conclusion.*
    1. Roman Catholics themselves declare purgatory is not in the Bible.
        a. W. E. Addis and Thomas Arnold, *A Catholic Dictionary*, p. 767, art. "Purgatory": "We would appeal to those general principles of Scripture rather than to particular texts often alleged in proof of Purgatory. We doubt if they contain an explicit and direct reference to it."
        b. Cardinal Nicholas Wiseman, *Lectures on the Principal Doctrines and Practices of the Catholic Church*, Introduction page 16, admits that a Roman Catholic "could not discover in it [the Bible] one word of purgatory." Thus, purgatory is not Scriptural.
    2. Matt. 15:9; Rev. 22:14. It is dangerous to accept the commandments of men.
    3. Isa. 1:18; Titus 2:11-13. Come to Jesus now; live righteously "in this present world."

MRS. CATHERINE LEBEDOFF.

The Work of Evil Angels

SATAN

John 8:44. Satan is a liar, a deceiver, a murderer.
Rev. 12:9, 10. He is an accuser of the brethren.
1 Peter 5:8. He seeks to tempt and destroy.
2 Cor. 4:4. He blinds the minds of unbelievers.
Rev. 12:12. He is very angry, for his time to work is short.

Satan is the originator of all the evil in our world, but he is so clever in his deceptions that few believe that he exists. He puts his spirit, his thoughts, into the minds of those who yield to his temptations. All the selfishness, greed, unhappiness, discouragements, doubts, fears, discord, quarrels, hatreds, and war—yea, every base and evil thing—are the result of his influence.

He stirs up man to rebel against God, to refuse to obey His law, or to do His will in any way. He tries to obliterate every trace of the image of God from the face, form, mind, and heart of man.

He especially delights to tempt the children of God to sin, for then he can accuse them to God and the holy angels as unworthy of mercy and salvation. In this work he never wearies, for he accuses "them before our God day and night."

He knows the human heart, because he has studied it now for nearly six thousand years, and he is adept at suiting his temptations to our desires, our weaknesses, our inherited tendencies. He is working with increased energy now because he knows that his time is short.

EVIL ANGELS

Ps. 78:49. Evil angels can trouble man only when God permits.
Job 1:12. The experience of Job is an example.
1 Sam. 16:14, 15. Evil angels come when the Spirit of the Lord is grieved away.
1 Cor. 10:19, 20. The worship of idols is the worship of devils.
Mark 5:1-20. Evil angels have complete possession of those who yield to their temptations.
1 Tim. 4:1. They work with special power in the last days.
Rev. 16:13, 14. They will gather rulers and people to the battle of Armageddon.

"We wrestle not against flesh and blood, but against principalities, against powers, against the rulers of the darkness of this world, against spiritual wickedness ["wicked spirits," margin] in heavenly places." Eph. 6:12.

All who are tempted have this comfort, that "God is faithful, who will not suffer you to be tempted above that ye are able, but will with the temptation also make a way to escape, that ye may be able to bear it." 1 Cor. 10:13. Only when we willfully sin against God, and thus grieve the Spirit of God and the good angels away from us, can Satan and his angels come near to trouble us.

Romans 1:20-32 tells how men became idolaters, of all the wicked things this causes them to do, and the degradation it has brought to the human race. We understand why this is so when we read that he who worships a false god is really worshiping a devil. The heathen fear their gods, and well they may, for these gods are demons in disguise. Because the devil and his angels are invisible to human eyes, they are no less real and to be feared by those who come under their power.

In the Old Testament there are many evidences of the work of evil angels; but when Jesus came to this earth, Satan increased his efforts to overcome the human race. He even tempted Jesus and tried to overcome Him, but Jesus never yielded in any way to his influence. Satan literally took possession of the minds and bodies of men and women, and controlled their words and actions. But Jesus overcame Satan and delivered them from his power.

In these last days many are "giving heed to seducing spirits, and doctrines [teachings] of devils." 1 Tim. 4:1. The world is full of false teachings, or principles, which the devil has put into the minds of men. As a result, the earth is full of suffering, bloodshed, and every evil thing. All this is the work of evil men who are possessed and inspired by evil angels.

Mediums

Gen. 3:1. Satan uses mediums to communicate with man.

2 Cor. 11:14, 15. He and his angels transform themselves into angels of light.

1 Sam. 28:11-16. They can simulate the form of the dead.

1 Chron. 10:13, 14. Saul inquired of an evil spirit, not of the Lord.

Acts 13:6-10. Sorcerers are children of the devil, mediums of evil angels.

Deut. 18:10-12. God condemns all wizards, familiar spirits, necromancers, and sorcerers.

Rev. 21:8. They will suffer the second death.

Satan is a deceiver, first, last, and always. Jesus said, "He is a liar, and the father of it." John 8:44. He wishes us to believe that he does not exist, for then he could the easier deceive. For this reason he never appears as he really is, but seeks for agents, or mediums, through whom to communicate his plans and principles. He spoke to Eve through a serpent, that she might not suspect who was really talking to her.

Since then he has used as mediums men and women—anyone who will give up his mind and will, and yield himself to the guidance and control of Satan. In the Old Testament these persons were called wizards, witches, necromancers, sorcerers, and those who had familiar spirits. God said back there that no such agent of Satan should live within the land of Israel.

For purposes of deception Satan can transform himself not only into an angel of light but into the forms of our dead friends. This he did in the days of Saul through a medium, the witch of Endor. It was not Samuel who came up out of the earth but a devil who impersonated Samuel. We are told positively that Saul inquired of a "familiar spirit; . . . and enquired not of the Lord." 1 Chron. 10:13, 14. The godly Samuel, had he been alive, would not have responded to the call of a witch—an agent of Satan. The message given was true, because Satan can foretell any event over which he has control. Saul sinned against God when he went to inquire of a witch, and he was then in Satan's power.

The Dead

Isa. 8:19, 20. All mediums seek communication with the dead.

Eccl. 9:5, 6, 10. But the dead know not anything.

All these mediums pretend to communicate with the dead, but the messages they receive are from the devil and his angels. Satan told Eve she would not die, that even the Creator could not take away the life He had given her. He has caused most of the human race to believe that they are immortal, that the dead are really more alive and have greater powers than when they lived on the earth. He teaches men that they will live forever, no matter how much they disobey God.

Protection Against Evil Angels

Eph. 6:11, 12. We need the whole armor of God.

Job. 1:9, 10. God puts a hedge around those who love Him.

Ps. 34:7. This hedge is the good angels.

James 4:7. Submit to God. "Resist the devil."

Jesus overcame Satan with the Word of God. This same weapon will protect anyone from Satan's deceptions and power if he will but use it. If we know what the Bible teaches, and obey it, Satan cannot deceive us. God puts a hedge of holy angels around those who love and trust Him. Satan's power to deceive is great, but God's power to protect is much greater.

Additional References

Job 1; 2
Lev. 17:7
2 Chron. 11:14, 15

Matt. 13:37-43
Mark 7:26-30
Matt. 12:22-30

Life in Christ 451

Deut. 32:17	2 Thess. 2:7-12
Zech. 13:1-3	Lev. 20:6, 27
Luke 11:14-26	Rev. 9:20, 21
Jude 6	Rev. 20:1-10
Luke 4:33-36	Matt. 25:41
Mark 9:17-27	1 John 3:8
Ps. 106:28, 37, 38	John 10:27-29
Matt. 13:18, 19	Rev. 3:10

ALMA E. MCKIBBIN.

Is Spiritism Scriptural?

It is not always necessary to teach spiritism in detail, but its main deceptions should be understood by all. Where there appears to be no particular confusion, it is better not to raise issues concerning this last-day deception. The Bible teacher should be prepared, however, to meet various problems which often do arise.

1. What statement was made by Satan to Eve in the first doctrine given to the family of earth? "Ye shall not surely die." Gen. 3:4.
2. What statement had God made? "Dying thou shalt die." Gen. 2:17, margin.
3. How does God describe death? Dissolution of man back to dust. Ps. 146:4.
4. How did Satan insinuate doubt on this point? Gen. 3:4, 5.
5. What does the Bible teach is fallen man's state? 1 Cor. 15:53.
6. What is the meaning of the word *mortal?* Subject to death.
7. In what state would a person be if he could not die? If he just entered another sphere of existence? This would be an immortal state.
8. Who only is immortal? God only. 1 Tim. 6:15, 16.
9. How was Adam's life to be perpetuated before sin? Gen. 2:9.
10. What was removed from Adam as soon as he sinned? Gen. 3:22-24.
    NOTE.—One member of the heavenly family in his effort to exalt himself—to be like God—had become acquainted with good and evil. He had led other angels to join him. Adam also had joined this fallen family. He was then excluded from the tree of life.
11. When Satan said that man would not surely die at death but would be changed to another form of existence, what was he? A liar, telling something that is not a fact. John 8:44.
12. By what means did the devil work to make it appear that his word was truth? By familiar spirits known under such names as

sorcerers, necromancers, witches, wizards, magicians, enchanters, soothsayers. 1 Sam. 28:8-15.
13. With what form of worship were these always associated? 2 Kings 21:5, 6; Ps. 106:28.
14. When Pharaoh resisted the message of Moses, for whom did he call? Ex. 7:11. Sorcery is witchcraft.
15. Whom did Nebuchadnezzar call on in his perplexity? Dan. 2:2.
16. What did God say about these mediums? Deut. 18:9-14.
17. What is meant by—
    a. Passing through the fire? Fire is a symbol of the sun. Ps. 106:37, 38; Lev. 18:21.
    b. Divination? Telling the future. Eze. 21:21.
    c. Enchantment? Incantation, sorcery, witchcraft, spell. Ex. 7:11.
    d. Witch? A Woman medium.
    e. Charmer? One who casts a spell over another.
    f. Consulter of familiar spirits? Spirits claim to be from the dead. Note the various forms in which this is done today; by trance medium; the seance or circle touching hands; or planchette; the writing mediums; transparent visions, etc.
    g. Wizard? a man medium.
    h. Necromancer? One holding communion with supposed spirits of dead.
18. How did God regard these practices? Deut. 18:12.
19. What was one of the civil laws of Israel? Ex. 22:18; Lev. 20:27.
20. What would happen to the individual that sought communion with these spirit beings? Lev. 20:6.
21. What did Isaiah say about seeking the dead? Isa. 8:19.
22. Can the dead communicate with the living? Eccl. 9:5, 6.
23. Can they return to their homes as ghosts? Job. 7:9, 10; 2 Sam. 12:23.

APPEAL: This study should not be left in a negative mood. God warns of deceptions so we may not be led astray by its errors. The light of God's Word dispels all doubt, error, and fear. Let us walk in it. Isa. 8:19, 20.

MYRTIS BEAMAN.

PART FOUR ★ CHAPTER EIGHT

Christian Stewardship

Stewardship embraces man's time, talents, means—everything God has given him. Tithing may be the main point in our study, but principles stressing the more abundant life must not be eclipsed. This subject is now widely discussed in various sectors of the Christian church.

The question of stewardship need not be reserved until the last of the series; because of the reader's personal interest in the subject, it may be touched on previously. But after God's claims on the Sabbath have been stressed, the question of stewardship will be seen in a new light. Not merely the paying of a tenth of our means is required by God, nor sacrificing for His needy cause. Tithing should become a responsibility involving a great privilege. We share in the blessing of cooperating with God for the hastening of His kingdom upon earth. We are debtors to those who do not know Christ. Such an approach appeals to thoughtful, earnest, zealous, and unselfish Christians.

Tithing—A Cycle of Love

1. Who is the rightful owner of the universe?
   Creator of heaven, earth, and man. Gen. 1:1, 27; Ex. 20:11.
   Earth is the Lord's and they that dwell therein. Ps. 24:1.
   Gold and silver also. Haggai 2:8.
   "Cattle upon a thousand hills." Ps. 50:10.
   All power belongeth unto God. Ps. 62:11.
2. What is man's relationship to God's family?
   Christ God's Son by nature. John 3:16.
   Man His son by adoption. Gal. 4:5.
   Adopted through Christ. Eph. 1:5.
   Children of God. Rom. 8:16.
   Now called sons. 1 John 3:1, 2.
3. How is the Father's love bestowed on us?
   a. Gives us gifts.

Gives us all things to enjoy. 1 Tim. 6:17.
Gives us strength and power. Ps. 68:35.
Gives us power to get wealth. Deut. 8:18.
  b. Makes us heirs.
    Rightful heir. Heb. 1:2.
    "Heirs of God, and joint-heirs with Christ." Rom. 8:16, 17.
4. How does God ask recognition of His ownership?
  a. In love and obedience.
    "If ye love Me, keep My commandments." John 14:15.
    Honor God with first fruits. Prov. 3:9.
  b. In tithes and offerings.
    One tenth is the Lord's. It is holy. Lev. 27:30, 32.
    God challenges us to prove Him. Mal. 3:10.
5. How is the tithe to be used?
  For priests (ministry). Num. 18:20-24.
  Ordained by God to support gospel. 1 Cor. 9:13, 14.
  To carry gospel message to others. 2 Cor. 11:7-9.
6. What examples of faithful tithing does the Bible teach?
  Abraham. Heb. 7:2; Gen. 14:18-23.
  Jacob. Gen. 28:20-22.
  Jesus exhorted tithing even from small produce. Matt. 23:23.
7. What are the special blessings of faithful tithing?
  The nine-tenths multiplied beyond need. Mal. 3:10-12.
  Plenty to spare. Prov. 3:9, 10.
  Everlasting riches. Luke 16:10-12.
  (Stress importance of God's blessing on His gifts, proper disposition of God's favors, cooperating with God in His work of salvation.)
  APPEAL: Ps. 116:12-14.   MRS. MAYME GIDDINGS.

God's Ownership

I. *God the Original Owner of the Earth.*
   For nearly 6,000 years man has been hoarding, but still he does not own a thing. Only way he will ever have anything is through Christ. Man "sold out" to Satan. Ps. 24:1; 50:10, 11; Haggai 2:8.

II. *We Are God's Stewards.*
   1. Parable representing our stewardship. Luke 19:12-27.
   2. God gave Adam use and care of Garden of Eden, with understanding that man would reserve to Him one tree, acknowledging God's ownership and rights. Gen. 2:15-17.
   3. *Tree* was a test of man's character in the matter of His possessions.
   4. *Sabbath* a test of man's character in matter of time.

Christian Stewardship

    5. In all ages God has maintained these two tests. Our possessions, time, life, health—all belong to God, and should be used in a way to honor Him.

III. *The Principle of Tithing.*
   1. Abraham paid tithes, acknowledging Possessor of heaven and earth. Gen. 14:18-20.
   2. Jacob understood this principle. Gen. 28:20-22.
   3. Tithing antedates Mosaic law and is not abolished. Heb. 7:5, 9.
   4. In days of Nehemiah all Israel paid tithe. Neh. 12:44, 47.
   5. Jesus taught this principle. Matt. 23:23; 22:21.

IV. *Use of the Tithe.*
   1. All tithe holy; to be used for sacred purposes. Lev. 27:30, 32.
   2. Old Testament church financed by tithe. Num. 18:21.
   3. Same plan for support of ministry today. 1 Cor. 9:13, 14.

V. *Failure to Pay Tithe Brings Curse.*
   1. Withholding tithe is robbing God. Mal. 3:8, 9.
   2. God removes physical blessings when unfaithful. Deut. 28:15-17, 21-24.
   3. Gives power to get wealth; can also remove power. Deut. 8:17, 18.
   4. Nontithepayers' wages put "into a bag with holes." Haggai 1:5, 6, 9.
   5. Riches will not profit in day of wrath. Prov. 11:4.
   6. What profit to gain world but lose soul? Mark 8:36.

VI. *Proving God's Promises.*
   1. Some think they cannot afford to tithe. Nine tenths with God's blessing will go farther than ten tenths without. Ps. 37:16.
   2. Not room to receive the blessings. Mal. 3:10-12.
   3. Barns filled with plenty. Prov. 3:9, 10.
   4. Seek first the kingdom of God, and "all these things shall be added." Matt. 6:31-33.
   5. David never saw "righteous forsaken." Ps. 37:25.
   6. "My God shall supply all your need." Phil. 4:19.

                                              MARJORIE VANSICKLE.

Should Christians Pay Tithe?

1. How are godliness and covetousness in contrast?
   God's people should be content; foster peace. 1 Tim. 6:6.
   A greedy Christian is spiritually sick. 1 Tim. 6:9-11.
   Covetousness is evil of last days. 2 Tim. 3:1, 2.
   Our loving Saviour warns us. Luke 12:15; Mark 10:17, 22-25.

2. Godliness—What does it mean to us?
   Bible says it is complete surrender. Rom. 12:1.
   How much did God give to save us? John 3:16; Phil 2:6-8; 2 Cor. 8:9.
   Same spirit should be in us. Phil. 2:5; 1 Tim. 6:17-19; Matt. 6:19, 20.
   Benevolence in early church. Gifts: Acts. 4:33-37.
   Tithe: 1 Cor. 9:14.
   Gospel work our responsibility. Mark 16:15; John 17:18, 24.
3. What does God's Word teach regarding liberal, systematic giving?
   Abraham and Jacob gave tithes. Gen. 14:18-20; 28:22.
   The tithe is holy. Lev. 27:30.
   New Testament advice. Matt. 23:23; 1 Cor. 9:13, 14.
   God's plan does not include church fairs, suppers, lotteries, etc. 1 Cor. 11:22; John 2:16.
   The Lord's rebuke to the unfaithful. Mal. 3:7-9.
   The blessing of tithe paying. Mal. 3:10; Luke 6:38.
   We cannot afford not to pay tithes. Hag. 1:5-7.
4. APPEAL:
   God's principles are always sound. Prov. 8:8, 9.
   His blessing is on condition. Mal. 3:10.
   The Lord longs to bless man. Deut. 11:27.
   Heed what God says. Isa. 48:17, 18.

S. A. BROBERG.

PART FOUR ★ CHAPTER NINE

Prophetic Topics

It is our prophetic teachings that give life and setting to our message. The prophecies provide an element of certainty and assurance. This helps our readers to sense quickly the point that our truth is more than just another idea of a Christian church. Presenting the prophecies of Daniel and Revelation provides the proper urgency for the acceptance of a whole chain of truth for this hour of history. The Bible instructor must know and feel in his own soul that prophecy is but history in advance. There is power in our instruction when these great themes of present truth will march forth in battle array. Let us become masterful teachers of the prophetic Word.

The Great Day of the Lord

I. *Earth's Last Days.*
  1. Terrible day of the Lord.
     a. In what words have prophets described this day of the Lord? Joel 1:15; 2:11; Zeph. 1:14.
     b. What brings this terrible day? Isa. 13:6, 9, 11.
     c. What two classes will be on earth during this time of visitation? Mal. 3:18.
  2. When does the day of Lord begin?
     a. What marks hour when God changes from *mercy* to *justice?* Rev. 22:11.
     b. Will either wicked or righteous on earth know decree has been uttered?
        (1) Wicked know not. Matt. 24:38, 39.
        (2) Believers know not. Matt. 24:42.
     c. After this decree is uttered, what happens? Dan. 12:1.
  3. During seven last plagues.
     What is included in this time of trouble?
     a. God's wrath visited on human family. Rev. 15:1.
     b. Armageddon. Rev. 16:16.
     c. Greatest earthquake of all ages. Rev. 16:18.

II. *End of the World, Coming of Jesus.*
  1. What event immediately follows earthquake? Rev. 19:11, 16.
  2. What do the wicked do when they see Jesus coming? Rev. 6:14-16.
  3. What will His glory do to the wicked? 2 Thess. 2:8.
  4. What becomes of their bodies? Jer. 25:33.
  5. How long will the wicked remain dead? Rev. 20:5, first part.

III. *After the Millennium.*
  1. Close of 1000 years.
     a. What raises the wicked at close of 1,000 years? John 5:28, 29.
     b. What will Satan do to this vast host of wicked? Rev. 20:7, 8.
     c. How does the beloved city come to be on earth? Where located? Rev. 21:2, 10; Zech. 14:3-5 (last part verse 5).
     d. When the wicked surround the Holy City, what will God show them? Rev. 15:4.
  2. Anguish of lost.
     a. What is revealed to each when God's judgments are made manifest? 1 Cor. 4:5; Jude 15.

      b. When each sees himself as God sees, what will wicked do? Isa. 45:23; Phil. 2:10, 11.
      c. When wicked see what they have lost, what will happen to them? Rev. 20:9.
      d. Who enters this fire with all the unsaved? Rev. 20:10.
      e. What is consumed by this fire? Mal. 4:1; Matt. 10:28; Eze. 18:4.
      f. End of all the wicked. Obadiah 1:15, 16; Ps. 37:10; Eze. 28:10.

IV. *End of God's Wrath.*
  1. What marks finish of great and terrible day of Lord? Isa. 65:17.
  2. What invitation shows all can escape destruction? Rev. 22:17. (Appeal.)

                                                      JENNIE IRELAND.

God's Last Warning Messages

(Condense by selecting texts or give in two studies.)

Text: Rev. 14:6-12.

PART I

I. *First Angel's Message.* (Supply S.D.A. history.)
  1. First angel with everlasting gospel. Rev. 14:6.
  2. Burden of message: "Judgment hour *is* come." Rev. 14:7.
  3. Judgment still future in Paul's day. Acts 24:25.
  4. Judgment connected with coming of Christ. 2 Tim. 4:1.
  5. Righteous "accounted worthy" *before* Christ comes. Luke 21:36.
  6. Christ brings His reward with Him. Rev. 22:12.
  7. "This message," based upon "little book," announces that time should be no longer. Rev. 10:10.
  8. Followed by a world-wide message, it must deal with prophetic time. Rev. 10:11.
  9. Daniel, the "little book." Gives longest prophetic period in the Bible. It ended in 1844. Dan. 8:14.
  10. Proclamation of this message compared to a lion's roar. Rev. 10:1-3.
  11. Parallel before earthly sanctuary cleansed, a warning was sounded throughout all Israel. Lev. 23:24.
  12. Disappointment of 1844 and parallel. Rev. 10:8-10; Luke 19:35-40; 24:20, 21.
  13. Lesson applying to 1844 disappointment. Heb. 10:32-34.

II. *Second Angel's Message.* (Supply S.D.A. history.)
  1. Many rejected first message; persecuted those who accepted. (Relate denominational history.)

Prophetic Topics

2. Second angel followed announcing fall of Babylon. Rev. 14:8.
3. Babylon an apostate church. Rev. 17:5, 18.
4. "Babylon is fallen," repeated; urgency of message. Rev. 14:8.

PART II

III. *Significance of Babylon, Beast, Image.*
  1. The beast power persecuted saints 1260 years. Rev. 13:5-7.
  2. Claims to have changed God's law. Dan. 7:25. (Catholic assertions.)
  3. God's law commands to keep holy the seventh day, Saturday, sunset to sunset. Ex. 20:8-11; Lev. 23:32.
  4. Obedience is the highest type of worship. 1 Sam. 15:22.
  5. As in Elijah's day, all now asked whom they will serve. 1 Kings 18:22.
  6. Only those who refuse to worship beast have their names in book of life. Rev. 13:8.

IV. *Third Angel's Message.* (Supply S.D.A. history.)
  1. Most solemn message in the Bible. Rev. 14:9-12.
  2. Last message before Christ comes. Rev. 14:14.
  3. Follows first and second messages and is world-wide. To "any man," none excluded. Warning against the worship of beast and his image.
  4. Babylon's fall complete. Rev. 18:1-5. The apostate church eventually becomes Babylon. She has confused her children. Rev. 17:5. While confusion of worship increases and Rome attempts to change the very law of God, God's solemn warning messages to the world become more alarming.
  5. Great power attends message. Rev. 18:1.
  6. Unlawful connection with nations crowning sin. Rev. 18:3.
  7. Christ is the head of this church. (Eph. 5:23.) Churches appeal to earthly governments to make religious laws; unfaithful to Christ. (2 Cor. 11:2.)
  8. The church guiding the state; drunk with blood of martyrs. Rev. 17:3, 6.
  9. Church and state union world-wide. Rev. 18:3.
  10. God now calls His people out of Babylon; all who refuse receive of her plagues. Rev. 18:4.

V. *Significance of Seven Plagues.*
  1. Those who obey beast receive his mark, drink of unmixed wrath of God. Rev. 14:10.
  2. The unmixed wrath of God in seven last plagues. Rev. 15:1, 7.

3. The seven last plagues on those who worship the beast and his image and receive his mark. Rev. 14:9, 10.
4. The righteous are shielded. Ps. 91:1-10.
5. Kept word of God's patience. Rev. 3:10.

VI. *Message Produces Two Classes.*
1. Two classes—commandment keepers and commandment breakers. Rev. 14:12; 22:11.
2. When message completed, Christ gathers earth's soul harvest. Rev. 14:14-16.
3. Only commandment keepers have right to tree of life. Rev. 22:14.
4. "Choose you this day." Joshua 24:15.

VII. *Appeal.*
"Do you recognize, Mrs.———, that the truths we have been studying together are important messages from God? Are you preparing to obey these solemn messages by taking your stand with God's faithful children, who are warning the world of the soon coming of Jesus? Obedience to God's last warning messages brings great joy and blessing; disobedience brings sorrow and destruction. Surely, we want to be found on God's side; do we not? Let us now pray that He will help us to make the right decision." (Close with prayer.)   MARJORIE MILLER GREENE.

Earth's Seven Last Plagues

Text: Prov. 26:2. "The curse causeless shall not come."

I. *God's Love Requires Justice.*
God is loving, merciful, long-suffering, forgiving, just. God's chastenings are to lead to repentance. He does not afflict willingly. Mercy has always been mingled with His wrath. But eventually God must "bare His arm." He then opens the armory of heaven to destroy Babylon. This "act," foreign to God's nature, is necessary. Texts for teacher's background: Ex. 34:6, 7; Rev. 3:19; Lam. 3:33; Hab. 3:2; Isa. 52:10; 28:21; Jer. 50:23-26; 25:30-33.

II. *Warning Against Earth's Last Plagues.*
1. Babylon's sins to reach a climax.
 a. In them is filled up the wrath of God. Rev. 15:1; 14:10; 18:4, 5.
 b. Her deceptions and persecutions then punished. Rev. 18: 6-8.
 c. No one still unsaved can be saved during these plagues. Rev. 15:8; 10:7; 16:17.
2. Warning messages precede plagues. Amos 3:7.

Prophetic Topics 461

    a. World-wide message first. Rev. 14:6, 7; Matt. 24:14.
    b. Next, a message to the churches concerning Babylon's fall. Rev. 14:8.
    c. Then all must decide on worshiping God or the beast. Rev. 14:9, 10.
    d. Another world-wide loud cry, second message to *come out* of Babylon. Rev. 18:1-4.

III. *Unparalleled Time of Trouble.* (Dan. 12:1.)
  1. Destruction from the Almighty. Joel 1:14, 15.
    a. All nature affected. Joel 1:17-20.
    b. Desolation of the earth. Zeph. 1:14-18; Jer. 4:16, 20; Isa. 26:21.
    c. Mighty men helpless.
    d. Wrath, trouble, physical distress.
    e. Darkness and gloominess. (Atmospheric and mental.)
    f. Wars affecting great cities.
    g. Blood poured out as dust.
    h. Whole land speedily devoured.
    i. Spiritual famine, mental distress. Amos 8:11, 12.
  2. Last plagues like Egypt's plagues. Rev. 16:1, 21; Job 38:22, 23; Isa. 30:25-30; Eze. 13:11; Ex. 7-11.
    a. Grievous sore upon all beast worshipers.
    b. Sea becomes as blood of dead man.
    c. Rivers turned to blood.
    d. Sun scorches men with fire.
    e. Darkness over seat of beast.
    f. Drying up of river Euphrates.
    g. Unprecedented earthquake, hail.

IV. *Protection Promised Righteous.*
  1. No plague to fall on righteous. Ps. 91:9, 10; Rev. 3:10; Ex. 8:22, 23.
  2. Other promises of protection. Isa. 28:17; 32:18, 19; 4:5, 6.
  3. God appeals to His people today to seek protection. Zeph. 2:1-3.

V. *Appeal.*
These seven last plagues are not of ordinary severity; nor are they just local. The whole world is involved in the final issue between worshiping God or the beast power. Repeated messages have foretold this destruction. Many signs have warned men not to ignore God's pleadings for salvation. Every individual will then understand the issues of the conflict between God and Satan and will have taken a positive stand for or against God. God's "strange act" of destruction will then be recognized as an act of love to redeem His obedient children from Satan's tyranny.

On whose side will *you* be found when these last plagues begin to fall? (On God's side, of course!) This solemnizes us, does it not? Let us bow before God, asking Him to impress us with the importance of this warning message and to help us to stand before Him at that time.

The True and the Apostate Church
(Advanced instruction for Catholics.)

I. *Church Compared to Woman—Pure or Fallen.*
   Jer. 6:2; 2 Cor. 11:2; Rev. 12:1-3; 17:1-6.

II. *The Church Pillar and Ground of Truth.* (1 Tim. 3:15; John 17:17.)
   1. Gospel church supports truth.
      a. Christ and church must agree on doctrine. Amos 3:3; John 15:10.
      b. Christ's Word, like Himself, is truth. John 14:6; 1:14.
      c. God's law is truth. Ps. 119:142.
   2. Apostate church departed from truth.
      a. "Cast down the truth to the ground." Dan. 8:12.
      b. Deceives; does not love or practice the truth. 2 Thess. 2:10, 12.

III. *Knowing True Church From False.*
   1. Pure church.
      a. Pure, loved of Christ. Rev. 12:1-3; Eph. 5:25.
      b. Love, fellowship, and obedience. 1 John 5:3; 1:7.
      c. Children taught of God. Isa. 54:13.
      d. Keep commandments; Spirit of prophecy. Rev. 12:17; 19:10.
      e. Dressed in Christ's righteousness. Rev. 19:8; Isa. 61:10.
      f. Crown of 12 stars—apostolic church. Rev. 12:2.
      g. Maintains high standard.
   2. Apostate church.
      a. Dressed in purple and scarlet. Rev. 17:4. Lacking Christ's righteousness Babylon wears her own dress of worldly pride and ambition. Isa. 59:6.
      b. Pride and violence. Rev. 17:6.
      c. Babylon and her children confused. Rev. 17:5.
      d. Unfaithful; adulterates truth, confuses Christians. Rev. 17:4; Matt. 15:9.

IV. *Judgment of Fallen Church.*
   1. "Come out"; her plagues in one day. Rev. 18:4-8.
   2. Her pride revealed. Rev. 18:16.

Prophetic Topics

3. Arts and pleasures fade. Rev. 18:22; 2 Tim. 3:4, 5.
4. Babylon's light becomes darkness. Rev. 18:23.

V. *Invitation to Join True Church.*
   1. An eternal, universal, commandment-keeping church. Heb. 12: 22, 23; Rev. 22:14; 14:12.
   2. True church invites all to prepare to meet Jesus. Rev. 22:14, 20.

VI. *Appeal.*
   To which church will you belong? Rev. 22:17.

Mrs. Henrietta Immergut.

God's Remnant Church

I. *God Has Always Had His Church.* (Acts 7:38; Eph. 5:23.)

II. *A Remnant Church in Every Crisis.*
   1. Examples:
      a. Noah. Gen. 7:1. Abraham. Gen. 12:1. Lot. Gen. 18:17-33.
      b. Israel. Rom. 9:27.
      c. New Testament remnant. Rom. 11:5.

III. *Characteristics of Remnant.*
   1. Remnant means last part.
      a. Noah last of his generation. Gen. 7:1.
      b. Israel a peculiar treasure. Ex. 19:5.
      c. Remnant called out of Babylon. Rev. 18:1-4.
   2. Remnant means small part.
      a. Lot's family. Gen. 19:15-17.
      b. Israel fewest of all people. Deut. 7:7.
      c. Noah and his family saved. 1 Peter 3:20.
      d. Few find true way. 1 John 4:4; Rev. 14:1; Matt. 7:14.
   3. Tests of God's remnant church.
      a. Agree with law and testimony. Isa. 8:16, 20.
      b. Keep commandments and have testimony of Jesus. Rev. 12:17; 19:10.
   4. God's last-day remnant. Isa. 11:10-12.
      a. No iniquity, lies, deceit. Zeph. 3:13.
      b. "Live soberly, righteously, and godly." Titus 2:12-14.
      c. Holy and without blemish, a glorious church. Eph. 5:27.
      d. Chosen generation, royal priesthood, holy nation, peculiar people. 1 Peter 2:9.
      e. No guile, without fault. Rev. 14:5.
   5. Message of last-day remnant. Rev. 14:6-11.
   6. Result of message. Rev. 14:12.

Addie Mae Kalar.

IV. *Remnant Church the 144,000.*
   Remnant sing a new song of redemption. Rev. 14:1-4.

V. *Appeal.*
   Having discovered God's faithful remnant church, are you now ready, Miss———, to join His true church in giving His messages of truth to the world before Jesus returns? We welcome you into our church and know that you will be very happy in our fellowship, etc. (Prayer.)

God's Plan for Israel

(For Anglo-Israelites, Dispensationalists, Zionists, etc.)

THE NAME

Israel means "a prince" of God, one who prevails with God. Gen. 32:27, 28.

The Lord said Israel should be the name of His people. I Kings 18:31.

The Lord commanded Israel to keep His law. 2 Kings 17:34.

The Lord said, "Israel is My son, My firstborn." Ex. 4:22.

Israel "shall dwell alone." Num. 23:9.

"The Lord hath spoken concerning Israel." Num. 10:29.

A true Israelite has no guile. John 1:47.

The Israel of God are those who have been born of God and thus become new creatures. Gal. 6:15, 16. They are the church of God in all ages—His true children. God has only one way of saving sinners, and only one people—Israel. One becomes an Israelite by being an overcomer, by prevailing with God to forgive his sins and accept him as His child.

Jacob is an example. Naturally, Jacob was full of guile, a deceiver; hence, his name, which means "a supplanter." He was shrewd and cunning in getting what he wanted. For many years this disposition caused himself and others much trouble, and sorrow, but in that night by Jabbok, as he struggled for his life with One who he thought was an enemy, Jacob realized his sin and gave it up forever.

Then the Lord said: Now you are Israel, a prince, a soldier of God; you must never be Jacob again. As Jesus said of Nathanael, "Behold an Israelite indeed, in whom is no guile," so it is said of the redeemed, the true Israel of God: "In their mouth was found no guile: for they are without fault before the throne of God." Rev. 14:5. The character of the true Israelite is open, frank, truthful, sincere. He is truly transparent.

God's Purpose for Israel

Israel is to be God's people forever. 2 Sam. 7:23, 24.
Earth was divided according to the number of Israel. Deut. 32:8.
To Israel were committed the oracles of God. Rom. 3:1, 2.
Israel receives the revelations of God in their fullness. Rom. 9:1-5.
A true teacher in Israel knows the mysteries of God. John 3:10.

The nation descended from Abraham, Isaac, and Jacob was called Israel. It was the church of God, and He intended, and desired that everyone in the nation should be an Israelite indeed; but many failed to perfect character. At times it seemed that they were not Israel but Jacob; but in the days of the worst apostasy there were always some who were true to God. At one time Elijah thought he was the only one, but God said He had still seven thousand. "The Lord knoweth them that are His."

Though true Israel is always a peculiar people and dwells alone, yet God meant Israel to be a light, a leader to all the heathen nations—to occupy among them the place of a first-born son in a family. They were to be a loving elder brother to all mankind, one who would invite them to share the blessings promised to Israel.

To Israel were revealed all the principles of the plan of salvation; therefore, its teachers should have been able to explain to the nations the plans and purposes of God. This the prophets and others did, and we have their teachings in the Old Testament.

True Israel

Not all are Israel that are called Israel. Rom. 9:6.
Only children of the promise are Israel. Verses 7, 8.
Israel is likened to an olive tree. Rom. 11:16, 17.
Some of the branches (Jews) were broken off. Verses 17-20.
A wild olive tree (Gentiles) was grafted into the root. Verse 17.
Gentiles should not boast. Verses 18-20.
Gentiles remain only if they continue faithful. Verses 21, 22.
Literal Israel (Jews) may be grafted in again. Verses 23-25.
"All Israel shall be saved." Verse 26.
Gentiles must become Israel to be saved. Eph. 2:11, 12.

At length Israel so far departed from God that He rejected them as a nation and accepted the Gentiles in their place; but the character of true Israel remained the same. The Lord has called Israel "a green olive tree, fair, and of goodly fruit." Jer. 11:16.

Paul uses this figure of speech to explain how a Gentile may become a part of Israel. Because of unbelief some of the original branches, the Jews, were broken off, and a wild olive branch, Gentiles, was grafted in to take their place. The root or trunk of the tree remains the same, so the new grafts partake of "the root and fatness of the olive tree." Thus the Gentiles receive a wonderful legacy of blessing, for to the Jews were given the law, the covenants, and the promises, especially of a Saviour from sin. Therefore, Gentiles who become Israelites should not boast or feel superior to the Jews, who were once Israelites. We should also be glad that the branches broken off, the Jews, may be grafted in again and become once more a part of true spiritual Israel. Thus "all Israel shall be saved"—those who comply with the plan of salvation, Jew or Gentile.

ADDITIONAL REFERENCES

Rom. 10:1-3
Rom. 10:11-13
Rom. 11:1-5
Rom. 11:6-16
Isa. 41:8-14
Gal. 6:16

Acts 28:17-29
Acts 13:44-48
Gen. 13:16
Gen. 26:4
Gen. 28:14
Jer. 11:16

ALMA E. McKIBBIN.

God's Promise to Israel Fulfilled

(For Anglo-Israelites, Dispensationalists, Zionists, etc.)

I. *Introduction.*

Gen. 12:1-3. Call to Abram.
Gen. 32:28. Name of Israel first given to Jacob.
Ex. 1:1-5. Later applied to his descendants.

II. *What Original Promises Were Made to Israel?*

1. On obedience and commandment keeping.
    a. Deut. 11:26, 27; 28:9, 12, 13. Temporal blessing.
    b. Jer. 17:24, 25. Jerusalem would stand forever.
2. Disobedience and commandment breaking. Deut. 11:28; 28:14, 15. Jerusalem must be destroyed. Jer. 17:27.

III. *What Resulted From Israel's Failure to Obey God?*

1. Prophecy of dispersion for disobedience.
    a. Eze. 23:28; 21:25-27.
    b. Jer. 25:8-11; 34:17; Deut. 28:58, 64-68.
2. Prophecy of separation of tribes and fulfillment.
    a. 1 Kings 11:29-33. (*ca.* 980 B.C.)
    b. 1 Kings 12:1-17. Israel (10 tribes) separated from Judah (2 tribes) *ca.* 975 B.C. Tribes continued until *ca.* 721 B.C.

Prophetic Topics

3. Prophecy of fulfillment of captivity of tribes.
   a. 2 Kings 17:13-18, 23. Israel (10 tribes) taken captive by Assyria, *ca.* 721 B.C.
   b. Jer. 25:1-4, 8-11; 2 Chron. 36:5, 6, 14-21. Judah (2 tribes) taken captive to Babylon *ca.* 606 B.C.
   All 12 tribes in Babylon—70 years captivity, about 606-536 B.C.
   NOTE.—It is accepted that the official "first year" of Nebuchadnezzar's reign began in 604 B.C., but archaeological finds show that he was reigning in the latter part of the year preceding. A Babylonian king's "first year" was the calendar year beginning on the new year's day (in the spring) following the accession (see Encyclopaedia Britannica, 1945 ed., vol. 5, p. 655). So 605 B.C. was the accession year of Nebuchadnezzar. This fits Daniel 1:1 and Jeremiah 25:1, and makes unnecessary the assumption of a two-year coregency of Nebuchadnezzar with his father, on which the 606 B.C. of older commentaries is based. 605-536 equals seventy years *inclusive,* as the Jews and other ancient peoples counted. (See editor's footnote in *Daniel and Revelation,* new edition, p. 19; for a fuller explanation see the Appendix A, part 1 in L. E. Froom's *Prophetic Faith of Our Fathers,* vol. I.)
   c. Promise to all 12 tribes in first year of captivity of return; its fulfillment. Jer. 30:3. (*ca.* 606 B.C.) Jer. 50:33-35.
      (1) Ezra 1:1-3. (536 B.C.)
      (2) Ezra 6:16, 17. (515 B.C.)
      (3) Ezra 8:35. (457 B.C.)
4. Prophecy of 70-week probation period for Jews and fulfillment. Dan. 9:24-27; Matt. 27:21-26, 50, 51; Acts 7:51-54, 57-59; 8:1-4; 13:46.
5. Final dispersion of the Jews was under Titus A.D. 70. Jer. 17:21-27; Deut. 28:64-68.

IV. *What Is Included in God's Repeated Call to Israel?*
1. Isa. 55:3-7; Rom. 10:21. Israel failed. They were disobedient and avaricious.
2. Israel—Jew and Gentile called through Christ.
   a. 1 Cor. 1:23, 24; Rom. 10:12. No difference—Jews and Greeks called.
   b. Rom. 11:11, 17-21, 23, 24. Salvation to Gentiles after Jews' fall.
   c. Gal. 3:6-9, 26-29; Gen. 26:4, 5. Children of faith now counted. Obedience required.
   d. Gal. 6:14-16; Rom. 2:28, 29. Not circumcision, but new creature.

V. *How Will the True Israel Be Gathered?*
   1. Isa. 11:11, 12; 43;5, 9. A remnant gathered from four corners of earth.
   2. Isa. 27:12, 13; Jer. 3:14. Gathered one by one.
   3. Rom. 9:24-28; Rev. 12:17. Remnant fulfills prophecy.

VI. *What Promises Are Then Fulfilled to the True Israel?*
   1. Gen. 32:28. True Israel an overcomer of all sin.
   2. Rom. 11:26, 27. In Christ all Israel saved.
   3. Rev. 21:7; 22:14. Overcomers are commandment keepers.

MARY E. SAXTON.

PART FOUR ★ CHAPTER TEN

Decision Lessons

There is great demand for various types of decision lessons which can be used by Bible instructors. Here are some very simple lessons, usable for the beginner in the Bible work. Not only the Sabbath truth but every progressive step in the Christian life presents tests and crises which call for forthright decision on the part of those who walk in advancing light. In an appealing way the apt Bible instructor learns to establish each point of truth as it is discussed with her reader. She helps the student of the Word to mark these personal decisions as milestones on the way to the full acceptance of God's revealed truth.

Just a Faith, or the Faith of Jesus?

The purpose of this study is to emphasize the need of the right kind of faith. Faith is more than a platitude; it is a saving transaction and involves our destiny. It must be the faith of Jesus!

Text: Rev. 14:12.

I. *Faith a Present Need.*
   1. "Shall He find faith on the earth?" Luke 18:8.
   2. Our faith now tested. 1 Peter 1:7; 4:12.
II. *What Is Faith? How Received?*
   1. Faith is believing. Heb. 11:1, 6.
   2. "Faith cometh by hearing." Rom. 10:17. "Hearing by the word of God."
   3. "To every man the measure of faith." Rom. 12:3.
   4. Faith "worketh by love." Gal. 5:6.
III. *Faith Accompanied by Works.*
   1. "Faith without works is dead." James 2:14-17, 26.
   2. "The devils also believe, and tremble." James 2:18, 19.
   3. "Be ye doers, . . . and not hearers only." James 1:22-24; Matt. 7:24-27.
IV. *Demonstration of True Faith.*
   1. Faith chapter. Examples of hearers and doers. Hebrews 11.
   2. Abraham showed his faith by obeying. James 2:21; Gen. 22:1-18.
   3. Rewarded according to our works. Rev. 22:12; Matt. 16:27.
   4. By works faith made perfect. James 2:22.
   5. Faith of Jesus requires obedience to commandments. Rev. 14:12.
V. *The Triumph of Faith.*
   1. "I have kept the faith." 2 Tim. 4:7; Rev. 14:12.
   2. Faith and salvation. 1 Peter 1:9.
   3. Our prayer: "Lord, Increase our faith." Luke 17:5.

MRS. THELMA A. SMITH.

Examining Our Faith

(Review of doctrinal points of our faith. Timely just before baptism.)

Text: 2 Cor. 13:5.

I. *Examining Ourselves in Light of Bible.*
   1. What description does God give of His people in the last days? Rev. 14:12, last part.
   2. To whom was this true faith given? Jude 3.
   3. Was this faith held by the church in Paul's day? Rom. 1:11, 12; Eph. 4:5.
   4. For what did Jesus commend His people when apostasy began to affect the church? Rev. 2:13.
   5. How were the deceptions of Satan to be resisted? 1 Peter 5:8, 9.

II. *Examining Our Christian Doctrines.*

Let us now examine ourselves to see whether we really have the faith of Jesus. Do we hold the points of faith as taught by Jesus? 2 Tim. 1:12.
1. Justification by faith. Gal. 2:16.
2. New birth in Christ. John 3:3-8.
3. Baptism by immersion. Matt. 3:13-17.
4. Imminent and visible coming of Jesus. Matt. 24:32, 33, 30.
5. Prophecies of Daniel and Revelation. Matt. 24:15; Rev. 22:7.
6. State of the dead and destruction of the wicked. John 11:11-14, 25; Matt. 10:28.
7. Perpetuity of the law. Matt. 5:17-19.
8. The true Sabbath. Luke 4:16; Mark 2:27, 28.
9. Health and dress reform. 3 John 2; 2 Cor. 6:16-18; 1 Tim. 2:9, 10.
10. Christian standards in reading and recreation. Rom. 12:2; 1 John 2:15-17.
11. Ordinance of humility and the Lord's supper. John 13:4-17; 1 Cor. 11:23-26.
12. World-wide missions and gospel support. Matt. 24:14; Mal. 3:10; Matt. 23:23.
13. Spiritual gifts. Eph. 4:11-15.

III. *Surrender to Jesus Means Obedience.*
1. What was the secret of Paul's life? Gal. 2:20.
2. What could he say at the close of his life? 2 Tim. 4:6-8.

IV. *Appeal.*

Let us accept the truth, the faith of Jesus. Will you determine today to be among those mentioned in Revelation 14:12?

FLORENCE KIMMEL.

Importance of Present Truth

Text: 2 Peter 1:12.

I. *Introduction.*

Our Bible study develops assurance that this wonderful Advent message is God's truth for this time. We want to believe the truth, but we often wonder just what is truth. This is the same question Pilate asked in John 18:38. It is the all-important question for each of us to settle. So we too ask, "What is truth?" Let us find the answer in God's Word. What is truth? The answer is, "Thy word is truth." John 17:17.

II. *Sanctification Through the Truth.*
1. God desires all to come to knowledge of truth. 1 Tim. 2:4.
2. Salvation and sanctification through belief of the truth. 2 Thess. 2:13; John 17:17.
3. Sanctification of the spirit embraces obedience. 1 Peter 1:22.
4. Obeying Bible truth indicates we are converted. 1 Peter 1:22, 23.

III. *What Is Present Truth?*
1. Urgency of truth.
    a. Peter admonishes to be established in present truth. 2 Peter 1:12.
    b. Abiding truth for every age:
        (1) God's *love* reaches all men.
        (2) God's *grace* saves all men.
        (3) Through Jesus all men may receive *salvation*.
2. Present truth has a time limit.
    a. Pertinence of Noah's teaching of the coming flood now past; was extremely important in Noah's time.
    b. Once timely, destruction of Nineveh preached by Jonah; now past truth.
    c. John's message fulfilled in Christ's day.
        (1) John bore witness of Christ. John 1:4, 6, 7.
        (2) Voice in the wilderness: "As said the prophet Esaias." John 1:23.
        (3) John knew the prophecies concerning his time. Today we must understand present truth. 2 Peter 1:12.
3. God's special message is present truth for our time.
    a. A threefold message of present truth today. Rev. 14:6-11.
    b. Points of message:
        (1) Jesus' second coming.
        (2) World to keep God's broken law.
        (3) Judgment-hour alarm.
        (4) Babylon's lawbreaking is idolatry.

IV. *Accepting Present Truth Message.*
1. "Thy word have I hid in mine heart." Ps. 119:11.
2. "I have chosen the way of truth." Ps. 119:30.
3. "Obeying the truth." 1 Peter 1:22.
4. "Truth . . . endureth for ever." Ps. 117:2.
5. "His truth shall be thy shield." Ps. 91:4.

V. *Appeal.*
Present truth must not be ignored; it awaits our acceptance. Its urgency becomes a life-or-death message deciding our eternal destiny. (Close with earnest prayer.)   MRS. MARIE SCHMIDT.

Our Responsibility to Bible Truth

I. *To the Law and Testimony.*
   What is the test of truth? Isa. 8:20.
II. *New Light and Its Responsibility.*
   1. What must be our relation to new light? John 12:36; James 4:17.
   2. For what are we held accountable? John 9:41; 15:22.
   3. Why will some people neglect studying the Bible? John 3:20, 21.
   4. How is new light revealed? Prov. 4:18, 19; John 16:12, 13.
   5. Where will this light be found? Ps. 119:105.
III. *True and False Teachers.*
   1. How does God teach us His way? Isa. 28:9, 10, 13.
   2. What description of the prophet fits into our day? Jer. 5:30, 31.
   3. How should we regard these false teachers? Jer. 23:16, 17, 20-32; Isa. 48:17, 18.
IV. *The Reward of Truth.*
   1. What is promised to those who obey? John 14:15, 16; Acts 5:32.
   2. What is the Christian's greatest joy? 1 John 1:4-7.
   3. What may follow our acceptance of new light? Heb. 10:32, 33.
   4. What is the final reward of a sound faith? Heb. 10:38, 39.

ETHEL MARIE HULL.

Walking in the Light

I. *The Privilege of Seeing New Light.*
   1. "In Thy light shall we see light." Ps. 36:9.
   2. "Light is sown for the righteous." Ps. 97:11.
II. *Light Brings Personal Responsibility.*
   1. Action for God.
      a. Light brings salvation or condemnation. John 3:19, 21.
      b. Light must be accepted. John 9:41; 15:22; Acts 26:18.
      c. Light may be for a limited period of time. John 12:35, 36.
   2. Following the light.
      a. The children of truth hear His voice. John 18:37; 15:10.
      b. They follow in the path of light. Prov. 4:18.
      c. Failing to walk in light brings spiritual darkness. Eph. 5:8; John 12:35.
   3. Why light is rejected.
      a. Men believe not God. John 6:64, 66.
      b. Not willing to do God's will. Matt. 7:21.
      c. Look to their leaders and teachers. John 7:26, 48.
      d. Follow traditions instead of God's Word. Matt. 15:9, 13.
      e. Will not submit to God's way of life. Matt. 23:37, 38; 7:14.

III. *Appeal.*
Let us believe in the light while it shines on our pathway. Delay is too serious. Each day must find us walking in all God's revealed light. Will you, Mr. and Mrs.———, walk in the new light He has given you? (Prayer for heavenly guidance.)

Children of Obedience and Disobedience

INTRODUCTION: Stress conflict between truth and error. Present issue of obedience is the Sabbath. No neutral ground.

Text: Matt. 13:38.

I. *Two Distinct Classes.*
  1. Since days of creation two families. Gen. 6:1, 2.
  2. Rebellious tendencies of man. Isa. 1:2.
  3. Satan the archrebel. John 8:44.
  4. Rebellion of wicked spirits. Eph. 6:12.
  5. God of this world blinds minds. 2 Cor. 4:4.
  6. Satan works through children of disobedience. Eph. 2:2, 3.
  7. "Will not hear." Isa. 30:1, 9.
  8. Are in bondage. Gal. 4:3.
  9. Are children of death. Ps. 102:19, 20.

II. *How Men Become Sons of God.*
  1. By receiving Him. John 1:12.
  2. By joining Jesus' family. Eph. 3:14, 15.

III. *Characteristics of Obedient Children.*
  1. If sheep, hear His voice. John 10:27, 28.
  2. Follow God as dear children. Eph. 5:1.
  3. Walk in truth. 3 John 4.
  4. Jesus is the truth. John 14:6.
  5. His law is truth. Ps. 119:142.
  6. Love Him, keep commandments. John 14:15.

IV. *Reward of Obedient Children.*
  1. "Eye hath not seen." 1 Cor. 2:9.
  2. See Jesus and be like Him. 1 John 3:1, 2.
  3. Reign with Christ eternally. Dan. 7:27.

MRS. ELIZABETH BECK.

Deciding Now for Christ

INTRODUCTION: Emphasize that Satan's tools against truth's acceptance are indifference and procrastination. God's Word warns us to act in favor of truth.

Text: 1 Kings 18:21. "How long halt ye?"

I. *The Problem of a Conflict.*
   1. "Double minded man is unstable." James 1:8.
   2. "No man can serve two masters." Matt. 6:24.

II. *Responsibility of Light.*
   1. Path of just is a shining light. Prov. 4:18.
   2. Light rejected becomes darkness. John 12:35, 36.
   3. By waiting we walk in darkness. Isa. 59:9; John 3:19-21.
   4. Light rejected invites deception. 2 Thess. 2:10-12.

III. *Importance of Prompt Obedience.*
   1. If we sin willfully, no more sacrifice. Heb. 10:26, 27.
   2. Prayer then an abomination. Prov. 28:9.

IV. *Responding to Present Truth.*
   1. "Consecrate yourselves to day to the Lord." Ex. 32:29.
   2. "Turn ye ... now." Jer. 25:5.
   3. "Return ye now." Jer. 35:15.
   4. "To day, ... hear His voice." Heb. 3:7, 8, 13.

V. *Uncertainty of the Future.*
   1. "Ye know not what shall be on the morrow." James 4:13-17.
   2. Dead cannot hope for truth. Isa. 38:18.
   3. "Seek ye the Lord while He may be found." Isa. 55:6.

VI. *Appeal.*
   "Choose you *this day*." Joshua 24:15.   Mrs. Thelma A. Smith.

Importance of Obedience

I. *The Two Contending Powers.*
   1. How do we show whose servants we are? Rom. 6:16.
   2. What is real proof of love to God? John 14:15; 1 John 2:3-6.
   3. Bible examples—why written? 1 Cor. 10:11.
      a. Saul. 1 Sam. 15:1-23.
      b. Religious leaders. Eze. 22:26, 28.
   4. How had the scribes and Pharisees reasoned? Matt. 15:3-9. (Attempted to change the fifth commandment by their traditions.)
   5. What did Christ say to them? Mark 7:9, 13. (Christ would surely say this today to those who are substituting a traditional sabbath in place of the Sabbath of the fourth commandment.)
   6. What prevented some of the leaders in Christ's day from accepting Him as the Messiah? John 12:42, 43. (This same reason prevents some today from fully obeying God.)

II. *Test of Obedience.*
 1. Should popular practice decide our relationship to the truths of God's Word? 1 Cor. 1:26-29; Matt. 7:13, 14.
 2. Should we allow anyone or anything to stand in the way of our obeying God? Matt. 10:37, 38; Acts 5:29.
 3. How does Christ compare those who obey Him with those who do not? Luke 6:46-49; Matt. 7:21.
 4. What promise does Jesus make to those who truly serve Him? Matt. 6:31-33. (Faith in God is needed. God never asks the impossible. "Now unto Him that is able to do exceeding abundantly above all that we ask or think, according to the power that worketh in us." Eph. 3:20. He said to Israel at the Red Sea, "Go forward!")

III. *Danger of Delay.*
 1. We cannot say no to God with safety.
  a. Awaiting a convenient season. Acts 24:25.
  b. Herod did "many things," but not *all* were what God wanted.
  c. "What shall it profit?" Mark 8:36. (What does a man gain in the end if he allows his business or church friends to stand between him and God? There is a time coming when he would gladly give every dollar he had ever earned if he could just have one more chance to obey God. Isa. 2:19-21.)
 2. What does God say of the one who knows and does not do His will? James 4:17; John 15:22; Heb. 10:26, 27.
 3. Why is it always dangerous to delay?
  a. The uncertainty of life.
  b. Danger of grieving away the Holy Spirit. ("Walk while ye have the light, lest darkness come upon you: for he that walketh in darkness knoweth not whither he goeth." John 12:35. After a light has been in a room and then extinguished, the darkness is greater than before. See 2 Thess. 2:9-11.)
 4. What will some be saying when it is too late? Jer. 8:20.

IV. *Blessing of Obedience.*
 Upon whom is God's blessing pronounced? Luke 11:28; Rev. 22:14.

V. *Appeal.*
 What excuse can we offer to God in that day? Excuses that seem plausible *now* will be flimsy *then*. Whenever we face a decision between truth and error we are at the crossroads of life, and our eternal destiny depends upon the path we choose. Let us surrender all to God and obey Him implicitly.   LILLIAN SANIFF.

Is God Particular?

Text: Isa. 28:17.

I. *Introduction.*
   1. Governments are particular. Income tax paid to the dollar. Rationing boards particular about orders to the public. Banks particular about checks we write. Highway patrol particular about our speed limit.
   2. God particular about His commandments. 1 John 3:4.
   3. Gave Son to die because He could not condone sin. John 3:16; 1 John 2:2.
   4. Present tendency to be indifferent to our own destruction.

II. *Examples Proving God Too Is Particular.*
   1. Eden lost because of disobedience. Gen. 2:16-19, 24.
   2. Cain's indifference caused his rejection. Gen. 4; Heb. 11:4.
   3. Mighty men of renown rejected in Noah's day. Gen. 6:4; 2 Peter 2:5; Luke 17:26, 27.
   4. Sodom and Gomorrah destroyed because of disobedience. 2 Peter 2:6; Luke 17:28, 29.
   5. Nadab and Abihu perished because of strange fire. Lev. 10:1, 2. ("What difference does it make?" preacher's boys reasoned.)
   6. Saul sadly learned God was very particular. 1 Sam. 15:22; 31:4.
   7. Lessons from Uzzah and the ark. 2 Sam. 6:6, 7; Num. 4:15-20; 7:9. Even an emergency does not excuse disobedience.
   8. Naaman to dip seven times in river. 2 Kings 5:13-15.
   9. Judas disobeyed to gain 30 pieces of silver. Acts 1:25; Matt. 27:3-10.
   10. Ananias and Sapphira disobeyed and perished. Acts 5.

III. *Acceptance of New Light Always Important.*
   1. Even good men like Cornelius needed added light. Acts 10.
   2. Light for limited period only. John 12:35, 36.
   3. Sabbath God's special light in last days. Rev. 14:12; 12:17; Ex. 20:8-11.
   4. Following majority is unsafe reasoning. Ex. 23:2; Matt. 7:13, 14.
   5. Even leaders not always safe guides. John 12:42, 43; Matt. 15:3-9.
   6. Must look to God, not man. Eze. 14:14; John 21:21, 22.
   7. Danger of procrastination. Acts 24:25.

IV. *Blessing of Obeying God's Word.*
   "Blessed are they that *hear* the word of God, and *keep* it." Luke 11:28. (Earnestly appeal to walk in all revealed truth. Close with prayer.)

Obedience and Life
or
Disobedience and Death

APPROACH: Weak faith, and lack of the right faith, a present-day danger. Unbelief another of Satan's strong tools to discourage Christian in stepping out on God's promises. Satan pictures problems and disasters that might result from stepping out on Bible faith. He worries us with doubt and fear. How can we meet our greatest enemy?

I. *Warnings Against Unbelief.*
   1. Israel's sin of unbelief. Heb. 3:17-19.
   2. Similar danger today. Heb. 4:1, 11.
   3. Unbelief separates from God. Heb. 3:12.
   4. Jews rejected because of unbelief. Rom. 11:19, 20.

II. *Victory Through Faith.*
   1. Our only hope. Heb. 3:14; Rom. 11:20, last part.
   2. "Believe in the Lord . . . , so shall ye be established." 2 Chron. 20:20, last part.
   "Unbelief whispers, 'Let us wait till the obstructions are removed, and we can see our way clearly;' but faith courageously urges an advance, hoping all things, believing all things." —E. G. WHITE, PP 290.

III. *Believe, Obey, Rest.*
   1. Rest and peace promised. Belief brings rest to the heart, and peace of mind. Heb. 4:3; Isa. 48:18.
   2. "Confidence . . . hath great recompence of reward." Heb. 10:35-37.
   3. Perfect peace result of trusting God. Isa. 26:3.
   4. Just shall live by faith. Heb. 10:38.

IV. *Two Ways of Decision.*
   1. Life or death. Jer. 21:8; Deut. 30:15; Rom. 6:23.
   2. Obedience or disobedience. Heb. 10:38, 39.
   3. God's Word must influence our choice. Prov. 14:12.

V. *Appeal.*
   What a privilege to truly believe God! Hebrews 10:35-39 is God's message to us today. Let us believe that God is able to give us a conquering faith. Then let us sweetly rest in Him knowing that "the just shall live by faith." VINNIE GOODNER.

Loyalty and Obedience

I. *Serving God by Choice.*
   1. Man placed on probation. Gen. 2:16, 17.
      The tree of knowledge had been made a test of Adam and Eve's obedience and their love for God. Without some test there would have been no development of character. God desired obedience prompted by their love to Him. He did not force the will but had created them capable of appreciating His wisdom and love.
   2. God has given all men the freedom of choice. Joshua 24:14.
   3. "Choose life." Deut. 30:19; 11:26-28.

II. *God Warns Against Disobedience.*
   1. Israel failed because of unbelief. (Margin of Heb. 4:11. "Unbelief" is "disobedience.") Heb. 3:17-19.
   2. Disobedience prevented Israelites' entering Canaan. Joshua 5:6.
   3. God's Word not "mixed with faith." Heb. 4:2.
   4. We are warned not to fail as did Israel. Heb. 4:1.

III. *Obedience Determines Loyalty to God.*
   1. "To whom ye yield yourselves." Rom. 6:16.
   2. Conquering all obstacles by obedient faith. 1 John 5:3, 4.
   3. Faith more than mere belief, requires works. James 2:14-24.
   4. "Faith which worketh by love." Gal. 5:6.
   5. Saul's partial obedience not genuine faith. 1 Sam. 15:10-24.
   6. Disobedient prophets unsafe guides. Deut. 13:1-4.
   7. Uzzah perished beside the ark because of disobedience. 2 Sam. 6:6, 7; Num. 4:15.
   8. Disobedience instigated by Satan. Eph. 2:1, 2.

IV. *Truth, Like Faith, Requires Obedience.*
   1. Living faith is known by its works. James 4:17.
   2. Truth knows no compromise or disguise. Must be obeyed. John 15:22; 9:40, 41.
   3. Light spurned becomes darkness. John 12:36-46.
   4. Rejection of light opens way for great delusions. 2 Thess. 2:9-12.
   5. Consequences of disobedience must be met in the judgment. Heb. 10:26, 27; Rom. 14:10.

V. *Love Prompts Obedience, and Conquers.*
   1. Love and obedience inseparable. John 14:15, 21.
   2. Must love God above all else. Luke 14:26, 27, 33.
   3. God will sustain His faithful children. Matt. 6:24-34; Isa. 41:10.
   4. Joyous reward of obedient. Rev. 22:14.
      (Appeal and prayer.)

God's Last Message and the Remnant Church

(This study, used by an evangelist in a community Bible school, has real point when truth needs to be reviewed.)

I. *A Special Preparatory Message Sounded in All the World Before Christ Comes.*
   1. The everlasting gospel in setting of judgment-hour message. Matt. 24:14; Rev. 14:6, 7; Dan. 8:13, 14.
   2. Warning against beast worship. Invitation to accept seal of God. Rev. 14:9-12; 13:15-18; 7:1-4; 14:1.
   3. It will call for obedience to God's commandments. Rev. 12:17; 3:14-18; James 2:10.

II. *Sabbath of God Rallying Truth for Remnant Church.*
   1. It will be an Elijah message. Mal. 4:5, 6; Matt. 17:10-13; Luke 1:17.
   2. Elijah's message emphasized obedience. 1 Kings 18:17, 18, 20, 21.
   3. Remnant church will keep all God's commandments including Sabbath. Isa. 56:1, 2; 58:12-14; Heb. 9:28.
   4. Keeping of commandments passport to city of God. Rev. 14:12; 22:14.
   5. Three angels' messages of Revelation 14 strikingly bring to view God's last efforts to save the world from complete rebellion and ruin. The first is announcement of beginning of investigative judgment, due in 1844. The second follows quickly. Confusion and "Babel" will fill the church and the world. Then follows terrible warning against the beast, his mark, and his image. We can only resist this mark by accepting God's seal, the Sabbath.

E. L. CARDEY.

Fleeing Out of Babylon

(Parallels between ancient and modern Babylon. Both incurable. This lesson should bring conviction to come out of Babylon without delay.)

I. *God's People Had to Flee Ancient Babylon.*
   1. Fled Babylon to worship God.
      a. Fleeing meant deliverance from Babylon's cup of iniquity. Jer. 51:6, 7.
      b. Babylon's sins had become incurable. Jer. 51:53, 56, 57, 62.
      c. She had "striven against the Lord." Jer. 50:24.
      d. Sun worship caused her to forget God. Eze. 8:16.

        e. A standard had been set up against Baal. Jer. 50:2.
        f. God's people left Babylon to build Zion. Jer. 51:8, 10.
        g. Came out willingly. Jer. 50:4-6.
        h. Entered into "a perpetual covenant" with God. Jer. 50:5.
        i. Could not remain on neutral ground. Jer. 51:50.
    2. Called out by a message.
        a. The trumpet call had rallied Israel to God's standard. Jer. 51:27, 12.
        b. God appointed the time and His "shepherd." Jer. 50:44.
        c. Babylon's "walls" offered no protection to God's people. Jer. 51:44, 58.
        d. They fled to escape punishment. Jer. 51:44, 45.
        e. A remnant responded to the message. Jer. 50:20.

II. *We Must Today Flee From Modern Babylon.*
    1. The last-day apostasy.
        a. Modern Babylon has confused world with false doctrines. Rev. 14:8; 18:1-4; 17:4, 5.
        b. She has wealth, display, and influence. Rev. 18:12, 13, 22, 23.
        c. Supported by many nations. Rev. 17:1-5; 18:23.
        d. Persecutes God's children who turn from her. Rev. 17:6; 18:20, 24.
    2. Heeding God's last message against Babylon.
        a. Message to flee Babylon follows judgment-hour message. Rev. 14:6-8.
        b. The call comes to His faithful children. Isa. 58:1-3.
        c. Sabbath truth is associated with call to flee Babylon. Rev. 14:8-11.
        d. The message brings a true Sabbath reform. Isa. 58:12, 13.
        e. It precedes the seven last plagues. Rev. 18:4, 8.
        f. A remnant will heed the warning message. Rev. 12:17; 14:12.
        g. Babylon to be utterly destroyed. Rev. 16:19; 18:21.

III. *Appeal to Leave Babylon Immediately.*
Let us not "stand still," but flee in haste to obey all God's commandments and to escape modern Babylon's wrath. Jer. 51:6, 50; Rev. 18:4; Ps. 119:59, 60.

Church Membership and Attendance

I. *A Reformatory Message.*
    1. Call out of Babylon. Rev. 18:1-4; 14:8.
    2. To unite with remnant church. Deut. 6:23; Rev. 12:17; 14:12.
    3. Entrance into church by baptism. 1 Cor. 12:13; Rom. 6:4.

II. *Church Membership Important.*
   1. Christ is head of His church. Rev. 1:13, 20; Col. 1:18; Eph. 5:23.
   2. Joining His spiritual body. 1 Cor. 12:14, 18-20; John 15:1, 2.
   3. Church has last message for world. Matt. 24:14; Rev. 14:6-12.
   4. Church members to give message. Ps. 68:11.
   5. Accepting Christ includes joining His church. Acts 5:14; 2:41, 47.
   6. Growth only when connected with His body. John 15:5.
III. *Fellowship With the Children of Light.*
   1. Walking in the light provides fellowship. 1 John 1:7; 1 Peter 1:22, 23.
   2. Symbol of fellowship—right hand of welcome. Gal. 2:9.
   3. God recognizes fellowship of commandment keepers. Rev. 14:12.
   4. Admonition to attend church regularly. Heb. 10:25.
IV. *Blessings of Church Membership.*
   1. God loves gates of Zion. Ps. 87:1-3.
   2. Members built into His spiritual house. Eph. 2:19-22.
   3. Church provides cleansing and protection from error. Eph. 5:27; 4:11-16; Acts 27:31.
V. *Appeal.*
   Christ has told us in His Word where His true church may be found. Rev. 14:12; 12:17. He regularly meets with His commandment-keeping children. Luke 4:16. He is pleased when we honor His holy day. Mark 2:28. How soon are you planning to be baptized and become a member of Christ's remnant church? Since this is a most serious question, it never pays to delay our membership. Will you now declare your intentions to do so by signing this beautiful covenant? (Have Baptismal Covenant on hand.)
VI. *Additional Proofs.*
   1. Christ recognized church of His day. John 2:16; Matt. 18:15-18.
   2. New Testament believers had church organization.
      a. Met in houses. 1 Cor. 16:19; Col. 4:15.
      b. Called flock of God. Acts 20:27, 28; Luke 12:32.
      c. Churches organized in Judaea. 1 Thess. 2:13, 14.
      d. Large church council at Jerusalem. Acts 14:27.

Attitudes Toward Bible Truth
(Based on New Testament texts.)

Text: Matt. 13:16.

I. *Purpose of Christ's Parables.*
   1. To impart heavenly truths. Matt. 13:35, 43.
   2. Obviates tendency to be indifferent to truth. Matt. 13:13-15.

II. *Lessons From the Gospel Sower.*
   1. Seed by wayside. Matt. 13:4, 19, 24, 25.
      a. Seed is Word. 1 Peter 1:23.
      b. God desires to plant truth in heart. Ps. 51:6; Prov. 23:26.
      c. Satan snatches away good seed. Matt. 13:24, 25.
      d. Satan's tools:
         (1) Unbelief. Matt. 13:58.
         (2) Obscuring light. 2 Cor. 4:4.
         (3) Persecution. Matt. 24:9, 10.
   2. Seed on stony ground. Matt. 13:5, 20, 21.
      a. Hardness of heart. John 6:60, 61.
      b. No depth of growth.
      c. Tribulation discourages many. Matt. 5:10-12.
   3. Seed among thorns. Matt. 13:7, 22.
      a. Cares choke gospel seed. Luke 21:34; Matt. 6:25-34.
      b. Worldly riches. Matt. 19:21-24.
   4. Seed on good ground. Matt. 13:8, 23.
      a. As one who heareth Word. Rev. 1:3.
      b. "Understandeth it." Luke 24:44, 45.
      c. "Bring forth fruit." John 15:16.

III. *Lessons From Wheat and Tares.* (Matt. 13:24-30.)
   1. Wheat and tares grow together.
   2. Good seed sown by Christ. Matt. 13:37.
   3. Unbelief and traditions sown by Satan. Matt. 15:9, 13.
   4. Harvest will reveal true nature of seed. Matt. 13:37-43; 7:21-24.

IV. *Lessons From Mustard Seed, Leaven.*
   1. Faith as mustard seed, may be small at beginning. Matt. 13:31, 32.
   2. Faith as leaven, works inconspicuously. Matt. 13:33.
   3. It comes by hearing Word. Rom. 10:17.
   4. Why some doubted in Christ's day. John 5:39, 40; 7:48.
   5. Faith is most necessary in our day. Luke 18:8.

V. *Lessons From Pearl of Great Price.* (Matt. 13:44-46.)
   1. Diligent searching secures God's treasure.
   2. Requires all to gain eternal life.

Day of Salvation Now
(To meet second-chance confusion.)

Text: 2 Cor. 6:1, 2.

I. *What Is Man's Condition in This Life?*
   1. He is born in sin. Ps. 51:5.

Decision Lessons

   2. Comes short of glory of God. Rom. 3:23.
   3. Must die for his sins. Rom. 6:23; Eze. 18:4.
II. *What Is God's Plan for the Sinner?*
   1. God has no pleasure in death of wicked. Eze. 18:23.
   2. God wills to save him. Isa. 43:25; 44:22.
   3. God saves through Jesus Christ. Luke 19:10.
   4. Saves freely by His grace. Rom. 3:24.
III. *When Will the Sinner Be Saved?*
   1. When he recognizes his condition as sinner. Luke 18:13.
   2. When he confesses his guilt. 1 John 1:7-9. Prov. 28:13.
   3. When he believes in the Saviour. Rom. 3:22.
   4. Before he dies. Eze. 18:23.
IV. *Will There Be Another Chance to Be Saved?*
   1. This life only chance for salvation. 2 Cor. 6:1, 2.
   2. After death no more saving. Eccl. 9:5; Isa. 38:17, 18.
   3. Neither after the resurrection. John 5:28, 29.
   4. No more chance during millennium. Rev. 20:4.
   5. After millennium, resurrection of wicked and second death. Rev. 20:4, 11-15.
   6. Only those who are saved now live eternally. Rev. 22:14, 15; Dan. 7:27.
V. *Appeal.*
   Come to Jesus *today;* let Him save you *now.* John 3:16.

Will Sinners Have a Second Chance?

I. *All Men Given Opportunity for Salvation.*
   1. Through Adam's transgression death passed upon all. Rom. 5:12.
   2. Death is an enemy all want to escape. 1 Cor. 15:26.
   3. In Christ all made alive. 1 Cor. 15:22; 1 John 5:11, 12.
   4. He lighteth every man. John 1:9.
   5. His salvation appears to all. Titus 2:11-13.
   6. No other way to be saved. Acts 4:12.
II. *The Judgment Follows This Life.*
   1. Judgment is as certain as death. Heb. 9:27.
   2. All appear before the judgment seat. 2 Cor. 5:10; Eccl. 11:9.
   3. Investigative judgment in heaven before Christ appears. Rev. 22:11, 12.
III. *God Desires Eternal Life for All.*
   1. No pleasure in death of wicked. Eze. 33:8, 9, 11, 15-19; 18:31, 33; 33:11.

2. Turning from sin to righteousness means life. 1 Peter 3:10-12.
  3. Continuing in iniquity results in death. Eze. 33:8, 9; Rom. 2:5, 6; Prov. 6:12, 15.
  4. God pays fair wages for the way man lives. Rom. 6:23.
IV. *Our Opportunity for Salvation Only in This Life.*
  1. No other opportunity after life. Eccl. 9:4-6, 10.
  2. "Seek ye the Lord while He may be found." Isa. 55:6, 7.
  3. Today and now the accepted time. Heb. 4:7; 2 Cor. 6:2.
  4. "Before the *decree bring forth.*" Zeph. 2:1-3.
     a. Divine decree settles each one's destiny. Rev. 22:11, 12.
     b. "The harvest is passed, the summer is ended." Jer. 8:20; Rev. 14:15-19; Matt. 13:37-43.
V. *What About the Heathen?* (Use only if necessary.)
  1. "The Gentiles, which have not the law, do by nature the things contained in the law, . . . are a law unto themselves." Rom. 2:14.
  2. God considers where a man is born. Ps. 87:4-6.
  3. Even the heathen without excuse. See creative works. Rom. 1:20.
  4. There are righteous heathen (obedient as far as they know). Jesus will tell them their first gospel story. Zech. 13:6. (See *The Desire of Ages,* p. 638.)
  5. The wicked discerned by their disobedience. Lev. 5:17; 4:27, 28; Luke 12:47, 48. (Disobedient to principles of God's law in relation to fellow men.)
VI. *Gracious Invitation to All.*
  1. The Lord not willing any perish. 2 Peter 3:9.
  2. "*Whosoever will,* let him take of the water of life." Rev. 22:17.

ABBIE DUNN.

The "Second Chance" Mirage
(To clear up confusion.)

I. *Introduction.*
  1. Illustration: Traveler in desert. Thirsty and tired, sees lake on horizon. Turns from his course toward lake. Expends all energy to get there. Finds it only a mirage. Had been traveling in right direction, but turned off because mirage seemed shorter and easier way to quench thirst; realizes he has been deceived by not following his compass.
  2. Last-day prophecy. 2 Tim. 4:3, 4.
     a. Some will not endure sound doctrine.
     b. They will seek smooth, pleasing doctrines.
     c. Finally turn away from truth to fables.

3. The religious world today is filled with *contradictory doctrines*, each claiming to be the true way of salvation. Fables, like mirages, are pleasant, but very deceiving and dangerous.
4. Of all doctrines preached today, doctrine of "second chance" most popular. Accepted by many sincere people. Does Bible teach a second chance for salvation?
   a. Second chance in some future time? During the millennium for world conversion?
   b. Second chance after death?

II. *Is There a Second Chance During the Millennium?*
   1. Millennium (1,000-year period) begins with resurrection of righteous. Rev. 20:4-6.
   2. Resurrection of righteous at second coming of Christ. 1 Thess. 4:16, 17.
   3. Jesus does not usher in a millennium of second chance so all will be saved. Rewards every man according to his works. Rev. 22:12.
   4. All chances of salvation forever past just before Jesus comes. Rev. 22:11.
   5. *No* second chance during millennium.

III. *Is There Hope of Second Chance After Death?*
   1. Isa. 38:18, 19.
      a. Dead cannot hope to learn God's truths. Too late.
      b. Life only presents opportunity to be saved.
   2. John 5:28, 29.
      a. Evil nature not changed during death.
      b. Jesus says evildoers come forth at resurrection of damnation.
   3. Eccl. 11:9.
      a. Many now live in pleasure, depending on a second chance after death.
      b. God says, "For all these things God will bring thee into judgment."
      c. The judgment decides our eternal destiny.

IV. *Can Last Opportunity of Salvation Now Be Lost?*
   1. By resisting the Holy Spirit we commit the unpardonable sin. Matt. 12:31, 32.
   2. Heb. 10:26, 27.
      a. No hope for one who knows truth and willfully continues in sin.
      b. No second chance. Only judgment and punishment.

V. *What Is the Future of Wicked After This Life?*
  1. Wicked will be destroyed. Ps. 145:20.
  2. Wages of sin is the second *death,* not second chance. Rom. 6:23.
  3. 2 Thess. 2:8-12.
      a. Those who fail to receive truth in this life consumed by brightness of His coming.
      b. The "second chance" a deceptive mirage that will fade away when Jesus comes.
  4. Eze. 18:23, 30-32.
      a. Lord has no pleasure in death of wicked.
      b. Wicked not to wait for second chance but turn from sin today.
      c. Iniquity of wicked will be their ruin.
  5. Mark 16:15, 16.
      a. If second chance in the future, why preach the gospel today?
      b. He that believeth not "shall be damned." Does that sound like a second chance?

VI. *Appeal.*
  1. 1 Peter 1:22, 23.
      a. Purified only by obeying truth of His Word.
      b. Important to study His Word.
  2. Must live righteously in this world if we expect to live with Jesus hereafter. Titus 2:11-13.
  3. There is no escape if we now neglect salvation. Heb. 2:3.
  4. *Now* is the day of salvation! 2 Cor. 6:2.

Mrs. Catherine Lebedoff.

Scripture or Tradition?
(For Catholics.)

Text: Ps. 119:30-38.

I. *God's Way—Scriptural Truth.*
  1. Faith. Heb. 11:6.
  2. New birth. John 3:5.
  3. Confession to God. Acts 2:38.
  4. Baptism. Mark 16:15, 16.
  5. God's Word—the Bible. Ps. 119:105.
  6. God's law. Rom. 3:31.
  7. Love. 1 John 4:8, 16.
  8. Tithing. Matt. 23:23.
  9. Sabbath. Mark 2:27.
  10. Spirit of prophecy. Rev. 12:17; 19:10.
  11. Sanctuary. Ex. 25.

12. Health reform. 1 Cor. 10:31.
13. Reward at resurrection. John 6:39.
14. Life in Christ. 1 John 5:12.
15. Feet washing. John 13.
16. Lord's supper. 1 Cor. 11:23-26.
17. Annihilation. Rom. 6:23.
18. New earth. 2 Peter 3:13.

II. *Rome's Way—Tradition, Apostasy.*
 1. Human works; penances.
 2. Infant baptism.
 3. Auricular confession.
 4. Sprinkling.
 5. Tradition.
 6. Tradition. dogma.
 7. Intolerance; persecution.
 8. State offices; bazaars, etc.
 9. Sunday; holidays of church.
 10. Church officials speak.
 11. Rome, St. Peters, the church.
 12. No restrictions in diet.
 13. Reward at death.
 14. Natural immortality.
 15. Holy water.
 16. Forgiveness through mass.
 17. Purgatory; everlasting punishment.
 18. Heaven or hell.

III. *Choosing to Follow Truth.*
 1. Prov. 7:24-27. "Go not astray in her paths."
 2. John 17:17. Being sanctified by truth of Scripture.
 3. 2 Thess. 2:3-13. Guard against deceptions of apostate church.
 4. Rev. 21:27; 22:12-15. Deceptions lead to destruction, not life.
 5. Rev. 14:12. God's saints are commandment keepers.
 6. Rev. 22:14. Only obedient enter Holy City.

The Reward of Forsaking All

I. *Accepting Christ's Invitation.*
 1. Parable of great supper. Luke 14:16-27.
 2. Christ's warning. Luke 14:33.

II. *Gospel Invitation Requires Self-denial.*
 1. Jesus was willing to leave heaven for us. John 3:16; Matt. 26:38-44; 27:46.

    2. Abraham left his kindred. Gen. 12:1, 4.
    3. Moses chose to suffer affliction with people of God. Heb. 11:24, 25.
    4. Paul's testimony: "I count *all things* but loss." Phil. 3:4-8.
III. *No Sacrifice Too Great.*
    1. "Let him deny himself." Luke 9:23-26.
    2. Loveth father or mother more than Christ. Matt. 10:34-38.
    3. "What is a man profited?" Matt. 16:24-26.
    4. "Left all . . . and followed Him." Luke 5:11, 27, 28.
IV. *Counting the Cost.*
    1. Through much tribulation enter kingdom. Acts 14:22.
    2. Those who have sacrificed. Ps. 50:5.
    3. Sufferings at present; glory hereafter. Rom. 8:17, 18.
    4. Suffer with Christ; reign with Him. 2 Tim. 2:12; 1 Peter 4:12, 13.
V. *Reward Now and Eternally.*
    1. Peace results from doing right. Isa. 48:18, 22.
    2. "Peace . . . , which passeth understanding." Phil. 4:7.
    3. Peacefully welcoming Christ's return. 2 Peter 3:14.
    4. Receive manifold now, and hereafter life everlasting. Matt. 19:27-29; Luke 18:28-30.
    5. "Fulness of joy." Ps. 16:11.   MRS. THELMA A. SMITH.

Persecuted for the Truth's Sake

INTRODUCTION: Persecution has been the common lot of God's faithful all down the ages. 2 Tim. 3:10-12; 1 Peter 4:12, 13; Rev. 17:6. The eleventh chapter of Hebrews lists a "cloud of witnesses" (Heb. 12:1, 2)—those who suffered and died for their loyalty to God.

I. *Example in Bible History.*
    1. Abel died a martyr to his faith. Gen. 4:1-8.
    2. Joseph chose confinement in a dungeon rather than break seventh commandment. Genesis 39.
    3. Daniel faced lions' den in honor of first commandment. Dan. 6:1-24.
    4. His three friends stood undaunted before infuriated king of Babylon and burning fiery furnace, in obedience to God of second commandment. Daniel 3.
II. *Sabbath a Last-Day Test of Loyalty.*
    "The Sabbath will be the great test of loyalty; for it is the point

of truth especially controverted. When the final test shall be brought to bear upon men, then the line of distinction will be drawn between those who serve God and those who serve Him not. . . . While one class, by accepting the sign of submission to earthly powers, receive the mark of the beast, the other, choosing the token of allegiance to divine authority, receive the seal of God."—GC 605.

1. Dragon wroth with God's commandment-keeping people. Rev. 12:17.
2. Boycotting and threatened death await those who maintain their allegiance to God of holy Sabbath. Rev. 13:2, 3, 6-8, 15-17.
3. God warns His people to come out of Babylon, not to receive her plagues. Rev. 14:9-11; 18:1-4.
4. God's faithful children will keep commandments of God and have the faith of Jesus. Rev. 14:12.
5. They will keep holy the Sabbath—sign of His authority as Creator. Rev. 7:1-3; Ex. 20:8-11; Eze. 20:12, 20.

III. Promises of ultimate glorious victory to faithful, even unto death. Rev. 3:10-12; 7:9-13; 2:10. "Those who are earnestly seeking a knowledge of the truth, and are striving to purify their souls through obedience, thus doing what they can to prepare for the conflict, will find, in the God of truth, a sure defense. 'Because thou hast kept the word of My patience, I will also keep thee,' is the Saviour's promise. He would sooner send every angel out of heaven to protect His people, than leave one soul that trusts Him to be overcome by Satan."—GC 560.

IV. *Appeal.*
What precious, comforting promises are found in the Bible! No matter how hard our lot, we can be assured that God will not forsake those who trustingly and courageously step out to keep His commandments. Our present conflicts will make our future bliss seem all the sweeter. Let us now claim His promise to those who have kept His commandments. Rev. 22:14. We want to be with them as they are welcomed by God to the Holy City; do we not? Mr. and Mrs. Brown, let us now commit your problem to our heavenly Father. He knows how to solve every perplexity. (Prayer.)

ABBIE DUNN.

PART FOUR ★ CHAPTER ELEVEN

Christian Standards

Our message must raise up the falling standards of the church at large. To us the principles of dress reform must be more than denominational teachings, and this is also true of amusements, reading, and so forth. Worldliness and pride are so prevalent today that the Bible instructor must be prepared to meet arguments outside and inside of the church. We should be able to present clear-cut, logical reasons why we have found it necessary to build certain reforms into our message. Dealing with the problem of dress reform in the light of a warning against the "idolatry of dress," makes this matter one of real importance and urgency. As health reform is a message for this hour, so dress reform too must be considered on this basis.

We have here included help in meeting some particular queries hardly discussed elsewhere in our literature. Bible instructors must meet these very problems more than other workers, and we should become well informed on our true principles.

Reformatory Message and Dress Standards

INTRODUCTION: Message of preparation for Christ's coming includes separation from world. 1 John 2:15-17. Message produces clean and holy people ready for heaven. Hope of Jesus' return incentive for reform. 1 John 3:1-3. Reformatory message helps us to find His true church. What are its standards?

Text: Isa. 62:10-12.

I. *Standards of Christian Church.*
   1. Purity and holiness characterize Christ's church. 1 Peter 2:9.
   2. Members separated from world. 2 Cor. 6:15-18.

Christian Standards

    3. Hold a high standard on all points. Phil. 4:8.
    4. Pride and lust overcome by gospel. 1 John 2:15-18.
    5. Church presented faultless at Christ's second coming. Eph. 5:25-27.

II. *Lowered Standards of Last Days.*
    1. Last days will be like Noah's time. Luke 17:26-28; Gen. 6:5, 12.
    2. Worldliness of church makes last day "perilous." 2 Tim. 3:1-5.
    3. Many refuse God's reformatory message. 2 Tim. 4:1-5.
    4. Prayerlessness, wrath, doubt; vanity of women pronounced. 1 Tim. 2:8, 9.
    5. Vanity of last-day church members. Isa. 3:19-26; 4:1.

III. *Need of Revival and Reformation.*
    1. True revival produces reformation. Hosea 14:1, 2, 4.
    2. Examples of genuine revivals.
        a. Bethel's reformation.
            (1) Change of dress; ornaments given up. Gen. 35:1-5.
            (2) Adornment and make-up heathen customs. Judges 8:24; Hosea 2:13; Jer. 4:30; 2 Kings 9:30.
        b. In Moses' day.
            (1) Worship of golden calf; licentiousness. Ex. 32:1-6.
            (2) Israel laid off ornaments. Ex. 33:1-6.
            (3) Gold and jewels were used for the sanctuary. Ex. 35:21, 22, 29.
    3. Reforms of remnant church.
        a. Reformation prophesied. Rev. 12:17; Isa. 62:10-12.
        b. Law of God and faith of Jesus basic in reforms. Rev. 14:12.
        c. Remnant a type of ancient Israel. 1 Cor. 10:1-11.
        d. Ancient Israel lusted after the world. (Compare 1 Corinthians 10:6 with 1 John 2:16.)
        e. Modern Israel warned against idolatry. 1 Cor. 10:7. (See section on idolatry of dress in last days. *Evangelism,* pp. 268, 269.)
        f. Remnant a special people; "royal priesthood." 1 Peter 2:9.
        g. Living in antitypical day of atonement. Rev. 14:7.
        h. Priest's garment changed on that day. Lev. 16:4, 23; Eze. 44:17-19.
        i. Modern Israel's effective reforms. Titus 2:11-13.

IV. *Appeal for Holiness and Simplicity.*
    "Be not conformed to this world, but be ye transformed by the renewing of your mind." Rom. 12:1, 2.

Standards for Dress and Deportment

Text: Isa. 62:10-12. "Lift up a standard for the people."

I. *Introduction.*

Though the church does not set up a censorship, it must exert influence to help men and women to live Christian lives.
1. Our own judgment on Christian standards not safe. Prov. 16:25.
2. God's Word our guidebook. 2 Tim. 3:16, 17.
3. Christ our example. 1 Peter 2:21; 1 John 2:6.
4. By our standards of dress and deportment we either confess or deny Christ. Luke 12:8, 9.

II. *Bible Principles on Christian Standards.*

Standards of dress, amusement, and so forth may be different today from those of Bible times, but Bible principles still our guide. Let us test our standards by the Bible.
1. Dress principles.
    a. Should we dress as we please, or conform to God's standards? Rom. 12:1, 2; 1 Cor. 10:31.
    b. Paul's advice to Christian women. 1 Tim. 2:9.
    c. God provided adequate clothing. Gen. 3:7, 21.
    d. Modesty and simplicity. 1 Peter 3:3-5.
    e. God's children are reformers. Ex. 33:5, 6.
    f. Jewelry and heathenism. Judges 8:24.
2. Cosmetics and apostasy.
    a. Appearing as heathen. 2 Kings 9:30; Jer. 4:30.
    b. Heathen practices associated with immorality. Eze. 23:40, 43.
3. Amusements.
    a. Books.
        (1) Fleshly lusts. 1 Peter 2:11.
        (2) Greeks at Ephesus burned evil books. Acts 19:18, 19.
        (3) Religious experience determined by books. 7T 204.
    b. Music.
        (1) Christian type of music. James 5:13.
        (2) Good music is a blessing. Col. 3:16. See 1T 506.
    c. Dances; movies.
        (1) From Catholic priest's confessional; nineteen out of twenty fallen people admit occasioned at dance. (Provide facts on the dance evil.) 1 John 2:14-16.
        (2) Illustration: Titles such as "Heaven Can Wait," "A Shot in the Dark," "Our Wife," laugh at sin—a Christian cannot partake; he must overcome questionable amusements.
        (3) God is not pleased with our foolish ways. Eccl. 5:4.

Christian Standards 493

   4. Applying the test.
      a. Test for all our actions. Phil. 4:7-9.
      b. Bible teaches separation from world. No neutral ground. 2 Cor. 6:17; James 4:4.
      c. Christian does not conform to the world. Rom. 12:2.

III. *Conclusion.*
   1. Diligence in holy living and godliness. 2 Peter 3:11-14.
   2. Jesus' coming near. Holy standards should be set. Isa. 62:10-12.
   3. Willingness to give up all. Luke 14:33.
   4. True joy and lasting happiness. Ps. 16:11.
   5. Bring peace of Jesus. John 14:27.   LENNA McCARTY.

The Christian and His Dress

I. *Warfare of the Christian.*
   1. A great warfare in progress. Eph. 6:10-17.
   2. Christ Captain of our salvation. Heb. 2:10.
   3. Satan a mighty foe. 1 Peter 5:8.
   4. Our part in the conflict. 2 Tim. 2:3, 4.
      In times of war armies of contending forces identified by their uniforms. We recognize postman and fireman by attire. As representatives of heaven, Christians should be known by their attire.

II. *From Glory to Apostasy.*
   1. Man in Eden clothed with glory and honor. Gen. 2:25; Ps. 8:5.
   2. Sin forfeited robe of glory; man substitutes. Gen. 3:7; Eccl. 7:29.
   3. After man's fall God provided adequate clothing. Gen. 3:21.
   4. Israel's dress symbolic of commandments. Num. 15:38, 39.
   5. Enemy also recognized by attire. Prov. 7:10; 2 Kings 9:30.
   6. Dress apostasy of last days foretold. Isa. 3:16-23; 2:2.

III. *Instruction for Overcoming Worldliness.*
   1. Christian distinctive from worldlings. 2 Cor. 6:14-18.
   2. Gold, pearls, costly array prohibited. 1 Tim. 2:9, 10.
   3. Paul's appeal to Christian wives. 1 Peter 3:1-5.
   4. Standards for Christ's true church. Eph. 5:26, 27.

IV. *Victory for Overcomers.*
   (Dress of righteousness typical of Christian's attire.)
   1. Saints clothed in righteousness. Rev. 19:7-9.
   2. Tribute to conquering grace. Isa. 61:10.
      (Provide General Conference leaflet on "Standards.")
                                                  RUTH S. LAMB.

Godliness and Sanctification

(Select texts or present in two studies.)

I. *Christian Temperance, Conduct, and Dress.*
   1. What does God desire of those who are waiting for the return of Jesus? 1 Thess. 5:23.
   2. How much of our lives will be affected by Bible religion? I Cor. 10:31; 6:19, 20.
   3. With what is true temperance classified? Gal. 5:22, 23.
   True temperance is the total abstinence from all that is harmful, and the moderate use only of that which is good.
   4. Where in Christian growth and experience is temperance placed? 2 Peter 1:5-7; 1 Cor. 9:25, 27.
   Temperance is rightly placed here as to order. Knowledge is a prerequisite to temperance and temperance to patience. It is almost impossible for an intemperate person to be patient.
   5. In what way does the Lord express His will for us? 3 John 2.

II. *The Relation of Diet to Health.*
   1. What is essential to good health? Prov. 4:20-22.
   2. What food was originally given to man? Gen. 1:29.
   Fruits, grains, and nuts comprised the original diet of man, and it was not until after the Flood that man was permitted to eat flesh. Gen. 9:2-4. God "intended that the race should subsist wholly upon the productions of the earth; but now that every green thing had been destroyed, He allowed them to eat the flesh of the clean beasts that had been preserved in the ark. PP 107.
   3. How are clean and unclean meats distinguished? Deut. 14:2-20; Lev. 11:2-22.
   4. What shows that the use of flesh had become a habit with Israel? Ex. 16:4. The Israelites in Egypt had adopted many of the ways of the heathen. Appetite, too, had been perverted. A fleshless diet soon became a problem to them. Num. 21:5; 11:4, 13, 31-33.
   5. What was God's reason for giving Israel restrictions in diet? Ex. 23:25; 15:26.
   6. Did this lapse affect their spiritual life? 1 Cor. 10:5-11.
   "That which corrupts the body tends to corrupt the soul. It unfits the user for communion with God, unfits him for high and holy service."—MH 280.
   7. What will be our fate if we defile the temple of God? 1 Cor. 3:16, 17.
   Daniel's noble example of true godliness (Dan. 1:8-20) is a lesson

for this age. "Daniel was blessed because he was steadfast in doing what he knew to be right, and we shall be blessed if we seek to honor God with full purpose of heart."—CH 156.
8. Against what evil does Christ especially warn us? Luke 21:34, 35; Matt. 24:45-51.
9. How will God deal with those who refuse to heed His call to complete sanctification? Isa. 65:2-4; 66:15-17.

III. *Reform in Habits, Amusements, and Dress.*
1. What else does God forbid beside unclean foods? Lev. 10:9, 10; Deut. 29:18 (margin), 19, 20; Prov. 23:31, 32; 20:1.
Every soul-defiling habit must and can be overcome by the grace of God. The use of drugs such as alcohol, tobacco, tea, and coffee unfit us to walk with God.
2. How will the true Christian relate himself to the things of this world? 1 John 2:15; Rom. 12:2.
One who is walking with God will not be found patronizing theaters, dance and billiard halls, or other places of worldly amusement. Such things as gambling, card playing, etc., deaden the spiritual senses.
3. What counsel is given concerning our attire? 1 Peter 3:3, 4; 1 Tim. 2:9, 10; Isa. 3:16-23.
Our attire "should have the grace, the beauty, the appropriateness of natural simplicity. Christ has warned us against the pride of life, but not against its grace and natural beauty. . . . The most beautiful dress He bids us wear upon the soul. No outward adorning can compare in value or loveliness with that 'meek and quiet spirit' which in His sight is 'of great price.'"—MH 288, 289.
4. To the overcomer what beautiful promise is given? 2 Cor. 6:17, 18; Rev. 21:7, 27.   R. ALLAN ANDERSON.

Coming of Elijah the Prophet

Christian education should be included in our instruction to new Sabbathkeepers. It fits into Elijah's message. Presenting a study on the work of Elijah provides a proper approach.

Text: Mal. 4:5, 6.

I. *"Spirit and Power of Elias."*
1. God's commandments had been forsaken. 1 Kings 18:18.
2. Sun worship introduced. Eze. 8:15-18.

3. Prophets of Baal tested. 1 Kings 18:22-28.
4. Elijah proved his faith in God's Word. 1 Kings 18:30-39.
5. Baal's prophets defeated. 1 Kings 18:40.

II. *John, the Elijah of First Advent.*
1. John called men to forsake sin. Matt. 3:2, 8; Isa. 40:3-8; 1 John 3:4.
2. Jesus declared John to be the Elijah. Matt. 11:7-15; 17:10-12.
3. Disciples understood this prophetic application. Matt. 17:13.
4. John's testimony, "I am the voice." John 1:21-23.
5. Leaders were blind to John's message. John 9:41.
6. People followed their blind leaders. John 7:26, 48.
7. Traditions in place of God's commandments. Matt. 15:9, 13.
8. Rejection of John's message meant destruction. Matt. 3:12.
9. John's mission fulfilled prophecy. Luke 1:13-17.

III. *Elijah Message at Second Advent.*
1. Elijah prophecy also applies to time of end. Mal. 4:5; Zeph. 1:14-18; Joel 1:14, 15.
2. Isaiah foretold this work of reform. Isa. 62:10-12.
3. Message includes call out of Babylon. Rev. 18:1-4.
4. "The voice of the day of the Lord." Zeph. 1:14-18.
5. Obedience to this message means salvation. Heb. 5:9.
6. Rejection leads to error. 2 Tim. 4:1-4; Ps. 119:142.
7. Fulfillment of Elijah message, message of Second Advent. Rev. 14:6-12.

IV. *Appeal.*
Texts: Matt. 7:20-23; 1 Kings 18:21; Joshua 24:14, 15; Rev. 22:14.

Reforms Under the Elijah Message

I. *Introduction.*
Definite reforms will today take place under present-day Elijah message. These will especially affect parents in training their children. John the Baptist a true type of such reform. It influenced his diet, dress, education. Mal. 4:5, 6; Matt. 3:1-6; Luke 1:15-17.

II. *Last-Day Conditions Affect Behavior.*
1. A reprobate mind produces disobedience. Rom. 1:21-23, 28, 30.
2. Disobedience of children in last days. 2 Tim. 3:1, 2.
3. Teachers turn from truth to fables. 2 Tim. 4:3, 4.
4. Develops scoffers and evolutionists. 2 Peter 3:3-6.
5. Heathen influences rule precious heritage (youth). Joel 2:1, 15-17.

Christian Standards

III. *Raising Standard for Advent Youth.*
  1. Obedience must now counteract disobedience. Rev. 14:12.
  2. Church must raise standard against enemy. Isa. 59:19.
  3. True education upholds God's commandments. Eccl. 12:12-14; Isa. 54:13.
  4. Children to be taught God's commandments. Deut. 6:4-9.
  5. Parents responsible for proper training of youth. Judges 13:12; Eph. 6:4; Prov. 22:6.

IV. *Need for Christian Schools.*
  1. Advent youth today called to God's work. Joel 2:28-32.
  2. "Seed" of church to teach Gentiles. Isa. 61:4-9.
  3. Influence of godly training.
      a. Early education influenced Moses and Daniel. Heb 11: 23-26; Deut. 34:10; Dan. 1:8, 17, 20.
      b. Schools of prophets influenced Solomon. 1 Kings 4:29-34.
      c. Mary's teachings influenced Jesus' life. Luke 2:46-52.
      d. Timothy's early training built character. 2 Tim. 1:5; 3:14, 15.
  4. Under sealing message parents must train their children. Isa. 8:15-20.
  5. Our task: finishing the gospel work. Matt. 24:14.

V. *Appeal to Parents.*
  To consider seriously a Christian education for their children. S.D.A. youth called to herald Advent message to ends of earth. This requires a special training, and the Christian school is in God's order. Parents must decide this matter on faith, dedicating their children to the closing work of the gospel. God is counting on all Seventh-day Adventist parents to do this. Jer. 13:20; Isa. 8:18.

Establishing a Happy Home
(For youth with S.D.A. background.)

I. *Introduction.*
  1. God's first gift to man. "God celebrated the first marriage. Thus the institution has for its originator the Creator of the universe. . . . It was one of the first gifts of God to man, and it is one of the two institutions that, after the fall, Adam brought with him beyond the gates of Paradise." PP 46.
  2. The Sabbath a twin institution. "Then marriage and the Sabbath had their origin, twin institutions for the glory of God in the benefit of humanity. . . . He enunciated the law of marriage for all the children of Adam to the close of time. That

which the eternal Father Himself had pronounced good, was the law of highest blessing and development for man." MB 99, 100.

II. *Marriage—Part of God's Plan.*
1. What was God's plan in providing the institution of marriage? Gen. 2:18.
2. As the Creator joined the hands of the holy pair in wedlock, what was His pronouncement? Gen. 2:22-24.
3. In God's plan, how many wives were provided for a man? Gen. 2:24, 22; Eph. 5:31; Mal. 2:14.
4. How should the marriage relationship be entered into? Mal. 2:14-16.
"The family tie is the closest, the most tender and sacred, of any on earth. It was designed to be a blessing to mankind. And it is a blessing whenever the marriage covenant is entered into intelligently, in the fear of God, and with due consideration for its responsibilities. Those who are contemplating marriage should consider what will be the character and influence of the home they are founding. . . . A relation so important as marriage and so far-reaching in its results should not be entered upon hastily." MH 356-358.

III. *Law of Love in Home.*
1. How binding is the bond of mutual relationship in marriage? 1 Cor. 7:3, 39; Eccl. 9:9. "Let the husband and wife study each other's happiness, never failing in the small courtesies and little kindly acts that cheer and brighten the life." MH 393.
2. Does the happiness of a home depend upon luxury or possessions? Luke 12:15; Prov. 15:17.
3. Should adversity affect the love of husband and wife? Eccl. 8:6, 7. "A house with love in it, where love is expressed in words and looks and deeds, is a place where angels love to manifest their presence. . . . There the humble household duties have a charm." 2T 417.
4. What is God's plan for the husband? 1 Tim. 5:8.
5. What are the God-given duties of the wife? Prov. 31:10-31.
6. What further counsel to both is given by Peter? 1 Peter 3:1-12. "Mutual kindness and forbearance will make home a paradise, and attract holy angels into the family circle." 1T 386, 387.
"Angels delight in a home where God reigns supreme, and the children are taught to reverence religion, the Bible, and their Creator. Such families can claim the promise, 'Them that honor Me, I will honor.'" 5T 424.

IV. *Place of Family Altar.*
   1. What was Abraham's daily practice for his whole household? Gen. 18:19.
   2. What was Timothy's early training? 2 Tim. 1:5; 3:15.
   3. How are parents admonished to care for the "little church" in their home? 1 Tim. 3:4, 5.
   4. Why is this counsel so important today? 2 Tim. 3:1-3.
   5. What is the promise to Christian parents in these last days? Mal. 4:4-6.

   "In too many households, prayer is neglected. Parents feel that they have no time for morning and evening worship. . . . From every Christian home a holy light should shine forth. Love should be revealed in action. It should flow out in all home intercourse, showing itself in thoughtful kindness, in gentle, unselfish courtesy. There are homes where this principle is carried out,—homes where God is worshiped, and truest love reigns. From these homes, morning and evening prayer ascends to God as sweet incense, and His mercies and blessings descend upon the supplicants like the morning dew. A well-ordered Christian household is a powerful argument in favor of the reality of the Christian religion,—an argument that the infidel cannot gainsay." PP 143, 144.

   Additional References: DA 150, 151, 144; 4T 503-508, 515; TM 180, 181; MH 356-359, 374, 376, 377; Wearner, *Fundamentals of Bible Doctrine* (Review and Herald), chap., "The Christian Home."

   MARJORIE MILLER GREENE.

PART FOUR ★ CHAPTER TWELVE

Presenting the Spirit of Prophecy

Teaching those who are unacquainted with spiritual gifts, or who may be greatly confused with spurious demonstrations, requires special skill to make the instruction effective as well as informative. For this reason a number of experienced Bible instructors have been selected to give their presentations in more detail. All workers will appreciate capturing their special techniques of argument, and will also be benefited by their more unique methods of appeal. The field is still wide open to the aggressive Bible teacher whose more than average background of the Spirit of prophecy will present a new appeal to the uninformed or skeptical. We would advise a wise selection of textual points, and a restraining of such as may not be necessary with some readers. Since the Spirit of prophecy is for the church, our teaching in this respect should reveal our continuous research in helping new believers, as well as our weathered saints, to a fuller appreciation of the gift in our midst.

The Church Militant

I. *Introduction.*
From the time sin first entered our world God's children have been in conflict with Satan. Gen. 3:15; Eph. 6:11-13. A line of demarcation was early drawn between the two classes of worshipers. Gen. 4:26; 6:1, 2; Heb. 11:4. As sin increased, God often called His faithful children to separate from the worldliness around them. Gen. 12:2; 13:12. His church was well organized in Old Testament times. Acts 7:38. It centered in the tabernacle. Jesus was prefigured in every sacrifice that was offered. Heb. 9:9-11. The Ten Commandments made ancient Israel a distinctive people. Ex. 19:5.

II. *The Apostolic Church.*
 1. Organization. Mark 3:13, 14.
 2. Figure of building. Eph. 2:19-22.
 3. Membership taught. Acts 2:47.
 4. Founded on law. Matt. 5:17, 18; 1 John 2:3-5.
 5. Church represented by symbol of woman. Jer. 6:2; 2 Cor. 11:2.
 6. John's view. Rev. 12:1, 2, 5.
 7. Church fled into wilderness. Rev. 12:6; 2 Thess. 2:1-4.

III. *The Remnant Church.* Rev. 12:17.
 1. Distinguishing features.
   a. Keep commandments. Rev. 12:17.
   b. Have Spirit of prophecy. Rev. 12:17; 19:10.
   c. To rise after 1798. Rev. 12:6.
   d. To give messages of Revelation 14:6-11; 14:12.
 2. Satan's bitter warfare. Rev. 12:17.

We invite you to view the complete
selection of titles we publish at:

www.LNFBooks.com

or write or email us your praises,
reactions, or thoughts about this
or any other book we publish at:

TEACH Services, Inc.
P.O. Box 954
Ringgold, GA 30736

info@TEACHServices.com

www.ingramcontent.com/pod-product-compliance
Lightning Source LLC
Chambersburg PA
CBHW060512230426
43665CB00013B/1490